Cubans in the Confederacy

Cubans in the Confederacy

José Agustín Quintero,
Ambrosio José Gonzales,
and Loreta Janeta Velazquez

Edited by Phillip Thomas Tucker

McFarland & Company, Inc., Publishers
Jefferson, North Carolina, and London

Library of Congress Cataloguing-in-Publication Data

Cubans in the Confederacy : José Agustín Quintero, Ambrosio José
  Gonzales, and Loreta Janeta Velazquez / edited by Phillip Thomas
  Tucker.
       p.   cm.
  Includes bibliographical references and index.
  ISBN 0-7864-0976-2 (softcover : 50# alkaline paper) ∞
     1. Quintero, José Agustín, 1829–1885.   2. Gonzales, Ambrosio José.
  3. Velazquez, Loreta Janeta, b. 1842.   4. United States — History — Civil
  War, 1861–1865 — Participation, Cuban.   5. Cubans — Confederate States
  of America — Biography.   6. Diplomats — Confederate States of
  America — Biography.   7. Soldiers — Confederate States of America —
  Biography.   8. Spies — Confederate States of America — Biography.
  9. Confederate States of America — Biography.   10. Cuba — Biography.
  I. Tucker, Phillip Thomas, 1953–
  E585.C8C83   2002
  973.7′42 — dc21   2001041054

British Library cataloguing data are available

Cover images ©2002 Art Today

Manufactured in the United States of America

*McFarland & Company, Inc., Publishers
  Box 611, Jefferson, North Carolina 28640
  www.mcfarlandpub.com*

Contents

Introduction

Phillip Thomas Tucker

Cuba and the American Civil War would seem to many American historians and Civil War buffs to have no connection whatsoever. Twentieth century events like the failed Bay of Pigs invasion and the Cuban missile crisis, which brought the world to the brink of a nuclear holocaust, remain dominant in the popular perceptions of Cuba's contributions to the American story.

Although Cuba and the United States share many years of history, that common history has been obscured by twentieth century political conflict between the two countries. Castro's revolution and Cuba's Cold War alliance with the Soviet Union placed the Cuban people in the historically unfamiliar role of enemies of the United States. The resulting anti–Cuban feelings have obscured the roles of Cubans in American history, especially in regard to America's most written-about conflict, the Civil War.

In truth, Cuba played an important role in America's formative years, exerting an influence out of proportion to the island's diminutive size. Concern for how events in Cuba might affect the institution of slavery in the states along the Gulf of Mexico played a part in leading the American nation into the Civil War. Most literature on the Civil War acknowledges the impact of the new western territories won from Mexico during the Mexican-American war, but Cuba, too, had a significant role, in regard to both slavery and expansion, in heightening the sectional tensions and divisions. Therefore, the fact that hundreds of Cubans served with distinction on both sides during the Civil War should not be surprising.

For the most part, Cuba's importance to the United States, including the impact of the island's turbulent history, can best be explained by its vital location. The west end of the more than 700-mile island of Cuba points like a dagger toward the Gulf of Mexico, while the east end looms only 90 miles

1

from the southern tip of Florida. In this strategic position, Cuba commands the all-important sealanes that connect the United States mainland to the Caribbean and the rest of the world.

In the April 1823 words of secretary of state John Quincy Adams in regard to the strategic importance of the position of both Cuba and Puerto Rico: "These islands are natural appendages of the North American continent, and one of them [Cuba] almost within sight of our shores, from a multitude of considerations, has become an object of transcendent importance to the commercial and political interests of our Union.... Its commanding position gives it an importance in the sum of our national interests with which that of no other foreign territory can be compared." From the beginning, the proximity of Cuba to the United States has always given it a strategic importance far beyond that of any other Caribbean Island.[1]

Beyond the island's unique geographical position, a commonality lies in the early history of both the United States and Cuba. In many ways, that history is much more alike than dissimilar. Before the Castro revolution, no nation south of the United States border — not even Mexico — had been more Americanized than Cuba. In political, economic, and cultural terms, Cuba had been the "most North American of the former Spanish colonies" south of the United States border. In fact, the people of Cuba lived under a constitution modeled after that of the United States.[2] Ironically, the roots and the ideological foundations of the Cuban revolution — the event that would so divide the Cuban nation from its northern neighbor — largely existed in the American struggle for independence, and America's own political and social idealism. Both of these ideological revolutions of exploited colonies were successful in overthrowing unpopular central governments of Europe — Britain and Spain — and in creating new experiments in nationhood based upon the lofty principles and visions of the American Declaration of Independence.[3]

As ideological and psychological fuel for his Cuban revolution Castro drew on the inspiration of the great national hero José Martí, the nineteenth-century Havana-born visionary of the dream of Cuban independence. Martí's primary historical influence in turn, had been the ideology of the American Revolution and such founding fathers as George Washington and Thomas Jefferson. Martí wrote that the United States was "the greatest [nation] ever built by liberty [and Cubans] have made of the heroes of this country their own heroes, and look to the success of the American commonwealth as the crowning glory of mankind.... We love this country of Lincoln."[4]

Even long before Martí, history was a common thread between the two nations. Centuries of history bound the thirteen English colonies and then the American republic with the island of Cuba. Americans died fighting on Cuban soil and for possession of the island. In 1762, "several hundred

Americans" in the service of the British died in the military effort that resulted in the capture of Cuba from the Spanish, when Britain and her colonial allies captured Havana during the French and Indian Wars.[5]

Following the establishment of American independence, however, a great concern of the United States was what Cuba would come under the domination of Britain. Hence, to address such realistic strategic concerns, the Monroe Doctrine was issued in 1823, with a special emphasis on Cuba because of its proximity to the United States and because of its strategic location. Most of all, the United States realized that Cuba must remain in friendly hands.

As Adams continued in his April 1823 letter to the American minister in Spain: "The transfer of Cuba to Great Britain would be an event unpropitious to the interests of the Union [and therefore] our right and of our power to prevent it, if necessary, by force, already obtrudes itself upon our councils, and the administration is called upon, in the performance of its duties to the nation, at least to use all the means within its competency to guard against and forefend it." Adams merely echoed the views of other Americans when he viewed Spanish domination of Cuba as an "unnatural connection."[6]

Ever expansionist, Thomas Jefferson coveted Cuba "for strategic reasons." He said that he hoped that Cuba would be extended into "our Confederacy," which was "an empire for liberty." Jefferson wrote: "I have ever looked on Cuba as the most interesting addition which could ever be made to our system of States [and] her addition to [the United States] is exactly what is wanting to advance our power as a nation to the point of its utmost interest." Like other Americans, Jefferson was concerned about British control of Cuba if taken from a weak and vulnerable Spain, whose once mighty empire had crumbled.[7]

Among the reasons that Americans feared a British controlled Cuba were racial factors rooted in the institution of slavery. In this regard, by 1823, American statesmen were focusing on a number of historical lessons of both the Caribbean region and the recent War of 1812. The greatest fear of the South and southern leaders during the antebellum period was that of slave insurrection, thanks to the great slave revolt on St. Domingue in the early 1790s. Considerable fear existed that the lessons of St. Domingue, the world's first black republic, would eventually affect Cuba, resulting in yet another black republic with British assistance. This was a primary reason why the United States for decades sought to purchase Cuba or looked for other ways to eliminate the threat of insurrection that would affect the slaves along the Gulf of Mexico.

Sparked by the idealism of the French, American, and Haitian revolutions, Americans early identified with the struggle of the Cubans against the Spanish. Henry Clay, in perhaps his greatest speech, declared how the valiant Cubans' struggles against Spanish rule were "animated by an American feeling

[and] they would obey the laws of the system of the New World, of which they would compose a part in contradistinction to that of Europe.... At the present moment the patriots of the south are fighting for liberty and independence — for precisely what we fought for" during the American Revolution.[8]

To Americans, Cuba was very much a paradox — both a potential threat and a potential territory and eventual state in the Union. While southerners of the antebellum period viewed Cuba as an extension of a great southern empire in the Caribbean, the North viewed Cuba as a threat because of its large number of slaves and the possibility it presented of the expansion of slave territory. American imperialists desired to obtain Cuba in the spirit of Manifest Destiny, while southerners coveted Cuba to expand an empire for slavery.

On the eve of the Civil War, the Democratic Party demanded the annexation of Cuba, a factor leading to the split in the party that helped to pave the way for Lincoln's election as president. In this way, Cuba contributed significantly to the polarization of North and South, helping to pave the way for armed conflict among brothers. These factors helped to set the stage for the forgotten role of Cubans in the American Civil War.[9]

Why is the story of Cuba's contribution in the American Civil War now important? Why does it need to be told? Ironically, one central factor to answer these questions lies in the America of today.

Here at the beginning of the twenty-first century, the ethnic composition and fabric of the United States is changing rapidly, while the nation moves forward to become a true multicultural society. For the first time in United States history, the Hispanic people, including Cubans, are the country's fastest growing minority and indeed are on the verge of becoming the largest ethnic minority in the United States. Therefore, it is especially ironic today that the role of Hispanics, and especially Cubans, in United States history remains overlooked by historians.

The Cuban heritage added vibrant, exciting stories to the annals of the American Civil War, yet it has been ignored by generations of America's historians and scholars. This is true even in some of the areas most heavily populated by Cubans — even in Miami, Florida, the largest center of Cuban culture in the United States. Nevertheless, these stories are vital to our understanding of Cuba and especially its nineteenth century relations with the southern United States.

Clearly, it is important that the role of Cubans in the Civil War be fully understood because it is an important part of the American story. Consequently, it is the overall purpose of this work to illuminate the roles, sacrifices, and accomplishments of representative Cubans who played distinguished but forgotten roles during America's fratricidal conflict — all for the Confederate army.

Actually, Cubans served in the armies of both the Confederacy and the Union. The eastern theater was the scene of active Hispanic and Cuban participation during the great clashes between the Army of Northern Virginia and the Army of the Potomac. In the first days of the war, enthusiastic Hispanics in the North joined up with the initial call to arms. One regiment of the Army of the Potomac, which contained Cubans as well as other Hispanics, was the 39th New York Volunteer Infantry. This distinguished command was known as "the Garibaldi Guard." However, "Lincoln's Foreign Legion" might have been a more descriptive sobriquet because this fine regiment was composed of soldiers from around the world.

This ethnically diverse New York City regiment contained what was called a "Spanish" company [D], which was originally led by Captain Joseph Torrens. In the ranks of this New York regiment could be found at least three soldiers from Cuba, Privates De Santiago Fernandez, Juan Herandez, and Felipe Pis. All in all, more than 100 "Spanish" soldiers, who in civilian life had been sailors, waiters, soldiers, painters, bakers, blacksmiths, and clerks, marched and fought with the "Spanish" company of the 39th New York during the bloody campaigns of the Army of the Potomac.

One Cuban who fought nobly for the Union was Lieutenant Colonel Frederic Fernandez Cavada, who led the finely uniformed Zouaves of the 114th Pennsylvania Volunteer Infantry, known as Collis's Zouaves, in the Third Corps's defense of the Peach Orchard in Gettysburg on July 2. Cavada and his men were caught in the wake of the fierce attack of General William Barksdale's Mississippi Brigade, which was part of the assault of General James Longstreet's Corps, Army of Northern Virginia. It was these Mississippi Rebels who overran the Peach Orchard to surpass "Pickett's Charge" in terms of both penetration and overall success.

Lieutenant Colonel Cavada was born in Cienfuegos, Cuba, in Las Villas Province, to a Cuban father and an American woman from Philadelphia, Pennsylvania. From the fall of 1864 to February 1869, he served as the United States consul to Trinidad, Cuba. Most of all, he was a Cuban nationalist, quitting his position to fight for Cuban freedom and independence. With his Civil War experiences, he soon led the guerrilla forces in the District of Trinidad, and then all troops fighting in the Las Villas Province. Eventually, Cavada became the commander-in-chief of the Cuban Revolutionary Army, earning a reputation as a hard-fighting general of distinction. By this time, his brother Adolfo was also aiding in the struggle for Cuban freedom, leading the Cuban patriot forces of the Las Villas Province.

As a cruel fate would have it, Cavada forfeited his life as a general of revolutionary Cuban forces for the goal of Cuban independence from Spain. Like so many other Cuban independence fighters and despite the intervention of high-ranking former Civil War officers, Cavada was executed by a Spanish firing squad on July 1, 1871.

But before Frederic's death in Cuba, the Cavada brothers both performed well in the Civil War. Along with many of his fellow Pennsylvania Zouaves during the assault of General Longstreet's First Corps in the Peach Orchard sector along the Emmitsburg Road, Frederic Cavada was captured by the rising tide of victorious Mississippians, when they surged across the Emmitsburg Road and smashed through the Union lines. A poet, author and enlightened reformer who was anti-slavery and an early advocate of women's rights, Lieutenant Colonel Cavada, whose brother, Adolfo F. Cavada, was now serving on General Andrew A. Humphreys's staff, was destined for confinement in the infamous Libby Prison in Richmond, Virginia, after he was captured by the Mississippi Rebels. Cavada later published the book *Libby Life: Experiences of a Prisoner of War in Richmond, Va., 1863–1864*, which told of the horrors of prison life.[10]

But it was the Spanish southeast that saw the most widespread Hispanic participation east of the Mississippi River. The heaviest Hispanic (including Cuban) representation in military service was from the Gulf Coast area along the Gulf of Mexico, including the states of Mississippi, Alabama, Louisiana, and especially Florida. More Cubans served in Florida units than in units from any other state.

By the time of the Civil War, the majority of Hispanics of the Gulf coast, including most Cubans, resided in the cities of New Orleans, Louisiana; Mobile, Alabama; Biloxi, Mississippi; and Pensacola, Florida. When Confederate guns opened their angry wrath on Fort Sumter in Charleston harbor, these Hispanics were prepared to defend their states and communities with their lives.

By any measure, the most obscure and least understood Hispanics and Cubans who fought in the Civil War were those who wore the gray. Stereotypes continue to exist that the average Southern soldier was a typical Southern "cracker" and Anglo-Saxon of a homogenous background, but such was not the case. In fact, the Confederate armies were ethnic melting pots, representing foreign soldiers and nationalities from across the world. A large part of the colorful mix consisted of the Hispanic and Cuban Rebels.

In the eastern theater, Cuban participation in the great conflict began with the opening volleys of the war. For instance, Cuban-born and New York City and Havana–educated Ambrosio José Gonzales was serving as one of General Pierre G.T. Beauregard's staff when the first shots were fired on Fort Sumter. With a law degree from the University of Havana and a South Carolina woman from a distinguished family as his wife, Gonzales had also been an active revolutionary against Spanish rule in Cuba. He served the Confederacy throughout the course of the war and was a member of the staffs of the most famous Southern commanders — Beauregard, Lee, Pemberton, Hardee, Johnston. As artillery commander he played a vital role in the all-important

Confederate defense at Honey Hill. Yet his participation is scarcely noted by most historians today.

Another example of an educated Cuban offering distinguished service to the Confederacy was Ramon T. de Aragon. The chief surgeon of General Matthew Duncan Ector's Texas and North Carolina brigade and the Army of Tennessee, de Aragon had migrated to the United States in the 1850s. He then settled in Moscow, Tennessee, and married a Tennessee girl, while acclimating to life in America and the local community. Not long after the Confederate guns opened fire on Fort Sumter, Ramon T. de Aragon enlisted in the 13th Tennessee Confederate Infantry as a private.

Evidently he possessed a Cuban medical education, because de Aragon became a medical steward for the Tennessee regiment by the time of the battles at Belmont, Missouri, and Shiloh, Tennessee. Subsequently, de Aragon was promoted to assistant surgeon of the 9th Texas Confederate Infantry, in which other Hispanics served, in June 1862. The Cuban medical man was promoted to regimental surgeon in April 1863, serving until the war's end. After the conflict, Ramon T. de Aragon became the major of Moscow, Tennessee.[11]

Cuban women also served with distinction in the Civil War. One of these was Lola Sanchez, who hailed from the St. John's River country of northeast Florida near the town of Palatka. Like most Florida Hispanics, she was strongly pro–Confederate, with a brother serving in the Rebel Army. She became especially passionate in her defense of the Confederacy after her aged father, Cuban immigrant Mauritia Sanchez, was imprisoned in St. Augustine, Florida, as a spy. In addition, the Sanchez hacienda was often raided by the Yankees, who also possessed a keen interest in the three attractive Sanchez sisters, Lola, Eugenia, and Panchita. As if to obtain revenge for these humiliations, Lola Sanchez served as an effective spy, providing the Confederates with intelligence of impending Federal troop movements, after a daring nighttime ride through swamp and forest on at least one occasion.[12]

However, the most famous Cuban woman who contributed in the field of espionage during the Civil War was Loreta Janeta Velazquez. Even more than Lola Sanchez, Velazquez played a remarkable role both as a soldier and a spy. She was Cuban-born and educated in Louisiana, and became the wife of a Confederate officer. Employing many false names and disguises, she is even said to have passed herself off as a man and fought on the battlefield of Bull Run.

This work presents new research on Velazquez and other Cubans whose stories add a new dimension to Civil War history. At a time when so much Civil War historiography lacks fresh insight, the long overlooked role of Cubans in the Confederacy presents an important story that needs to be told.

8   Introduction

Notes

1. Harry F. Guggenheim, *The United States and Cuba: A Study in International Relations* (Westport, Conn.: Greenwood, 1934), pp. 1–4.

2. Ramon Eduardo Ruiz, *Cuba: The Making of a Revolution* (New York: W. W. Norton, 1968), pp. 1–9, 19.

3. *Ibid.*

4. Philip S. Foner, editor, *Our America: Writings on Latin America and the Struggle for Cuban Independence* (New York: Monthly Review Press, 1977), p. 235.

5. *Ibid.*, p. 8–9; Thomas Fleming, *Liberty: The American Revolution* (New York: Viking, 1997), p. 41.

6. *Ibid.*, p. 4; Ruiz, *Cuba*, p. 19.

7. *Ibid.*, p. 2; Dumas Malone, *Jefferson and His Time: The Sage of Monticello* (6 vols., Boston: Little, Brown, 1981), vol. 6, pp. 22, 339, 429; Ruiz, *Cuba*, p. 19.

8. Michael J. Kryzanek, *U.S.-Latin American Relations* (New York: Praeger, 1985), p. 6; Guggenheim, *The United States and Cuba*, pp. 8–20.

9. Ruiz, *Cuba*, pp. 19–20; Guggenheim, *The United States and Cuba*, pp. 20–22.

10. Oliver Wilson Davis, *Sketch of Frederic Fernandez Cavada* (Philadelphia: James B. Chandler, Printer, 1871), pp. 3–16; Harry W. Pfanz, *Gettysburg: The Second Day* (Chapel Hill: The University of North Carolina Press, 1987), pp. 45, 55, 92, 132, 330, 365; Edward J. Hagerty, *Collis' Zouaves: The 114th Pennsylvania Volunteers in the Civil War* (Baton Rouge: Louisiana State University Press, 1997), p. 297; Frank de Varona, *Hispanic Presence in the United States: Historical Beginnings* (Miami: Minemosyne, 1993), pp. 165–1970.

11. Family papers of Robert M. Webb, Chattanooga, Tennessee.

12. Ella Lonn, *Foreigners in the Confederacy* (Gloucester: Peter Smith Publishers, 1965), pp. 378–379; Anne Funderburg, "Women of the Confederacy," *Southern Partisan* (1994), pp. 18–19, 22.

1

José Agustín Quintero: Cuban Patriot in Confederate Diplomatic Service

by Darryl E. Brock

The Mexican governor regarded his old friend, the Confederate confidential agent, with patient interest. The agent discussed Texas border trade, shipping into the port of Matamoros and even the need to restrain bandits who preyed on everyone, whether they be Mexican, Confederate or Yankee. Of course, the new Southern nation sought good relations with governor Santiago Vidaurri. It well recognized he effectively headed the States of Nuevo León and Coahuila, but also exercised important influence over the other states bordering the Rio Grande. A states' rights adherent, Vidaurri understood the motivations of his Confederate neighbors. Sharing their secessionary interests, he too felt little in common with the Federal government in far-away Mexico City. The independent-minded *caudillo* governor had long nursed hopes of breaking away northern Mexico and forming a distinct new nation, Sierra Madre. Now this grand Southern Confederacy presented new possibilities. Vidaurri began his discussion with the Confederate diplomat, Cuban-born José Agustín Quintero.

Agreeing that both nations stood to gain much from working together, the governor stressed the mineral wealth of his region and his admiration for the industrious American people. Vidaurri then proposed something so ambitious, so unexpected, Quintero no doubt gasped in amazement: Secession of northern Mexico and a petition to join the Southern Confederacy as several new states.

José Agustín Quintero had already seen and experienced many remarkable things in his uncommonly full life, yet he had never encountered such a stunning, unanticipated turn of events. In his first diplomatic assignment for his new president, Quintero had already achieved an unprecedented coup.

How was it this talented Cuban found himself employed in the Confederate diplomatic service? Why had President Jefferson Davis entrusted him with such an important delicate mission? Just who was this Cuban-Confederate agent?

ISLAND GENESIS

Quintero's relationship with the United States and its Southern leaders began years earlier in his native homeland, Cuba. Born in La Habana (Havana) on May 6, 1829, as José Agustín Quintero y Woodville, he was to find that the union of his parents' cultures presaged a life transitioning between the Spanish and English-speaking worlds.[1] That is, his father, Antonio Quintero, was a well-to-do Cuban tobacco plantation owner, yet his "lovely and accomplished" mother, Ana Woodville, was of British parentage.[2] His parents "were people of sensibility, fond of culture." Young José grew up bilingual, his mother ensuring his facility in English.[3]

A bright student, Quintero had Don José de la Luz y Caballero as his first teacher and mentor. There the "immortal maestro" directed the College of San Cristóbal de Carraguao, one of the two exalted schools in Havana.[4] His reputation extended well beyond the Caribbean. An 1845 issue of the *Southern Quarterly Review*, published in Charleston, spoke highly of Cuba's *Patriotic Society*, declaring Don José de la Luz "among the most efficient and valuable members of this society."[5] Don Pepe, as his students affectionately called him, had a passion for education.[6] He taught his boys strict morality, "resistance to every form of oppression and injustice, [and] of self-sacrifice on the altar of duty." For these radical thoughts, the Cuban government branded him "the patriarch of the Cuban revolution," accusing him of "preparing the boys for conspiracy and the scaffold."[7] The *Southern Quarterly Review* noted this: "We regret to learn that Del Monte and De la Luz have, more recently, fallen under the ban of the colonial government, on suspicion of having been concerned in fomenting the late discontents among the slaves."[8] Actually, the Spanish view of his liberal teachings was accurate. In future years, his students José Agustín Quintero and Juan Clemente Zenea were among those who would both take active roles resisting Spanish oppression.[9] One critic accurately summed Luz y Caballero's influence on Quintero: Without doubt, the maestro's "teachings firmly stamped the course of his literary and political life."[10]

HARVARD DAYS

At the young age of 12, Quintero's parents sent him to Harvard College at Cambridge, Massachusetts, to continue his education.[11] Among his academic pursuits, he may have studied European literature under Henry Wadsworth Longfellow; nevertheless, at the same time he also took a few law courses.[12] At Harvard he perfected German, adding this language to his facile command of English and Spanish.[13] While yet a student still adjusting to a new life in a foreign land, tragedy struck: Quintero's father died in Cuba. As if this were not a serious enough blow, his father's estate then came into question. Consequently, young José Agustín Quintero now found himself thrown upon his own resources.[14]

The young man decided not to immediately return to Cuba, but instead resolved to continue studies at Harvard. He financed this effort by tutoring Spanish.[15] As the *Daily Picayune* would one day report, "Handsome, accomplished, genial, the boy-teacher was a favorite in society and made many friends among the literati [*sic*] of Boston and its vicinity."[16] It was, in fact, at this time Quintero published poems in local Boston newspapers. These "attracted the favorable comment of such men as Longfellow and Emerson."[17]

Most accounts of Quintero's life in fact report he became intimate friends with Longfellow and Emerson. One sketch asserts that among the correspondence at the Longfellow home and museum are Quintero's letters later written from Havana.[18] Certainly Longfellow did correspond with at least one Havana bard. During Quintero's years at Harvard, Longfellow grew impressed with Rafael María de Mendive's *Pasionarias* and sent an autographed copy of his own work to the Cuban.[19] There is no doubt but that Quintero favored Longfellow's work in later years. Quintero would eventually translate into Spanish and German many of the poet's major efforts.[20]

There is some basis to give credence to these assertions of friendship. When Quintero arrived at Harvard in about 1841, Longfellow was only 34 years old and had been the head of the modern languages department for half a dozen years. The poet-professor supervised four native instructors and taught many lectures himself. The students particularly liked their dapper, gaily dressed professor. They respected his effects to make classes lively and interesting, quite unlike the dry, disciplined lectures of others. No doubt Quintero also noted Longfellow's recent shift in emphasis from prose to poetry. Longfellow followed the German language and literature closely, but Spain was his "land of dreams, his lost country of cloudy places."[21] Of course, this provided a likely attraction to the new Cuban student. In 1840, just before Quintero arrived, Longfellow had immersed himself in Cervantes and Calderon and drafted a comedic play — *The Spanish Student*. During Quintero's tenure, Longfellow continued work on this opus, finally publishing it in 1843.[22] No doubt Quintero, a colonial subject of Spain, found this project of great interest. In fact, as a study of the "popular traits" and "manners of a remarkable people," the young Spanish student's perspective may have been useful to Longfellow.[23]

As for a possible relationship with the eloquent spokesman for the transcendentalists, Ralph Waldo Emerson, the evidence is less substantial. By the time Quintero arrived at Harvard, Emerson lived at nearby Concord as a lecturer and writer. Emerson did not have official ties at Harvard, nor was he particularly welcome. In the Divinity School graduation address just a couple of years earlier, Emerson had created a firestorm of controversy with his radical assertions against Christianity, as practiced by the clergy, and encouragements to future ministers to look beyond the church for true spirituality. He would be *persona non grata* at Harvard for decades.[24] Even though Emerson would not have lectured in any of Quintero's classes, he could easily have read of the Cuban's work in the local press. Furthermore, as Emerson and Longfellow had been close friends for years, this could have facilitated the young student's introduction.[25] Regardless of Quintero's possible intimate friendship with Emerson, it would be Longfellow whom the Cuban would translate and emulate throughout his life.

A beautifully scripted handwritten essay of Quintero's from about this time — his Harvard years — survives at the Boston Public Library. It is called *Lyric Poetry in Cuba* and, surprisingly, is written in English.[26] This is unusual since most of Quintero's writings on Cuba are typically in Spanish. In the manuscript's introduction, the young Cuban declares the "great inspirations" for poetry:

> Every one knows that Poetry has three great inspirations, love to the Divinity; love to country; and love to woman. These inspirations languish if she sing not of God, with all his grandeur, of country, with all its magnificence, and of woman, with her virtues, beauty and attractions. Kindled with these holy themes, Poetry has crowns of flowers for woman, laurels for her native land, and soars on golden and chrystaline [*sic*] wings to Heaven.[27]

Having proclaimed these inspirations, Quintero launches into a survey of more than a dozen notable lyric poets of his beloved isle. Among these are one of Longfellow's favorites, Rafael María de Mendive, as well as such greats of the past as José María Heredia and José Jacinto Milanés. Included also are Quintero's contemporaries with whom he would later come to be identified: Miguel Teurbe Tolón, Leopoldo Turla and Juan Clemente Zenea. Quintero's short paragraph on Turla would later be quoted by José Manuel Carbonell in his important 1930 work *Los Poetas de "El Laúd del Desterrado."* Misinterpreted handwriting or typesetting, however, would introduce a puzzling English original along with the Spanish translation: "Turla writes with the philosophy of the *thinwing* man."[28] The correct, completely translated citation is typical of the fluid, concise style Quintero employs in these sketches: "Turla writes with the philosophy of the thinking man. He meditates, and turns his eyes to humanity. He is the cypress-tree, ever green, that looks to heaven, and speaks to us with mute eloquence, of a happy resurrection."[29]

Placing a date to this composition is a challenge. Quintero's choice of English implies he wrote this as a student, perhaps near the end of his college days — say, when 18 or 19 — possibly under the tutelage of Longfellow. This is reinforced by the essay's long residence in Boston at the public library. Actually, a tentative somewhat later date of 1850 has been traditionally assigned to this treatise. At first, this would seem improbable. Upon graduation, Quintero's life would soon become embroiled in turbulent change and difficulty; certainly one would expect this effort to have been completed during the more tranquil days before his 1848 departure from Harvard.[30] Alternatively, one might conclude he sent it to Longfellow, as part of correspondence, shortly after returning to Havana that year. This could explain why it yet resides in Boston.

Examination of the sketches for internal evidence helps settle the question of when Quintero wrote this. One clue is his sober reference to José Jacinto Milanés: "A few years since the powerful intellect of Milanés destroyed itself, and mentally killed him...."[31] In fact, Milanés went insane in 1843 after only a relatively short publishing life.[32] Quintero's "few years since" are probably more than three but less than ten years, narrowing the date of composition to within perhaps a trio of years from 1850. Reinforcing this time frame is a glancing reference to Pedro Santacilia, an only slightly older poet who would figure importantly in Quintero's future. Santacilia's efforts as a writer in Cuba began no earlier than 1845 when he moved from Spain to the Caribbean. Only two years later he would have already helped establish new literary magazines on the island and gained critical recognition.[33] If Quintero knew only of Santacilia's budding reputation while at Harvard, he would come to know him personally in 1848 upon return to Havana. The third and most compelling piece of internal evidence is mention of Juan Clemente Zenea. At 17 years of age, only in 1849 did Zenea publish his first articles in Havana newspapers under a pen name.[34] Thus Quintero's *Lyric Poetry in Cuba* could not have been written prior to 1849, much less at Harvard, and yet still allude to Zenea. As events will prove, it is virtually impossible that Quintero wrote this in Cuba, but he must have written it in Louisiana or Texas in the 1849–50 time frame, or even possibly a couple of years later. Regardless, it is still more than likely the essay had been sent to Longfellow.

Carbonell, the aforementioned Cuban scholar, wrote of Quintero's early inclinations as a poet: "Since very young he felt the vibration of his heart in the entreaty of the motherland and art, the two great loves that revealed his temperament and filled his life with roses and thorns."[35] Certainly Quintero's closing lines of his short tome confirm the young man's compulsion towards this noble calling, yet they almost betray an uncertainty regarding his prospects: "In the end we make mention of the Señora Avellaneda, Roldan, Clemente Zenea, Velez, Santacilia, Guiteras, Baralt, Garcia de la Huerta, Losada, Fornaris, and, if futurity shall concede the name of poet to him who writes these lines, he will be able to say, without humility, that he was born, as they were, beneath the beautiful sky of the young Cuba."[36]

Harvard has no record of José Agustín Quintero's attendance or matriculation.[37] His father's early death may have contributed to his taking classes irregularly as he could pay for them, and could have resulted in this uncertainty. Quintero may not even have graduated, for he would soon continue his education in Havana. He returned to Cuba in early 1848.[38]

CLUB DE LA HABANA

Quintero completed his studies at Havana and there began a career he would follow throughout his life. In the year of his return to the island, he was graduated at the age of 19 with a law degree, probably granted by the University of Havana.[39] Genteelly educated and having already demonstrated considerable native talent, Quintero apparently wrote for several publications. More significantly, he also secured editorship of an important magazine, *El Faro Industrial*.[40] He assumed this position from Cirilo Villaverde, who had held the editorship the previous six years.[41] Villaverde would be an important comrade during future, sometimes difficult, years. It may be that Villaverde recommended Quintero for the editorial position, or it could be through this magazine that their important friendship developed.

At this time in Cuba, the excesses of harsh Spanish rule fired a new generation to finally take action, to realize Luz y Caballero's dream of a free Cuba. Quintero soon numbered among the adherents to this cause, Cuba Libré. That spring, these young patriots formed the *Club de la Habana* (Havana Club), a broadly based secret society comprised of plantation owners, intellectuals and journalists. Well traveled and knowledgeable of a world beyond the beaches of Cuba, they aimed to overthrow the government in favor of the North-American democratic model. Members used code names, perhaps emulating Masonic ritual. Quintero employed the alias *Felipe Morton*, while his friend Villaverde went by two alternating names, *Simón T. Paz* and *Carlos Padilla Bravo*.[42]

Quintero's cadre of conspirators included notable literary figures, among which many would play important roles in the Cuban's future. An "intimate friend," the journalist John Sidney Thrasher was half Latin like Quintero, his mother from Cuba. Known as *El Yankee,* Thrasher also edited the daily newspaper *El Faro Industrial,* probably taking over from Quintero later in 1848. A weekly edition of the paper *The Beacon of Cuba* also favored Thrasher as editor. Extremely well connected to New York publishers Moses and Alfred Beach of the sensational *The Sun* newspaper, Thrasher introduced this style of reporting into the repressive environment of Cuba. In fact, the Beach brothers had already allied with other Cuban exiles in the New York *Consejo Cubano* (Cuban Council) and recently founded the insurrectionary *La Verdad.* Like "packages of truth," the New York Cubans smuggled this pro-annexation organ into Cuba to fuel the emerging revolution.[43] In June, three of these council members, Gaspar Betancourt Cisneros, Alonzo Betancourt and José Aniceto Iznaga, through the assistance of Mississippi senator Jefferson Davis, gained an audience with President Polk. The president, however, offered no promises of assistance for the impending revolution.[44]

Another leader in the cabal, a professor at the University of Havana, may have associated with Quintero as an instructor or merely a sympathetic new friend. Alias *Don Germán,* Professor Ambrosio José González (later changed to Gonzales) hailed from the city of Matanzas, the son of a noted educator-journalist.[45] Although a decade older than Quintero, the two shared law degrees from the University of Havana and the experience of having been educated at a young age in the United States. In fact, when only nine, Gonzales attended military school in New York. There he established a lifelong friendship with his Louisiana classmate, Pierre Gustave Toutant Beauregard, the future Creole Confederate general.[46] When Quintero met Gonzales, this professor of languages and mathematics had recently returned to Havana.[47] In the preceding two years he had been traveling abroad in the United States and Spain. The professor now embraced the liberal philosophy of his late father and may have even recruited Quintero into the Havana Club.[48]

The Havana Club also boasted poets and writers. Among these numbered the novelist Ramón de Palma and the poet José Antonio Echeverría. Longfellow's favorite, Rafael María de Mendive, also resided in this august group.[49] Mendive, as noted previously, appeared in Quintero's *Lyric Poetry in Cuba.* It may be that this manuscript had been written during or soon after the days of the Havana Club, rather than a few months earlier at Harvard. Longfellow certainly maintained a Cuban correspondence with Mendive at about this time. As has been suggested by at least one biographer, it may be that Quintero also penned letters to his Boston literary mentor, one of these possibly including the *Lyric Poetry of Cuba* manuscript.[50] It may be, as the conspiracy developed, Quintero feared the piece would be lost and sent it to Boston for safekeeping, not realizing that the city's public library would preserve it for future generations.

During these days of heady plotting, Quintero contributed to a subversive magazine called *La Voz del Pueblo Cubano* (The Voice of the Cuban People).[51] It is reported his "bold and eloquent pen made him so obnoxious to the authorities," they arrested him three times.[52] His intimate comrade Pedro Angel Castellón may have directed this publication. Regardless, by 1850 Castellón had left the island using a false passport. Only three years later the revolutionary junta *Orden de la Joven Cuba* — The Order of Young Cuba — was established in New Orleans with Castellón as secretary and John S. Thrasher presiding.[53]

Two other poets cited in Quintero's *Lyric Poetry in Cuba* soon lived as exiles in the United States, but whether they joined the Havana Club is uncertain. As the club prepared for revolution, Pedro Santacilia circulated as a manuscript his *Canto de Guerra* (Song of War), urging his brothers "to arms" against "cruel oppression " from Iberia. He was arrested by 1851. Deported to Spanish prisons, he finally escaped Gibraltar to New York. Later in New Orleans, he rejoined the movement in concert with Thrasher, Castellón and others.[54] On the other hand, young Juan Clemente Zenea was only 16 years old as the Havana Club organized. His first writings in Havana newspapers, under a pen name, did not occur until the following year, 1849. The impressionable youth simply witnessed the events unfolding. This also reinforces that Quintero could not have written his *Lyric Poetry in Cuba* at this time and yet speak of Zenea, but most likely drafted the manuscript a year or two later in the United States. Regardless, when 20 years old, Clemente Zenea abandoned Cuba for New Orleans, where he too allied with Thrasher and Castellón as a member of the *Orden de la Joven Cuba*.[55]

The Havana Club proposed "to add another star to the flag of the United States," that is, to resolve their problems with Spain by annexation. Admittedly, some members feared that Spain would soon free Cuban slaves, thereby ruining the sugar economy. As part of the United States, they felt the Negro traffic could be protected, with order preserved. Other conspirators, paradoxically, saw in the United States the promise of ultimate liberty for all Cubans, slave or not. They reasoned a union with their North-American neighbor would bring an influx of white settlers, machinery and capital to displace the current system of slavery practiced by the rich. Yet another group seemed not so strongly influenced by arguments concerning slavery, but simply admired the United States, its freedom of speech, material wealth and democratic institutions. The various factions united in agreement on annexation and committed to bringing this to fruition.[56]

To overthrow the Spanish colonial government and achieve annexation, the Havana Club looked to an armed invasion by North-American volunteers. The Mexican War had just ended, providing a fertile recruiting ground for thousands of seasoned yet disbanding troops still in that country. Although

Mexico had ceded two-fifths of her territory to the United States, some proponents of "manifest destiny" felt this inadequate, casting avaricious eyes to Cuba. The timing could not be better. The earlier meeting arranged by Senator Jefferson Davis of the New York *Consejo Cubano* with President Polk did result in an initiative to buy Cuba, but Spain ridiculed the idea. Not relying solely on this prospect, in May the Havana Club had already dispatched its leader to Mexico to negotiate with North-American general William Worth, namesake of Ft. Worth, Texas. The club stood ready to offer him three million dollars to personally head an army of liberation. The proposal requested an invasion force of 5,000 U.S. veterans.[57]

LÓPEZ AND MINA ROSA

Even as the Havana conspirators moved forward, across the island at Cienfuegos a prominent Spanish general had already organized a revolt, scheduled for June 24. Born in Venezuela five decades earlier, the charming, dashing Narciso López had fought with the Spanish against Simón Bolívar and had withdrawn to Cuba with the army upon Bolívar's victory. Moving to Spain, he supported the queen in the Carlist War of Succession against her uncle Don Carlos. Honored and rising to the rank of major general, he had even served as governor of Madrid for a short time. Returning to Cuba in 1841, López prevailed upon his long friendship with the island captain-general and secured the governorship of Cuba's important Trinidad region, as well as presidency of the Supreme Military Tribunal. Ironically, in his military capacity López imposed harsh sentences on political dissenters. By 1843, his political fortunes waned as a new captain-general replaced his friend. Stripped of his lucrative post and influence, López endured the humiliation of a general without duties. This fateful turn forced him into private business. Near Cienfuegos, he managed mines and plantations with little success, sliding ever further into debt.[58]

Even before his descent from power, López had intrigued against the Spanish government. In Spain he had earlier been a member of the liberal party. In Cuba he desired independence for the island, but feared this might bring abolition. The large, uneducated, black population, if freed, could result in a Negro Republic the likes of Haiti, with its problems of anarchy and instability. López felt the United States presented a potential solution to this dilemma. About the same time that the New York *Consejo Cubano* communicated with President Polk, López spoke openly of separation to U.S. consul Robert Campbell of Havana. Though desirous of acquiring Cuba, Campbell could only reiterate official U.S. policy of nonintervention regarding Spain; President Polk made it clear there would be no war over Cuba.[59]

General López moved ahead anyway, believing the United States would in the end step in once the revolution commenced. The uprising would occur simultaneously at several locations on the island, including Trinidad, Villaclara and Cienfuegos.[60] Remembered as the conspiracy of the *Mina de la Rosa Cubana* (Cuban Rose Mine), it took this name from one of the general's mines near Cienfuegos. Among his most ardent supporters, Matanzas professor Miguel Teurbe Tolón (alias *Lola la* in the conspiracy) would take a special place among the patriots and followers of López. In his *Lyric Poetry in Cuba*, Quintero spoke of this "tender and melancholy poet," one who "in the clear moonlight, weeps gazing at the stars." Teurbe Tolón would later translate many important pieces, including Thomas Paine's *Common Sense*.[61] Another key advocate was Cirilo Villaverde of the Havana Club. Villaverde met López in 1846. Like Tolón, with whom he would closely work in future years, Villaverde would dedicate his life and talents to serving López and the cause.[62]

The *Mobile Tribune* of Alabama would later observe of the intelligent, persuasive Narciso López that "his dark eyes ... fix the attention and convince you he is no ordinary man."[63] So this gaze transfixed the compatriots in Havana. López quickly assumed a leading role in the Havana Club, assuming the secret alias *El Capo*. The club, however, convinced him to delay the insurrection until North-American general Worth and his troops arrived. López reluctantly agreed it made sense to coordinate efforts.[64]

Only days away from launching the strike, the Spanish colonial government learned of the conspiracy. President Polk, having only recently discussed the plan with the New York *Consejo Cubano*, requested U.S. consul Campbell inform the authorities in Havana. The president did not want to jeopardize negotiations underway to purchase Cuba. As a further precaution against U.S. involvement, he ordered General Worth to withdraw his troops from Mexico to New Orleans and then himself proceed to Washington. López might have gained warning by Campbell, but the general was not in Havana at the time.[65] At about the same time, a young conspirator named José Sánchez Iznaga (nephew to José Aniceto Iznaga of the New York exiles) mentioned the conspiracy to his mother. The boy's father consulted the family attorney and then decided to inform the government, hoping for leniency. The colonial authorities moved quickly and imprisoned young José (only to let him quietly escape to the United States).[66]

The crackdown netted several conspirators and scattered the others to the winds. General Narciso López grew suspicious when the Cienfuegos governor summoned him on July 6 for an important meeting. Having already learned of young José's arrest, López fled, barely managing to escape on a ship to Rhode Island.* Similarly, only weeks later Havana professor Ambrosio José Gonzales would leave Cuba for New Orleans, brazenly boarding a ship without a passport.[68] Matanzas professor Miguel Teurbe Tolón also abandoned the island in August and by the 15th assumed editorship of *La Verdad* in New York. Many of those who did not face immediate arrest found the political climate so repressive they emigrated to the United States within two or three years. These included the poets Pedro Angel Castellón and Juan Clemente Zenea. Other supporters did not fare quite so well. The failure of Mina Rosa did not result in Pedro Santacilia's immediate arrest, but as alluded to previously, by December of 1851 he was incarcerated in Havana and quickly transferred to prison in Spain. Santacilia, however, eventually escaped and rejoined his comrades in the United States. Similarly, John S. Thrasher was imprisoned about the same time, in October 1851. The Savannah *Morning News* called this "fraud upon justice" against an "unoffending, whole-souled American"; nevertheless, Thrasher somehow avoided an eight-year African sentence in chains and instead later emerged as a liberation force in New Orleans.[69]

MORRO CASTLE

The authorities imprisoned Quintero and Cirilo Villaverde, along with many others. In comparison, Quintero's sentence proved light: only four years in an overseas prison. (Some biographers, though, claim his sentence to be death by firing squad.)[70] Villaverde, on the other hand, faced ten years of incarceration, to be followed by a barbaric death at the garrote. Narciso López too received the death sentence, while young José Sánchez Iznaga, who in confiding with his parents probably caused the disaster, could look to six years in prison. In subsequent years the Permanent Military Commission and other tribunals meted additional punishments: Pedro Angel Castellón to die of bloody strangulation at the garrote, Miguel Teurbe Tolón (and his revolutionary wife, Emilia) with deportation, and Pedro Santacilia earning permanent banishment. In many cases these "bookkeeping" judgments were made in absentia — years after the fact — long after the defendants had escaped the colonial grasp. Despite broad involvement in the Havana Club, the actual

Narciso López and Ambrosio José Gonzales would initially resume their efforts based in New York City, where they would design the modern Cuban flag (and its inversed image, the present-day Puerto Rican flag). Soon thereafter they would move operations to New Orleans and the more sympathetic South. They would approach Mexican War heroes Jefferson Davis, Robert E. Lee and Mississippi Governor John Quitman to lead the proposed Cuban revolutionary army.[67] The future liberation efforts of the López Movement, and the important role played by Gonzales, are further treated in Michel Wendell Stevens's in-depth chapter "Two Flags, One Cause—A Cuban Patriot in Gray: Ambrosio José Gonzales," located elsewhere in this volume.

charges often stemmed from a number of other official misdeeds; in Quintero's case, he and others received sentence on November 13, 1852 over their publication of *La Voz del Pueblo Cubano*.[71]

In October of 1848, after *Mina Rosa*, 19-year-old José Agustín Quintero suffered imprisonment at the Morro fortress in Havana. At about the same time, a much older Cirilo Villaverde joined his fellow conspirator. Villaverde could have been speaking for both of them when he described the experience: "Locked up like a wild animal in a dark and humid dungeon cell, I remained there for six consecutive months...." This dismal period greatly affected Quintero. He wrote the poem *Esperanza* (Hope) on his cell wall, dedicated to his prison comrades:[72]

> If today in the black, lonely obscurity
> you are oppressed by the pain of the merciless yoke,
> and you sadly lament a dead hope
> of a somber and ominous destiny,
> perhaps tomorrow will yield a sparkling brilliance,
> your noble brow girdled with laurels.

Less than a year at the castle jail, in early 1849 Quintero and 37-year-old Villaverde both escaped to the United States. The circumstances of Quintero's flight remain a mystery. Not so with Villaverde. He would one day emerge as Cuba's penultimate historical novelist, the author of the exceptional period piece *Cecilia Valdéz*; thus, his life is well chronicled. The details of Villaverde's departure from Morro prison are a simple matter of record. A ready presumption is that the two simply exited together on the night of March 31.[73] The fact is that jailer Don Juan Garcia Rey (perhaps more widely known by his alias, Juan Francisco Rey) aided the escape of Villaverde as well as Vincente Fernandez, a man held for fraudulent bankruptcy. Villaverde states he escaped on April 4, but this must refer to his departure from Cuba. U.S. consul Campbell confirms this. On April 2, the consul had already reported the escape to the Secretary of State; no doubt Villaverde took refuge in Havana for four days before leaving the island by boat.[74]

This otherwise minor escape created an international incident. Three months later, on July 5, agents of the Spanish consul in New Orleans seem to have abducted the former jailer Juan Francisco Rey and spirited him back to Havana. Crescent City newspapers, fanned by the Cuban press in exile, widely repeated the victim's landlord in his statement of the kidnapping. U.S. sovereignty had been violated! Popular demand required arrest of the wily, scheming Iberian consul. A trial ensued. Jurisdictional problems arose and Washington soon stepped in, demanding the return of Juan Francisco Rey. U.S. consul Campbell then extended the U.S. flag to protect the hapless Cuban.

These measures proved effective. The colonial captain-general finally pardoned Garcia, alias Rey, returning him to the United States.[75]

Behind the scenes of this diplomatic affair, an unresolved element is Quintero's potential involvement. The various accounts of the Cuban's life glance over the escape, silent on the specifics; however, Julian Divanco's comprehensive sketch provides the same date as that of Villaverde's escape. Perhaps this is only an assumption. The routes of escape do seem to differ. Villaverde took a schooner to Apalachicola, Florida, before heading to New York. Quintero's schooner reportedly steered a course to New Orleans and then to Texas. Interestingly — perhaps more than coincidentally — Juan Francisco Rey and Señor Fernandez also proceeded to New Orleans after Villaverde separated at Apalachicola. In major reports of the Rey episode, including U.S. president Zachary Taylor's June 14, 1850, report to Congress on the abduction, no mention is made of any other Cubans — only Rey, Villaverde and Fernandez.[76] Yet, certain New Orleans newspapers noted Rey "had aided in the escape of three prisoners in March, 1849."[77]

On the surface, it would seem Quintero did not escape with Villaverde. The differences in boat routes, the intense press coverage and government dispatches never mentioning Quintero do not beg plausibility for his involvement. Yet, the particulars do seem very similar, as well as the timing. Villaverde and Quintero had served together in the Havana Club as close comrades. No doubt Villaverde would have helped his friend, if at all possible. Not to be overlooked is the intriguing report in some newspapers of a third prisoner escaping. Furthermore, it seems incredible Quintero could have eluded the likely increased vigilance after Villaverde's escape. A possibility may be that the jailer also engineered Quintero's escape — at the same time as Villaverde — and if Quintero did not accompany Juan Francisco Rey to New Orleans, he may have taken a different ship, somehow his tracks more effectively obscured.

NEW ORLEANS AND TEXAS

Quintero's life and whereabouts in the half dozen years after escaping Cuba prove elusive to the historian. Biographers in both English and Spanish offer numerous, indeed conflicting, accounts of his later years, but almost uniformly gloss over the decade leading to Southern secession with but a single passing sentence. There is general consensus Quintero first traveled to New Orleans, then to Texas.[78] The record nevertheless leaves many unanswered questions: How long did he stay in New Orleans? What was his Texas destination? Why did he go there? Plus, how did he occupy himself in these two cities?

New Orleans would one day prove Quintero's home where he would permanently settle and raise his family; however, that time had not yet arrived. It is possible, though, that he did spent some time in New Orleans in 1849 and perhaps even into the following year. If so, 20-year-old Quintero found himself largely on his own. His fellow Cuban conspirators and prisonmates had widely scattered. Cirilo Villaverde, who had escaped Morro Castle at apparently the same time as Quintero, had quickly joined the translocated liberation movement now in New York City, there working with Ambrosio Gonzales and Narciso López. Miguel Teurbe Tolón too resided in New York, now editing the aforementioned revolutionary organ *La Verdad*. In Cuba, John Thrasher, *El Yankee*, somehow yet continued as a journalist—for the time being anyway—despite his involvement as a leader in the Havana Club. In fact, Thrasher, Castellón, Clemente Zenea and Santacilia still wrote for and served the cause in Cuba, their looming exiles reserved for the future.[79]

So Quintero apparently stood alone, now separated from his revolutionary comrades; yet, perhaps he chose this fate. If Villaverde could find his way back to López and Gonzales, no doubt Quintero could have rejoined the movement as well. A bit younger than his colleagues, it thus seems likely he decided not to. Prison may have had a sobering effect on his revolutionary impulse. Perhaps he now concluded a military expedition had little chance of success. If so, Quintero's future poetic efforts would nevertheless show continued admiration for López and the cause of Cuban liberation; but, it may be he simply felt called to pursue a separate destiny and serve by the pen rather than the sword.

By winter of 1850, Mississippi Governor John Quitman assumed a leading role in the efforts to support López's expeditionary plans to liberate Cuba; the focus of planning thus shifted from New York and Washington to the South, especially to New Orleans. López, Gonzales, and Villaverde, along with large numbers of North-American recruits, feverishly organized a filibustering expedition to invade Cuba that spring. Filibuster, at that time, referred to irregular military adventurers who often fought more for political motives than pecuniary gain. The prospect of liberating Cuba—and annexing her to the United States—greatly excited the locals, and Southerners in general. The press covered these inspiring liberation activities in great detail, yet Quintero appears nowhere in the record. Similarly, none of the many historical accounts reveal Quintero as involved in the New Orleans preparations. As a previous leader in the original Havana Club, Quintero no doubt would have risen to a position of leadership as the new expedition materialized. It thus seems likely he no longer resided in New Orleans, if indeed he had resided there at all since his prison escape. By this time Quintero surely had left for Texas, if not already in the previous year.[80]

A likely Texas destination would have been the port of Galveston and the nearby Houston area. Quintero biographers do generally agree he proceeded to Texas. The major port of entry — then as now — would have been at Galveston. Beyond this, some references indicate Quintero actually made his home at Richmond in Ft. Bend County, near Houston. Here he is reported to have partnered with or studied law under the Texas Republic's second president, Mirabeau B. Lamar, who had just gone into retirement at his Richmond plantation. Lending credence to this, one of the Spanish-language sources indicates Quintero had the "title of attorney from the University of the State of Texas, District of Richmond." *The Handbook of Texas* further notes Quintero "lent valuable assistance in the study of Spanish manuscripts now included in the Lamar Papers." More colorful, New Orleans *Times-Picayune* biographer John S. Kendall wrote that Quintero went to Texas where "he met and became intimate with Mirabeau B. Lamar; ... no ordinary man might long be friends with that extraordinary old firebrand."[81]

PRESIDENTS AND CONSPIRATORS

Despite a paucity of objective evidence to support this, it is probable Quintero did meet, study and possibly work with Lamar beginning as early as late 1849, continuing at least on and off over the next half dozen years. By the end of the decade Quintero and Lamar were demonstrably close friends; indeed, Quintero publicly championed Lamar in the years just prior to secession. Such a close relationship obviously had a genesis and a gestation. The one period in Quintero's life which proves relatively undocumented, and where his residence is uncertain, is these early years of the decade. Circumstance implies this is when he came to know Lamar and where their warm friendship developed.

The people of Texas knew Lamar as the poet-president, their recollections ranging from admiration to derision. A cultured man originally from Georgia, as Texas president a decade earlier, Lamar had strongly advocated education but implemented grandiose impractical projects, almost bankrupting the state. Later, as ex-president, he served in the Mexican War under General Zachary Taylor, gaining plaudits for gallantry at Monterrey. He then filled one term in the legislature before retiring in the summer of 1849 to his poetry, writings on Texas history, and the study of Spanish. How Lamar met Quintero is uncertain, but the two had much in common. They would certainly have been drawn to each other.[82]

In fact, Quintero's body of Spanish poetry seems to have been largely written during this decade, and a sensitive man like Lamar could have catalyzed this activity. In prison, Quintero had penned verse capturing his isolation and despair; he would likely have continued his active writing after arriving to American shores. His *Lyric Poetry in Cuba* shows strong evidence of having been written soon after he left the Caribbean. In later years, Quintero proved an advocate of Lamar's own significant efforts at verse, very likely returning the favor of the president's presumed early interest and support.

In a larger sense, Lamar's strong interest in Cuba provides particularly fertile ground to speculate on the Quintero connection. Soon after López's failure and withdrawal from Cuba in the 1850 Cárdenas expedition, Lamar received a June 15 letter written in New Orleans by Quintero's past Havana associate, José Sánchez Iznaga. This was the very same young patriot who had inadvertently exposed Mina Rosa in Cuba — resulting in Quintero's imprisonment — and whose uncle had helped found the revolutionary publication *La Verdad* in New York. Sánchez Iznaga complained to Lamar of General López's arrest. Indeed, López had barely eluded a Spanish warship before reaching the sanctuary of Key West. He nevertheless soon found himself arrested by American authorities and transferred to New Orleans for trial, charged with violation of Neutrality Laws. Addressing the former president with the military title "Genl Lamar," Sánchez Iznaga informed him "We can communicate nothing new to you." The Cuban operative nevertheless asked the president to "always keep us posted of the place where you are going to stop, and the method of addressing you...."

Lamar, at the very minimum, had already been a trusted, if not clandestine advisor to the Cuban independence movement. Sánchez Iznaga's letter makes this very clear: "I would also like you to communicate to us the ideas which may occur to you concerning the matter, for the advantage of the enterprize." In actuality, as with Jefferson Davis, Robert E. Lee, and Governor Quitman, the Cuban resistance group courted President Lamar for his influence, leadership and support — financial and otherwise.

The arrest of López led to a series of three trials held in New Orleans early the next year, beginning in January 1851. Lamar was in the city and actually married his second wife there in February; he no doubt would have followed developments and may have met with some of the principals. Judah Benjamin, the brilliant future Confederate Secretary of State, led the prosecution. In cross-examination he expertly pressed Quintero's professor-friend, the Cuban adjutant Ambrosio José Gonzales, another future Confederate officer and a chief witness for López's defense. The jury deadlocked; a mistrial had occurred. Two more trials ensued with the same result, the last ending March 6. A sympathetic populace would not convict López, Gonzales and Governor Quitman.[83]

Efforts to mount another expedition, ongoing even during the period of the filibuster trials, now accelerated. Hardly a week later, Quintero's old comrade Gonzales wrote from Macon, Georgia to President Lamar who was also in the city at the time with his new bride. Gonzales virtually gloated on the mistrials: "... You know already, in all probability, we have all been discharged, under circumstances amounting to an acquittal." The Cuban further reported on sales of Cuban Republic Bonds and arrangements to purchase armaments, hundreds of horses, and a couple of steamships to support their next expedition. Noting "the *high functionary* you introduced me to has been very friendly & *liberal* with me," Gonzales now asked for Lamar's "moral influence" with their friends in Columbus and Macon, Georgia, as well as Lamar's cousin Charles in Savannah. Now was the time for Lamar to go public, since "*just now* your letter upon Cuban matters would be most opportune." Gonzales also requested assistance in securing funds, stressing the need "to beg and entreat for the redemption of the hundreds of thousands of Cubans who labor under Spanish tyranny and the selfishness of a few of their own people...."[84]

In response to Gonzales, a few weeks later President Lamar wrote from Macon offering regrets that he could not support the project:

> I will explain to you in person, when we meet again, the imperious circumstances which place it entirely out of my power to cooperate with you in your noble endeavors for the good and glory of your deeply injured and oppressed country, and this inability on my part you will please communicate to the incorruptible old veteran and patriot Genl. Lopez, for whom I entertain the highest friendship and esteem, and whose cause, being that of God and Liberty, I sincerely hope may be as triumphant as his heart can desire.[85]

Apparently that same month, now in Philadelphia, Lamar wrote a lengthy, apologetic letter in Spanish to Narciso López, going into great detail why he felt the movement had little prospect of success. "I am resolved," Lamar wrote, "at the risk of being considered impertinent, to venture some observations and reflections which have occurred to me on contemplating the revolution, which it is said, is bound to occur in that turbulent Island." Lamar felt López was courting disaster, that the Cuban people had been degraded by political and religious tyranny for so many centuries they had no conception of or even desire for liberty. "The Cubans have not yet manifested any inclination to unsheathe the sword," Lamar argued, "and until they make some demonstration of this nature it is futile to try to help them and to give freedom to them as we would give rewards to children." Believing López deceived himself that a small filibuster army could spark a revolution among such a people, Lamar asked his friend to open his eyes to this dangerous course. Eerily prescient, Lamar predicted the outcome of the invasion:

> .... If you should land there with a handful of foreign volunteers — they would be weak and insignificant to fight their opponents, [and even] counting upon the cooperation of the natives of the country, I am certain that your ruin and that of your valiant companions would be inevitable, because no one would come out to your assistance, nor even lift a finger in defense of you or your

cause. In the hour of danger the terrified inhabitants would seek their own safety, and deliver you and your courageous army over to the government, and you, forsaken and deceived by the perfidy of pusillanimous friends, would be hanged as a criminal, and with you would perish the best hopes of the country. Condemned and executed as a traitor, you would descend to the grave without a single friend to eulogize you or vindicate your fame, tormented in your last moments with the bitter reflection that you have sacrificed your life for an ungrateful people who are incapable of appreciating your virtues or of avenging your death.[86]

Early the following August, leaving behind an ill and recuperating Gonzales, López precipitously invaded Cuba upon hearing of an uprising in Camaguey. A Kentucky regiment commanded by Colonel William Crittenden — nephew of the U.S. Attorney General — accompanied the Cuban filibusters. They landed, but as Lamar predicted, no one joined the would-be liberators; instead, disaster, capture and firing squads greeted the outnumbered Kentuckians. Their leader López, alone and humiliatingly displayed in Havana's public square, suffered execution as a traitor at the hands of his Spanish captors. Lamar's prediction erred on only one point: López did not enjoy the simple mercy of hanging, but the cruel strangulation of the garrote.[87]

A KINDRED INTELLECT

Quintero thus found himself influenced by a thoughtful, sincere statesman who had predicted the filibuster outcome and had earlier informed López, "I cannot advise my friends and compatriots to go with you to Cuba...."[88] Quintero may have consciously sought a new life independent of the Cuban revolutionary movement, possibly meeting Lamar for the first time in Texas or even in New Orleans upon the general's marriage. On the other hand, the Cubans in New Orleans may even have assigned Quintero to serve as liaison to Lamar. Regardless, once exposed to a kindred intellect who so clearly perceived the folly of the enterprise, Quintero must have been similarly convinced. Lamar's influence may have imprinted a new mindset onto the Cuban. A patriotic Quintero continued dedication to the cause of Cuban liberation, but he would now exhibit this ideal in stirring poetry rather than radical revolutionary action.

It would be 1853 before President Lamar would return to Texas for anything like an extended period. If indeed Quintero had made his acquaintance and fell into Lamar's coterie of friends and colleagues in Richmond, their intercourse would have been greatly interrupted by Lamar's travel. Other than the latter part of 1849 and portions of 1850, Lamar spent a great deal of time

Georgia and elsewhere. Thus, it may be that the two maintained contact on a sporadic basis, or that Quintero did not actually establish a relationship with Lamar until the general and his bride returned and finally settled at Richmond beginning in 1853. It is entirely possible Quintero did not fall into Lamar's sphere until after the López fiasco, but had been otherwise engaged in New Orleans or Texas for some two or three years after escaping Havana. Supporting this is a *Daily Picayune* citation claiming Quintero lived in New Orleans for 34 years. While this could not have been continuous residence, this implies the Cuban first arrived there in 1851. Indeed, one biographer actually states Quintero renewed his friendship with Pedro Santacilia in New Orleans during this time, about 1853. If so, Santacilia may have introduced Quintero to his new friend, former Mexican governor and future president Benito Juárez. In his humiliating exile, Juárez then rolled cigars for a living. Juan Clemente Zenea and other Cubans had also befriended the Mexican, even sending arms to liberal forces then vying for control of his country's government. Quintero would have had a warm camaraderie with the *Order of Young Cuba*, and such old friends as Thrasher, Castellón, Villaverde, Santacilia and Clemente Zenea. The New Orleans city directories for the decade before secession — specifically 1849 to 1860 — do not include Quintero as a resident, any Quintero for that matter. Of course, this is not definitive. A young man of little means, Quintero could very well have informally roomed with any of his Cuban friends, thereby preserving no permanent record of any period he might have lived there.[89]

Contentedly wed and no longer harboring further political ambition, Lamar now focused on historical and poetical interests. Since his days as vice-president of the Texas Republic almost 20 years earlier, he had been collecting materials and writing on various Spanish era topics. One of these was Philip Nolan, the turn-of-the-century adventurer who had attempted to wrest Spanish Texas from the Empire. While Lamar would never publish any of his projected historical volumes, Quintero would years later emerge the recognized expert on Nolan. Perhaps Lamar instilled in the Cuban this early interest in Texas history. Quintero's future publication may have been a direct outcome of this early collaboration and friendship.[90]

Another aspect of Lamar's mid–1850s life comes into clearer perspective when Quintero is presumed an intimate of the ex-president, at least by this time. From New Orleans in January of 1855, John S. Thrasher sent President Lamar an annotated Spanish-language manuscript on the life of Mexican General Santa Anna. Writing of his old nemesis had been one of Lamar's favorite topics for a book. Thrasher, who had been so active in conspiring with Quintero in Havana — only to later be jailed and expelled for writings sympathetic to López — now wrote on Cuban annexation in *De Bow's Review* and actively conspired with Mississippi Governor John Quitman for a new filibustering expedition. In fact, Quitman relied heavily on both Thrasher and Lamar's Savannah cousin, Charles. Even with the filibuster imperative, Thrasher also translated historical literature. By the following year, he would publish a translation from Spanish of Alexander Humbolt's *The Island of Cuba*. Thrasher's letter to Lamar begins: "As my young man became somewhat confused in arranging the papers you handed him, I have taken the liberty of going through them myself...." Clearly, a collaboration between Thrasher and Lamar had been established. Lamar's use of Thrasher to assist in his Santa Anna research could have been suggested by a trusted young friend, Quintero himself. In fact, two years later Quintero (mis-indexed as J. N. Quintero in the Lamar Papers) would correspond with Lamar on this very same topic: "Sending a biographical sketch of Santa Anna sent by Antonio Navarro...."[91]

Election of James Buchanan as president in 1856 revived Lamar's interest in a political appointment. The new president had strong Southern support and shared with Lamar a keen interest in Cuba. As a diplomat to Britain, Buchanan had earlier co-authored the Ostend Manifesto, the declaration that the United States had the right to seize Cuba by force if the Spanish refused to sell her. Encouraged, Lamar traveled to the inaugural and met with influential party leaders. Mississippi Governor Quitman helped draft a letter recommending Lamar for a ministerial assignment in Europe or South America. That summer Lamar received an Argentine appointment, but at the last moment a more highly compensated position combining Nicaraguan and Costa Rican posts materialized. Just after Christmas, in 1857, Lamar departed for Central America.[92]

Coincidentally — or not — by this time Quintero established himself across the state in Bexar County in the town of San Antonio. Sketchy accounts indicate Quintero had studied law under Lamar, "was admitted to the practice" in Texas and had taken U.S. citizenship in 1853.[93] Regardless, Spanish Queen Isabel II proclaimed amnesty a year later in 1854, but Quintero did not return to Cuba.[94] At least one biographer indicates Quintero served as law partner to Lamar in San Antonio.[95] The two may have been partners, but they certainly never worked together in San Antonio. The former Texas president never lived there. What is certain is that the summer of 1856 found Quintero editing a San Antonio Spanish-language newspaper called *El Ranchero*. Its first edition arrived Independence Day, 1856.[96] Such an undertaking certainly fit Quintero's talents. How and exactly why he came to take this position is uncertain. Nevertheless, this move coincides with President Lamar's stirring from retirement into a more active political role once again. Quintero needed to be established independently. Lamar's days at his Richmond plantation would soon yield to diplomatic service in Central America.

TEXAN KNOW-NOTHINGS

A new national party, the American Party, emerged in the 1850s and took root in Texas. It reacted against strong waves of immigration and growing populations of Roman Catholics. The party encouraged that only long-established and native-born Americans be considered for public office. By the early 1850s, it was organized as a series of secret orders, absolutely mystifying political party bosses in New York City. When questioned, suspected members declared they knew nothing. Called "Know-Nothings" after that, the movement carried Massachusetts and nearly took New York State in 1854. Attracting Whigs and disgruntled Democrats, that year the movement extended its influence into the South.

Across the country, the Know-Nothing party proved a distraction from the argument over slavery, providing a common menace to cement the Union — immigration. In Texas, the party attracted those who did not want to see disunion over slavery, but paradoxically the party also came to be viewed as proslavery and pro–South. The logic went that the large German population was antislavery, thus restriction of immigration would preserve proslavery sentiment.[97]

Nationally, the party attracted such notables as former president Millard Fillmore and telegraph inventor Samuel B. Morse; locally, in Texas, the most significant convert was none other than Sam Houston. The Texas patriot had long promoted a pro–South Unionist course and opposed repeal of the Compromise of 1850 lest "the extremes of Abolitionists and secession parties ... convulse the Country from Maine to the Rio Grande." Disenfranchised from both major parties, yet with presidential ambitions, Houston saw in the American Party a platform he could support. He soon began clamoring against immigration. The Texan warned of the half million yearly European immigrant "paupers and criminals" who opposed slavery and would swell the Northern political ranks. He also argued against the power of the Catholic church and its oppression of American Catholics by its own priesthood and Pope. Texas, with a large population of German and Spanish-speaking immigrants, provided an excellent field with which to reap political gain.[98]

A rash of newspapers rose in Texas taking strong positions on the Know-Nothing Party. In Austin, celebrated physician, ranger, and Quitman filibustering supporter John Salmon "Rip" Ford's *Texas State Times* took a pro–Know-Nothing stance, as did the *Herald* and *Sentinel* in San Antonio. In that city, the three ethnic groups took sides along party lines, with the Germans favoring the Democrats. At the Bexar County Democratic convention in June, 1856 the Spanish speakers split. One group of delegates afterwards used the *Bejareño*, founded in the previous year, to promote its side. Presenting Quintero's faction, one historian wrote: "The rival group responded by founding *El Ranchero*, edited by José Quintero, to present their views. *El Ranchero* took an almost hysterical view of the Know-Nothings, warning that they planned violence against the Spanish-speaking and planned to tear down the Roman Catholic churches."[99]

The Know-Nothing *Herald*, headed by an intelligent, social activist, 18-year-old editor named James P. Newcomb, translated and printed one of Quintero's more "incendiary" editorials. The Know-Nothings reacted strongly. They "charged Quintero with printing false and libelous material" and demanded retraction if he valued his life. Doctor James M. Devine, the local mayor, grew concerned that tensions would explode. He advised citizens of San Antonio, "regardless of party," to arm themselves, not just for their own protection, but to safeguard Quintero, the editor.

Into Mayor Devine's drugstore at Commerce Street and Main Plaza, on the northeast corner, soon stormed John S. McDonald. A staunch Know-Nothing, and also a former mayor himself, he originally owned the press from which the *Sentinel* and its Know-Nothing successor the *Herald* had sprung. McDonald challenged Devine, apparently on his protection of Quintero, whereupon Mayor Devine killed McDonald. The Mayor then placed himself in jail to await a legal judgment on his actions.

The *Herald's* co-owner, J. M. West, would not stand for this. A questionable character himself, he had previously fled Ohio and a murder charge. West led a mob to the jail and urged his compatriots to drag the mayor out of the cell and hang him there on the spot. Fortunately for Mayor Devine, the mob did not have the nerve to do so. Afterwards, the judge ruled Devine had only acted in self-defense.

Bloodshed seemed to calm passions in San Antonio over Quintero's editorial. The locals agreed Mayor Devine had no choice but to kill McDonald, yet they nevertheless missed the old fellow. James Newcomb received a great deal of criticism for translating Quintero's article and starting the controversy, so he sold the paper and after a while "went east" supposedly to improve his education. Eventually Newcomb returned and continued a brilliant career at the *Herald*. As for West, the partner, he skipped town just before arrest on the Ohio murder charge. In the following year he joined William Walker's filibuster in Nicaragua, was wounded during the 1857 expulsion from the capital Granada, and afterwards settled in New Orleans.[100]

PRESIDENT LAMAR—POET COMRADE

Quintero's time in San Antonio seems to have been relatively brief. On Christmas Day, 1857, from Austin where he now resided, Quintero wrote a letter to President Lamar. The Cuban reported his new position: "I am at present Assistant Clerk in the House of Representatives."[101]

Again, Quintero's life had taken a new direction, with typically few clues left to unravel the circumstance. Actually, he did translate various legal documents for the state, and one of them does provide a hint as to what might have happened. Quintero, listed as lawyer (abogado), prepared the Spanish version of an 1856 map of the city of San Antonio. This map is shown as a publication of the San Antonio *Ledger*. The map appears as a supportive document for the Texas charter document for the city. It may be that Quintero's contacts and skills — journalistic, linguistic and legal — had been recognized in San Antonio. Initial work in San Antonio may have led to a more substantial position in Austin.[102]

In fact, aside from his statement of serving the legislature as assistant clerk, Quintero prepared two other state documents in 1857. One of these, issued in Spanish, had the title "Report of the Governor of the State of Texas and documents relative to attacks against Mexican highwaymen." It was translated by J. A. Quintero in Austin, of John Marshall and Company, state printers. The other document was less colorful: "Penal code of the State of Texas. Adopted by the sixth legislature. Spanish version by J. A. Quintero, lawyer and legal advisor. Austin: Printed by order of the government in the office of the State Gazette, contracted to Marshall and Oldham. 1857 ... 112 p." Quintero has been said to have worked for a land office in Austin about this time, so perhaps he found himself employed, as needed, as a translator for the company of Marshall and Oldham.[103]

Living in Austin, the state capital, and working for the legislature gave Quintero access to important Texas icons. A 1937 centennial year *Times-Picayune* account remembered Quintero and reported "he became a friend of Sam Houston." If true, it is surprising a late nineteenth-century *Daily Picayune* retrospective, some 50 years earlier, failed to note this friendship.[104] Did Quintero know Sam Houston? Probably. Senator Houston would have been frequently seen at the Austin capitol. Of course, Houston's flirtation with the Know-Nothing party would not have set well with Quintero. By the time the Cuban arrived in Austin, though, Houston had drifted from the movement. After all, the party had the audacity to pass over the "Father of Texas" in its nomination for president![105] Regardless of political shifts, nothing could change that Houston represented Mirabeau Lamar's longtime mortal enemy. The passionate, loyal Cuban would never countenance betraying his intimate friend, President Lamar. On this basis, the *Picayune* reference is surely specious, the error of an unfamiliar writer decades later who confused one Texas hero, Lamar, with another, Houston.

As former president Lamar left Washington for Nicaragua, Quintero's correspondence indeed reveals their close friendship and how much Lamar had come to rely on the Cuban's help. In the same Christmas Day letter, Quintero reports on the status of a biographical article in the *Texas Almanac*, lamenting "the engraver and the printer ought to be hung or at least indicted for libel" for sketching "an awful engraving purporting to be your portrait." Ever attentive, he promises to forward a poem in Spanish dedicated to Mrs. Lamar, to be published in "any of the newspapers" of Central America. Similarly, Quintero asks for Lamar's address to send a biographical sketch of Mexican general Santa Anna. Furthermore, Quintero does not neglect to furnish the latest intelligence on the near lifeless stirrings of the Know-Nothing party.

This letter also reveals Quintero's less intense, lighter side. He playfully wrote, "I have not done my duty to the State or obeyed the Bible (Gen. Chap. 1, v. 28). So, you will perceive that times are glorious with me. I have many dimes and no children." Of course, Quintero referred to his not fulfilling the biblical admonition to "be fruitful and multiply." The result: Free of children, he yet retained ready funds — "many dimes" — for whatever suited him. Since Quintero brought up familial matters, the implication is that he is married by this time. In fact, in the postscript Quintero mentions a book of poetry written by Lamar "stolen ... from my wife's room," apparently by one of Lamar's female admirers. The Cuban reinforces this with a reminder: "My wife wishes to be kindly remembered by you."[106]

Actually, Quintero had been married some eight months by this time. On April 13, 1857, in her home city of New Orleans, he married Eliza Bournos.[107] Biographers report little on her and how she and Quintero came to know each other. Some records present her as Eliza Frances De Tazier (Bournos).[108] A few accounts indicate the Cuban spent some time in New Orleans in 1857 prior to the War.[109] Perhaps he did move to the Crescent City for a short time during the 1850's — even as late as early 1857 — and met his wife there. Among the range of possibilities is that Mirabeau Lamar may have had some role in their introduction. After all, Lamar had also been married in New Orleans not so long before; furthermore, Quintero's Eliza did wish to be "kindly remembered" by the former president. Interestingly, there are conflicting accounts of an unnamed Mexican woman Quintero married a handful of years later.[110] It may be that Eliza Bournos was of Spanish descent — certainly a long-established ethnic group in old New Orleans — and the Hispanic biographers simply presumed his wife came from south of the border.

Regardless of this important move to gain a wife, Quintero still viewed poetry as vital. Lamar, his friend and mentor, also pursued verse, so in the Christmas Day letter Quintero sensitively followed the president's publishing successes: "I also enclose an article on your family published a few weeks ago and your beautiful poem 'Grieve not sweet flower &c.' which I clip from the Charleston Courier. Doña Carmelita, My Gem of Delight and many of the poems contained in the Verse Memorials are going the round of the newspaper press almost every day."[111] Quintero's enthusiastic report conveys greater optimism than a review he wrote earlier that year. In September 1857 Lamar had published his life's poetic output in a slender volume entitled *Verse Memorials*. Quintero, truly in his element, promoted the book in a lengthy, eloquent promotional piece. He opens defining the same three inspirations to poetry outlined in his *Lyric Poetry in Cuba* a decade earlier, and then transitions to an unmistakable advocacy: "…We are now rejoiced to see a new contribution to Southern literature, and hail it as the harbinger of that lustre which genius is destined to shed over our land of beauty, enterprise and valor." Lamar the soldier and statesman, "like of Knight of old has laid aside his trenchant sword…." And his poetry? "His poems are like the violets that bloom on the way side and regale the traveller with their delicate perfume." His emotion? "He sometimes weeps but his tears are the morning dews that brighten the rose and double its fragrance." To wit, "Would you present a rose to the Lady that you love?" asks Quintero. "Who has ever done it more gracefully than Lamar in his lines beginning — 'Grieve not sweet flower to leave these shades.'"

Of course, "Poetry has never been the study and pursuit of Gen Lamar." The Cuban defender apologizes for the "melodious expression of natural feelings…." He argues that had Lamar "cultivated poetry as an art" rather than indulge "only in moments of leisure and relaxation," his "poetry would have been characterized by all that boldness of thought, vigor of expression and fierce ardor which so abound in his political writings." Quintero thus makes his case for Lamar: "As a poet, therefore, of accident, and not by profession — as one who has only tuned an unambitious harp for the momentary gratification of those he loved and respected — is he to be judged; and without hesitation we proclaim it, that he is not surpassed by any American poet within the walk which he has chosen for himself." Underscoring this fairness he asks for Lamar, and admitting one could not liken Lamar to the "satire of Holmes" or the "scholarship of Longfellow," Quintero asks if one would "compare the Paradise Lost with the Irish Melodies."[112]

Lamar's *Verse Memorials*, a little more than 200 pages long, contains over 60 of the general's poetic works. He dedicated the volume to the wife of one of his faithful friends of Lone Star Republic days: "To Mrs. William L. Cazneau — so favorably known to the public by her pen, as 'Cora Montgomery'…."[113] Interestingly, during the López conspiracy days Cora Montgomery had provided a respectable front as "publisher" of the New York revolutionary periodical *La Verdad* in loose connection with John Thrasher. Quintero's past Havana conspirators, Miguel Teurbe Tolón and then Cirilo Villaverde at this time had actually edited the patriotic organ, which was routinely smuggled into Cuba.[114]

Regardless of past threads linking Lamar's group of intimates to Quintero, his book offered a broad collection of poems: they ranged from "On the Death of My Daughter" to "Ode to Fishing Creek." One work written in 1833 Georgia, entitled "Arm for the Southern Land," captures a mood more readily associated with the secessionary crisis of 1850, or even of 1860.[115] The opening stanza:

> ARM for the Southern land,
> All fear of death disdaining ;
> Low lay the tyrant hand
> Our sacred right profaning !

Quintero's review does much more than defend President Lamar's creative work; it provides insight into the Cuban's absolute devotion to his new homeland, to his Southern homeland. In chastising Georgia for not better recognizing her own son, he first hints at this: "We have met with some of the Georgia papers and ... not even a solitary piece has been admitted into their papers...." Quintero continues: "Had the most indifferent piece of Lamar appeared" in *Harper's Magazine*, there is no "doubt it would have been copied throughout the South...." In alluding to this acquiescence of the South's cultural subjugation by the North, Quintero then pays tribute to South Carolina as a unique Southern state:

> She is the Bulwark and protector of the American Constitution — the bold, consistent and uncorrupted defender of its original and unperverted principles; and at the same time she is almost the only State of the South which has manifested any disposition to protect her own literature — to emancipate herself from the dogmatism of the North, and to build up a character of her own.

Quintero subsequently chastises his fellow Southerners for neglecting the *Southern Literary Messenger* in favor of "its more presumptuous and arrogant, yet less meritorious rival, 'Harper's Magazine,'...." More broadly, he cautions: "Without a literature of our own, we can have neither dignity, self-respect or any security of rights." Now a fervent Southerner, he warns of becoming "social inferiors and political dependents" to "our enemies in intellectual pursuits." What started as a tribute to Lamar's creative endeavor ends as a virtual call to action: "To be second rate in the arts, sciences and literature is to be second in Civilization and second in everything else. If we would maintain political equality in the Union it is indispensable to establish social and mental equality. Without the arts, sciences and literature, there can be neither permanent prosperity nor security for liberty."[116]

So Quintero, the ardent Cuban revolutionary, has virtually completed the transition to Southern nationalist. His allegiance to the South is not superficial, nor is it a half-hearted result of obligation to dear friends. Now a Southerner by choice and conviction, Quintero argues for cultural independence from his region's "enemies" to the North. He falls just short of proposing political independence. As the "fiery trial" inexorably approached, there would be no question where Quintero stood.

BEFORE THE STORM

The year 1858 brought renewed contact with old friends. Quintero no doubt corresponded with colleagues from the Havana conspiracy days, or at least with their New York publisher. This collaboration yielded publication of the seminal work *El Laúd del Desterrado* (The Lute of the Exiled). This collection had been forged in the idea of Cuban independence, featuring Quintero and six other poets who had been martyred or exiled as heroes to the cause. Of course, such a volume would naturally have been a publication of the revolutionary group in New York, printed by their periodical *La Revolución.*[117]

The following year saw expanded horizons in the Hispanic world. While yet an Austin resident, Quintero crossed paths with an important Mexican leader who would soon play a pivotal role in his life and career. Santiago Vidaurri, the governor of the combined Northern Mexican States Nuevo León y Coahuila, had abandoned his capital of Monterrey due to pressure from President Juárez's liberal forces during the War of the Reform. Professing himself a liberal, Vidaurri had only attempted to secure his own position, nominally supporting the liberal government against the church conservatives who still held Mexico City. The result: Governor Vidaurri had been arrested, followed by a short, self-imposed exile for two weeks in Austin. There, early that fall, he met several Texas leaders, one of them proving none other than Quintero. The two became friendly and even corresponded occasionally. The next year, from Austin, Quintero wrote to the Mexican governor, both in June and as late as October of 1860.[118]

Further south, in Central America, Minister Lamar had actively attempted to advance United States interests, but his diplomacy proved inconclusive, particularly facing lingering resentment engendered by the William Walker filibustering coup in Nicaragua. In an apparent goodwill gesture, Lamar had even donated to the new Nicaraguan public library 200 copies of his *Verse Memorials*. By late 1859, Lamar's assignment had ended. He returned to Richmond in October where he again hoped to complete his long-delayed works on Texas history. One morning only two months later, at a Christmas celebration on his plantation, Mirabeau B. Lamar observed to an examining doctor: "I feel very queerly, I believe I am going to die." Moments later he expired of a heart attack.[119]

The Texas patriot had influenced Quintero immeasurably. As the sun set on the old Georgian, the dawn had only risen for Quintero. He would take the rich experience and mentorship bequeathed by Lamar — legal, historical, literary, even Southern partisan — and make it a source of strength in his own life.[120]

The Cuban would never forget Mirabeau Lamar. Perhaps in a kind of tribute, Quintero's future publications on Texas history may have been intended to complete works Lamar had earlier envisioned. More personally, Quintero would ensure his friend's name lived on to the next century. In just a few years, the Cuban would proudly welcome his firstborn into the world, giving him the only name possible from one poet-comrade to another: Lamar.

The death of Lamar — coupled with the draw of old island friends — may have catalyzed Quintero's decision to make a new start. In his October 27, 1860 letter to Governor Vidaurri, Quintero provided details of his plans:

> I write you not only to acknowledge receipt of your letter [of the 14th], but to reveal to you that the 1st of next [month] I shall leave with the destination of New York where they call me to be editor of "El Noticiero." This periodical's accounts today are $30,000 in capital and thousands of subscribers in Spanish America. I believe it will have a fair influence.
>
> My aim is to stay in that city only a year, because I will never abandon … Texas. I desire, nevertheless, that during my residence in the North, you write me frequently.[121]

Records conflict somewhat, but general consensus is that Quintero moved to New York. This correspondence with Governor Vidaurri settles the issue, even to the date: November 1, 1860. Some biographers report that Quintero worked as a notary public in New York at this time. He had the legal credentials, no doubt, but it may be that these accounts confuse his later years as a notary public in New Orleans.[122] The position he actually relocated for involved editorship of *El Noticiero* (The Reporter), an apparently well-financed startup magazine or newspaper. Whether or not this offer and prospect materialized, biographers typically agree that Quintero's great journalistic achievement in New York proved to be his association with the renowned newsman Leslie. Publisher of the widely read *Frank Leslie's Pictorial Weekly*, he put Quintero's journalistic and linguistic skills to excellent use on the Spanish version of this popular newsletter, *La Ilustración-Americana*.[123]

Of course, now Quintero would have had great opportunity for camaraderie with his Havana prison companion Cirilo Villaverde, who returned to New York in 1860 after two years in Havana. In fact, Villaverde would later assume editorship of this same Leslie Spanish-language publication.[124] There is more than speculation to support this reestablishment of ties to the

Cuban junta in New York. Very faintly visible on the letter to the governor is an apparent forwarding address. It refers to "J. S. Thrasher, Esquire" at one of the New York hotels.[125] It may be that Thrasher in fact recruited Quintero to New York. Regardless, Quintero indeed renewed connections to a dedicated Cuban patriot, one who historically had had excellent ties himself to the publishing world. In fact, Quintero, Thrasher and Villaverde had each alternated editing Havana's *El Faro Industrial* about a decade earlier. By association, the Cuban from Texas quickly found himself consorting with revolutionaries, if only to enjoy their friendship and perhaps publish in their various journals.

In some ways, Quintero's move to New York would seem to defy good judgment. The nation's two great sections — North and South — were on a collision course. Radical abolitionists and fire-eating secessionists stood ready to rend the nation to defend their principles. Quintero could not have been oblivious to the storm brewing. Perhaps, like many, he could not comprehend the unthinkable, and somehow hoped the trial would pass. In hindsight, this move to New York for one of his sectional ardors represented an imprudent course. Regardless, Quintero would find himself in this "enemy" terrain as the results of the presidential election that year unfolded.

El Laúd del Desterrado

Quintero must have reflected on his goals and achievements as the guns of secession turned his world on end. Had he not survived the coming conflict, evidence of his passing would be limited to a few creative works of poetry and literary critique. On this basis, a pause to take assessment of Quintero, the writer and poet, provides useful perspective.

Motivated in great part by the revolutionary struggle of his Havana youth, poetry served as Quintero's great creative outlet. Nevertheless, he sometimes wrote essays on general topics of importance to him. Unlike his poetry, the surviving, readily available essays are typically in English. Already considered have been his works *Lyric Poetry in Cuba* and his advocacy piece, "Verse Memorials by Mirabeau B. Lamar."[126] Another essay — possibly a book — symbolizes Quintero's virtual transfer of allegiance from Cuba to the American South, just as filibuster leadership shifted from the Cuban López to the Southerner Quitman. This work is, in fact, a biographical treatment of John Quitman. An extremely rare publication, Quintero possibly wrote the piece after Quitman's 1858 death, but before the War of Secession. Biographers provide virtually no detail on this book, other than its name, and even here there is disagreement. Some report it as *Apuntes Biográficos*, while one authoritative source calls it *Biografía del jeneral [sic] John A. Quintman [sic]*, recording it published in New Orleans.[127] Obviously penned in Spanish, the title "Biographical Points" implies it had the character of an essay, perhaps even a handwritten manuscript like his *Lyric Poetry in Cuba.*

Quintero's poetry and other essays — largely of patriotic nature — appeared extensively in the Spanish-language press, at least according to a 1955 Havana publication from *El Sol.* This in-depth treatment of Quintero's life, *El Primer Periodista y un Gran Educador,* is quite unique. While virtually every other biographer redigests previous, brief outlines of the Cuban's life, this article is rich in detail. Its extensive inventory of magazines and clandestine revolutionary publications presents Quintero as an ardent voice for Cuban freedom during his exile. The titles and subjects of these reputed writings are not presented; nevertheless, the list is wide-ranging. In 1852, as the article goes, Quintero "collaborated" in the separatist periodical *La Voz de Pueblo Cubano,* while the following year he appeared in Cuba's *Revista de la Habana.* (Of course, the Cuban tribunal sentenced Quintero after publication in *La Voz* in the same year.) At an undetermined date, Quintero also figured in other Cuban magazines, *El Fanal, La Aurora del Yumuri* and *Aureola Poética.* This article also mentions Quintero's publication in his friend Cirilo Villaverde's *La Verdad,* which moved to New Orleans in 1854. Later, the transplanted Cuban is reported as contributing to the *Revista Habanera,* a publication which began in 1861 as war in the United States erupted. More interestingly, *El Ariguanabo* and *Diario Mercantil* began at the same time, and Quintero is said to have been an editor and "intense collaborator." Another war-era publication in which he published, this one "property" of his friend Cirilo Villaverde, was *La América.* By 1868, the Cuban patriot was writing for the New York magazine, *La Revolución,* and he is said to have been editor of *El Boletín Comercial* in 1871. Another New York patriotic organ associated with Quintero is *El Nuevo Mundo.*

There may be great accuracy in that listing, but no other Quintero essay, among the many surveys of Cuban poetic literature which are readily available, mentions this remarkable list of publications with such specificity. Furthermore, this article is incorrect on many other aspects of Quintero's life. Some of the conflicts this article presents, when compared to other established sources, are that Quintero is reported in New Orleans before the war working on Leslie's magazine, that he lived in Mexico into the 1870's, and that he received a law degree in New York after the war, at which time he moved to that city.[128] With this many inconsistencies, an examination of this large number of listed publications for actual submissions by Quintero would be a prudent step to determine the true extent of his work. Of course, it may not be as simple as this. Quintero had been sentenced by the Spanish authorities — even condemned to death, by some reports — so it may have been wise for his publishers to have him write under pseudonyms.

It is Quintero's appearance as one of the luminaries in *El Laúd del Desterrado* that secures him a permanent place in Hispanic literature. More than any other work, *The Lute of the Exiled* captured the voice of Cuban exiles and their plea for liberty in *la patria*, the homeland. The individual tomes, collected in unison, offered to the world a powerful cry of anguish against Spanish tyranny. Published in 1858, this collection had genesis with Quintero's revolutionary companion in Havana, Pedro Santacilia. Two years earlier in New York he had published his own solitary work, *El Arpa del Proscrito* (The Harp of the Banished). Now, the new collection featured Santacilia along with Quintero and other contemporary exiles: Pedro Angel Castellón, Leopoldo Turla and Juan Clemente Zenea. In addition, two fallen comrades completed the collection: Miguel Teurbe Tolón, who had edited *La Verdad* and had died in Cuba the previous year at the tender age of 37, and José María Heredia, a widely respected "prophet of our revolution," whose writings a generation earlier had inspired his literary descendants. Of course, the assemblage could open with none other than Heredia's *Himno del Desterrado* (Hymn of the Exiled). Its optimistic vision had long motivated the conspirators, but would not come to pass for several decades:

> Cuba, at last thou shalt be free and pure as the air thou breathest,
> as the sparkling waves which thou dost see kissing the sand of thy shores.[129]

This important collection featured three of Quintero's pieces: *A Miss Lydia Robbins, Adelante* and *Poesía*. The editor described the exiled poet as a "talent in bloom, which began to unfold in prison." Others have ascribed to Quintero's work a "biblical character in the language of Poe." The eminent authority José Manuel Carbonell, in his evaluation of Quintero and colleagues, *Los Poetas de "El Laúd del Desterrado,"* provided this assessment: "The poetic inspiration of Quintero is one of a fluid enchanter when he evokes nature and describes, invaded by intense longing for his homeland port, the landscapes and scenes which shine in his soul, the lantern of memory."[130]

A Miss Lydia Robins, written "with his eyes full of his homeland and its horizons, and his heart burning with rage," represents the freedom fighter's retrospection "illuminated by the prospect of combat." One of the quartets in this poem captures the pathos of longing for his homeland:

> Oh Lydia! Sweet Lydia! The icy wind
> wounds me here with its quick edge,
> I enjoy the liberty that I yearned
> but my sad heart is dying.[131]

The other two works, *Adelante* and *Poesía*, represent the patriotic ardor which animated Quintero so much in his earlier years. *Poesía* is "one of his most vigorous compositions, by its bitter beauty of depth and grave solemnity of form." Written at the time of the López expedition, after the liberator's capture and hideous execution in Cuba, Quintero lamented the futility of the sacrifice:

> —What will you do, blacksmith?—The soil lasts
> where coffee and sugar bloom.
> —Vain is your industry, your toil is madness!
> Fatigue and bitterness is yours
> the gold and harvests are Spain's![132]

One of Quintero's famous poems, *Memorias del alma (Memories of the Soul)*—written after the Confederate War and dedicated to "his adored" but otherwise unidentified Rebecca—features a tribute to his dear old friend, Texas president Mirabeau B. Lamar:

> Lamar, incomparable on the rostrum,
> inspired poet, in combat a thunderbolt;
> to you, my good friend,
> that you knew to share
> your home and bread with me,
> I consecrate a memory to you! Your name
> how indifferent, the victor does not hail,
> with my lute, in the Spanish tongue,
> I will carry to the fields of fame.[133]

Quintero's penultimate work is *El Banquete del Destierro, The Banquet of the Exiled*. Logically, this should have been the feature piece in *El Laúd del Desterrado*, but it was written some time afterwards. In fact, it was probably written in postwar New Orleans, where at least one source indicates Quintero published "his best verses." Another major scholar speculated this may have been inspired by Longfellow. Described as "frightful and macabre," it is "a strange song which puts ice in the soul." Carbonell wrote: "The vision of the poet is absorbed in the cruel reality of an unredeemable homeland, subjected to the furor of tyrants." Quintero rails against "outrages by the brutal soldiery" to his homeland, the "sorrowful virgin of his love." The opening pensive stanza captures his despair in exile, coupled with admiration for the fallen:

> Severe and bitter destiny
> to strange lands sends us;
> look how dark the sky is!
> There is not even a ray of hope!
> But let us laugh at the sorrows,
> raise the foaming cup,

A toast for the ones that have died!
Hurrah for Liberty![134]

In addition to these more familiar poetic works, Quintero produced other major efforts. These include *El Tiro, Al Aura, El Retorno al Delirio, A Fanny, Desaliento, El Látigo Español, Quintana en Cuba, El Pasado, El Paraíso del Corazón, Al Volver a Verte, Amor Perdido, Inocencia y Pasión, Patria, En la Muerte de Castañada,* the sonnet *Jerusalem* written in English, and the aforementioned *Esperanza,* composed in Havana's Morro prison. Quintero also penned *En la Muerte de Narciso López* (In the Death of Narciso López); interestingly, *El Laúd* contains an identically named 1851 work by Tolón, though of different verse. Beyond this important body of creative work, Quintero's fine linguistic ability also found broad expression. He translated into Spanish several key English and German works by major poets, including Henry Wadsworth Longfellow (El Amanecer), a paraphrase of a German sonnet by Friedrich Rückert, as well as works by the German poets Johann Schiller and Johann Uhland, and the Englishman Tennyson.[135]

Quintero's work has been compared to that of one of late-nineteenth-century Cuba's most notable poets, Julián del Casal. Never exiled from Cuba, Casal nevertheless engaged in a kind of self-imposed exile of spirit. Inspired, perhaps even obsessed, by French and Japanese literary traditions, his home even exuded Oriental elegance. Casal was a "forerunner of the *modernista* movement" and in turn influenced his friend, the eminent Rubén Darío. Quintero's life work interested Casal greatly. One critic reported that Casal hoped Quintero's son, Lamar, would one day "give light to the complete work of a meticulous and original artist, who in a supreme outburst of vehemence, composed a tragic song, mournful and funerary that carries the title *El Banquete del Destierro....*" That an artist of such distinction as Casal "admired" Quintero is notable, significantly more so coupled with "great praise from Manuel Sanguily." Of course, Sanguily was a great writer of the days just preceding the Spanish-American War, and later rose to Secretary of State for Cuba. Long belated accolades from a representative of the Cuban government itself![136]

The echoes have long since died from Casal's plea to bring together the works of José Agustín Quintero into a single volume; alas, his wish has not yet come to pass.

SECESSION

Quintero no doubt arrived in New York City in November 1860, just as Abraham Lincoln secured the presidency. The Democrats had split the vote, paving the way for a radical new party, the Republicans. Quintero's "Bulwark and protector of the Constitution," the State of South Carolina, led the way in seceding from the Union by the end of the following month. Weeks later, early in 1861, her sister states of the deep South followed. By February 1, over the protest of Sam Houston, Quintero's adopted State of Texas seceded by a vote of 166–8. A week later, the newly formed Confederate States of America adopted a provisional constitution in Montgomery, Alabama. These states wished to peacefully leave the Union, exercising the right of secession — a right claimed by the New England states on more than one occasion in the preceding decades.[137] President John Buchanan did not challenge secession. In his waning days as president, Buchanan perceived no legal Constitutional remedy to coerce the parting states to remain in the Union. Despite a widespread impression that the new president Lincoln planned to end slavery in the South, his inaugural speech claimed no such goal. In fact, Lincoln would tolerate constitutionally sanctioned slavery where it already existed; his concern had to do with prohibiting extension of slavery into the new territories.[138] The South viewed this as a threat. Over time, the shift in alignment of states in favor of the North would condemn the agrarian South to economic servitude of Northern industrial interests. Tariff Acts in the past had raised the cost of European manufactured goods in a way to ensure a captive Southern market and vast profits for the North. This tendency to concentrate national wealth in the North, it was thought, would accelerate under the Republican Party. As a separate country, the South reasoned it could trade with the United States and Europe as equals. One Massachusetts historian wryly captured the sense of the times: "Slavery was the cause of the war, just as property is the cause of robbery."[139] Echoing this sentiment, British Prime Minister Lord Palmerston later observed that Lincoln, in the carefully worded Emancipation Proclamation of 1862, "undertook to abolish slavery where he was without the power to do so, while protecting it where he had the power to destroy it."[140] Of course, Palmerston referred to Lincoln's proclamation applying only to states of the Confederacy, but not to the five Union states yet practicing the institution.

Against this backdrop, Quintero decided to join his comrades in Texas and "cast in his lot with the Southern people." This decision no doubt occurred soon after the early February Lone Star secession. The *Daily Picayune* would report: "He took this step at great personal sacrifice, with characteristic generosity of impulse, despite the protests and warning of his Northern friends and employers."[141] Implicit is that Frank Leslie and Cirilo Villaverde attempted to dissuade Quintero; yet, John Thrasher probably lent his support. Thrasher would soon prove himself more than sympathetic to the South.

Various sources indicate Quintero enlisted as a private with the Quitman Rifles or Quitman Guards in San Antonio, Texas. This unit is said to have soon proceeded to Richmond for service in Virginia. While several Confederate units in Mississippi and Georgia employed this local designation, none of the Texas infantry companies officially claimed this title.[142] It may have been an informal appellation, or Quintero may have even joined a state militia unit. At the same time, no José or Joseph Quintero appears in the Compiled Military Service Records. These records do list a corporal John A. Quintero in Co. A, 3rd Texas Infantry, also cited as Juan Quintero. This is not the Cuban recently of New York City, though. Twenty-three-year-old Corporal John Quintero, probably of Mexican descent, mustered in on May 25, 1861; by this time official records place the much older Cuban José Quintero on special assignment. Furthermore, this John Quintero deserted the cause on March 17, 1862, a disgraceful act hardly in character with the noble patriot of Cuba. An additional level of confusion exists, though, in placing José Quintero's actual service. The indexers of the *Official Records of the War of the Rebellion* made a significant error. They listed him as "Juan" Quintero, an inaccuracy often promulgated in contemporary treatments. Regardless, Quintero seems to have served for a short time with a Texas infantry unit, and by spring of 1861 he found himself in Richmond.[143]

In an historical sense, the idea of Hispanics embracing the Confederate cause runs counter to American mythology related to the war. After all, the Confederacy has often been presented as the bastion of the Southern white plantation class, or perhaps the adventurous refuge of uneducated "crackers." Even a more charitable view might simply consider the Southern nation as one attracting conservative Protestants of the states' rights school. Thoughtful adherents to an eighteenth-century vision of America, these secessionists felt destined to reestablish the agrarian nation of the Founding Fathers — the true America. Whatever one's view, none of these perspectives brings to mind Hispanics and a new nation comprised of a diverse citizenry.

Yet, the Confederate States did claim and attract citizens from Northern and Southern Europe, Canada and every Northern state, not to mention American Indians, free (and slave) Negroes, and even Hispanics. Attractions to the "cause" ranged from sheer adventure and mercenary interest, to noble conviction. These Spanish-speaking Confederates originated from Mexico, Cuba and as far away as Spain. Former Texas Ranger Santos Benavides would rise to the rank of Colonel, the highest ranking Confederate officer of Mexican extraction. Quintero's Cuban professor friend of the López era, Ambrosio José Gonzales, would serve General P.G.T. Beauregard with distinction as his artillery officer in Charleston.[144] Another past Havana colleague of Cuban ancestry and recent colleague to Quintero in New York City, John Sidney Thrasher, would uniquely contribute to his young nation's cause as superintendent of the Confederate Press Association, a "Pioneer News Agency."[145] Quintero's devotion to the South is not an aberration, but reflective of a broad mosaic of peoples who believed in limited government, the right of self-determination, and in defending a staunch Constitutionalist peoples against invasion by the powerful majority. Of course, with the López conspirators there was another attraction: the Southern people's very own sons had died for Cuba Libré just a decade earlier.

The Confederate States, portrayed as a pariah nation-state by the victors of the secessionary struggle, gained notable defenders from many quarters, including the Hispanic world. One of these, the "national hero of Cuba," José Martí would fire the resistance that Quintero and others had kindled decades earlier, setting in motion by sheer force of personal conviction a crusade the Spanish would finally yield to. In Martí's *Obras Literarias* (Literary Works) is an unapologetic tribute to the "brains of the Confederacy," Secretary of State Judah P. Benjamin. Martí does not assail Benjamin's Southern Confederacy or note any unsavory taint. He instead speaks admiringly of Benjamin's service and loyalty. Impressed by this Jewish Confederate's "model of integrity," Martí encourages every young man in moments of weakness and despair to "turn and gaze at the portrait of Judah Benjamin."[146]

MEXICAN DIPLOMACY

The newfound Confederacy bordered on the United States and one other foreign nation, the Spanish-speaking land to the south: Mexico. President Jefferson Davis recognized the value and opportunity Mexico presented. A neutral country with a land border, Lincoln's naval blockade could not cut off trade and supply for a desperate Confederacy. Indeed, Mexico would be the window for European supply of war matériel and vital goods to sustain its economy.

Against this new Confederate military-political interest on the landscape remained a history of uncertain Mexican nationalist and North American expansionist tendencies. As a result of the Mexican-American War and subsequent Texan independence, Mexico had lost over half of her national territory, counting Texas. In the "manifest destiny" tradition, the United States desired to purchase the northern Mexican border states as well. By the same token, Mexico was just emerging from its most recent Civil War, the liberal Indian President Benito Pablo Juárez just reestablishing his government in December 1860. The war with the United States, and its own internal struggle, had placed Mexico in desperate debt to Great Britain, France and Spain, the balance as much as one hundred million dollars. The Mexican government pleaded insolvency, unable to pay even the interest on its debts. The United States, at war with itself, presented a wonderful distraction. Conveniently overlooking the Monroe Doctrine, by the end of 1861 the European nations would descend on hapless Mexico to extract legitimate payment, and perhaps a bit more to boot. Not oblivious to European designs, both the United States and the Confederacy considered the virtual inevitability of European intercession. Even so, they jockeyed for influence and opportunity in Mexico. They looked to this nation to help sustain the long-term interests of their own countries.[147]

Both North-American nations sent diplomatic commissioners to President Juárez's seat of power in Mexico City. The United States assigned this vital task to Thomas Corwin, who would prove adroit and resourceful in thwarting Confederate prospects with the Juárez administration. As inept as Corwin was capable, the Confederates entrusted its relations to John T. Pickett. Experienced in Mexico, having for some years been consul to Veracruz, the ill-tempered and imprudent Pickett nevertheless represented a poor diplomatic choice. Interestingly, the Kentuckian Pickett had served at Cárdenas in 1850 as part of the López filibuster.[148]

On May 17, Secretary of State Robert Toombs appointed Pickett as Confederate agent to the Juárez administration in Mexico City. While attempting to establish good relations and mutually advantageous treaties, Pickett was to inform the Mexicans "the Confederate States declared themselves an independent nation" and stood ready "to guarantee Mexico against foreign invasion." The Confederate States would be the buffer and protector for Mexico from the designs of the United States. Pickett was also to "watch the proceedings of the representative of the United States," and should Mexico make agreements with that nation, ensure strict neutrality by Mexico for both belligerents.[149]

Pickett arrived in the capital to find a cool reception and a populace clearly favoring the United States. He reacted badly. His questionable judgment and prejudice might have been predicted: Pickett had had the State Department endorse an addendum to his orders, openly declaring that a million dollars "judiciously applied" could buy diplomatic recognition. "The Mexicans are not overscrupulous," Pickett argued, "and it is not our mission to mend their morals at this period." Now in the capital, the agent managed to offend most in power. He ridiculed Juárez, declaring, "My business is to recognize Mexico — provided I can find a government that will stand still long enough." Soon after arrival, Mexican Congress gave the United States permission to march through Northern Mexico from California to Arizona, claiming it did not realize the Confederacy also claimed Arizona. Unsure of this development, Pickett countered that if the rumor were true, the Mexicans would soon face 30,000 Confederate diplomatic agents crossing the border. Of course, even the slightest jest of Confederate invasion could only chill already bad relations even further. Abandoning hope of developing a productive relationship with the liberal administration, Pickett sought to have himself thrown out of the country. In this way he might impress the Conservative "Church Party" who yet controlled portions of Mexico. Picking a fight with "hands and feet" against an equally rash Yankee named Bennet, the Mexicans instead threw him in jail as a common criminal. After 30 days, he bribed the judge and secured release. Barely escaping an assassination attempt, Pickett returned to Richmond on May 6, 1862 — nearly a year after his posting. The government had received few of Pickett's dispatches and had little idea of his activities in Mexico. After reading the duplicate file of dispatches now delivered in person, an outraged President Davis literally closed the door in Pickett's face.[150]

U.S. minister Thomas Corwin, also a fellow Kentuckian, had engineered Pickett's failure from the beginning. Little did Pickett realize his confidential dispatches were being sent back from Matamoros to President Juárez for review. The Confederate's wild statements and contemptuous opinions regarding Mexicans were known in the Mexican capital months before read in the Confederate capital. On the other hand, the Mexicans favored former Ohio Governor Corwin even before he arrived — "a *Yankecito* after Mexico's own heart!" It was Corwin who had objected to the Mexican-American War of 1846, hoping "the Mexicans would receive the invading American army with bloody hand and hospitable graves." Corwin quickly went about inflating rumors of Confederate plans to foment revolution and overthrow the elected government. Only the United States could guarantee the safety of Mexico. Should the Union not be restored, the new Southern Confederacy's next conquest would be Mexico. So successful was Corwin in alarming the Mexicans and gaining their goodwill, the Mexican Congress unanimously voted to allow U.S. troops to march across Sonora to reach Arizona. Thus, the hapless Pickett found his poor reception, jail term and assassination attempt largely orchestrated by the influence of the U.S. agent.[151]

Had Juárez intercepted and read Corwin's dispatches quite so diligently as he did the Confederate's, chagrin might have yielded to a different political alignment. Corwin's designs on Mexican territory were no less ambitious than what he claimed for the Confederacy. The agent's superior, Secretary of State William H. Seward, was an expansionist of first order who dreamed of a nation encompassing Mexico, Central America, the Caribbean and even Canada. Rumors that the Confederates planned to seize Lower California (Baja) alarmed Corwin, only because they might take it first. A Confederacy stretching coast to coast, challenging the "Pacific interests of the United States," could not be tolerated. He endorsed the idea of seizing this territory rather than allow that "the filibustering secessionists should get possession" first, even trumping Pickett's one million dollars with an eleven million dollar loan offer masking interest in Mexican annexation. The loan ostensibly would allow payment of European interest, holding at bay European intercession while neutralizing Confederate influence. The loan, however, required Mexico to pledge all her public lands and mineral rights in Lower California, Sonora, Chihuahua and Sinaloa. Of course, if the Mexicans could not make their payments, these lands "become absolute in the United States" at the end of six years. Before long, Corwin even advocated using Mexican public lands for postwar colonization of freed Negroes, a plan Lincoln favored. During the remaining time Juárez yet enjoyed power, Corwin dangled this loan prospect, rendering the Confederacy impotent. It never came to pass, though, as the French would not be held at bay with U.S.-financed interest payments. They demanded both principle and interest and would proceed to take it by force.[152]

Corwin deftly parried the best Confederate efforts towards Juárez. So overwhelmingly had the South been trounced in Mexico City, Richmond would not bother to send a replacement agent for Pickett until the administration changed. In his friendship with Juárez, Corwin also convinced the president to order the governors of the northern border states to refuse trade with the Confederate States. Fortunately for the South, a fiercely independent *caudillo* governor named Santiago Vidaurri paid little heed to the dictates of a weak president in faraway Mexico City. At the same time, the Confederacy had in reserve an untried new diplomat who would soon match and exceed the finest Lincoln and Seward could offer.[153]

QUINTERO AND VIDAURRI

Not quite 32 years of age, Quintero somehow made acquaintance of leaders in the Confederate State Department, apparently soon after his Texas unit transferred to the Virginia theater. Hispanic biographers often claim that he had a close relationship with President Jefferson Davis.[154] This is not out of the question, but Quintero probably had first to prove himself before gaining ready access to the chief executive. Regardless, a multilingual Harvard-educated journalist-attorney of Hispanic descent could only be viewed as a unique commodity. That Quintero could boast well-placed Texas connections, not to mention personal correspondence to an important Mexican border governor, must have seemed extraordinary to the State Department. The fact is, on May 22, 1861, within a week of Pickett's assignment as minister, Quintero received appointment to entreat with Governor Santiago Vidaurri.

Secretary of State Toombs introduced his "agent and special messenger" in a letter written to Vidaurri from the Confederate capital at Montgomery:

> I have charged J. A. Quintero, Esq., to proceed immediately to the seat of your Government to assure you of the amicable disposition of the people of the Confederate States toward those of Mexico.... Although an accredited political

agent of the Confederate States has been sent to the City of Mexico, I have thought it proper, owing to the distance of your residence from that city and the absence of speedy and constant communication with the central Government, to send you this special message.

Quintero's mission, expected to last only a few weeks, entailed solving border problems with lawless bandits. Renumerated at $200 per month, Secretary Toombs charged Quintero: "You will therefore represent to Governor Vidaurri in terms of kindness, but with firmness, the necessity that he shall take active steps to defeat expeditions planned within his jurisdiction against our citizens...."[155] In his separate letter to Vidaurri, Toombs stressed this same point:

> It is credibly reported to this Government that evil-disposed Mexican citizens residing within the limits of your jurisdiction have planned predatory expeditions against the citizens of the State of Texas. I feel assured that it is only necessary to bring this fact to your notice ... to prevent any such invasion of the soil of the Confederate States....[156]

Quintero recognized he possessed unique advantages, so unusual there could not be found anyone in the Confederacy with better prospects in this assignment. A Cuban, he shared the native language of Mexico, yet stood apart from its politics and factions. Furthermore, he had maintained a warm correspondence with Vidaurri and had provided "some personal services" to the governor during his exile in Austin. Optimistic that the Mexican's "reception of me will be cordial," Quintero departed Galveston on June 5. Traveling through Brownsville and taking the stage from Matamoros, on June 17 he arrived some couple hundred miles later at Nuevo León's capital, Monterrey (often spelled "Monterey" in period accounts).

Only a couple of days after presenting letters of introduction from Secretary of State Toombs and Texas governor Edward Clark, an invitation came for an audience with his excellency at the palace. The governor's personal physician, South Carolinian J. H. Means, facilitated scheduling this meeting. Quintero found Vidaurri more than willing to discuss issues of interest to the Confederacy. The *caudillo* chafed at President Juárez's attempts to rein in distant states; he hoped to find a strong ally in the Southern Confederacy. Encouraged, Quintero wrote: "General Vidaurri feels a great friendship for the South."[157]

The confidential agent and the governor soon met again, on June 26. Now Quintero raised the issue of border security against bandits. This had been the motivation of Texas governor Clark in urging President Davis on the matter of appointing someone like Quintero, lest Sam Houston's partisans succeed in establishing a new Texas Republic. The Cuban-Confederate's specific concern centered on Juan N. "Cheno" Cortina. The "folk hero" had raised a large force in Mexico, possibly ready to invade Texas; Quintero implored the governor to take measures against him. Texans well remembered 1859, just two years earlier. The desperado Cortina had captured Brownsville and held it until driven out by Texas Rangers and U.S. regulars commanded by Colonel Robert E. Lee. Vidaurri responded positively. He had been active against Cortina since the time of the Brownsville incident, and only in the April just past had decreed such outlaws subject to arrest. Unfortunately, this "irresponsible man" had eluded Vidaurri's forces. Confederate Colonel Santos Benavides had just dispersed Cortina's bandits in the previous month, but the leader yet remained at large. Nevertheless, Quintero could enthusiastically report after this meeting an agreement on reciprocal extradition. He hoped this accord would reduce the number of border crossings by criminals seeking to elude capture.[158]

Successful on this point, Quintero proceeded to raise other issues, particularly the prospect of Union troops invading the Confederacy from northern Mexico. Confederate leadership feared Juárez would grant permission to march through Sonora from California. Pickett, in Mexico City, argued against this as if assailing the wind, but Quintero enjoyed greater success. Governor Vidaurri knew the other Northern governors well and could influence them. He ensured the Confederacy that their enemy would "never get consent to march troops through northern Mexico to attack," regardless of whether Juárez agreed or not.[159]

Flush with unexpected and generous concessions on each point, Quintero decided to tackle trade as well. The Davis administration noted that President Lincoln's blockade, if effective, could soon deprive the South of needed weapons for defense, as well as vital lead for bullets and saltpeter for gunpowder. Richly blessed with natural resources, Mexico could be a new source of trade for war supplies as well as other civilian goods. Governor Vidaurri shrewdly recognized a great opportunity. He could aid his Confederate friends while his people and government profited from high tariffs and selling goods at inflated prices. It just so happened his son-in-law owned a leading commercial house. Strengthening the otherwise poor northern economy and cementing ties with the Southern Confederacy could only increase his ability to oppose Juárez. Vidaurri expressed regret to Quintero that he possessed less than a dozen cannon and 10,000 rifles; these had to be preserved, in light of disagreements with Juárez, for "local defense." Otherwise, he could offer the mineral resources of his domain to promote manufacture of military implements. Arrangements could be handled through his physician, Dr. Means.[160]

A last major discussion point Quintero broached concerned transportation. The governor assured Quintero that shipping could be handled at Matamoros of the bordering Atlantic state Tamaulipas. Vidaurri exercised such a "moral influence" over that state's governor, he may as well have been chief executive. Neutral ships from Europe could readily supply the Confederacy from this point. As for land transportation, Quintero proposed a railroad from Matamoros to the Pacific coast. Attractive routes could be conceived through the states of Chihuahua or Durango, leading through rich mineral areas and ending at the deep-water harbor at Mazatlán in the state of Sinaloa. Such a prospect excited Vidaurri. He desired economic development of the North. Of course, Quintero realized such investments would tie the *caudillo* closer to the Confederacy.[161]

Finally, the Mexican governor raised an unexpected issue of significant import: annexation. Vidaurri had long envisioned secession leading to formation of the northern Republic of Sierra Madre. Now a more attractive option existed. Vidaurri proposed an extraordinary union of his own Nuevo León y Coahuila, with Tamaulipas, as new states within the Confederate nation. Perhaps Chihuahua and Sonora could also be induced to secede as well. The governor suggested broad mutual advantages. The north really had more in common with Confederate Arizona and Texas than the jungles of tropical southern Mexico. The combined Confederate-Mexican sections could build on significant American influence by expanding mining, textiles and agriculture, particularly with Confederate technical skills. Negotiations could commence at the earliest convenience. Of course, Juárez would not acquiesce, but 1,000 men from Texas and some "flying artillery" ought to handle the difficulty.

Totally unprepared for this offer, a stunned Quintero had no ready Confederate position to present in response to this amazing possibility. His diplomatic orders never conceived of such a proposition. The Confederate agent listened carefully and assured the governor every detail would be conveyed to the State Department. Of course, this would be held in the strictest confidence.[162]

The governor could not resist visiting with Quintero one more time the night before the agent's departure from Monterrey. An hour-long visit at the Confederate's hotel room ensued. The Mexican leader again stressed "his friendship and good will" towards the Southern Confederacy. He requested this visit be considered "a call on his Excellency Jefferson Davis." Soon after Quintero left, Vidaurri protected himself with a vague letter informing Juárez of the diplomatic visit. He also published Quintero's correspondence in the official government newspaper *Boletín Oficial*. This exposed the confidential nature of the Confederate assignment, but would not diminish its effectiveness. Justifiably proud of his achievement, Quintero reported to Assistant Secretary of State William M. Browne that "We have gained an ally." To Texas governor Clark he concluded: "I have been entirely successful in my mission."[163]

A STAR RISES IN RICHMOND

Leaving Mexico, Quintero inspected the Bagdad port facility near Matamoros in greater detail and then proceeded to Brownsville, Texas. From here he wrote Assistant Secretary Browne that he would soon proceed directly to Richmond. Suspicious of Union spies sprinkled in the postal service, Quintero had "communications of *great importance* to our Government which I have not thought safe to send by mail." Richmond did not yet know of Vidaurri's fantastic offer.[164]

Arriving August 17 in Richmond, the new seat of Confederate government, Quintero began detailed letters to Robert Hunter, the newly appointed Secretary of State. In several reports the Cuban wrote over the next five days, he covered the extradition agreement, blocking Federal troop movement through Mexico, trade opportunities, land and water transportation, and, of course, the bombshell — annexation of Mexico.

Soon after his June interviews with Vidaurri, and while still in Mexico, Quintero had determined the trade potential of Nuevo León y Coahuila. He had found reasonably priced military items in good quantity: lead, copper, saltpeter and gunpowder. Other items, such as coarse cloth, could also be readily obtained.[165] On August 29, soon after Quintero returned to Richmond, Assistant Secretary of State William H. Browne informed Pennsylvania-born Major Josiah Gorgas, brilliant chief of the Confederate Ordnance Bureau, of Quintero's reports:

> ...This Department has received intelligence that the Government ... can procure from the Province of New Leon, Mexico, almost unlimited supplies of copper and lead, the former at $15.50 per quintal (100 pounds) and the latter at $10.50 per cargo (300 pounds), and that both can be delivered at Roma, Texas, at an advance on the above-named price of 20 per cent. From the same source it is ascertained that large quantities of powder can be obtained at a moderate price and with thirty to forty days' notice. You will be good enough to inform this Department whether you require any of the articles above named; ... this Department can communicate the wishes of the War Department to our agent, now in this city, but about to return to his post. For obvious reasons it is desired the information herein contained shall be kept secret.[166]

Quintero's reports deeply impressed the State Department and President Davis. No word had yet come from Pickett in Mexico City. On the other hand, Quintero had given the government something tangible and optimistic. Possibilities in Northern Mexican now captured their imagination. On September 3, Assistant Secretary Browne informed Quintero of his new permanent assignment:

> The report of your recent mission to the governor of New Leon ... [has] received
> the entire approval of this Department, and if affords me pleasure to inform
> you that the President, appreciating the skill, prudence and ability which you
> displayed in the discharge of your duty, has appointed you confidential agent
> of this Government in northeastern Mexico, to reside at Monterrey.[167]

In this letter, Browne continued with Quintero's charge. As confidential
agent, he would determine whether the Mexican government authorized transport of Union troops across her territory to attack the Confederacy. If so, he
would persuade Governor Vidaurri to "use his power and influence" to prevent "the disastrous consequences which must necessarily ensue." Quintero
should also engage in "diligent enquiry as to ... purchasing small arms, powder, lead, sulphur, saltpeter," and, in fact, is "authorized to contract for 500
tons of lead...." Similarly, the "saltpeter in natural formation ... near the Rio
Grande, opposite Eagle Pass" necessitated "especial pains" and losing no time
in ascertaining the supply opportunity. Of course, Quintero must determine
the best means of land and water transportation of these goods purchased in
Mexico. Browne cautioned Quintero of the "secret and confidential nature"
of the mission, encouraging prudence in whom he acquainted with the fact.

As for the startling annexation offer, President Davis had given the matter considerable thought and finally decided to politely decline. It would "be
imprudent and impolitic in the interest of both parties ... in regard to the
proposition by Governor Vidaurri...."[168] This wonderful opportunity to
expand the territory and wealth of the Confederacy came fraught with numerous entanglements. At the very best, this could only deprive the Confederate
States of its "neutral" port at Matamoros. That is, Lincoln's blockade would
surely be extended to this new Confederate city. Much worse, the Confederacy would no doubt soon be at war with Juárez. Vidaurri, in relying on the
Confederate States to maintain his northern empire, offered little strength of
his own. Furthermore, Davis believed the Europeans would likely intercede.
Rather than deprive Napoleon of the spoils and later incur French wrath, it
would be better to let the Europeans come and embroil themselves in a war
with the United States over the Monroe Doctrine. This would guarantee the
independence of the Confederacy.[169]

REVOLUTION AND INTERVENTION

Stopping in New Orleans for several days on account of rumors that
Vidaurri had been deposed, careful inquiries dispelled these stories; Quintero
continued to Brownsville, arriving in late October. Here he met Fort Brown's
commander, Colonel John S. Ford, a South Carolinian who had long before

adopted Texas. The commander introduced him to local commercial agents who endeavored "to smuggle out of New York" a number of arms. Quintero offered his support. Only a few years earlier in Austin, "Rip" Ford's *Texas State Times* had promoted the Know-Nothing Party, while in San Antonio Quintero had argued against the movement as editor of *El Ranchero*. On the other hand, they had both worked towards Cuban liberation; Ford had diligently organized Texan recruits for Governor Quitman's abortive filibuster of 1855. Now they united for the Confederate cause, Quintero praising the one-time Texas Ranger: "[He is] a gentleman of fine intellect and an old veteran. He is thoroughly acquainted with the Mexican character and Spanish language and ought by all means remain permanently at this post. He can be of *great service* to our government."[170]

Upon arrival in Monterrey on October 24, Quintero grew concerned to learn Juárez had closed the border to trade with both contending sides, Union and Confederate. Union minister Thomas Corwin's efforts in Mexico City now reached to the frontier. The Southern agent lost no time in consulting with Vidaurri. The governor, though ill, welcomed the visit and assured his Confederate friend: The border would be protected and maintained open to Confederate commerce. The following month Quintero reported his satisfaction to the State Department: "Governor Vidaurri is much feared, not only by President Juárez but also by the people of the interior states. For years he has ruled supreme and the states of New Leon and Coahuila have under his administration been prosperous and happy. Hence his popularity on the frontier. He is our faithful friend and ally."[171]

Santiago Vidaurri's rise to power began 20 years earlier as secretary to the then liberal governor of Nuevo León. In fact, in service to General Mariano Arista, Vidaurri spied on Texas President Lamar's ill-fated Santa Fé expedition to take over the New Mexico area. Serving successive conservative governors, Vidaurri seized on disillusionment after the disaster of the Mexican-American War. In 1855, the national Revolution of Ayutla provided opportunity for the liberals to take power in the north, with Vidaurri as their leader. As governor of Nuevo León, he quickly annexed Coahuila. Vidaurri instituted needed reforms and taxed the church. The governor emulated North-American democratic institutions, protected the border, and in 1857 began the Civil College which two years later boasted faculties in law and medicine. Militarily, his vision of a northern country, Sierra Madre, stalled. While he exercised considerable influence over the neighboring states of San Luis Potosí, Chihuahua, Durango and Tamaulipas, an 1855 expedition to extend his unofficial control over the latter by annexation had failed.[172]

Tamaulipas erupted again as Quintero returned from Richmond. The contested governor's election there threatened another revolution. The pro–Confederate, newly elected governor, Jesús de la Serna, also received backing from President Juárez. The opposition candidate, Cipriano Guerrero, challenged this decision.

An armed conflict brewed. Elected governor Serna relied on General José María Jesús Carvajal to command his forces. North Americans liked Carvajal, who spoke flawless English and had studied in the South at Virginia's Bethany College. He played to Confederate admirers in Brownsville, noting he had two sons engaged in protecting a "Southern school" from Yankee invasion. On the other hand, the challenger Guerrero also claimed a well-respected, superior commander in General Guadalupe García. An editor from Brownsville reported that the general "speaks with confidence, and denies all possibility of ... failure."

Of course, a Mexican revolution just did not fit the Confederate agenda. Thriving trade in Matamoros now "ground to a halt." The Yankee blockading ships had not yet arrived at Brownsville, so the loss of Matamoros was not critical — yet. Increasing the tension, General García virtually extorted "loans" from Matamoros merchants he believed supported the elected governor Serna, and then expelled them from the city. These businessmen gathered in Brownsville and plotted their revenge. The Confederacy found itself on the verge of being dragged into the revolution. Colonel "Rip" Ford favored Carvajal, a fellow Mason with whom he served in 1851 filibustering excursions, and Quintero also preferred the pro–Confederate Serna administration; yet, both sought to avoid sympathetic Texans entering the conflict, undermining the Confederate position. In fact, Ford dispersed Carvajal's troops as they organized near Brownsville and made it clear that "strict neutrality" would be observed.[173]

During November Carvajal attacked Matamoros. The Brownsville *Flag* noted the charge drew attention across the river in Brownsville, sounding like "three thousand muskets had all exploded at once." Behind their hastily constructed barricades, García's several hundred defending troops held their own. The Confederate military refused crossings across the Rio Grande, except for Carvajal's wounded. The engagement proved indecisive. Further skirmishes decided little, their key impacts being to curtail Matamoros trade. This deprived the Confederacy of needed materials to sustain its nation and army in the Trans-Mississippi region, while Vidaurri's revenue stream gave out. The governor had to resort to pressing merchants in Monterrey for loans, particularly the German-Americans who had left Texas to avoid supporting the Confederacy. Quintero spoke harshly of these "avowed enemies" who "have not spared any means to poison the minds of the Mexicans against us." In a January 27, 1862 letter to then Colonel Henry McCulloch, Commander of the Western District of Texas, Quintero complained: "They are constantly taunting and deriding the military weakness of the South and circulating rumors calculated to do us harm." He vehemently denounced one such German spy, Parson Lyons, who fled San Antonio "with Christ upon the lying lip, and Satan in the soul."[174]

Assistant Secretary Browne, on January 14, 1862, wrote Quintero to inform him of completed transactions with a Mexican gunpowder merchant Quintero had suggested, and he also reported that the "Trent Affair" had been resolved. Britain had almost gone to war with the United States over the abduction of Confederate commissioners Mason and Slidell, but their recent releases averted this. Browne expressed appreciation for recent dispatches "relative to political disturbances in Mexico," and he asked that the State Department be kept "advised of the progress of events in that country." Reflective of the importance attached to the evolving Mexican situation, and how it might fit in the emerging geopolitical context, Browne requested explicit detail:

> A succinct and intelligent outline of the position, strength, and resources of the parties contending against the General Government of Mexico; reliable information as to the ability of the latter to maintain its authority; the state of the revolution, which is understood to be progressing in Tamaulipas — and how far the anticipated difficulty with Spain will unite the local governors and conflicting parties in Mexico in a common cause against that kingdom will enable this Department to form a clearer idea of the complications that now exist in Mexican affairs, and the power of that republic to extricate itself from them.[175]

As Jefferson Davis predicted, President Juárez now faced intervention by the European powers. The Spanish had occupied Veracruz in early December, and by January 7 the Allied fleet of Spain, France and Britain landed. Ostensibly, they sought payment on their outstanding loans, but Spain and France saw opportunities to flaunt the Monroe Doctrine and seize a bit more. Facing challenge at the seat of power, Juárez sought to consolidate defenses in the north. Setting aside the legal election in Tamaulipas, he declared martial law there and ordered Vidaurri to take full command. The governor raised an army, but Carvajal and president-elect Serna would not give up. They instead took refuge in Brownsville where they sought aide from sympathetic Confederate friends.

Quintero faced a decision: Should the Confederacy support the pro-Confederate, legally elected Governor of Tamaulipas whose commanding general enjoyed long friendship with the Texans, or instead back President Juárez's choice of military ruler, Santiago Vidaurri, a man who had already proven friendship to the South? In Quintero's mind the choice could not be clearer: Support Vidaurri. At Vidaurri's request, Quintero proceeded to Brownsville to forestall Carvajal. There Quintero met with acting commander Philip N. Luckett, temporarily in charge during Colonel Ford's rest leave. Luckett sought to maintain neutrality. During a Carvajal crossing into Texas, Colonel Luckett seized their arms and provided two companies of cavalry to patrol the Rio Grande. Coincidentally, Luckett commanded the 3rd Texas Infantry. It may be that Corporal Juan A. Quintero of this regiment — the soldier-Quintero of presumed Mexican extraction — participated in efforts to safeguard the border on behalf of the diplomat-Quintero.[176]

Early March brought two new problems: Lincoln and Ford. Two ships of the Union president's blockade finally arrived at Brownsville. "One of them is the Portsmouth, a sloop of 22 guns," Quintero wrote to Assistant Secretary Browne on the 4th. The *Portsmouth* seized a Mexican-owned schooner from Havana, laden with tobacco. She also captured an English steamer taking on cotton. Quintero reported the English consul's inability to gain satisfaction, "only that the cotton was contraband." The consul petitioned the English fleet at Veracruz "demanding the presence of a man-of-war at the mouth of the river." Quintero wisely followed suit, taking advantage of the intervention: "I am endeavoring to get the Spanish and French merchants to apply, through their respective consuls, for protection, so that war vessels may be sent also to the mouth of the river and the commerce of Matamoros be protected." These efforts paid off. On March 16 the heavily armed H.M.S. *Phaeton* arrived at the Rio Grande, followed the next day by a French corvette H.I.M. *Berthollet*. The Federals concluded they could not prevent the "illicit trade" without seizing Brownsville. As a result, U.S. Secretary of Navy Gideon Welles ordered that no more vessels be captured at the mouth of the Rio Grande.[177]

The other problem that month came in the person of Brownsville commander John S. Ford. The colonel now returned from his rest in San Antonio. Ford had strong ties to Carvajal, going back to 1851 when they jointly led an army to invade northern Mexico to establish a separate buffer country between the United States and Mexico. Now Carvajal had been supplied cannon by someone in Texas. The Mexican general attacked the town of Reynosa at the head of 500 men. Rumors abounded that Ford supported Carvajal. Quintero now had doubts about the former ranger. An uneasy Vidaurri penned letters to President Davis and other Confederate leaders, reminding them of friendship and his interest in providing munitions.

With no resolution forthcoming, the situation deteriorated. Quintero wrote to the State Department in late March that "friendly relations with the Mexican frontier ... [were] fast dying away." Completely exasperated, he all but resigned, asking if there might not be another person with "more influence" on the military. On April 6, Governor Vidaurri himself wrote to Texas governor Francis Lubbock, urging disarming of the revolutionists so that they might "live honestly." Two days later, a Confederate sympathizer attempted to cross the border only to be told by Vidaurri's secretary, Manuel G. Rejón, that it had been closed. Vidaurri's patience had worn thin.[178]

The border soon reopened, but Vidaurri's retaliation included a duty of two cents per pound on cotton. The governor denied to Quintero that the duty had anything to do with border troubles, but asserted he simply needed to maintain his army of 7,000 in the field. The Cuban knew how to deal with a fellow Latin. Informing him that he understood exactly what the governor meant, he warned of "killing the goose that laid the golden egg." Brought to reality by Quintero, and having gotten Confederate attention, the duty dropped by half the day following Quintero's interview. Faced with this unanticipated impediment to trade, the State Department finally took actions their confidential agent had been recommending. Ford soon received orders to arrest Carvajal. When the Brownsville commander did not comply quickly enough, Quintero proposed to the new Matamoros *commandante* to charge Carvajal with violating the international border. An affidavit to this effect, sworn in Brownsville, could not be ignored. Carvajal's filibusters were disbanded that month, but warned by Ford, Carvajal fled to New York for the duration of the war. Border tensions eased. Within a few months, Quintero convinced Vidaurri to fully remove all export duties.

In May, a change of command to Quintero's liking occurred. Ford's insubordination resulted in a transfer to Austin where his charge had more to do with paperwork than supervising troops. Quintero's influence in Richmond had been felt. Secretary of State Benjamin wrote Quintero that "the fact stated by you that General Vidaurri has reason to believe that Colonel Ford is connected ... with Carvajal has not been without influence in the adoption of this course." Brigadier General Hamilton P. Bee assumed command in South Texas. He appointed Colonel Luckett to manage Ford's previous duties on the border. Since General Bee was extremely familiar with Mexico, fluent in Spanish, and a "most popular and efficient officer," Quintero felt that he would have avoided many of the problems Ford exacerbated.[179]

COTTON ON THE BORDER

Brigadier General Bee, in his initial tour of the border area during the fall of 1861, recognized the importance of Brownsville and the Rio Grande. He astutely wrote to the Secretary of War: "By proper encouragement every necessary supply, either for our Government or people, can be brought to Matamoras [*sic*] from abroad, and we have no other outlet so long as the supremacy of the seas is against us." Quintero, at this same time, seized opportunities to establish this trade for his new country. He quickly identified the Monterrey firm of Oliver and Brothers as a preferred supplier. Experienced with New Orleans and Texas, the company's large capital and extensive business network made it an excellent choice. This was the firm which could deliver lead to Roma, Texas — about 100 miles up the Rio Grande — as well as sulphur, saltpeter, blankets and even small arms from Cuba, England and neighboring

Mexican states. Quintero also contracted with Vidaurri's son-in-law, Patricio Milmo, for flour. By November, the confidential agent had identified reasonable sources for cannon and rifle powder. Early the next month he further located a supplier for 370 rifles, carbines and muskets, encouraging Texas Governor Lubbock to quickly purchase these arms before a speculator snatched the deal from Richmond.[180]

This excellent start had slowed to a trickle with the Tamaulipas revolution and Ford's apparent intrigues with Carvajal. After the Mexican filibuster fled to New York, trade recovered, albeit slowly. During the early months of 1862, Quintero achieved some modest successes in trade other than cotton. He acted quickly to obtain 40,000 rifles from New York. The Mexicans had ordered these arms, but could not pay for them. Vidaurri's secretary Rejón also assured Confederate access to 2,500 pounds of saltpeter per month at good prices, with "any quantity of ship building timber" also available for cash. Even Vidaurri soon offered "all the ammunition" the Confederates might desire.[181]

Of course, to finance much of the trade, the Confederates relied on "King Cotton." Despite the European market for the crop, many obstacles challenged its shipment. At this time the Rio Grande water level had dropped too low to support loading and unloading of ships, at least without hazard. A supply of at least two months of cotton stood on the wharf ready to be loaded. Complicating this, the "want of steamboats under neutral flags add[ed] ... to the embarrassment." The delay had increased expenses of merchants who tried to pass along additional costs to unwilling buyers. The multiplicity of private and government agents trying to broker deals also worked at cross purposes to the interests of the Confederacy. In April the *Ft. Brown Flag* reported "there are no transactions taking place...."[182]

Getting the cotton to Matamoros in the first place proved a significant challenge. Some shallow-draft schooners flitted among the Texas coastal lagoons and barrier islands, but as enemy vigilance increased these water routes fell into disfavor. There being no rail or interior water routes, transportation of cotton to the border from the plantations of Texas, Louisiana and as far away as Arkansas and Mississippi typically resorted to slow, expensive, plodding wagon trains traveling over hundreds of miles of semiarid and desert lands. The key and most easterly route began at the Alleyton cotton depot, about midway between Galveston and Austin, and continued through King's Ranch, near Corpus Christi, on to Brownsville. Planters with cotton to haul often found difficulty locating teamsters to transport their goods, the military and speculators having contracted with a great many of them. To solve this problem, a Confederate purchasing agent arranged for Mexican teamsters to assume responsibility for two-thirds of the route. One 14-year-old lad, John Warren Hunter, wrote of his experience in traveling on the route to Matamoros from the King Ranch. "Ox trains, mule trains, and trains of Mexican carts, all laden with cotton coming from every town in Texas" came together at Brownsville, creating the "greatest shipping point in the South" and developing in "Matamoros ... a great commercial center." He further described the 125-mile stretch as "a broad thoroughfare along which continuously moved two vast, unending trains of wagons; the one outward bound with cotton, the other homeward bound with merchandise and army supplies."[183]

Another major trail covered central and west Texas, passing through Austin. It led through San Antonio and from there either to King's Ranch or any of the Rio Grande border towns such as Eagle Pass, Laredo or Roma. On either side of the river more wagon trains paralleled the waterway, carrying goods to Brownsville or, across the river, to Matamoros. The river became navigable at Roma, and specially built steamboats provided an alternative to these wagon trains to complete the trip. San Antonio emerged a major cotton depot for this traffic. One of the few women to make the trip, Eliza Ripley, described the scene presented at the city: "...Hundreds of Chihuahua wagons ... 'parked' with military precision ... waiting their turn to enter the grand plaza, deliver their packages of goods, and load with cotton" for their return to Mexico. Mrs. Ripley further noted the destitute land they passed through as "so barren that the only growths were prickly-pear and mesquite...." "Rip" Ford, who had by then passed from Quintero's favor, supported this assessment, finding around several water holes "hundreds of domestic animals, dead, their flesh seeming dried up on their bones...." Drought in the following year would create an even more desolate freighting passage. As if the brutal elements posed insufficient hazard, along these routes preyed Mexican outlaws, Union renegades and Confederate "sulkers."[184]

Against this complex logistical and economic backdrop, Quintero attempted to impose some order. Earlier that year Quintero had complained to Richmond: "The waste, inefficiency, and lack of unity had provided dishonest cotton brokers to monopolize the trade in a way that was detrimental to the interests of the government." In particular, speculators made huge profits on cotton sold at Matamoros, but corresponding return military supply shipments often failed to materialize. General Bee and his subordinates imposed an export certification system. This limited export permits to authorized government agents and merchants who facilitated army supply imports. These efforts would prove largely unsuccessful, as private profiteers would nevertheless dominate the trade throughout the war.[185]

Mexican export fees also stifled Confederate cotton trade. A $10 per bale tariff impacted competitiveness of cotton shipped from Matamoros. Earlier in 1862, Quintero convinced Vidaurri that lower duties could only increase import revenues. The governor realized the logic of this, and further recognized that his son-in-law, Patricio Milmo, could reap enormous profits from increased trade through his large export firm. In April, Vidaurri cut the duty in half, crediting a letter from "citizen J.A. Quintero" and the "heavy expense incurred by merchants who introduce cotton for re-exportation...." Soon thereafter, the Carvajal incident resulted in Vidaurri reimposing prohibitive tariffs; Quintero faced down the Mexican and again secured the lower rates. As a further concession, Vidaurri agreed to establish Monterrey as a "free depot" for cotton awaiting transit. In neighboring Tamaulipas Quintero similarly dealt with a succession of new military commanders and governors in keeping the tariffs stable so that trade could flourish.[186]

Despite challenges and short-term setbacks, the Matamoros trade took on a huge scope. Union authorities took notice of successful arrangements of the Confederate authorities — especially efforts by Quintero and Vidaurri — in establishing Matamoros as the South's "great thoroughfare," having the same importance in the Confederate Trans-Mississippi Department as "New York ... to the United States." As if to confirm this assessment, by August ships arrived in larger numbers, removing the glut of cotton that had accumulated earlier. At this time, Quintero wrote the new Secretary of State Judah Benjamin regarding munitions purchases: "Texas is well supplied with ammunition." He further reported: "The State of Texas has for some time been purchasing blankets, power, lead &c from Mexico. The house of Oliver Bros. of Monterey have sixty waggons running from that city to San Antonio, Texas."

That September, Quintero reported in his ongoing assessment to Benjamin the "trade is immense" and the "commerce between New Leon and Coahuila and the Confederate States grows larger every day." He amplified this evaluation: "There are numerous Mexican teamsters and waggons engaged in the trade. Powder — of excellent quality — lead, copper, tin, blankets, coffee, sugar, shoes, hides, cloth, brown sheeting for negro clothing &c are abundantly exported from the State." In communications with foreign consuls, Quintero learned their governments stood ready to provide up to 500 wagons to haul cotton from Southern depots, and would pay "any amount of specie for cotton." The activities that autumn of San Antonio quartermaster Major Simeon Hart also underscored the scope of the trade. As Hart had just assumed responsibility for Trans-Mississippi Department supply purchases from Mexico, Quintero reported the agent bought "over a million dollars of army supplies" in just two weeks. Even visiting British Colonel Arthur Freemantle in his *Diary* described "seventy vessels ... constantly at anchor outside" Bagdad, the port for Matamoros, and "for an immense distance" along the shore "endless bales of cotton."[187]

In November Brig. General Bee recognized the success of the Mexican trade. "With the glittering attraction of our cotton, the whole available resources of Mexico are being brought to us." He suggested that if the commanding general "will authorize cotton to be purchased and stored at San Antonio every article manufactured in Mexico in required quantity will be brought here and exchanged for it."

The Confederate authorities might have been pleased to also read frantic Yankee dispatches reporting continued consternation over the success in Mexican trade. About this same time late in the year, Quintero's Union counterpart in Monterrey, Consul M. M. Kimmey, complained of this trade to U.S. Secretary of State Seward. Citing the broad range of goods shipped by large wagon trains through Eagle Pass and elsewhere, he lamented they provided "almost everything needed to supply the wants of the rebels." The frustrated consul further warned that "within the past three or four months the trade has grown to be of great magnitude, and as it is increasing every day it is difficult to say to what extent it may be carried or what proportions it may assume if the Government does not interfere in the most prompt and energetic manner." Even in faraway England, the United States consul at London, F. H. Morse, complained of the "contraband trade with the Confederates" to Secretary of State Seward. The "trade through Matamoras [*sic*] and Texas" is of much importance, he lamented, based on a "genuine" letter enclosed which should "not be made public as it would compromise friends here and do far more harm than good."[188]

Another aspect of the Matamoros trade worked against Union interests: illicit Confederate trade with New York. Each year during the war the number of ship clearances from the Northern port to Matamoros rapidly increased. Described as "heavy and profitable," during the war more than 152 ships of aggregate 35,000 tons made the passage. Ostensibly sent to Mexican merchants, various munitions, war supplies and civilian goods quietly transferred to Confederate interest. Texas newspapers advertised "garden seeds fresh from New York via Matamoros," noted that Southern men wore shoes "made by these Massachusetts men long after the War began," and commented that gold to pay debts "bears the Philadelphia mint mark." In Rhode Island, cotton manufacturer and Senator William Sprague — the future son-in-law of Chief Justice Salmon P. Chase — gained exceptional profits from the trade. In order to circumvent charges of trading with the Southern enemy, in many cases a broken-voyage system via Nassau, Havana or other "neutral" ports came into use. Often sanctioned by political brokers in Washington, the British did not fail to notice this double standard. They remarked of "large stocks of goods at Matamoros, constantly replenished by direct shipments from New York and Boston, for use in the Rebel States." Later the British foreign minister would challenge Secretary of State Seward on molestation of British ships engaged in legitimate trade at Matamoros, even while the New York trade prospered unhindered. Should hostilities against British vessels continue, it would be regarded "as little less than a calamity." In short, the illicit New York trade not only exposed a certain Yankee hypocrisy, but strengthened the Confederate cause while increasing Federal tensions with a powerful British nation.[189]

NEUTRAL BORDER VIOLATED

As the second year of the war, 1862, came to a close, Quintero faced new border incursions and the political complications they created. Threats and rumors abounded of Unionists in Mexico planning raids on Texas, aided by unsavory Mexican friends with grudges against the Confederate States of America. Quintero suspected the Union consul in Matamoros, Leonard Pierce, of fomenting these border troubles. On December 18, a Confederate wagon train suffered attack across the river from Las Cuevas. The Mexican bandits murdered three teamsters. Another party of desperados crossed into Zapata County and killed the chief justice there. Retribution proved swift. Confederate Captain Santos Benavides and his Confederate-Mexican cavalry crossed the river and violently punished the outlaws. Benavides reported 18 robbers killed and 14 wounded. The retrieved items included 58 horses, almost as many saddles and a number of documents implicating Pierce in encouraging the bandits.

Quintero resolved to expose Pierce and maintain peace on the border. Appeals to Vidaurri had little effect. The *caudillo* governor wished to help, and did send letters to influential political friends, but President Juárez had removed Vidaurri as military governor in Tamaulipas, the neighboring state where Pierce had orchestrated these transgressions. The new governor, wealthy businessman Albino López, seemed to wish resolution and invited Quintero to a meeting in Matamoros. Quintero hastened to Tamaulipas and learned from the governor no Mexican troops were involved, as they had been withdrawn from the border to begin preparing for a French invasion. López promised to expel Pierce if Quintero could provide documentation linking the U.S. consul to these crimes. Quintero would report in late January one firm concession: Confederate authorities had permission to cross the border to pursue and even punish any outlaws found. Quintero and General Bee conferred on the matter in Brownsville and agreed an extradition agreement with López would be helpful. López officially stated an international treaty could not be signed by the two states, Texas and Tamaulipas, but he felt a "principle of reciprocity" with the Confederacy to be consistent with Mexico's federal policy. On February 28 he did secretly issue an extradition agreement meeting Confederate interests. Quintero reported that although no proof materialized with which to expel consul Pierce, the public and secret "treaties" considerably improved border relations.[190]

Just days later in March a Confederate action occurred which threatened to undo this careful diplomatic achievement. General Bee had not given up his pursuit of consul Pierce, and on March 10 he outlined to Governor López how Pierce had raised Federal recruits in Mexico and "incited them to commit rapine and murder on this side of the border," causing "much injury and mischief" to "loyal citizens." This frustration might have been more believable to Governor López except for subsequent charges of Confederates themselves violating the Mexican border only five days later. At 4 o'clock A.M. several Southerners and a few off-duty soldiers crossed the Rio Grande into Matamoros and seized half a dozen Yankee refugees. These included a "treasonous" Texan, former district-court judge Edmund J. Davis who would later serve as Reconstruction governor of Texas. A colonel in the Union's First Texas Cavalry (known in some quarters as the First Texas Traitors), the raiders also abducted his lieutenant, William W. Montgomery. Crossing the river back into Brownsville, several prisoners were conveniently executed as they "escaped." They hung Montgomery from a mesquite tree, but took Davis to Ft. Brown at the pleadings of his wife, the daughter of a respected local Confederate. Speaking of Davis's comrades, Quintero reported to Benjamin that month: "I have reasons to believe that they will not commit treason again in this world. They are permanently located in the soil of the country. Deserving as their fate has been, the occurrence at the mouth of the river is deeply to be regretted, as it may lead to new complications."

An astute observer, Quintero's concerns proved more than justified. He reported Vidaurri's views that "authorities in Tamaulipas are ... controlled by an unprovoked hostility to the Confederacy, thinking themselves capable not only to cope with France but with the Southern States. He laughs at their conceit and ignorance." The account of reactions in Matamoros supported Vidaurri's assessment. That night of the abductions, "bands of music paraded the streets with *vivas* to Lincoln and death to the Confederates. Governor Lopez was hissed at the theater because he feared the Confederates." A flurry of correspondence ensued between Governor López and General Bee. The governor did not accept as fact the evils ascribed to the U.S. consul and his agents, declaring "What appears to you indisputable is not clear to me...." In attempting to balance his citizens' outrage against a more prudent course, he pleaded "The reciprocity manifested by me, will be useless if your subordinates do not act with more prudence, or if mine do not obey orders." Though clearly furious at outrages perpetrated under the Unionist Davis's authority, General Bee realized one man should not jeopardize the Matamoros trade. Just three days after the incident, he released the prisoners from Ft. Brown. In his letter to López, the Confederate commander could not resist reiterating the indignities and outrages "by persons operating under ... this same E.J. Davis" and that the decision to release him "might perhaps be justly led to a different determination."[191]

With the fall of Vicksburg on July 4, the Trans-Mississippi emerged an autonomous region of the Confederacy, completely cut off from eastern supplies and thrown upon its own resources. Trans-Mississippi commander General Edmund Kirby-Smith now recognized existence of an "absolute want of army supplies in the Trans-Mississippi Department," admitting, "the Rio Grande [is] the only channel by which they are to be introduced." The cotton trade emerged more important than ever, and the need to restrain border difficulties could not be overstated.[192]

In September the value of the reciprocity agreement with López proved itself. The feared *bandolero* Octaviano Zapata had attacked and routed a Mexican army unit in the Tamaulipas town of Guerrero. The mayor of the town appealed to the Confederacy for help. Recently promoted Confederate Major Santos Benavides quickly responded, crossing the Rio Grande with 79 cavalrymen. The following day he located Zapata's camp. After a brief, furious exchange of fire, the desperados fled into the sparse countryside, their leader Zapata counted among the abandoned dead. The Confederates suffered not a single casualty. Consul Pierce had been thought behind Zapata's border atrocities, so an elated General Bee reported there would "be no trouble with this emissary of the Lincoln government...." The secret "treaty" established by Bee, Quintero and López allowing such pursuit and justice had served cross-border interests well, preserving peace while helping to maintain uninterrupted the vital Matamoros trade.[193]

September in Matamoros proved memorable to Quintero for another, more personal reason. On the 7th his first-born son came into the world. In tribute to his departed Texas friend, Mirabeau Lamar, the son also received the name Lamar. Sketchy records actually indicate Lamar to have been born in Matamoros. This certainly coincides with Quintero's need to work closely with Governor López in dealing with the *bandolero* Zapata. The birth of Lamar does raise the issue of whether Quintero's wife lived with him in Mexico during the diplomatic assignment. Of course, the birth of her son in Matamoros unambiguously reveals her residence that September. As for the previous December, nine months earlier, Quintero's correspondence clearly places him in Monterrey dealing with Vidaurri and López regarding border incursions. Thus, the implication is that Quintero's wife did remain in Mexico with her diplomat husband. In fact, on January 29, 1864, four months after Lamar's birth, the Cuban wrote to an old friend, "Eliza sends you her regards," further placing her at the Confederate's side. Alternatively, if she had originally stayed in New Orleans at the outset of Quintero's posting, she might have abandoned the city when it fell in early 1862. Her presence in Mexico may have provided a basis for some biographers claiming Quintero married "a local Mexican woman." A name such as De Tazier (Bournos), and a son born in Matamoros, could make such an assumption appear reasonable. Regardless, as Quintero continued to face diplomatic challenges on behalf of his new Confederate nation, he no doubt felt his efforts now assumed an even nobler purpose, that of providing new hopes and directions for the next generation.[194]

Throughout this period of diplomatic challenge, Quintero nevertheless established strong friendships and pursued broader interests. After all, before the war he already published extensive poetry and worked on important journalistic projects. Quintero may not have known that during this same year his old friend and Havana prisonmate, Cirilo Villaverde, extended the Confederate perspective through linguistic efforts. In New York, Villaverde translated *Richmond Examiner* editor Edward Pollard's *History of the First Year of the War in the South* (*Historia del primer año de la guerra del Sur*).[195] It is not surprising that such an engaging personality as Quintero, though separated from such old friends as Villaverde, would seize new-found scholarly opportunities in Mexico.

Don Manuel G. Rejón provided these new perspectives. Quintero described his friend as "a gentleman of fine appearance, an eminent lawyer and a member of the Mexican Congress." Rejón, at this time, also served Vidaurri as Secretary of State of Nuevo León y Coahuila. It had been Rejón who informed the Confederates of border closure during the Carvajal controversy earlier in the war. Obviously, Quintero had occasion to work closely with Rejón and come to know him well, both professionally and personally. The Mexican official had come into possession of many even then old documents which had previously resided for some years in the Mexican archives at Monterrey. These comprised "a collection of historical documents in reference to Texas, Louisiana, New-Mexico and California...." Among these documents were details of the fabled San Saba Silver mines, which Jim Bowie had planned to explore had he not met an untimely demise defending the Alamo. Apparently this set also included the diary and correspondence of Philip Nolan, the early Texas adventurer of some notoriety in whom Texas President Lamar had earlier shown interest. These no doubt appealed to the Harvard-educated Quintero. He must have realized their value in the world of literary attainments and perhaps even then committed to publish them after the war.[196]

Interestingly, in the literary world late this same year appeared Edward Everett Hale's perennially popular story *The Man Without a Country*. Designed to foster Union patriotism against "every Bragg and Beauregard who broke a soldier's oath two years ago, and of every Maury and Barron who broke a sailor's," this story specifically sought to inflame opinion against the "copperhead" Confederate sympathizer, Ohio gubernatorial candidate Clement L. Vallandigham. The disparate threads of Rejón's documents and Hale's story would juxtapose in postwar years, catalyzed by none other than Quintero himself.[197]

MONTURIOL'S "ICTÍNEO"

Only a couple of weeks after the incident of the Davis abduction the previous spring, Quintero sent to Secretary of State Judah Benjamin what might arguably be the most unusual letter written during the entire war by anyone on either side.[198]

MONTEREY, *April 9, 1863.*

SIR: Narciso Monturiol, a scientific Catalonian, has invented a vessel for submarine navigation. She is called "Ictineo" (fish-like vessel).

As a man-of-war she can prevent not only the bombardment of the ports, but also the landing of the enemy. If the services of Mr. Monturiol are secured and the necessary number of vessels built, no Federal squadron would dare to approach our coasts, since an unseen enemy can leave our harbors and destroy their ships. The "Ictineos" have guns which fire under water and also rams and torpedoes. They can navigate in a depth of about twenty-five fathoms.

The want of atmosphere to support animal life in the depth of the seas, which has been the great drawback to submarine navigation has been obviated. The inventor creates an artificial atmosphere and shutting himself up, like a larva, carries with him the elements of existence.

Several of the Spaniards here are well acquainted with Mr. Monturiol and are satisfied that he is not an idle talker. He had lately made experiments at Barcelona which prove his success.

Mr. Monturiol resides in Barcelona, Spain, Santo Domingo del Call Street (No. 1, room 2).

I have the honor to be, your obedient servant.

J. A. QUINTERO

P.S.—I enclose an able letter from Mr. Monturiol recently published by the Prensa de la Habana.

An extraordinary letter reading more like science fiction than a Confederate diplomatic dispatch, Quintero would seem to have identified the means to smash the Federal blockade. Could such an advanced submarine have actually existed in the world of 1863, or had Quintero's normally good judgment lapsed as he all but endorsed the crackpot scheme of a charlatan?

Actually, Narciso Monturiol, the Father of Spain's submarine, did develop the *Ictíneo*. Other than firing guns underwater, it could deliver almost everything Quintero claimed. First launched in Barcelona to great public acclaim during 1859, in the ensuing two years she had made 50 more dives. By the time Quintero wrote to Benjamin, the prototype had already yielded to construction of *Ictíneo II* in the previous year, the vessel Quintero no doubt spoke of. This larger more advanced double-hulled version, at 56 feet long, would carry 20 men to depths of 100 feet for up to seven and a half hours. Monturiol and his designers had developed a sophisticated chemical reaction system to produce oxygen for breathing, and steam for an underwater engine. Despite the amazing ingenuity of his invention, Monturiol would never interest a single nation in adding this vessel to their naval armadas. He would die penniless, but not completely forgotten. While his countrymen of Spain's Catalan region still honor their native son, it is likely the *Nautilus* of Jules Verne's *20,000 Leagues Under the Sea* had genesis in the *Ictíneo*. Verne researched the book in the 1860s and probably came across any of the numerous press reports on Monturiol's achievement.[199]

No record is evident regarding the Confederate State Department's response to this unusual offer. Review of the *Official Records of the Union and Confederate Navies in the War of the Rebellion* does not reveal a response, nor do the naval archives of Spain include correspondence between Monturiol and the Confederate States.[200] It may be that Secretary of State Benjamin may not have had the imagination to conceive of the vessel's military possibilities, or he may not have able to gain the War Department's or the president's attention on the matter. Not understanding Monturiol's success, they may have simply decided Quintero had been duped. At best, the Richmond authorities may have concluded Quintero ought to leave naval planning to those who had proper training and experience. Perhaps, in the end, the lack of Confederate interest is more simply traced to the fact that the Confederacy, in "straining every nerve," already had an imaginative submersible program underway. The semisubmersible *David* took shape in Charleston even as Quintero penned the letter. She would prove, before year's end, the value of torpedoes (submarine mines) — the brainchild of eminent Confederate States scientist Commodore Matthew Fontaine Maury — as she gravely wounded the Union flagship *New Ironsides*. In the next year, the Confederate submarine *H.L. Hunley* would sink the USS *Housatonic*, the first such action in history.[201] A young nation of limited resources, the Confederacy could not chase every will-o'-the-wisp, especially those apparently redundant to her own innovative, if desperate, programs to exploit every technological advantage possible against an industrially superior enemy.

Quintero, in forwarding this exceptional report, again proves his outstanding talents and abilities. Though Monturiol's vessel had been in existence since just before the war, there is no mention of it in any of the official navy reports of the Union or Confederacy. Only Quintero, in exploiting his Hispanic cultural affiliations, reported of the invention. A man not content to fulfill the narrow sense of his mission, Quintero took the broad view. He perceived the value of this intelligence in gaining a powerful weapon to assault the blockade which choked his nation. Quintero did what he could to advance this possibility; the fact that his nation did not act does not diminish his contribution.

STATE OF THE NATION

On September 16, scarcely a week after the birth of Lamar, Quintero wrote to Secretary of State Benjamin an insightful, sensitive overview regarding Mexican woes at the eve of French occupation of the north. The Cuban's sympathy for Mexico, his ability to synthesize large geopolitical trends and yet look to the interests of his own Confederate nation underscored his unique value to Richmond. He began: "Since my last dispatch to the Department, under date of July 23 (No. 49), this country has been in a state of great disorder." Quintero then recounted how the new cabinet of President Juárez had fallen apart as a result of a "violent altercation" between the president and General Manuel Doblado.

> General Doblado is an able statesman and a sagacious politician. He was considered the last hope of the Republic, and as such called by President Juarez, at the request of various of the States, to restore order and authority in Mexico.
>
> In the meantime the condition of this country is a sad one. The General Government is very unpopular, and has neither means at home nor credit abroad to prosecute the war. Aside of a large party which favor French intervention, patriotism seems to be dead in the heart of the people. The truth is the Republic has ceased to be.
>
> Governor Vidaurri favors the dissolution of the Mexican Union, that the different States composing the same may resume their sovereignty. His plan, however, has not been accepted. He has withdrawn the brigade of this State from the Mexican army. The latter is now reduced to ten or twelve thousand men.

Quintero continued in relating a succession of ministers to Washington, and then summarized President Lincoln's position on Mexican sovereignty:

> Señor Romero [who was formerly the Mexican chargé d'affaires in Washington] has stated to his acquaintances here, that the Government of the United States have promised to lend their aid to Mexico in her present troubles. He says that the United States had not ere this acted because they had relied upon the French disclaimers of all political designs against the Republic of Mexico; that the news of the establishment of a throne and monarch from Europe could not but arouse the North and compel President Lincoln to undertake a war with France. He says that while in Washington a few months ago, Mr. Seward assured him that the United States as a neighbor of Mexico, and having a similar form of government, deemed it important to their own safety that no foreign power should conquer this country and establish a monarchy.
>
> The French forces which are to occupy Matamoras [sic] are daily expected. It is believed that they will also take possession of Monterey, as they have recently

done with Tampico and Minatitlan. It is known that the expedition which is to occupy a portion of the Mexican States on our border is coming directly from France. I am satisfied that no armed resistance can be offered them.

The Confederate diplomat then proceeded at length to discuss United States seizures of an English steamer and intercession requested and granted by the new Tamaulipas governor for its release as a "neutral vessel." He further explored impressment of cotton by individuals, bringing the matter back to the French: "As soon as the French shall occupy Matamoras [*sic*] the necessary steps will be taken to have the free use of that port. Under their rule most of the present obnoxious duties on cotton will be repealed. Governor Vidaurri is to yield calmly to the force of circumstances and he will neither offer resistance nor obstruct commerce with Matamoras [*sic*]."[202]

As autumn of 1863 approached, Quintero and Vidaurri obviously concerned themselves with how the impending French occupation would affect their charges. Little did they know that a number of other political and military challenges would occur before the French occupation would number among their chief concerns.

YANKEE VEXATIONS AND MEXICAN OPPORTUNISM

On July 29, only a few weeks after the twin Confederate losses at Vicksburg and Gettysburg, President Lincoln challenged his Secretary of War Edwin Stanton on the lucrative Confederate border trade. "Can we not renew the effort to organize a force to go to Western Texas?" he asked. "I believe no local object is now more desirable." Taking Texas would free the 150 ships of the West Gulf Squadron to pursue such high seas commerce destroyers as the CSS *Alabama*. Furthermore, a Federal show of strength might give notice to the advancing French. By late October, 1863 nearly 7,000 Union troops landed at Brazos Santiago, the port for Brownsville some 30 miles away.

The Confederates could not hold Ft. Brown with no more than the 200 soldiers available. Though criticized by some, General Bee followed standing orders "to destroy what might fall into the hands of the enemy...." On November 3, about noon, he dispatched a large wagon train of army supplies north to King's Ranch, and sent his wounded to Matamoros. His men turned back wagons shipping cotton into the city. Waiting until the Federals were within ten miles, he then had the post destroyed, burning some 600 bales of cotton and throwing about as many into the river. According to Quintero's later report, some unknown person "without authority, fired the buildings." As the fire reached the ammunition supply, some 8,000 pounds of powder exploded, burning a block of city buildings. As the Confederates withdrew north, bandit General José María Cobos, who had been living in Brownsville, organized a force of 200 men "with the ostensible purpose of extinguishing the fire," according to Quintero. Women and children crossed the river to Matamoros on the ferry, but as the powder exploded a large firebrand struck the boat, setting it afire. On the 5th, 3,000 Federals under General Nathaniel P. Banks took the city. General Cobos relinquished command and the next day invaded Matamoros with the infamous Juan Cortina at his side, arresting the governor. Cortina in turn would execute Cobos within 24 hours, on charges of "refusing to recognize the Juarez government." Following several weeks of revolution in Matamoros, by January the pro–Yankee bandit Cortina would emerge as governor of Tamaulipas.[203]

In some ways the Confederates wondered why it had taken the Yankees so long to come; contingency plans had been established for just such a disaster. On November 9, General Bee informed Quintero of his safe escape "from the smoking ruins of Ft. Brown...." As the cotton wagon routes would shift west in favor of Laredo and Eagle Pass, further upriver away from Yankee control, Quintero needed to arrange Vidaurri's assistance. The Cuban delivered the vital aid. At the Piedras Negras depot across from Eagle Pass, Vidaurri stationed a large force to protect Confederate trade. This also served to assure his lucrative revenues of $40,000 to $50,000 per month. Bee felt shipping cotton through Monterrey to Matamoros would be successful "as I presume that even Yankee influence could not stop the usual commerce of Mexico." The alternative route through Eagle Pass soon thrived with activity. The customs collector there noted that "scarcely a day [passed] that hundreds of bales [of cotton] were not unloaded" there. Within a couple of months a huge inventory of some 5,000 bales accumulated, waiting for shipment across the river into Mexico. Safeguarding the Confederate side of the border stood Santos Benavides, now a colonel, and his cavalry.[204]

More disruptive to cotton trade than Union interference would prove the Milmo Affair, involving Vidaurri's son-in-law, Patricio Milmo. Immediately after the Yankees seized Brownsville, on November 6 Treasury Agent Clarence C. Thayer diverted to Matamoros after a dangerous voyage through blockading fleets with a shipment of seven cases of Confederate Treasury notes, amounting to $16 million. Intended to address a money shortage in the Trans-Mississippi Department, the money needed to complete shipment to San Antonio and Shreveport. Thayer, with some difficulty, finally located in Matamoros a Confederate Major Charles Russell. The major presented himself as the ranking Confederate officer on the frontier. Russell agreed that with so many unscrupulous characters about, including the bandit Cortina as *commandante*, he would ensure that the cases quickly left Matamoros and reach Eagle Pass, care of Milmo and Company. Russell, an unscrupulous quartermaster himself who had fled Brownsville and hid in Matamoros as much from the Confederates as the Yankees, revealed to Milmo the contents of the cases. Russell had engaged in scurrilous lining of his pockets on inflated Mexican contracts before, and this windfall opportunity could not be overlooked. Patricio Milmo informed the Confederates on December 11 he had confiscated the funds, as well as all Confederate cotton in transit within Mexico and that stored at Piedras Negras. He justified this as due to Confederate debts to his and other Mexican firms. By the 20th, Quintero had unsuccessfully appealed to Vidaurri on several occasions, reporting "[I] exerted my energies to the highest pitch in order to have said property released." Milmo lamely explained to Quintero that inflation of Confederate currency had caused him some loss. Vidaurri may have already been thinking about a comfortable, well-financed future after the French arrived. He apparently believed the Confederates hardly stood in a position to retaliate after losses incurred at Gettysburg and Vicksburg. Not believing a word from these two scheming relatives, Quintero concluded to quartermaster Simeon Hart, "I suspect the plot to take possession of the funds in question was conceived in Matamoros." The Cuban agreed that Milmo "is determined to take advantage of the situation of our government," but the agent nevertheless advised "prompt action in the matter." After all, "A day will come when we will be able to redress wrong."

That day did come, more or less. Quintero recommended a harsh line lest such seizures continue. His advice: Stop the shipment "of all cotton both public and private" in Nuevo León, instead diverting the revenues into Tamaulipas though Laredo. Facing lost revenues at Piedras Negras, Vidaurri "would be compelled to come to terms." Trans-Mississippi Department commander General Edmund Kirby-Smith did just this. On January 12, 1864, about two months after the hijacking of the Confederate currency, Kirby-Smith wrote Vidaurri: "A refusal to release the funds after their attention had been called to their illegal detention would seem to raise for discussion" whether a "hostile attitude" were intended against the Confederate States. He authorized no further payments until these "unpleasant matters" were disposed of. In fact, in Special Orders No. 8 the Trans-Mississippi commander ordered: "The exportation of all Government and private cotton from Texas by way of the Rio Grande is for the present prohibited." He took a step further than Quintero proposed and also seized all Mexican assets in Texas. To soften this stance, Kirby-Smith appointed a commission to Monterrey to negotiate a settlement. This delegation included Judge Thomas J. Devine. A previous delegate to the Texas secession convention, he was brother to the Mayor Devine who less than eight years earlier had defended Quintero's editorial in *El Ranchero*, even though it resulted in the shooting of publisher McDonald.

A frustrated Quintero cast his sights beyond Monterrey to the Juárez administration. In a secret January 29 letter, written in Spanish to a well-placed friend named Pedro Santacilia, the Confederate complained of Vidaurri's duplicity. In detailing the outrages against Texas and the Confederacy, Quintero implicitly dangled the carrot before Juárez: 7,000 bales of cotton taxed and shipped through Nuevo León just in the previous month, engagement of 3,000 wagons supporting the commerce, and three million dollars in trade having occurred since the war began. Quintero concluded, "Frankly speaking, the conduct of Mr. Vidaurri has not been that of a statesman, that the support of the unjust claim of a sole individual has sacrificed the great interest of Nuevo León."

Against General Kirby-Smith's ultimatum, and under pressure from the Confederate commission, Vidaurri finally capitulated. Politically he stood somewhere between Juárez and the French, committed to neither, and he relied heavily on the Confederate friendship and revenues. By February 24, a settlement provided Milmo and Company 500 bales of cotton, plus another 200 delivered in San Antonio as interest. A partner to the firm also received 1,500 bales. The Confederate currency proceeded on to the Trans-Mississippi Department. Confederate Major Russell found himself relieved of responsibilities by none other than President Davis. Quintero advised all to "put aside their pride, revenge or passion, and set themselves about the work of securing for the cause and country the greatest advantages possible to be obtained."[205]

POWER STRUGGLES ON THE BORDER

As the redirected cotton trade flowed along newly established primary routes, the military labored to contain the Yankee invasion. Brownsville had fallen. The order went out that Laredo, Eagle Pass and other Rio Grande trade crossings must be defended. General John Magruder, commander of the Department of Texas, on December 22 ordered Colonel John Ford to raise a force in San Antonio to retake south Texas from the Yankees. In outfitting the enterprise, Ford requested permission for use of "the camels now here as pack animals," believing they "would answer admirably for the expedition." No doubt, these camels remained from innovative experiments conducted only a few years earlier by Jefferson Davis, then U.S. Secretary of War. He had imported camels for trials in Texas and further Southwest; the war interrupted this promising work. Whether or not Ford employed camels, by January, 1864 he expected a mobile force of 1,600 soldiers for field operations in the chaparral. He planned to link up with Colonel Benavides at Laredo and other Confederate forces further west at Eagle Pass.

The Yankees did not rest on their laurels. Newly promoted General Edmund J. Davis — the very same Davis whom the Confederates had abducted from Matamoros and then released the previous year — had moved his cavalry upriver, taking Roma. Davis, an old friend of Colonel Benavides, had been miffed in not being selected for the Texas secession convention; he had quickly abandoned the Southern cause and sided with his friend's enemy. Now a Union general, one of his units ironically threatened Laredo and its defender, Santos Benavides.

The unusually harsh winter drought had brought a desolate, bitterly cold aspect to Laredo, only matched by the exhaustion that had kept Colonel Benavides bedridden for days. On March 19, a vaquero named Cayetano de la Garze furiously rode a lathered horse into Laredo's cotton-lined San Agustin Plaza. He reported a large force of Federals approaching. Benavides had scouts everywhere and did not believe this; he would later realize the Yankees had violated Mexican neutrality by traveling on the south side of the Rio Grande. Two days earlier, these units, led by guerilla Cecilio Valerio, had attacked an advance unit of Colonel Ford. Attracted by cotton stockpiles and the intelligence that Benavides was ill, Valerio now moved on Laredo with his 200 men. Defending the city, an unsteady Santos Benavides and the companies of his two brothers, Refugio and Cristobal, about 70 men in total, faced the enemy. As Santos left town to meet the Federals, he reminded his brother Cristobal that the 5,000 bales of cotton "belong to the Confederacy," and ordered: "If the day goes against us fire it." In a corral on the eastern outskirts of town, they met the Union forces in a three-hour pitched battle, badly outnumbered. These Federals, who only two days earlier had inflicted the loss of "much blood and property" on Ford, now retreated in disorder. Amazingly, Benavides's command suffered not a single fatality. In winning the battle of Laredo, Colonel Benavides preserved the cotton trade and repulsed the one Federal assault that might have unraveled the movement of Confederate "white gold" across the border.[206]

In Richmond, the administration sought to further protect the border by allying itself with the new French-installed Mexican Empire. On January 7, 1864 the State Department had appointed General William Preston as Envoy Extraordinary and Minister Plenipotentiary, assigned to Mexico City after the long absence of Minister Pickett. Secretary Benjamin informed Minister Preston of Quintero's role as "general agent" on the Rio Grande frontier. Preston's mission included "reciprocal free trade," but he also needed to help the new Mexican government understand the true designs of the Union; that is, if the United States could subdue the Confederacy it would then "extend their conquests by the annexation of Canada on the north and Mexico on the south." Taking "one war at a time," they will "commence with what they deem the easiest prey." Benjamin warned of historical examples regarding ambitious nations: "The danger is tenfold increased where a government, like that of the United States, has become so debased as to be under the control of the lowest classes, ready to sacrifice all justice and principle for the gratification of the lust of conquest."[207]

Though the Confederates held control of their border, President Juárez finally threatened Vidaurri's northern Mexican empire. Earlier, the French had taken the capital city; now the president retreated before their advancing armies. Juárez had expressed interest in the previous year of establishing a temporary government in Monterrey, but Vidaurri gave no encouragement to this. Finally, on January 9, Juárez set up his government less than 100 miles away in Coahuila's capital of Saltillo. Desperate to maintain his army and government, Juárez demanded Vidaurri's revenues from Confederate cotton moving through Piedras Negras. Vidaurri vacillated and Juárez decided to move on Monterrey. Juárez sent ahead his son-in-law, Pedro Santacilia, to feel out the *caudillo*. The governor seemed hospitable, issuing a letter of "most chivalrous cordiality" welcoming Juárez's wife to Monterrey. Cautiously encouraged, the president stationed an army of 1,300 near the city, while he and his ministers entered the Nuevo León capital on February 12. The governor had in reality only tried to buy time; with 22 cannon, he had already withdrawn into the fortified *Ciudadela* at the center of the city. Two days later, the president and governor met to discuss the city's transfer. At this conference, Vidaurri's son drew a pistol and encouraged open rebellion; President Juárez left in haste for Saltillo.²⁰⁸

Ever the astute diplomat, Quintero engaged in his own consultation with President Juárez during this tense period. To Secretary Benjamin, the Cuban reported being "on the eve of making private arrangements *with the President of the Republic* in order to continue ... trade through Camargo and Laredo." By January 29, Quintero had already engaged in aforementioned correspondence with the president's secretary, Pedro Santacilia, referencing the Milmo Affair as a vehicle to dangling Confederate trade inducements to Juárez. Timing and providence on his side, Quintero now approached the president when finances preyed heavily on the administration. Vidaurri had held back his share of revenues, while loans promised three years earlier by the United States had never materialized. The Confederacy offered the only significant source of income to prop the rapidly disintegrating legally elected government.

The tidal forces of Mexican civil war finally cast Vidaurri's tranquil empire on shoals of uncertainty. Viewed a traitor by the president, on February 26 Juárez officially deposed the governor and separated Coahuila from Nuevo León. This latter step would facilitate collecting custom duties from Confederate trade at Piedras Negras. Vidaurri soon found Juárez's saber balanced by threat's from French General Achille François Bazaine. Only a day after the president's action, a letter from the French general claimed the "fratricidal war" nearly over, the forces of "ex–President Juárez" scattered into small bands. Now Vidaurri must join the French for the sake of the "union of all the Mexican nation...." If Vidaurri made war on Napoleon III, it would be "disastrous" for the governor. Ever indecisive, Vidaurri placed the decision before the people as a referendum — support the President or welcome the French.

Quintero recognized the governor's dilemma and feared a desperate action to force Confederate assistance; he thus reinforced Eagle Pass lest this key port of entry be held hostage by Vidaurri. This proved unnecessary. The referendum settled in the president's mind that Vidaurri was indeed a traitor. Juárez dispatched a large force to Monterrey. Warned in advance, Vidaurri escaped through Laredo into Confederate Texas with the state treasury and archives. The former governor visited with his old friend Colonel Santos Benavides for some days, then proceeded to Houston. There General Magruder provided a warm welcome, hosting Vidaurri at one of the city's fine hotels. The governor may have had a selfishly independent streak, certainly traitorous from the Mexican president's viewpoint, but the Confederates owed a great deal to the faithful *caudillo*.[209]

JUÁREZ IN MONTERREY

On April 2, the president's army of between 5,000 and 6,000 entered Monterrey. Led by General Miguel Negrete, the commander arrested many of Vidaurri's officials, including Patricio Milmo, the governor's "partner in mercantile transactions." Milmo's arrest concerned many, as he enjoyed British citizenship. Quintero approached the general without hesitation to inquire regarding the policy towards Confederate trade and how its agents would be treated. The general assured Quintero on both counts. The following day President Juárez arrived to set up his government. Quintero sought a meeting with the president, who cordially greeted the Confederate diplomat. In fact, Juárez invited Quintero to dinner that very night and introduced the Confederate to the Mexican cabinet. The president further confirmed his general's promise of continued Confederate border trade.

Despite these assurances from Juárez, Quintero would soon have doubts. At the time Vidaurri had evacuated Monterrey, his former secretary of state Manuel G. Rejón had fled to Federally occupied Brownsville in hopes of there securing passage on to Havana. Here he proved victim to a rumored secret agreement of the previous January between Andrew J. Hamilton, Union Military Governor of Texas, and Mexican officials in the state of Tamaulipas (where the port of Matamoros resided). Hamilton arrested Rejón per orders of Major General Francis J. Herron. By turning Rejón over to the *Juaristas* on March 27, they seemed to honor this alleged agreement. From a postwar retrospective in *The Texas Almanac*, the words of Quintero:

> Rejón ... fled to Brownsville, Texas, and thought himself secure under the protection of the United States flag.

José M. Iglesias, one of President Juárez's Ministers, was at the time in Mata-moros, and solicited the extradition of Rejón. General F. J. Herron, command-ing the Federal forces on the lower Rio Grande, turned him over to the Mexican authorities. The famous Cortina was then Governor of the State of Tamauli-pas, and, in obedience to the order of Minister Iglesias, caused Rejón to be shot.

General Herron, after having surrendered Rejón, applied for the extradi-tion of a certain Confederate agent who resided at Monterey, but his wishes were not granted by the Mexican authorities.

The surrender of a political refugee like Rejón, that he might be put to death by his enemies, never occurred before in the United States. A father's prayer's, a woe-stricken wife's tears, and the piteous wailings of his children did not avail to save the unfortunate Rejón.

Quintero's good friend Rejón, who the year earlier had given his Con-federate *amigo bueno* treasured documents from the Mexican archives, was indeed shot as a traitor on March 28 — some said shot in the back. The fate of his friend concerned Quintero, for the Union authorities had also requested the Confederate's extradition. Only three days after Juárez's arrival, on April 6, Quintero met again with the president on this matter. Juárez clearly stated his neutrality to both Unionists and Confederates, giving assurances of Quin-tero's safety. The postwar vignette from *The Texas Almanac*, in referencing a "certain Confederate agent who resided at Monterey," could only have been Quintero writing of his own assignment. This reminder of an earlier Mexi-can rebuke may have been a subtle postwar tweak at then occupying Federal authorities, or perhaps Quintero simply wished to diminish his role as he looked to a then uncertain future in the Reconstruction South.[210]

In understanding Juárez's change of heart from caustic indifference to virtual friendship with the Confederacy, historians typically credit a certain pragmatic reality to the president. The acute need for government revenues, the lack of promised United States assistance and the unique ability of the Confederate nation to fulfill this need drove a relationship in direct conflict with the president's own earlier directives. No doubt these considerations did largely dictate the course Juárez took, but a neglected factor is the Cuban con-nection. Since the president's 1853 New Orleans exile, Cubans played a vitally important role his life. Quintero's one-time Havana Club compatriots Juan Clemente Zenea, Domingo de Goicuría and Pedro Santacilia had assisted Juárez in those days of exile, with Goicuría later officially representing the Mex-ican government in the United States during the War of the Reform and after the French invasion. Also fighting in the late 1850s for Juárez were the Cubans Carlos Manuel de Céspedes and Manuel Quezada — future Cuban indepen-dence heros who would continue Quintero's early Caribbean struggle. Quezada had fought for Juárez against the French, while de Céspedes had accompanied the president to Saltillo in the retreat from Napoleon's advancing troops.[211]

The Confederate diplomat may have benefited from the warm regard this close association with Cubans may have engendered, but the special relationships Quintero and Juárez shared with Pedro Santacilia present keener insight into the dynamics of the Monterrey occupation. Santacilia apparently met Juárez in 1853 while buying cigarettes on Bourbon Street and subsequently introduced him to the Cuban exile community, possibly including Quintero. Santacilia, with the Cuban businessman Goicuría, provided arms to Mexico during the War of the Reform, and in 1863 he married the president's oldest daughter, Manuela ('Nelita). Now as Juárez's son-in-law, he served as secretary and the president's closest confidant, as their extensive correspondence attests. Quintero, on the other hand, had mentioned Santacilia almost 15 years earlier in his aforementioned *Lyric Poetry in Cuba*. Both Cuban freedom fighters suffered imprisonment, and both escaped prison to New Orleans. A patriotic Latin poet of Quintero's mold, in his 1856 *El Arpa del Proscrito* (The Harp of the Banished) Santacilia set the stage for the mournful *El Laúd del Desterrado* (The Lute of the Exiled) which just two years later featured both Quintero and Santacilia. Only six years after this joint cry for freedom, they now met again serving different nations yet both espousing the same cause of self-determination and constitutional liberty.

These ties of *la patria*, suffering, friendship, and literary kinship no doubt played a key role in the events surrounding the president's occupation of Monterrey, a role completely overlooked in accounts of Confederate and Mexican history, as well as in the many biographies of President Juárez. Quintero's bold stance in remaining at Monterrey to face the president and his generals is more understandable in light of the Santacilia connection. Quintero had already written to his old friend at Saltillo in January. In this letter he referenced "our old friendship" and assured Santacilia he could count on "a very fond friend and dear countryman." At about this time — when Santacilia visited Vidaurri in Monterrey — Quintero and Santacilia no doubt met and discussed whether the Confederate should remain or not. As close advisor to the president, Santacilia may have also suggested a policy of warm "tolerance" to the Confederacy; regardless, Juárez would have been loath to hand over his son-in-law's countryman to the Yankees for hanging. In the dinner invitation with the president, and the introductions to his cabinet, may likely be traced the invisible hand of Santacilia. The commercial agreements between Juárez and Quintero may also have been facilitated by the Cuban son-in-law.[212]

Another aspect of the Monterrey occupation takes on interesting significance with Quintero's and Santacilia's presence noted. The president's finance minister, Guillermo Prieto, shared with the two Cubans a passion for poetry. In fact, Prieto stood as the esteemed national poet of Mexico. In Saltillo, Prieto and Santacilia had jointly directed the *Diario Oficial*, and now in Monterrey began a "weekly literary sheet of respectable poetry, romance, and satire, *El Cura de Tamajón*." It may be no accident the two confidants of the Mexican president chose to direct their considerable energies in such a project. Joining in critical mass with a noted Cuban poet in gray, this could help explain the genesis of such a literary undertaking even as powerful forces raged in two fratricidal wars, threatening the tenuous circumstance bringing these erudite souls together. In fact, within the month, Santacilia left the city, either to visit his wife or to pursue other business for Juárez. Minister Prieto may not have felt confident in tackling such a project alone; someone of Quintero's caliber, ready to stand in for the president's talented secretary, at least as an advisor, could have been significant in sustaining the effort.[213]

The relations between Mexico's Juárez government and Quintero's Confederacy proved mutually advantageous. Commerce provided vital revenues for the four and a half months Juárez found it possible to maintain a government in the state of Nuevo León. Indeed, the Confederate States provided for the continued existence of Juárez's nation, allowing him to virtually hang by a thread until the French could one day be expelled. In a report to Secretary Benjamin, Quintero remarked "the commerce between Texas and Mexico is quite brisk," a tribute to his dealings with the Indian president of Mexico.

In seeking to further expand trade, Quintero set up a meeting between Juárez and Kentucky's former "Know Nothing" governor Charles S. Morehead who then passed through Monterrey on his way to Europe. Morehead attempted to counter Yankee "sinister influences" against the trade in lead, sulphur and saltpeter. Absolutely confident, the Kentuckian stressed the "certainty of ultimate success" in Confederate nation-building as much as he touched on trade issues. Regardless, Juárez gave "promise to observe strict and impartial neutrality" but offered no further Confederate concessions.[214]

As if to lend credence to Morehead's confidence, Colonel Ford's summer offensive against the Yankees provided renewed Confederate optimism. In June, Benavides and other Southern forces joined Ford for an excursion down the Rio Grande. They surprised and punished two companies of Federal cavalry, securing "badly needed" additional saddles, weapons, wagons and horses. Skirmishing as close as five miles from Brownsville, Ford established positions "in as close quarters as possible" to intimidate the occupying Union forces. Three weeks later, flush with ordnance and other supply reinforcements purchased from Matamoros, Ford took the offensive. Yankee columns suffered losses in small furious engagements. By July 20, Union General Herron decided Brownsville could not be defended. He withdrew to the coast. The next day, a grateful mayor welcomed Ford's liberation force, and the ladies of the city presented a new Confederate battle flag to the colonel. The border cotton trade now resumed at Brownsville.[215]

Earlier that same month, United States Secretary of State William Seward received from the consul-general at Havana, Cuba a confidential dispatch detailing a secessionist scheme in California. Mr. Joseph A. Frink, a Connecticut trader living in Chihuahua, fell in with "rebels [who] have taken it for granted that he is one." In Monterrey the previous April, Frink "discovered that a scheme is on foot to strike a blow in Southern California." A Confederate Colonel Collins, a "native of Georgia or Missouri" assigned to raise a force in this project, commissioned Frink "a major in the Confederate Army." It seems "many wealthy and influential men in California had urged the rebel government in Richmond to cooperate with them, in order to wrest the southern portion of the State from the U.S. authority.... The conspirators expect pecuniary assistance from French mercantile houses." Frink had been ordered to proceed to Acapulco to learn details of Union mail steamers, and he stopped in Havana on the way. "The seizure of one or more of our steamers, laden with treasure, forms a part of the scheme." Frink actually had some evidence to back his claims. He presented to the consul-general a letter written on May 1 by one J. Quintero, "said to be the rebel agent in Monterey, to his brother, Antonio J. in Havana," in which Frink is confirmed a Confederate major. Per this communiqué, Quintero informed Frink of C.S. State Department Agent Charles Helm's location in the city. Frink asked nothing more of the U.S. consul-general than reimbursements for his trip to Acapulco. The consul wrote to the State Department that the "man appears honest in his purpose," so he instead provided fare to New York on the steamer *Liberty* to confer with Secretary Seward. About a week later, Seward wrote to Secretary of War Edwin Stanton of the "alleged plan of the insurgents" and recommended Frink be employed in Federal service.[216]

Meanwhile, in Monterrey events marched steadily toward continued border conflict and further disintegration of the Mexican president's position. Key bureaucrats and army officers resigned, or even joined the French as traitors. One of his generals defied orders in engaging a pro–French Mexican general at San Luis Potosí, suffering a defeat. As if the inexorable French advance posed insufficient threat, Vidaurri's Colonel Julián Quiroga camped north of Monterrey with 200 troops. Considered by many to be Vidaurri's illegitimate son, Quiroga now cut off important Confederate trade with Piedras Negras. Unwilling to challenge Quiroga's Mexicans as the French drew nearer and nearer, Juárez finally decided to abandon Monterrey. On August 15, "amidst a shower of bullets" hailing from Quiroga's guns, the chief executive fled northwest to Chihuahua. A triumphant Colonel Quiroga then occupied the city. Per Vidaurri's decree "issued from Houston," Quiroga assumed the acting governorship, proceeding to extort loans from merchants. This moment of power lasted but ten days, for the French at last marched into Monterrey on August 26.[217]

FRENCH ADVANCE, BORDER INTRIGUES

As French general Armard Alexandre Castagny occupied Monterrey, the bandit-governor Cortina at Matamoros blustered against Confederate Colonel Ford; French forces under Mexican Indian General Tomás Mejía would oust the troublesome *bandolero* one month later. The French welcomed the Confederate representatives in Monterrey at a "grand ball," according "great consideration" to their "distinguished" guests. Quintero renegotiated trade agreements with General Castagny, finding the French "quite cautious and reserved" in their interactions. The accommodating general nevertheless repealed duties on cotton. By late August, the visiting Ford noted of Matamoros: "There were millions of dollars of merchandise in the place." An enthusiastic Quintero reported to Benjamin in late October: "We have never been in such a favorable condition as we are at present in regard to our intercourse with Mexico. There will be no difficulty to export (in a quiet way) any arms and ammunition we may purchase in this country."[218]

Just a month earlier, the United States consul at Chihuahua had come to the same conclusion as Quintero. He complained of continued Confederate success in the Mexican trade: "...[The] cotton trade between Texas and Mexico is very active, and the rebels are now supplied with money and arms far more plentifully than at any past period.... The presence of the French on the frontier will not impede, but on the contrary encourage this trade, and we may safely conclude that the rebels are obtaining in large quantities those supplies which are now most needed by them." As if to underscore this assessment, in October and November of 1864 at least 600,000 pounds of ordnance shipped through Matamoros into Texas.[219]

Quintero informed Secretary Benjamin of the "warmest feelings of friendship toward the Confederacy" by the French, any political or commercial arrangements favorable to the South within the range of possibility. Napoleon certainly desired a Confederate victory over the Union, if only to help maintain his recently installed Austrian puppet's shaky Mexican throne, the Emperor Ferdinand Maximilian. On the Texas border, though, French interest rested primarily on what had motivated Vidaurri and Juárez in earlier days: profits from trade. In an expensive war of conquest over vast Mexican territories, the Matamoros border trade represented a vitally important source of revenues to help support the enterprise. Vidaurri's solution worked just as well for his successors; furthermore, a talented Quintero stood ready in each case to adroitly manage the consecutive parade of border powers.[220]

Only the following February of 1865 in the last year of the war, General Lew Wallace, the future author of *Ben-Hur*, reported to General Ulysses S. Grant his concerns regarding Confederate trade presence in Mexico: "Matamoras [*sic*] is to all intents and purposes a rebel port, free at that, and you can readily imagine the uses they put it to. There is never a day that there are not from 75 to 150 vessels off Bagdad, discharging and receiving cargoes."[221]

The Matamoros Trade still prospered, but the militarily besieged Confederacy nevertheless entered its twilight days. Desertions in the armies rose, and even public officials betrayed their trusts. Brigadier General James E. Slaughter, commanding at Brownsville, reported on February 8 to General Mejía at Matamoros regarding Judge George W. Palmer, depositary in San Antonio, who "has decamped with a large amount of Government property." Slaughter asked that Palmer be detained in Monterrey until proof of his guilt could be obtained to justify extradition. The next day, General Mejía promised "great vigilance" on the matter, assuring the Confederate commander if Palmer slipped through Monterrey "it would not be difficult to effect his capture in San Luis Potosi, or in Queretaro." The next week the arrest order arrived from the Confederacy. Regarding the "crime and flight of Judge Palmer" Mejía responded that he had taken several steps, including "informing the Hon. Agustin Quinterro [*sic*] of the circumstances, that he might not lose the said judge from his sight." On the 19th, Quintero himself wrote from Monterrey that he missed Palmer at Matamoros; however, learning he was at nearby Saltillo, "I immediately called on General Lopez and requested him to order his arrest." The disintegrating state of affairs weighed heavily on Quintero. "Most of the Americans now in this city are men who, after having left the Confederacy not to render military service, seem to be keeping their arms to the elbow in the most disgraceful transactions." The diplomat nevertheless expressed hope of Palmer's capture. "The miscreants who sympathize with him in this place, and will no doubt turn to be my enemies, can at no time intimidate me in the discharge of my duties."[222]

As the realization that the end of the Confederacy would come ere long, various schemes anticipated ultimate Union victory. The same Federal General Lew Wallace now ingratiated himself with General Grant, arguing that many disheartened Texas Confederates stood ready to join with Unionists to aid Juárez. Wallace arranged a meeting with Confederate Rio Grande Commander Slaughter near Brownsville. Provisioned with "a supply of refreshments" courtesy of U.S. Secret Service funds, the imbibing assemblage of enemy officers discussed "the Mexican project" for two days. Wallace reported to Grant that Slaughter believed his officers might "get honorably back in the Union" by conquering a few Mexican states from the French and "annex them ... to the United States." Colonel "Rip" Ford's report to Slaughter's superior differed; the Confederates viewed Wallace's various claims with suspicion. Ford's version credited Wallace advocating the armies should take over civil authority and that many Unionists "consider the Emancipation Proclamation a great mistake," in fact a "nullity." Slaughter's commander Major General John Walker communicated by letter with Wallace, then in Galveston, on March 27. Having already reprimanded Slaughter for engaging in such meetings related to "the blackest treason to the Confederacy," Walker angrily chastised the Yankee Wallace:

> When the States of the Trans-Mississippi united their destiny with the Confederacy of Southern States we pledged ourselves to share their good and evil fortune…. It would be folly in me to pretend that we are not tired of a war that has sown sorrow and desolation over our land; but we will accept no other than an honorable peace. With 300,000 men yet in the field, we would be the most abject of mankind if we should now basely yield … nationality and the rights of self-government. With the blessing of God, we will yet achieve these, and extort from your own Government all that we ask.[223]

Against this backdrop of Wallace's filibustering peace scheme, the Confederates jockeyed for position in case the "blessing of God" did not yield all General Walker hoped for. General Slaughter surrendered documents detailing the Wallace scheme to Imperialist General Mejía, a move that could only enhance Slaughter's standing with the French. Even General Edmund Kirby-Smith, commander of the Trans-Mississippi Department, sent confidential communiqués to Maximilian as early as February. He offered his services to the Emperor, should the Confederacy fall, and suggested he might induce intelligent Southern soldiers to defend His Majesty's nation if war came with the United States. By early May, a few weeks after General Robert E. Lee's surrender at Appomattox Courthouse, Kirby-Smith refined his plans. The Confederate nation in the east had dissolved with Lee's surrender and President Davis in flight; Kirby-Smith's relatively intact Trans-Mississippi Department represented the last hope of the Southern nation. He offered the Imperialists an agreement "for mutual protection against their common enemy," suggesting his noble troops would "rally around any flag" promising a fight against their "former foe" while aiding the Imperial cause. Kirby-Smith even held an army of 15,000 ready for President Davis to command and offer to Maximilian — if only the president could escape to the Western Confederacy.

The last battle of the War Between the States occurred in the Brownsville vicinity, and the Confederates happened to win it. An informal truce had been in force since March, about the time Wallace began consulting with the Confederates. On May 12, an ambitious yet inexperienced Federal Colonel Theodore Barrett decided to disregard orders and initiate an action against the Confederates. His 800 troops marched from the coast to Ft. Brown. General Slaughter left the fort to counter expected actions by the Mexican bandit Cortina. Quintero arranged an agreement with Imperial General Mejía that if Cortina joined the Yankees in their attack, Mejía's French and Mexican cavalry would cross the border from Matamoros, "in citizen's dress, and come to

1. José Agustín Quintero

our assistance." Captain A.J. Aldrich, assistant adjutant-general of Ft. Brown, would write some 25 years later, "Señor Quintero remained with me throughout the night, ready to go to Matamoros with the summons upon which they were to move." The next day, the 13th, the Federals engaged Colonel "Rip" Ford's 350 determined cavalry at a rise east of town called Palmito Ranch. Ford would later write that his spirits sank upon seeing the numbers of Federals. He believed he would lose the war's last battle, certain "I am going to be whipped." During the thick of the ensuring engagement, a determined Ford actually galloped past a unit of French volunteer cannoneers and cried "Allons!" to encourage them emphatically, "Let's go!" In heavy fighting the reported casualties were as many as 30 Yankees killed, over 100 prisoners taken and only a few minor Confederate injuries. Thus, the Confederates won a victory in the last battle of the war, and Quintero managed to have been involved as a potentially vital participant.[224]

Winning battles the Confederates could do — and had done for years — but winning wars proved another thing. General Kirby-Smith finally yielded to fate and surrendered the Trans-Mississippi Department to the Federals on June 2. In doing so, the Confederate Matamoros Trade finally ended. Only two days later, on June 4, United States agent A. H. Cañedo wrote from Matamoros to the Chief of Staff in New Orleans, Major General J. P. Osterhaus, regarding the nefarious activities of one "Mr. J. A. Quinterro [*sic*]." Cañedo mentioned Quintero "as one of the parties concerned in the affair" of the "Lone Star project," having met with French General Achille François Bazaine "last January in relation to it." Carefully tracking Quintero's activities, Cañedo reported: "Mr. Q. was here last week in close conference with General Mejia, and returned again immediately to Monterey, and will be here again in a week. He is ostensibly enlisted in the Imperial cause, but in reality is working for an uprising in Texas, the French and Mexicans to hold the frontier." Adding details to the conspiracy, the agent continued: "An officer formerly in the rebel service is now here, engaged in raising a regiment of Texans for service with the Imperialists. To sum up, it seems the enterprise I spoke of has received a sudden shock from the rapid success of the Federal arms, but is by no means extinct." Cañedo finally warned that the Confederate and Texan feeling "is most decidedly in favor of an uprising in Texas, at least assisting the Imperial against its enemies, particularly in the United States."

Certainly Cañedo depicted Quintero as intimately involved in the machinations set in motion by General Kirby-Smith. In reality, though, these activities occurred just prior to the general's surrender of the Trans-Mississippi Department. Cañedo had reported old news. In just a short week, the entire border situation had irrevocably changed. The commander at Federally occupied Brownsville, Brigadier General E. B. Brown, forwarded the Cañedo letter on to New Orleans just three days later, but prefaced it with its own disarming note: "My information is that there is now no desire on the part of the Government of Mexico to interfere with the affairs of Texas. General Mejia informed me in a personal interview I had with him yesterday that the services of former Confederate officers had been offered to him, and that they had been declined, and that his instructions were to cultivate amicable relations with the Government of the United States."[225]

The impact of the Matamoros Trade can not be overestimated. The millions of dollars of cotton traffic supported the Trans-Mississippi Department of the Confederate States, and to some extent, the eastern Confederacy. Any number of Texans grew wealthy, such as the New Yorker who adopted the South, Richard King, owner of the vast King Ranch through which the main cotton trade route passed. Similarly, financial empires rose in Mexico. José Oliver and Patricio Milmo garnered enormous fortunes; Milmo, who died in 1899 at the age of 75, had accumulated an estate worth as much as $15,000,000. Among the European firms, Droege, Oetling and Company garnered exceptional profits. The British Lieutenant Colonel Freemantle reported, "Mr. Oetling is supposed to have made a million of dollars for his firm by bold speculation" by the year 1863. In Monterrey, the accumulated fortunes established a foundation for the modern city's economic power as the third most populous city in Mexico, the second industrial city after the capital, and the key financial center in the north. The development and stability the Confederates provided to Vidaurri's regime also fostered his Civil College, now a major Latin American educational institution, the Universidad Autónoma de Nuevo León. Not to be overlooked, Confederate trade revenues also supported President Juárez's government at a vital time when the United States issued but empty promises to its neighboring democracy. Juárez thus kept his government and army solvent, and his treasury intact. This no doubt contributed to maintaining his precarious existence among fiercely independent northern *caudillo* governors, while biding time to strike back at Emperor Maximilian and the French.[226]

QUINTERO, THE DIPLOMAT—AN ASSESSMENT

Frank L. Owsley in his seminal *King Cotton Diplomacy* concluded that Quintero "and Henry Hotze, propagandist chief, sent to England in 1862, were perhaps the ablest and most successful Confederate agents sent to foreign countries...." Owsley credits Quintero with supplying munitions and other supplies to the Trans-Mississippi Confederacy: "It was he more than any of the military leaders who had the necessary tact to straighten out the difficulties which arose to disturb the friendly relations on the frontier, and to maintain this trade and prevent border incursions. He proved shrewd and successful in his dealings with all the Mexican authorities, one after the other — Governor Vidaurri, President Juárez, and, lastly, the French imperialists." Owsley further compared the Cuban Confederate to the celebrated commissioners of the Trent Affair. "Actually Quintero accomplished more tangible, material results than did either Mason or Slidell. The Confederacy might have got on without either of these agents, but Quintero's presence on the Mexican border was indispensable...."

Secretary of State Judah Benjamin also offered unstinting praise for his diplomat to Northern Mexico. "Mr. Quintero's services are highly appreciated by the Department and he has frequently received the commendation of the Government for his zeal and for the address with which he has managed to maintain cordial relations with all the functionaries on the Mexican border."[227]

Indeed, there could hardly have been a better example of an individual securing the assignment most suited to his unique talents. Quintero's appearance at the State Department early in the war must have seemed almost providential. No foreign mercenary or simple opportunist introduced himself; instead, Confederate bureaucrats met a young Hispanic man of the most profound and sincere dedication to Southern nationalism. There probably could have been found no one in the entire Southern nation to rival Quintero's education, language skills, literary attainments and political connections as justification for a delicate Mexican assignment. Further, while many a promising aspirant would fall short of his potential in the diplomatic, political and military arenas, few could later claim to have so far exceeded expectations. Of all the Hispanic Confederates, Quintero most capitalized on his unusual skills and background in service to his Confederate nation. Admittedly, John Thrasher made fine contributions as superintendent of the Confederate Press Association, but his journalistic prowess made this possible, not his Latin background and language skills.[228] Similarly, Ambrosio José Gonzales excelled as Beauregard's artillery chief, but again, not because he spoke Spanish.[229] Quintero's native intelligence, education and diplomatic talent provided the basis for his success, but his Hispanic heritage and cultural understanding enabled a level of achievement well beyond most of his Confederate diplomatic colleagues.

Aside from Quintero's achievements during the war, its personal meaning to him is poignantly preserved in his poetry. In *Memorias del Alma (Memories of the Soul)* he captures key moments of his life, commemorating "in the Spanish tongue" Texas president Lamar, but largely focusing on the days of secession, even while yearning for a perhaps allegorical lost love. Carbonell captures the sense of the work: "In his beautiful poem 'Memories of the Soul' which is dedicated to his beloved Rebecca, Quintero sings the glories and reversals of battle, and the bitterness and sorrow of defeat."

I saw you then, Rebecca, quivering
between love and the virtuous fighting,
with your face in broken tears...
And far away the evening star
trembling like the joy inside the heart.

Those sweet moments
of deep emotions...
If in love kisses may be used to deceive
tears are always truthful.

We parted, Alas!, perhaps never to see each other
on this earth, when the cruel
war rose her head
and roared alongside the horrid tempest.

I hastened to fill a place in the ranks
of a heroic legion, my life
consecrated at the altar an enlightened people
might have established for their sacred independence.

At the explosion of the fearful cannon
at the sight of inflamed bombs cleaving
the bluish sky, how much then
I remembered you! Fate more desired
that brutal force, not heroism,
might decide the struggle, as justice and patriotism
do not always manage to prevail.[230]

WAR'S END: SERVING JUÁREZ

One of the most difficult periods of Quintero's life to unravel is the year or so beyond the Confederate surrender. After the sunset and fall of the Confederate nation, Quintero may have served Mexican president Juárez in some capacity. The record is unclear on this point, but no doubt Quintero could have been useful to the president, his English and Spanish language diplomatic abilities having proven themselves to the Confederacy.

Many sources — mostly Hispanic — do place Quintero fighting at Benito Juárez's side. José Antonio Fernández de Castro's important essay on Quintero — one of the few in-depth treatments in the literature — insists Quintero abandoned the Confederacy at mid-war to join Juárez. Of course, this is a patent impossibility based on Quintero's extensive dispatches to Richmond and within the Trans-Mississippi Department. Other historians more or less state that after completing diplomatic work for President Davis, Quintero fought for Mexican democracy until Maximilian's defeat. Many of these accounts further implicate Quintero leaving for Cuba in 1868 after living in Mexico since the end of the U.S. War of Secession.[231]

Much of this record is incorrect — as will be shown, Quintero can definitely be placed in New Orleans prior to 1868 — but repeated references to serving under Juárez should probably not be ignored. The Spanish-language sources provide rich perspective on his revolutionary youth and on his life as a poet, information not found in English-language accounts. The details may be untidy, but the broad canvas rings true. Applying this filter to the Juárez connection, a reasonable working assumption is that Quintero did serve under Juárez, but the details of when and how this occurred may be viewed with skepticism.

There is also circumstantial evidence to support Quintero remaining in Mexico and joining the *Juarista* forces. First, he knew Juárez's son-in-law, confidant and secretary — the Cuban poet, Pedro Santacilia. Quintero and Santacilia had both been jailed for supporting Narciso López so many years earlier in Cuba, and they together comprised two of the seven Cuban revolutionary poets featured in the aforementioned seminal collection of Cuban patriotic verse, *El Laúd del Desterrado*, published in 1858. During the four and a half months the Juárez government remained in Monterrey — sustaining itself on revenues from taxing Confederate trade — it is not inconceivable Santacilia invited his old comrade to join him and other Cubans in another Hispanic revolution. An honorable man, Quintero no doubt felt duty called him to serve his second homeland to the end — his Confederate homeland — but with the fall of his new nation he could adopt another cause. A second bit of circumstantial evidence is that Quintero simply found himself in northern Mexico at the end of the war. Finding himself not far from Chihuahua, where the *Juarista* government had fled, Quintero knew the politics and major players, was a learned, accomplished diplomat, and he, of course, spoke Spanish as his native tongue.[232] Further, he might have expected that the now-victorious United States would rattle its sword on Juárez's behalf and that the tide might swing in the president's favor. Joining the *Juaristas* would have been a very logical choice for him. A third consideration is that Quintero very well may have been afraid to return to the United States. President Lincoln had previously excepted Confederate diplomats in his amnesty proclamation, and now President Johnson on May 29 additionally excluded "all persons who left their homes within the jurisdiction of the United States to aid the Confederacy."[233] Quintero could naturally have assumed he would find a jail cell waiting for him in the United States. He would not be the only Confederate seeking refuge out of the country.

Should Quintero have stayed in Mexico and served Juárez immediately after the war, he could have found himself in an unaccustomed position, namely, allied with U.S. general Philip Sheridan's Yankee cavalry. Had the

French not withdrawn their support for Ferdinand Maximilian, the puppet Emperor of Mexico, Federal forces might conceivably have interceded on behalf of Juárez. Furthermore, in such a fight Quintero would have found among the enemy several recent comrades in gray. Confederate General Jo Shelby had offered his several hundred remaining Confederate troopers-in-exile to serve Emperor Maximilian. Also among the emperor's newly faithful numbered other prominent leaders of the defeated nation: Generals Edmund Kirby-Smith, Hamilton Bee, John Magruder and Missouri's Sterling Price, a former governor. Commodore Matthew Fontaine Maury, too, served as the newly installed Imperial Commissioner of Confederate Colonization. On the other hand, some Confederates joined the legally elected president Juárez. Prentiss Ingraham of Mississippi fought for Juárez, and just three years later would also serve the Cuban revolution of 1868.[234] Colonel "Rip" Ford also emerged a *Juarista* brigadier general in the Mexican Army. He served under his old Mexican friend General José María Carvajal, who returned to Matamoros from New York exile in 1866; in fact, Ford thus allied himself with Union general Lew Wallace who had likewise recruited a volunteer corps for *Juarista* service.[235]

These possibilities of Quintero joining Union forces in this fashion did not occur, though, as Napoleon III seemed to have no stomach to face Juárez's forces, combined with the battle-hardened U.S. troops under General Sheridan. The French Emperor abandoned Maximilian. The Austrian nobly defended his regime rather than escape to safety. Juárez's troops captured him, with execution following on June 19, 1867. Soon thereafter, the new president of the emperor's cabinet, longtime *caudillo* Santiago Vidaurri, suffered betrayal and similar death as a traitor.

If Juárez represented the legal government of the country, were Quintero's former Confederate colleagues now supporting the wrong side? Not necessarily. While their association with Maximilian was largely driven by political necessity — he and the French had been friendly to the Confederate States and they did seem in control of the country — the truth is that Juárez and Maximilian were both reformers, each trying to improve the lot of the Mexican people. Maximilian did a lot of good for Mexico and had hoped to do a great deal more on their behalf. To Confederates, the stature of scientist-commodore Matthew Fontaine Maury, Maximilian's vision of new Mexican museums, observatories and expanded universities would have had a great deal of appeal. Juárez's execution of Maximilian drew an international outcry as an undeserved, barbaric act.[236]

There is another bit of evidence which seems to support Quintero living in Mexico, presumably at or after the time he served Juárez. In late 1868 Quintero will be reported in Havana, Cuba trying to establish attorney credentials with a law degree revalidated in Mexico. This is most puzzling and may indeed simply be an error in the historical record, repeated by one Hispanic biographer after another. Since Juárez would not reenter Mexico City until July 15, 1867, there would not seem to be an opportunity for Quintero to study in Mexico City until afterwards. Yet, as will be demonstrated, the record clearly places him in New Orleans at this time. The most likely time period for Quintero to serve Juárez would have been the last half of 1865 and part of 1866. It seems unlikely he would have pursued legal studies during a revolution, especially with the government on the run. Another possibility is that these Mexican studies were conducted prior to the recent U.S. war; however, Quintero can largely be placed in Texas, New York and possibly New Orleans since his escape from Havana's Morro Castle. There would have been little opportunity to live in Mexico during these years. Intriguing, but one other time remains: his years in Monterrey as a Confederate Diplomat. Perhaps Quintero attended the law school at the civil college Santiago Vidaurri established in Monterrey just before the Confederate War. In fact, Quintero is yet placed in Matamoros at the end of the war; he might have spent the uncertain first several months of Reconstruction studying law. A degree from a new, unproven college might help explain why this validation required some scrutiny in Cuba before a decision would be rendered. All in all, the idea of a Mexican legal validation for Quintero seems unsupportable, but like many things there may be a germ of truth in it, and it may add slight support to the notion Quintero lived in Mexico at some point after the War of Secession.[237]

CRESCENT CITY ATTORNEY

Regardless of Quintero's possible service to Juárez — or pursuit of Mexican legal studies — by the beginning of 1866 he had firmly established himself back in the United States. He had obtained a presidential pardon, having earlier traveled to Washington, D.C., probably in January of that year. This additional measure of travel to the capital may have been necessary due to his service beyond the United States border. The *Daily Picayune* of February 2 announced Quintero's arrival in New Orleans to pursue a legal career. Interestingly, *The Daily Southern Star*, the following day, ran a virtually identical notice, under the title "Personal":[238]

> Among the late arrivals in our city is Mr. J. Quintero, formerly of Texas, and late Confederate agent at Monterey, Mexico. He has just returned from Washington City, with the President's pardon, and informs us that he intends locating here, in the legal profession. Mr. Quintero is a native of Cuba, and was compelled to leave there for his participation in the Lopez movement. He is a gentleman of fine literary attainments.[239]

Quintero had been a lawyer before the war, so he naturally would have hoped to assume a legal career afterwards. The *Daily Picayune* clearly states, "After reading for some months in the office of the well known firm of Semmes a [*sic*] Mott he graduated in the law school of this city." The paper adds that he met with "a fair degree of success" as an attorney before "drifting again into journalism." The *Times-Picayune* centennial issue narrows the time frame for this, citing Quintero's graduation from legal studies in 1866. The *Revista Cubana,* unlike most Spanish-language sources, also supports this chronology. Its obituary notice for Quintero shows him graduating in law this same year. Surprisingly, though, the Havana publication places its revolutionary son at Harvard, having obviously confused Quintero's prewar studies. The landmark 1899 *Confederate Military History* series — a solid and accurate source on Quintero — lends further detail: "Then he made his home at New Orleans and entered the office of Senator Thomas J. Semmes." These sources are sufficiently consistent to establish the likelihood of Quintero's legal studies and practice in New Orleans.[240]

Quintero made an excellent choice in studying under the distinguished Thomas Jenkins Semmes, a first cousin to C.S.S. *Alabama* commander Admiral Raphael Semmes. Thomas grew up in Washington society, his mother, Matilda Jenkins, said to have entertained presidents Monroe through Lincoln, as well as statesmen the like of Calhoun, Clay and Webster. He graduated as a Harvard lawyer, a classmate of Rutherford B. Hayes, and moved to New Orleans five years later in 1850. Soon prominent, he served in the Louisiana legislature for a term. Afterwards, President Buchanan appointed Semmes United States District Attorney, proving an ironic assignment considering Quintero would one day study under him. That is, in this capacity Semmes prosecuted William Walker for violation of neutrality laws during the Nicaraguan expedition. Fate strangely decreed that Quintero, follower of the century's other famous filibuster, Narciso López, would find himself mentored by an enforcer of Caribbean neutrality. During Abraham Lincoln's War, then Louisiana Attorney General Thomas J. Semmes helped author the state's ordinance of secession and served the Confederacy as a Louisiana Senator. Described a "master pragmatist," Semmes proved flexible in Richmond, even advocating arming and freeing slaves if it would save "part of the cargo." Heading a socially prominent family, at his mansion Semmes entertained leading writers, artists and politicians, including Judah Benjamin and John Slidell before the war, and afterwards President Grover Cleveland. In postwar New Orleans, Semmes taught at Tulane University Law School, figured prominently in the 1879 Louisiana constitutional convention and, in an unprecedented tribute for a one-time Confederate Congressman, ascended to the presidency of the American Bar Association in 1886.[241]

Thomas J. Semmes personally touched the lives of at least two future

Picayune luminaries. Near the end of the war, in March 1865, then Senator Semmes appointed Thomas Gwynn Rapier as a midshipman in the Confederate States Navy. A month later, the young Rapier participated as a temporary infantryman in the desperate effort to save the Confederate treasury during the capital's evacuation. By June, with the war over, Rapier secured employment at the *Daily Picayune*. During Quintero's tenure, he rose to its business manager by 1879, and later president of the company in 1904. Ultimately, Rapier helped found and served as long-time director of the Associated Press.[242]

Of course, the other *Picayune* notable proved none other than José Agustín Quintero. Details of his association with Semmes are sketchy, and the preparatory legal studies are admittedly cited as lasting only a few months; nevertheless, Semmes had already proven a leading attorney by the reconstruction era, even if his greatest cases and achievements lay in the future. Quintero no doubt received excellent preparation to complete work at a local law school, attending what surely must have been the law department of the University of Louisiana, predecessor to Tulane University.[243]

Quintero's legal training established, his practice of law in New Orleans is less clear. The various sources imply he served as an attorney, but they conflict with other reports claiming his service just after the war was as a journalist. Somewhere during this time Quintero emerged as a reporter at the *Daily Picayune*. Teasing the most likely possibilities out of the historical record provides an interesting challenge.

QUINTERO JOINS THE *DAILY PICAYUNE*

The circumstances — even the year — of Quintero's original association with the *Daily Picayune* elude his biographers' grasp, or better said, their consensus. Prior to the *Picayune*, English-speaking writers typically place Quintero in New Orleans practicing law immediately after Confederate service, although some chronicle his destination as possibly Texas or New York, working as a journalist.[244] Hispanic biographers gloss over this period, almost uniformly stating Quintero remained in Mexico, fighting at the side of Juárez. It may be that *Picayune* biographer John Smith Kendall's general assessment represents a more solid basis than most for considering this time: "Finally, Quintero arrived in New Orleans, and there he spent the last nineteen years of his life, nearly all of them in the employ of the *Picayune*."[245]

Kendall seems largely correct. Quintero did finally arrive at New Orleans a year after the war — probably studying with Senator Semmes as early as 1866, 19 years before his death — and he spent most, but *not* all, of these years at the *Picayune*. Implicit in Kendall's summary are the key questions: Where was Quintero in the immediate years after the war? How did he occupy himself? What attractions lured him from the *Picayune* during these 19 years, and for how long? The Spanish-language sources, however, do prove Kendall and countless others wrong in one respect: Quintero did *not* live in New Orleans continuously these last 19 years, but attempted a return to Cuba at one point.

Culling unsupported, contradictory accounts, there remain a few anchors to piece together Quintero's elusive whereabouts in the several years immediately after the war. Fayette Copeland in her treatment of the reconstruction era New Orleans press provides one such starting point: "The *New Orleans City Directory* for the years following 1866 listed Quintero as "lawyer and Consul for Costa Rica, 66 Camp." That address was the office of the office of the *Picayune*." Reinforcing these details, Quintero's *Picayune* obituary is specific on dates, declaring Belgium appointed him their consul in 1867, "at which time he had already been for some months consul for Costa Rica, a post which he retained up to his death." This evidence clearly substantiates Quintero's residence in New Orleans by 1867, apparently working for the *Picayune* as well. The record further implies he lived there for some years "following 1866."[246]

Another historical anchor supports this implication, placing Quintero in New Orleans during late 1867, perhaps through 1868. Quintero's two articles in *The Texas Almanac for 1868*, published in Galveston and associated with *The Galveston News*, lend credence to Ronnie Tyler's assertion, in his excellent *Santiago Vidaurri and the Southern Confederacy,* that Quintero moved to Galveston after the war to work in newspapers and with the *Texas Almanac.* Yet, the almanac itself challenges this interpretation. Published sometime after December 27, 1867 — based on the preface by W. Richardson & Co., Publishers — a New Orleans legal firm advertisement in the almanac provides additional perspective: "J.A. Quintero, Attorney and Counsellor at Law, Notary Public and Commissioner of Deeds, For Texas, Virginia, South-Carolina, Alabama, Mississippi, Georgia and Maryland, No. 143 Gravier Street, New Orleans."[247]

Thus, the *Texas Almanac* firmly places Quintero in New Orleans at the close of 1867 and apparently during 1868. Ample precedent existed for him living in New Orleans and yet writing for a Texas-based almanac. The same edition claimed other contributors from out of state, the preface even citing a gentleman from New York State "who has been a contributor to our ALMANAC for many years." Indeed, Quintero had been closely associated with Texas before and during the war. Thus, it is not surprising that even in New Orleans he might maintain Lone Star ties, especially since both his articles explored Texas history based on the documents provided by his "ill-fated friend" Rejón: One concerned Philip Nolan's life, the other regarded the legendary San Saba silver and gold mines. Not that Quintero's association with the almanac was unusual: New Orleans advertisements abounded throughout the issue, the cover page prominently touting Geo. Soule's commercial and telegraph college in New Orleans.[248]

The *Texas Almanac* cements Quintero's location in New Orleans during this time, but leaves his occupation uncertain. Did Quintero practice law, or was he a journalist — and, regardless, for whom? It would seem Quintero seriously attempted to reestablish his legal career, which he had begun in Texas before the war in Austin when working with one-time Texas republic president Mirabeau Lamar, and apparently resurrected during his 1866 studies with New Orleans attorney Thomas J. Semmes. The evidence: The New Orleans city directory lists him as an attorney, he had advertised in the *Texas Almanac* as an attorney, and his role as consul for Belgium and Costa Rica would imply these countries recognized his ability to represent their legal and commercial interests in New Orleans.

As for Quintero the journalist, it would appear the seeds for a transition from the legal profession to full-time journalist had also been sewn. He had written widely before the war as a poet, journalist and writer, and proved loath to give up this avocation. The newly published articles in the *Texas Almanac* clearly support this. The circumstantial evidence for this transition is also strong, in that the *New Orleans City Directory* places Quintero's attorney address at the *Daily Picayune* office. Perhaps the missing tie is an unsupported but nevertheless intriguing statement by *Picayune* biographer Kendall: *viz*, "Quintero was in charge of court-reporting."[249] Consistent with the Cuban exile's prewar habits, everything in life could be an opportunity for writing, and so a new thrust into the legal profession provided new opportunities for journalist insight: court reporting for the *Daily Picayune*.

A NEW START, A NEW REVOLUTION

Quintero proved serious about reestablishing his legal career; he must never have ceased thinking of his first homeland, so he earnestly sought to reestablish his life in Cuba. Not many years before Confederate secession, in 1854 the Spanish Queen Isabel II had issued a general amnesty for past revolutionaries; Quintero finally resolved to act on the opportunity. Apparently during late summer of 1868, he departed New Orleans for Havana and petitioned the Spanish authorities there to recognize his legal credentials and authorize his practice on the island. While waiting for the slow wheels of Spanish bureaucracy in Cuba to grind, Quintero accepted a position editing the *Boletín Comercial*, a Havana-based mercantile publication.[250]

Spanish Cuba had been friendly to the Confederacy in past days, and Quintero represented but another in the parade of disenfranchised Confederates drawn to Havana. Indeed, in the desperate days after Appomattox, noted exiles sojourning briefly in the capital city included Secretary of State Judah Benjamin, European Agent and naval researcher Matthew Fontaine Maury, as well as General John Cabell Breckenridge, a former U.S. vice-president.[251] Other Confederates yet remained on the island, potentially available to welcome Quintero. Perhaps the Cuban knew French-born Pierre Soulé, a one-time United States Minister to Spain who co-authored the controversial 1850s era Ostend Manifesto which declared the U.S. right to seize Cuba at will. Regardless, the two shared a revolutionary perspective. Soulé previously supported Narciso López, and later represented William Walker in his Nicaraguan filibustering trial; the irony of Quintero having studied law under Semmes — legal nemesis to Soulé in the Walker case — could not have been lost on them, if perchance they had opportunity to discuss these old days.[252] Another compatriot also resided in Cuba after the war. Well-known to Quintero, but a contrast to Soulé, General Hamilton Bee had worked closely with Quintero in the Texas cotton trade during the years of Confederate service. He left Mexico with the fall of the Confederate colony, Carlotta, and found new engagement as a Cuban ship broker. Bee's commander, General "Prince John" B. Magruder, would also work in Havana for a period in the following year, his tenure on the island perhaps coinciding with Quintero's. Magruder had also served Maximilian in Mexico — in his case as an army general — whereas Quintero apparently supported the opposing *Juaristas*.[253] Quintero certainly remembered Magruder as commander of the Texas District during the difficult days of Confederate Diplomatic Service. Last, another veteran now worked as U.S. consul in the south Cuba port city of Trinidad, having been established there for some years, since 1864. Quintero may have known of him during the Confederate War. Betraying a somewhat different background than these others, Federico Fernández Cavada was Cuban, like Quintero, but a Yankee officer who had served notably at Gettysburg.[254] Cavada is easily placed at Cuba during this time, but the tenure of the other veterans is unclear. Regardless, a conceivable reunion of the North-American War veterans Quintero, Magruder and Bee — with Soulé and Cavada thrown in for good measure — would no doubt have led to remarkable conversation and recollections.

Later that year, in proceedings room no. 70 at the local university — presumably the University of Havana — Quintero passed the examination necessary to practice law. On October 5, 1868, his Excellency, Superior Governor Joaquín Vigil de Quiñones provisionally authorized Quintero as an attorney, subject to the opinion of the High Superior Council of Public Instruction. His success proved short-lived. The council suspended his certification on the last day of the month, apparently effective November 2. The official proceedings give no reason for the action, but simply declared they no longer accredited the solicitant titled as a lawyer from the State of Texas, in the District of

Richmond, whose qualifications had been revalidated at the University of Mexico.

Interestingly, despite this dubious University of Mexico revalidation, none of the Spanish-language sources cites his petition referring to a more recent New Orleans legal degree. It may be that an early biographer casually assumed Quintero would have moved directly from Mexico to Cuba, being unaware of his postwar move to New Orleans. This seems to have been repeated essentially verbatim in various accounts, consistent with other aspects of his life similarly treated this way. Some English-language writers also made such errors, in certain cases relaying Quintero's postwar environs as either Texas or New York. Nevertheless, supporting evidence for his New Orleans studies abounds, but Quintero had practically no opportunity to pursue law in Mexico, unless he somehow accomplished it during the years of Confederate diplomatic service.[255]

Regardless of how the petition presented his legal training, Quintero insisted on his claims, appealing to Cuba's chief Spanish executive, captain-general Francisco Lersundi. Finally, a couple of months later on January 2, 1869, Lersundi decided to authorize Quintero's exercise of the legal profession "by virtue that it is decreed by article 169 of the Plan of Studies in force." The order took effect a week later on the ninth of January.[256]

The island son could not have picked a worse time to return to the Pearl of the Antilles. Soon after his arrival in the previous year, the shaky throne of Queen Isabel II toppled on September 29, the "Glorious Revolution" banishing her into Parisian exile. A presumably more liberal government took its place, headed by reform-minded former captain-general Francisco Serrano. At the same time, islanders had reacted negatively to the new captain-general Lersundi's harsh rule and to the heavy burden of taxes collected by the far-off Spanish peninsular government.[257]

In New York City, by this time, Caribbean exiles had reorganized under the *Sociedad Republicana de Cuba y Puerto Rico*, established in 1865. This revolutionary council included many of the original López conspirators, such as its vice-president, the Cuban novelist Cirilo Villaverde with whom Quintero had languished in the Morro Castle prison two decades earlier. The junta, assisted by Chilean historian and "confidential agent" Benjamín Vicuña Mackenna, gained strong impetus as the South American agent financed their early work and personally adopted their cause. Vicuña Mackenna's interest sprung from a desire to divert Spain from Chile as it defended against new Pacific incursions by the former mother country; thus, he fostered a second front in the Caribbean. Junta plans included uprisings in the two last Spanish colonies, Puerto Rico and Cuba, while Puerto Rican attorney Segundo Ruíz Belvis met the then-recalled Vicuña Mackenna in Chile to explore additional funding sources.[258]

The "Glorious Revolution" may have accelerated Caribbean rebellion, perhaps with the prospect of like-minded progressives now in charge; on the other hand, it may be that Caribbean and peninsular upheaval may have simply coincided due to broad-based resistance throughout the Spanish realm. Regardless, Puerto Rican insurgents led the way on September 23 with the *"Grito de Lares"*— the Lares Cry — organized by the eminent Puerto Rican physician-writer, Ramón Emeterio Betances. The plot discovered, Spanish troops crushed the new Puerto Rican republic within 12 hours. Hardly two weeks later, Cuban revolution erupted, completely taking Quintero by surprise. On October 10, Cuban attorney, landowner and former Juárez defender Carlos Manuel de Céspedes declared the free *República de Cuba* at his sugar plantation, *Demajugua*, located at the village of Yara. Striking at the symbol of Spanish tyranny, he freed his slaves who then rallied to the revolutionary army, inaugurating what would be remembered as the *"Grito de Yara."* Originating in the eastern Cuban provinces, the revolution did not surrender to Spanish authority, but grew threateningly, attracting newly freed slaves, landowners, Puerto Ricans and even some North Americans to the cause. In just a few weeks, more than 10,000 rebels took to the field. Unable to ignore the crisis, captain-general Lersundi instituted marshall law and created a corps of civilian *voluntarios*, ruthless death squads. Armed with 90,000 Remington rifles purchased from the United States by the Madrid government, the *voluntarios* terrorized the island, torturing, raping and even murdering suspected civilians. Two days after Quintero's legal certification was finally issued, Madrid replaced Lersundi with a liberal, Don Domingo Dulce. The new captain-general called for moderation. The *voluntarios* ignored these pleas, convinced that the rebels must be brutally crushed. Before the end of the month, on January 22 two hundred *voluntarios* stormed Havana's Villanueva Theater, punishing the hapless audience to repeated volleys of terrifying gunfire simply because they had insulted the Spanish flag. A three-day orgy of looting and terror followed.[259]

FINAL EXILE

The revolutionary forces Quintero had helped breath life into during the López era, now resurrected, proved his undoing. As a past conspirator, Quintero knew the authorities viewed him with suspicion. He decided to abandon Cuba. Even as he must have prepared to leave, an old López comrade — and fellow Confederate — arrived in Havana: Ambrosio José Gonzales. Gonzales had earlier served López as adjutant. This Cuban-Confederate was actually the first Cuban to shed blood for the island's liberation from Spain, and he had also helped design Cuba's future national flag, and thus its reversed image, that of Puerto Rico. Gonzales, like Quintero, had adopted the American South as his new, cherished homeland, serving Confederate general P.G.T. Beauregard with distinction as his artillery officer in Charleston. Gonzales had not come to take arms, but, like Quintero, simply wanted to establish his family in his native land, in his case, reentering the teaching profession.[260] The literature is silent on whether Quintero had an opportunity to greet his old comrade; yet, the historian can wistfully anticipate the day an obscure letter or a forgotten journal will reveal that the two Cuban-Confederates did meet for an evening, momentarily casting aside their travails, revisiting memories of another time.

Consistent with Quintero's departure from Cuba, the *Revista Cubana*, in Quintero's obituary, indicates Quintero reestablished himself as a journalist in New Orleans in 1869. The magazine also credits him with editorship of the *Democrat*. Of course, this is impossible; the conservative *Democrat's* first issue appeared six years later in 1875, near the end of Black Republican reconstruction. Nevertheless, the *Revista Cubana* reinforces other Spanish-language sources citing Quintero's departure due to suspicions his presence raised. Unreliable are other conflicting sources which cite Quintero's residence in Mexico, or even Cuba, until the end of the Yara-inspired Ten Years War.[261] Spain signed the treaty ending the revolution in 1878; Quintero could not have been residing on the island or elsewhere these several years when the record clearly places him in New Orleans throughout this decade. In considering his 1869 departure, the eminent José Manuel Carbonell touches on the Cuban patriot's mindset: "Relatively young still, and accustomed to combat, there is no suspicion of the reason he did not lend his arm to Cuba, but not for that should we suppose his love for the land of his birth extinguished."[262]

What were the views of this Cuban patriot whose revolutionary-inspired collection in *The Lute of the Exiled* saw publication just ten years earlier? He watched developments from afar in New Orleans, no doubt reading about and even reporting on the events transpiring. By June, his old prison comrade Cirilo Villaverde, and the newly reorganized *Junta Central Republicana de Cuba y Puerto Rico*, had delivered "20,000 small arms, twenty-two small cannon, and a large number of men, most of whom were Cubans and other veterans of the Civil War."[263] Quintero's Confederate colleagues — and not an insignificant number of Yankees as well — had joined the fight for various reasons: mercenary interest, lack of U.S. prospects, or conviction that assisting the revolutionaries was simply the right thing to do. Confederate general Thomas Jordan accepted the junta invitation to organize the Cuban rebel army. Commander-in-chief by the following year, 1870, he routed a twice-larger Spanish army in true Confederate fashion; the Spanish reacted by placing a reward of $100,000 for his capture.[264] Quintero too must have read of Jordan's eventual successor. If he had not recently met him in Cuba, Quintero could not fail to note the parallels: Federico Fernández Cavada, also a veteran of the late unpleasantness, had ironically served the Yankees as a Gettysburg commander; yet, he too hailed from Cuba and had proven himself a fine writer, having published the penultimate history of Confederate prison experience, *Libby Life.*[265] Year after bloody year, Quintero must have followed the procession of Confederate colleagues sacrificing for the new cause: Prentiss Ingraham serving Cuba as he did Juárez before; Southern navyman John Newland Maffit, of the CSS *Florida*, commanding the *Cuba (Hornet)* in dangerous supply operations; Captain Joseph Fry, Yankee George Washington Ryan and Pedro Céspedes, younger brother to the Cuban revolutionary president, all suffering capture and execution for the *Virginius* expedition to arm the insurgents. These deaths presaged the 200,000 who would perish over the decade of the war. The whole American nation sympathized with the revolutionaries and chafed at Washington's decision — wise or not — to refuse material aid to the revolutionaries. In fact, after the *Virginius* incident, the clamor for war against Spain almost precipitated the eventual U.S. conflict by 30 years.[266]

Why did Quintero not fight for the Cuban rebels, as he did 20 years earlier? Time itself may be the reason: Quintero of 1868 was not Quintero of 1848. Older, perhaps even wiser, but not yet even 40, he now had a wife and a son. Perhaps this made all the difference. Perhaps he doubted the Cuban people would rally sufficiently to throw off the Spanish, a bitter lesson López, Crittenden and others paid for with their lives. Perhaps Quintero had no choice: Under guard, the Spanish deported many revolutionaries at this time, and Quintero may simply have lacked means to join the insurgents to the east, deep in the field. Finally, it may be after long service to López, Davis and possibly Juárez, a weary Quintero preferred others to now shoulder the burden. Regardless, Quintero returned to New Orleans and resumed a civilian career as a journalist for the *Daily Picayune*.

As Carbonell wrote, in his heart Quintero may have yet belonged to *la patria* and hoped still to aid her in some way. Guillermo Prieto of Juárez's administration further revealed that Quintero's home in New Orleans would later serve as a center for the revolutionary and intellectual Latin thought in the city. It seems Quintero resumed his association with the *Picayune*, but yet found ways to serve his native land.[267]

RETURN TO THE *PICAYUNE*

The *Daily Picayune* experienced a tumultuous series of financial demands and ownership changes during the reconstruction era. Poor business conditions in the late 1860s, following the crop failure of 1867, contributed to the

Picayune's difficulty, and Republican rule in New Orleans revoked the *Picayune's* short-lived position as official government newspaper. Officials redirected all such funds for public announcements to the radical *Republican* and the recently organized Negro paper, the *Tribune.* The *Picayune* editor, Vermont-born Alva Morris Holbrook, purchased an interest in the paper when 29 years old in 1837; he assumed both business and editorial control in 1860, nursing the paper through secession and early reconstruction, but in 1872 finally succumbing to these financial pressures. A short-lived business partnership afterwards took over but failed to prove good on their investment, partly due to internal squabbles. The result: Rival New Orleans *Herald* purchased the *Picayune* late the following year, its editors bringing with them a tradition of "vigorous assaults" on the Black Republican leaders "chiefly responsible for the present unhappy condition of our state." Holbrook returned as president, the *Times* of New Orleans commenting: "A cycle in the checkered history of the Picayune is closed with the return of A.M. Holbrook. Extremes have met and mingled in the directory during his absence, much after the fashion of oil and water."[268]

Quintero lived through this difficult, transitional phase of the *Picayune.* During these years, on March 7, 1871, he and his wife Eliza had a second son, John Marshall. Some accounts indicate there may have been two more children. Regardless, perhaps to counter the press of familial and somber business responsibilities, his keen pen sought mischief as a diversion.[269]

One such spirited article appeared on April 1, 1875, entitled "Festal. Great Banquet at the Picayune Office." He richly characterized "A Feast of Reason and a Flow of Soul" held "In Honor of the Members of the Press," explaining that editor and proprietor Holbrook had invited representatives from all the city newspapers to a great banquet in their honor. In a warm gesture of magnanimity, those in attendance even included the radical reconstruction press from the *Republican.* The honored guests enjoyed "liberal expenditure of powder and fireworks, bonfires, music and other devices," beautiful floral work adorning the table and especially the band's "sweet and flowing measures" of Strauss, Hatton and Verdi.[270]

Of course the "Bill of Fare" proved exquisite, the table "spread with everything the market affords." Furthermore, the tailored menu commemorated the assembled diverse individuals. The hors d'oeuvres, for example, acknowledged leading editors Stoutmeyer and Armstrong, but seemed to indelicately reflect on Henry Ward Beecher, the abolitionist; however, New Orleans' prominent, distinguished attorney Thomas J. Semmes, whom Quintero once studied under, received a favorable sobriquet: "Canape of anchovies a la Stoutmeyer; marinade of tunny a la Henry Armstrong; Sausages a la Beecher; Shrimp Salad a la Semmes (the Saladin of the Southern Bar); olives, celery, oysters."

The guests savored the feast of "costly viands and rich dainties," the blissful evening meandering to its midnight climax. The narrative continued: "It was nearly 12 o'clock P.M. when the cloth was removed. Mr. A.M. Holbrook rose. There was a religious silence. One of the guests dropped a pin, and we heard it drop." Holbrook quoted the wisdom of a Spanish writer and read letters from some "friends" in the current administration in Washington. These gentlemen had sent their regrets at not being able to attend. At the same time, these leaders conveyed a remarkably frank assessment of their political affairs and a keen recognition of the lack of affection felt in New Orleans and the South for their party and administration:

President Grant wrote on March 23, 1875:

> *Dear Friend*—I regret that it is not in my power to accept your polite invitation.... You have made yourself felt in journalism as one of the great powers in the South. If you have ever erred, it has been in abusing my administration, for you know full well that I personally sympathize with poor, suffering Louisianans. I have not deprived your people of their rights. I did not send Gen. Sheridan to New Orleans that he might goad you into rebellion, to crush you down afterwards. I am a true Republican, and for that treason I favor a third term. You know that I am slandered when I am charged with perpetuating myself and the members of my family in the possession of the best offices in the gift of the people.

Secretary of State Hamilton Fish similarly apologized that he could not leave Washington City without a dereliction of duty, and Attorney General George H. Williams wrote on March 25:

> *Dear Sir*—I am truly sorry I cannot be with you.... lately I differed with you on public questions; but I have never distrusted you or for a moment doubted your faithfulness to your convictions. I know that in recalling great services to liberty and civilization in the United States you cannot mention any rendered by me; but believe me, dear sir, that I am not altogether to blame, having since I accepted office from a Radical Administration been a docile instrument of my party.
>
> These letters elicited applause only from Cols. Burwell and Tracy, of the Republican.[271]

A series of rather spontaneous and often long-winded orations by the illustrious newsmen present continued for some time after Mr. Holbrook's remarks. Several men shared compelling insights worthy of excerpt:

> Mr. Armstrong, of the Times, who commanded a Confederate war vessel during the "late unpleasantness," next spoke in answer to calls. He said he had been like a bark driven on the breakers without compass or chart. During the last

war he once had hung his flag of distress, but a piratical looking cruiser (a Yankee admiral) had handed him into harbor. {Here he advanced up to Mr. Stoutmeyer [his boss] in a rocking-the-deck kind of gait.} I have since then, sir, encountered many a breeze, but no blow has done more injury to the rigging of my heart than to have been led into the Galveston shoal water by false lights.... In the future, I mean to keep right ahead, without making a tack either to windward or leeward. I will no more move round about.... I will remain here to take the wind from the sails of any journal. I drink to the prosperity of the United States. I am reconstructed.

[Music — Sailor's Hornpipe]

Col. Tracy, editor of the New Orleans Republican, rose and said: The United States represent constitutional government, "Relying upon God, the justness of their cause, ... and their good swords," the American people struck for freedom and independence.... As you well know, I am a Republican.... It is not a perfect party, nor what it should be, but we mean to toil on to make it what its great destiny demands it shall be. The Colonel was very pathetic in his appeals for help to re-elect Grant, and concluded his remarks with a toast to the New Orleans bar and the enforcement of the civil rights bill.

[Music — Glory Hallelujah, John Brown]

Col. Halsey, of the Bulletin ... said that despots yield to the moral influence of liberty.... The blessed rays of freedom always penetrated into the dark dwelling house of oppression. He felt instinctively that the heart of the people of Louisiana must rage with fury when they look back into the mirror of the past ten years; but the horizon was trembling with the light of liberty, and our State would soon be redeemed.... The North ... will never themselves become slaves to prevent our people from enjoying pure freedom. Our brethren there will never combine under the leadership of Grant.

[Music — "My country 'tis of thee," America]

Mr. Weichardt, so well known in this community ... Said "Here's to the German gazette," filling a tumbler with champagne and draining it at a draft.... Then having tossed the contents of his glass and refilling it, he said: "But it would be impolite on my part not to drink to the other newspapers," and he went on with a succession of toasts until he was quite full — Got tam!

About 2 o'clock in the morning Mr. Nicholson, the business Manager of the Picayune, having the floor suggested that it was now proper to adjourn.

No doubt, after reading this extraordinary account of a fabulous dinner, *Picayune* adherents, well acquainted with the paper's caustic view of the carpetbag city regime, picked up on the relevance of the date. One sharp reader suggested in the next day's paper: "The menu of the Picayune banquet was prepared by Don Jose A. Quintero, one of the most accomplished caterers of the profession." On the third of April, the *Picayune* admitted the confection: "Our contemporary is correct. The readers of the Picayune were indebted to the facile ingenuity, fertile imagination and exquisite talent of invention of the gentleman named for the unique description of that apocryphal banquet, which appeared in our columns on the 1st inst."[272]

The following year, Quintero seems to have repeated the feat, the paper of that same date headlining: "A Public Calamity! Fall of the City Hall Front. Narrow Escapes — Assistance Proffered."[273] The article opened:

> Our readers, we trust, will indulge us for the somewhat later appearance of our paper than usual. This delay is owing to our form [*sic*] having undergone the greatest disaster known to a printing office under the name of pi. Added to this at the hour of 2:25 o'clock this morning, in the midst of our troubles came to us the appalling news, that the fine portico, and indeed, the entire front of the City Hall had toppled to the earth.
>
> ...there were palpable clouds of pulverized mortar and venerable dust floating through the air. The crash, the echoes of which had been heard at the Picayune office had roused the whole neighborhood with its louder report. The echoes which reached our office passed over to the St. Charles Hotel and startled many of its inmates from their peaceful rest.
>
> The scene was sad beyond imagining. Those who had been startled from the sweeter rest of the morning time stood mute, wondering and almost palsied by the sight of the sudden ruin.
>
> The rich tympanum with its delicately relieved *bassi relievi*, the stately columns shattered in their precipitous fall, strewed the street even up to Lafayette Square, crashing through its iron railing with their massive fragments.

A shocking story indeed, New Orleans residents must have greedily devoured details of late-working City Hall clerks rescued by an alert night watchman, and the "great gallantry and judicious action" to save the contents of the neighboring mansion owned by "the benevolent Mrs. Slocum." How many readers once again fell for one of Quintero's "April's Fool" hoaxes, the record does not reveal.

The Man Without a Country

The ink had hardly dried on the April's Fool issue, when the famed writer Edward Everett Hale passed through New Orleans a week later on his way to Texas. This spring 1876 trip revolved around research on a new novel whose opening scene would occur in the city, the environs of which Hale waxed ecstatic in a letter home: "If I had come here, rather than to Washington when I was twenty-two, I should have lived here ever since."[274] Hale would have been even more enthusiastic had he realized the answer to his search could be found at the *Picayune* offices in the person of José Agustín Quintero, rather than hundreds of miles west on rail and stage.

The genesis for Hale's literary quest began with publication of his beloved story, *The Man Without a Country*, just 13 years earlier in December 1863. A virtual American myth — believed a true story by many — every school child at one time could tell the story of Aaron Burr's pathetic disciple, Philip Nolan. Charged with treason in the Burr conspiracies, the military court condemned Nolan to live his life transferred from one naval vessel to another, never to hear of or see the United States again. Nolan's deathbed confession of patriotism and love for his homeland stands as one of the most touching and poignant scenes in all of American literature.

In court-martialing his fictitious Philip Nolan, Edward Everett Hale did not realize he slandered the real Philip Nolan. A man with actual connections to Burr, but long dead since shot by the Spanish in 1801, the historical Nolan had been the first American filibuster to Texas. An educated Irishman based in Mexico's State of Texas, he had illegally traded with Americans in Natchez since 1775. Louisiana's Spanish governor encouraged such trade and Anglo immigration, but Texas governor Manuel Muñoz emphatically did not. In 1797 Nolan presented Louisiana's governor Baron de Carondelet with the first accurate map ever made of Texas, at least by an Anglo-American; the governor winked approval and provided a contract and passport to mustang wild horses (illegally, of course, in Texas) to supply a New Orleans Spanish regiment. At the same time, Nolan also secretly contracted with the crafty United States Army general James Wilkinson to organize some men to secede Texas from Spanish America. Wilkinson, essentially a self-serving double agent for both the Spanish and Americans, interested Aaron Burr in this scheme on an even broader basis; then, to later extricate himself as the Spanish became suspicious, Wilkinson would secure a scapegoat, exposing Burr's "treachery" to Thomas Jefferson.

Even as Wilkinson schemed, Philip Nolan spent seven months in the Texas frontier, possibly working to turn the Comanche and other Indian tribes against the Spanish. Finally, a force of 100 Spanish regular troops and volunteers caught up with him on March 21, 1801, wherein a fight ensued. Nolan died from a cannon blast. The Spanish imprisoned his small force of about 20 men in Mexico, on the charge of invasion, only one of them ever making it back to the United States. Nolan's escapade served to redouble Spanish efforts to populate and defend Northern Mexico, including Texas; however, the Louisiana purchase just three years later put even larger numbers of rapacious Americans on the border, accelerating the eventual move of Texas into the United States' sphere.[275]

The historical documents "From the old Spanish Records in the Archives of Mexico" relating these facts actually rested in Quintero's possession. He apparently obtained these letters during the "late unpleasantness" from his Mexican friend Don Manuel G. Rejón, whom the *Juaristas* later executed.[276]

Quintero wrote of this in *The Texas Almanac* of 1868 under the title "Philip Nolan and His Companions." His style, while engaging, proved unusually direct and factual for a Latin poet, quite remarkable for lack of embellishment; nevertheless, Quintero could not resist expressing his admiration for Nolan in the closing paragraphs:

> The diary kept by Nolan, and many of his letters, which are in my possession, show conclusively that he was not only a gallant and intelligent gentleman, but an accomplished scholar. He was thoroughly acquainted with astronomy and geography. He made the first map of Texas, which he presented to the Baron de Carondelet on returning from his first trip to Texas. Had he lived to see his plans carried out, Texas, the land he loved, would have been proud of him.
>
> Nolan is buried in a spot between Springfield and Waco, where his fight with the Spaniards took place. If that spot could be found, it might not be inappropriate to mark it with a slab and the following inscription: "SISTE, VIATOR, HEROEM CALCAS."[277]

Edward Everett Hale learned of this true Philip Nolan in the years following publication of *The Man Without a Country*. Many readers, even navymen, reported fond memories of their times with Philip Nolan on the USS *Levant*, not remembering news accounts of the ship's actual loss at sea two years before Nolan's reputed death on board in 1863. As Hale put it, of the entire navy and 4,000 newspaper editors throughout the nation, only a Philadelphia correspondent and a news writer in New Orleans noted the problem with the dates.[278] Surely this exceptional Crescent City newsman was Quintero. In the afterward to the story, later written in 1888, Hale elaborated:

> A writer in the New Orleans "Picayune" in a careful historical paper, explained at length that I had been mistaken all through; that Philip Nolan never went to sea, but to Texas; that there he was shot in battle, March 21, 1801; and by orders from Spain every fifth man of his party was to be shot, had they not died in prison. Fortunately, however, he left his papers and maps, which fell into the hands of a friend of the "Picayune's" correspondent.[279]

There can be no doubt but that Hale referred to Quintero. The details of this account match Quintero's *Texas Almanac* article exactly, this surely being the "careful historical paper" alluded to. Despite this, Hale may not have been acquainted with whom Quintero's friend had been. Had he known of the sad circumstances of Rejón's execution, Hale might have concluded he had in hand another excellent story to write about.

Hale continued in this book's afterward to explain how he came to make the mistake with Philip Nolan in the first place, and how Quintero (presumably) helped set the record straight:

I remembered ... in General Wilkinson's ... "Memoirs" ... frequent reference to a business partner of his of the name of Nolan, who, in the very beginning of this century, was killed in Texas.... Finding this mythical character in the mythical legends of a mythical time, I took the liberty to give him a cousin, rather more mythical, whose adventures should be on the seas. I had the impression that Wilkinson's friend was named Stephen; and as such I spoke of him in the early editions of the story. But long after this was printed, I found that the New Orleans paper was right in saying that the Texan hero was named Philip Nolan.[280]

A public declaration did not salve Edward Everett Hale's sensitive conscience. The historical injustice to Philip Nolan festered and bothered him over the years. Showing it still played on his mind, Hale made glancing reference to Nolan in a story entitled "The Brick Moon," published in an 1872 collection of tales, *His Level Best*. A light story of a scientific expedition to the moon — actually, a "brick" moon — the characters use a job wagon of a teamster P. Nolan to move astronomical equipment. They declare, "We always employ P. in memory of dead old Phil."[281]

Not satisfied until he had done all possible to rescue the true Nolan "from the complete oblivion which hangs over him," Hale finally decided to write a novel to set the matter straight once and for all. So 1876 found Hale and his daughter Ellen traveling through New Orleans on the way to Texas, researching the project. In Austin, Hale had a letter of introduction to a banker of dubious historical background. Scouting beyond this questionable contact, at the Secretary of State's office Hale quickly stumbled on the Spanish consul's turn-of-the-century report regarding Nolan's expedition.

Now on the scent, and quite frankly delighting in his western adventure, Hale braved the hazards of prairie travel and proceeded to San Antonio. In her excellent work on Hale, Jean Holloway reports on a meeting between Hale and Quintero:

> In San Antonio he found a gentleman of more "historical firmness" than the Austin banker, a Mr. J.A. Quintero, who shared Hale's avocation and who had "taken the most careful interest in the fame of Philip Nolan." Quintero was able to furnish the author original documents concerning the trial of some of Nolan's friends by the Spanish authorities, and probably showed him Nolan's diary and many of Nolan's letters.
>
> It was a treasure-trove of evidence which Hale put to good use in his novel.[282]

The value of Quintero's materials to Hale is beyond dispute; however, the certainty that such a meeting took place, at least in San Antonio, is questionable. Quintero had just published the April's Fool issue of the *Picayune* in New Orleans. It is not out of the question that Quintero could have journeyed to San Antonio about this time, but no evidence is cited to support this. Indeed, the conclusion is gleaned from a footnote in Hale's subsequent book *Philip Nolan's Friends*: "We owe these particulars to the very careful researches in Monterrey, of Mr. J.A. Quintero, who has taken the most careful interest in the fame of Philip Nolan."[283]

That a meeting between Hale and Quintero occurred in San Antonio thus seems unlikely, but simply appears a natural assumption by the biographer. More likely is that the two corresponded on the matter of Nolan's history, Quintero informing Hale of the 1868 *Texas Almanac* paper. Perhaps Hale did know of Quintero prior to this 1876 trip and took advantage of his itinerary to meet with the Cuban in New Orleans. In fact, 40 years later Hale's son wrote of this trip, lending some credence to this possibility: "My father found much valuable help in the studies of early Louisiana and Texas which were his main object here [in New Orleans]." Whether the two met in person, or merely corresponded, they probably established an excellent rapport. Both had attended Harvard, Hale having graduated a couple of years before Quintero's arrival. It is likely they both studied German there under a favorite teacher: Longfellow. Furthermore, they both shared the distinction of having been boy-students: Hale enrolling when only 13, Quintero at 12.[284]

Regardless of the circumstance of Hale's and Quintero's acquaintance, Hale did utilize this "treasure-trove" of material. He published *Philip Nolan's Friends; Or, "Show Your Passports!"* which appeared serially in *Scribner's Monthly* that year. The title is notably similar to Quintero's 1868 *Texas Almanac* article, but a more direct, if unidentified tribute to Quintero occurs at Nolan's appearance in Chapter III. The first sentence begins, "To *Philip Nolan and his companions* is due that impression of American courage and resource...." (emphasis added); this, of course, is identical to Quintero's article title, the original documents of which Hale had put to such good use.[285]

In this new novel, Hale finally explains the historical Philip Nolan, rescuing him from the oblivion he felt so undeserved. While introducing the facts of Nolan's life in a careful way, Hale did not hesitate to introduce fictional characters and romance throughout. It was a novel, after all. The clever ending served to indelibly tie together the two novels, resolving the historical injustice. In the last scene, Hale's characters drink a final toast to a young Ensign's health: "To Ensign Philip Nolan, ladies and gentlemen. May the young man never know what it is to be 'A MAN WITHOUT A COUNTRY.'"[286]

SPANISH INTRIGUE

In the following year, 1877, as the Ten Years War stilled raged in Cuba, Quintero somehow aroused suspicions of the Spanish consulate in New Orleans. A conspirator of some three decades past, his political conduct now became the subject of secret, official reports to Havana. Quintero may never have even known his activities had been watched and motives analyzed by agents of his former country.

In Dispatch number 21 of June 24, the consul notified the governor general in Cuba of several "particulars" which were in agreement with what the Havana chief of police had previously asserted. Soon thereafter, a July 5 report "of secret character" to the police specified the charges: Insurgents on the island spoke of "the help of the American subject, don José A. Quintero, Notary Public of New Orleans" and also editor of "The Picayune." The report continued about possible nefarious travels originating in New Orleans: "[Quintero]... left for there with the proper passport last June 12, and to which person is imputed the dispatch of certain false telegrams received in that city, harmful to the cause of Spain." Later from Havana Police Headquarters came the following:

> Don José Agustín Quintero ... arrived at this port June 20 on the steamer Margaret, coming from New Orleans and Bone Key [Key West], disembarking about ten in the morning with the interpreter from the Hotel Pasaje, with whom he lunched with an American who accompanied him in the trip. Afterwards he went to the house of Señor Spencer, Agent of the Associated Press, with whom he conferred a long time, reembarking the same day in the mentioned ship in the direction of the points of its origin. A native of the same name and surname, who now would be 47 years old and who is an American citizen, figured in the Narciso López conspiracy, for which he was sentenced to the fortress, managing to escape abroad, and therefore it is no surprise concerning the reports speaking of him which the Governor General has received. This is as much as I have been able to find out referring to the aforesaid individual that I have the honor to inform fulfilling your executive order.[287]

Were the Spanish overly paranoid or had Quintero managed to continue a strike for his homeland? Could it be that Quintero, the light-hearted reporter and author, led a double life and in some way assisted the revolution in his first homeland? Indeed, his Mexican poet-bureaucrat friend from Confederate days in Monterrey, Guillermo Prieto, had visited New Orleans in late March and declared Quintero's home "the center of conspirators and the cenacle of the literary." Among these literary exiles numbered another Cuban poet of *El Laúd del Desterrado*, Leopoldo Turla, who had corresponded with revolutionists and tried to aid their cause from New Orleans. Turla had died "two or three days" after Prieto's visit, and only a few months before Quintero's trip to Havana.[288] Could Quintero have been trying to fill the vacuum left by Turla, or were his interests truly more literary, his association with poet-revolutionists a simple matter of Latin hospitality?

Actually, nothing in the Spanish reports details furtive activities, deliveries of arms, or collusion with known revolutionaries. In fact, Señor Spencer of the Associated Press was no doubt Santiago S. Spencer. He currently edited the same *El Boletín Comercial* which Quintero had briefly edited a decade earlier — hardly a revolutionary publication. In fact, Quintero is said to have published in this journal, as well as an earlier journal of Spencer's, the *Diario Mercantil*. The entire meeting — a public lunch at that, replete with hotel interpreter — looked more like a business interview than one engaged in chicanery.

The Spanish were not convinced. A final dispatch of September 18 indicated that if Quintero returned to the island, "Be vigilant of his conduct."[289]

DUTY, DUELS AND HONOUR

Since before revolutionary times, an unwritten code governed personal conduct — especially in affairs of honor — and persisted throughout the nineteenth century. Rooted in Scott's romantic medieval era, Europeans brought to America this custom of the French and British military, and of the English landed gentry. Dueling came to be viewed as a Southern tradition, yet its practitioners included such august personages as Andrew Jackson, Henry Clay and Alexander Hamilton, the latter succumbing to the agile trigger of Aaron Burr. Indeed, the practice survived until well after the War of Secession. Confederate physician Hunter Holmes McGuire, director of "Stonewall" Jackson's medical corps, found his postwar patients unable to meet their bills; nevertheless, he managed well enough providing surgeon's services for Union officers, receiving $100 for each of their duels.[290]

This dueling code, the "code duello," evolved as a kind of gentleman's etiquette. It prescribed redress of offense, a protocol where a principal's "second" managed the affair of honor — apologies, challenges, even duels — to mitigate an insult. By midcentury, various writers captured the diverse rules of the code in print.[291]

"The hero of a dozen duels" in both his adopted and native lands — at least by one account — *Picayune* editor José Agustín Quintero wrote just such a little reference volume, *The Code of Honour*. Whom else might give justice to the task of reducing the "unwritten code" to the written form than a Latin poet from Cuba described as "a dashing, swashbuckling, romantic individual, as ready with the sword as with the pen?" Indeed, the same account, some half century later, would answer this question: "Quintero was a picturesque old fellow, just the kind of chap whom you would expect to take dueling seriously."[292]

Of course, when the New Orleans printing house of Clark and Hofeline published his little code in 1873, Quintero had only just passed his prime.

Picturesque or not, only in his mid–40's the *Daily-Picayune* editor was hardly yet an "old fellow." In fact, publication of his short manual may have increased demand for his services. Later that year, Quintero doubly served his avocation and his employer as a second for E.C. Whitney of the *Picayune*, reported December 17 in the New Orleans *Herald*—Whitney suffered a wound in the contest.[293]

The full title of Quintero's 1883 revised compact guide presages its contents: *The Code of Honour: Its Rationale and Uses by the Test of Common Sense and Good Morals with the Effects of Its Preventive Remedies.*[294] Indeed, the extended introduction addresses the nature of "honour" itself. Titled "Its Rationale and Uses," Quintero opens with a statement of how "individual rights" and "personal grievance" are matters beyond mere law:

> It is the remark of a distinguished moralist that "we desire both to be respectable and to be respected. We dread both to be contemptible, and to be condemned."
>
> Honour is the sentiment by which a high estimate is placed upon individual rights, social repute and personal self-respect. These are not always adequately protected by the laws and tribunals of the civil organisation. There are cases of insults grievous and degrading, for which there is no action at law. At common law a woman's chastity and a man's truth and courage, which are the foundations of all character, may be maliciously impeached, and the aggressor be free from legal challenge or issue. The injurer may enjoy impunity at law, while his victims are dragged down to degradation and despair. And in cases where suit would lie for damages, a legal investigation may involve for the insulted person, at best, shame, ignominy, perhaps ruin; and for the assailant, at most, insignificant pecuniary loss. Even the law's delays may work intolerable hardship and mortal injustice, touching character. And, against the baleful effects of "the world's dread laugh," what money will avail to protect, or will compensate the insulted?[295]

The subject of "honour" thus introduced, Quintero proceeds to define the "conservative and humane" rules of the Code of Honour, a process "to promote justice" and "designed to preclude hasty and passionate resort to sanguinary violence":

> The Code of Honour consists of rules for the government of gentlemen involved in such personal grievances. It is a digest of approved usages. It has the sanction of time and experience, and derives its authority from custom, among the refined, in the most enlightened nations, during several centuries, to this day. It is for civilised communities, and prevails among men of gentle manners. It, therefore, recognises no necessity for gentlemen to wear concealed weapons, and gives no countenance to that barbarous and homicidal practice. It urges, that an insult in public, by word or behavior, should not be resented there; and that a good quarrel will always keep for appropriate settlement. Its spirit and

purpose are wholly opposed to sudden and reckless affrays, engaged in without warning or consent. Its aim is, not to make strife, but to prevent it; not to
precipitate personal issues, but to control them in the interest of peace; not to
perpetrate wrong, but to promote justice.[296]

Rather than apologize for the mortal threat of injury inherent in duels,
Quintero argues it is this threat which discourages violence and promotes
gentlemanly resolution of offenses through civilized means. He claims that
"laws without vindicatory provisions are idle."[297] Quintero justifies this assessment by the result: "In three cases out of four, where risk of life is thus
imposed by consent, and incurred under the Code of Honour, the result is
either bloodless or not fatal." The advantages of mortal threat "incurred under
the Code" are thus explained:

> The Code of Honour authorises respectful calls upon persons, believed guilty
> of injuries, to make reparation by explanation, retraction, or apology, accord-
> ing to the nature of the case. And it supports the force and seriousness of such
> calls by sanctioning, as an alternative held in reserve, the formal proposal of
> RISK OF LIFE, by consent, to the persistent aggressor, at the hands of the aggrieved.
> As a safeguard, however, against abuse by groundless or frivolous issues, and in
> fairness to the person charged, it imposes upon the party invoking the vindi-
> catory provision of the law, THE SAME RISK OF LIFE to which he subjects the
> party charged with offense.[298]

To underscore and justify this "risk of life," Quintero touches on the
nature and value of life itself: "Now, among the refined, virtue with women
and honour with men are more valuable than life — are more worthy of the
last defense." He further added: "Self-protection is a right of nature. To protect one's carcass, is not the paramount purpose and entire scope of self-protection. Character and standing may be more valuable than life and as worthy
of defense."[299]

Quintero understood that some gentlemen would denounce the Code
as "bloody, cruel and barbarous...." He chided them to "understand the subject they deal with":

> It is their duty first to ascertain what the Code of Honour is; to recognise that
> it consists of the usages of the most refined classes and foremost men in the last
> three centuries of enlightened civilisation, and during the purer days of these
> United States, in the management of personal difficulties; to observe the iden-
> tity of moral status in public war and in duelling; to mark the great number
> of personal quarrels adjusted honourably and amicably by explanation, retrac-
> tion or apology, under advisements of seconds or through referees or courts of
> honour; to bear in mind how few such correspondences result in duels, and,
> of the duels fought, how small a number end fatally to life; to consider the

conservative purpose and elevating tendency of the Code; and to remember that affrays and street fights are the sole and inevitable alternative. Instead of discriminately damning the duello and all who act under the Code, it would better accord with good sense and Christian charity to subject each particular duel to examination, and to pronounce as the facts warrant.[300]

Indeed, Quintero seems to refer to the recent Yankee carpetbag occupation in noting that the current perfidious "regime" opposes the Code. No doubt, the "decline in morals and manners" in the United States is the result of abandoning the "code." Citing a "vast tide of immorality," he laments: "Men notoriously guilty of lying and peculation have been occupying the highest places in the land." Quintero paints this decadent, national guilt with a broad brush, even claiming the corruption of the divine, but then concludes with a hopeful thought:

> Undermining the sanctity of the pulpit and respect for the calling, we have had the spectacle of a great preacher tried for prostituting his high vocation to debauch the wife of a friend and member of his congregation; crowds of gaping church-women daily attending the Court House to hear the filthy details of this vile amour; and these daily published to gratify the prurient curiosity of the men and women of the country.
>
> *   *   *
>
> So long as the foul flood of radical aggression does not overwhelm true civilization in the United States — so long as radical licence does not render all too deeply degraded to be sensible of their own degradation — so long as radical levelling does not reduce all to the semi-savage state of the social hog — so long as the gentleman is not eliminated from existence — until the advent of the millenium, the Code of Honour will be used.[301]

The nature and value of the code firmly and extensively introduced, Quintero provides eight short chapters on "Rules for the Government of Principals and Seconds in Personal Difficulties."[302] Excerpted with the Cuban master's own headings are several of his gems regarding conduct:

Chapter I — The Person Insulted, Before Challenge Sent
- Whenever you believe you are insulted, if the insult be in public, and by words or behavior, never resent it there, if you have self-command enough to avoid noticing it. If resented there, you offer an indignity to the company, which you should not.
- When you believe yourself aggrieved, be silent on the subject, speak to no one about the matter, and see your friend who is to act for you as soon as possible.
- Never send a challenge in the first instance, for that precludes all negotiation. Let your note be in the language of a gentleman, and let the subject

matter of complaint be truly and fairly set forth, cautiously avoiding attribut-
ing to the adverse party any improper motive.

Chapter V — Duties of the Principals and Seconds on the Ground
- If, after an exchange of shots, neither party be hit, it is the duty of the second of the challengee to approach the second of the challenger, and say:
  "Our friends have exchanged shots, are you satisfied, or is there any cause
  why the contest should be continued?"
- If the insult be a serious character, it will be the duty of the second of the
  challenger to say, in reply to the second of the challengee: "We have been
  deeply wronged, and, if you are not disposed to repair the injury, the contest must continue."
- If either principal on the ground refuse to fight, or continue the fight when
  required, it is the duty of his second to say to the other second: "I have come
  upon the ground with a coward, and I tender you my apology for an ignorance of character; you are at liberty to post him."

Chapter VIII — The Degrees of Insult and How Compromised
- When words are used and a blow given in return, the insult is avenged, and
  if redress be sought, it must be from the person receiving the blow.
- Insults at a wine table, when the company are overexcited, must be answered
  for; and if the party insulting have no recollection of the insult, it is his duty
  to say so in writing, and negative the insult. For instance, if a man say: "You
  are a liar and no gentleman," he must, in addition to the plea of the want of
  recollection, say: "I believe the party to be a man of the strictest veracity and
  a gentleman."
- Intoxication is not a full excuse for insult, but it will greatly palliate. If it
  was a full excuse, it might well be counterfeited, to wound feelings or destroy
  character.
- Can every insult be compromised? — it is a mooted and vexed question. On
  this subject no rules can be given that will be satisfactory. The old opinion,
  that a blow must require blood, is not of force. Blows may be compromised
  in many cases. What those cases are, must depend on the seconds.

Quintero, having introduced the code and its practice, agreed "nothing
short of a great religious revival can raise the standard of public opinion"; however, as a practical matter he offered the additional suggestion that the Code
of Honour presents a "simple, certain and searching remedy, for the bad morals
and bad manners now prevalent." He implored his countrymen:

A correct appreciation and the encouragement of its use would enlist hon-
ourable men North, East, South and West in the cause of honour. It would do
more to eradicate promptly the rottenness consuming the Union — more to ele-
vate the people to a healthy state than all the party changes, legislative enact-
ments and judicial judgements which a hundred years may compass.[303]

Quaint and old-fashioned, citizens of the information age may easily dismiss the Code, yet the question remains as to whether or not it fostered a more humane civilization. Perhaps it did — or perhaps the nineteenth-century gentleman inherently claimed a chivalrous nobility superior to post–Victorians. In his delicious 1940 survey, "The Humors of the Duello," veteran *Picayune* newspaperman John Smith Kendall recounts an illuminating classic incident of the Code, originally printed in the 1859 weekly newspaper, the *Coast Journal:*

> On Thursday the 22nd ult., F.C. Aubert, of the Independent Vigilant, and E. Supervielle, of the Drapeau de l'Ascension, left here on the Vicksburg packet en route to Mississippi, to fight a duel. The Affair came off at Fort Adams, and resulted in the wounding of Mr. Aubert in the right hip. His wound is not considered dangerous. Mr. Supervielle was not harmed.
>
> A pleasant incident in the matter marked the dealings of the two principals. Perceiving that Mr. Aubert would be obliged to remain at Fort Adams because of his condition, his adversary kindly offered to attend to the editing of the Vigilant until Mr. Aubert recovered sufficiently to return to his post; and Mr. Aubert gratefully accepted the offer. Courtesy like this can be appreciated by everyone and is creditable to both parties.[304]

A dozen years later, even after the War, the Code still reigned. North or South, it seemed to matter little. An incident in Washington, D.C., proved this, the participants' actions scripted precisely according to the Code, as Quintero had captured it. Colonel Beverley Tucker had returned from Mexico after the collapse of the Confederate Carlotta colony, and found his dinner interrupted one evening by the angry bellowings of a Northern colonel, seated at a nearby table. Tucker ignored insults against the beauty of Southern women, but would not stand the vile accusations that hardly a single virtuous lady was to be found in the entire Southland. Tucker rose, offered his card and challenged the cur to a duel. The following day found the principals, their seconds and their surgeons assembled in the woods on the Virginia side of the Potomac River, near Arlington city. Tucker apparently had not yet calmed a whit, but the Yankee colonel had a change of heart. The offender's second asked if Tucker would accept an apology, as the officer now realized his slanders had been carelessly declared while he had been "in his cups." Of course the Confederate agreed to this, but honor yet remained to be satisfied. As demanded by Tucker, that evening the Federal colonel again appeared at the Metropolitan hotel restaurant, during the exact hour of his previous public outrage, and in an equally boisterous voice as before, retracted his remarks and apologized to the women of the South.[305]

In 1911, The Ruskin Press of New Orleans would reprint Quintero's *Code of Honour,* under the guidance of his son Lamar. A colorful newspaperman in his own right who virtually inherited his father's post at the *Daily Picayune*, Lamar was born in Matamoros during the heady days of Confederate diplomatic intrigue with Mexican governor Santiago Vidaurri. Now, he inherited the mantle of his father's reputation for honorable settlement of disputes. Though the Code no longer reigned, republication of his father's book gave Lamar a national reputation on "honor." Many a Northern newspaper consulted the new master in New Orleans on matters of etiquette and offense, duly publishing his dictums to wide public approval.[306]

As Knights to Their Ladies

The *Daily Picayune*, during carpetbag reconstruction, published the poem entitled "A Chirp from Mother Robin" on March 22, 1868. No doubt many poems and stories saw print in those days, yet this one differed: the author, under the pseudonym "Miss Pearl Rivers," was a woman. Defying Victorian strictures, Eliza Jane Poitevent, born in 1849 Mississippi, wrote for pay. At age 19, she further appalled local sensibilities in accepting the position of *Picayune* literary editor. Colonel Holbrook at the *Picayune* seemed little concerned, though, and wed Eliza in 1872. His former wife, however, did not take it so well. As one account put it: "A month after Eliza's marriage, the first Mrs. Holbrook, after failing in two attempts to shoot Eliza, hit her over the head with a bottle of bay rum. Servants intervened and Eliza ran next door, whereupon the attacker seized an ax and smashed the furniture."[307]

When a business partnership purchased the *Picayune* that same year, the 63-year-old Colonel and his young wife traveled extensively, but regained ownership of the paper in December, 1874. They assumed the $100,000 debt incurred by the previous owners in their failed venture. Tragedy struck and Colonel Holbrook then died in early 1876, less than a year after Quintero's apocryphal dinner banquet — Eliza now faced bankruptcy.[308]

The young widow of 27 considered her dilemma for three months. Her family desired that she give up business — her association with "tobacco-reeking men in an office" — and return home to Mississippi. Aware of the challenge, Eliza nevertheless preferred journalism and considered the prospect of managing the paper an attractive one. Several *Picayune* employees encouraged her to take charge of the paper. Most notable among these were the business manager, George Nicholson, and the chief editorial writer, José Agustín Quintero. Finally, Eliza Holbrook made up her mind to stay and made an announcement to her staff: "I am a woman. Some of you may not want to work for a woman. If so, you are free to go, and no hard feelings. But you who stay — will you give me your undivided loyalty, and will you advise me truly and honestly?"[309]

For a second the silence was tense. Then, "Why the little 'old' lady is going to stick!" someone gasped. Thomas G. Rapier, who'd started a few years ago as a handy-boy, gave a soft "Hurray." Page Mercer Baker and George W. Lloyd showed their clasped hands in token of support. But there was an uneasy shuffling of feet. Chief editorial writer Don Jose Quintero, once known as the Longfellow of Cuba, as adept with pistols as with pen, rose with the bearing of his grandee Spanish ancestors and announced grimly: "If anyone craves satisfaction for what The Picayune says, I'll meet him."

A few left. And a few of those who stayed grumbled. To prove that she could, Eliza fired them.

Of those who remained, she said, "Nowhere are there men so true and chivalrous." The Picayune became known as "The Old Lady of Camp Street" and Quintero taught the art of dueling to other members of the staff.[310]

"As knights to their ladies," Quintero and his Picayune comrades had loyally defended their lady. They worked for her, and they stood ready to fight for her.[311]

Heavy new responsibilities thrust on her inexperienced shoulders, Eliza would write years later: "I never felt so lonely and little and weak in my life as on the first day when I took my seat in Mr. Holbrook's big editorial chair...." Only a few months later, her widely respected business manager, George Nicholson, demonstrated his confidence and extended his support by acquiring a reported one-fourth interest in the newspaper. His and Quintero's faith in her proved well-founded. Eliza Jane Holbrook grew in the position, surmounting challenges of lawsuits, debt and the long carpetbag rule of the city. She restored a sense of vision to the paper, lacking during the years her husband had cautiously worked simply to keep the enterprise afloat. The *Picayune*, under her leadership, championed business development, prison reform and cultural projects such as monuments to Confederate heroes and establishment of the Southern Historical Society; yet, she received and then ignored criticism upon inviting former Yankee officers to join her staff when the *Republican* ceased publication.[312] Furthermore, she introduced other women writers, including Mrs. Elizabeth Meriwether Gilmer, who would take the famous pen name "Dorothy Dix" and achieve national fame working for Hearst's New York *Journal*. In 1879, publisher Eliza Jane Holbrook married her partner, George Nicholson. Their futures linked, the two effectively worked together, leading the paper until the century's end.[313]

The team of Eliza Jane and George Nicholson inherited legal wrangling brought on by the debts incurred from Mr. Holbrook's era. Investors in the failed business group of 1872–74 brought lawsuits beginning in 1875, lasting through José Quintero's life and carrying on to 1886, by which time his son Lamar had succeeded him. In fact, when the Louisiana Supreme Court finally judged against these claims in January, 1888, Lamar telegraphed Mrs.

Nicholson at her home in Bay St. Louis, Mississippi with news of the stunning victory.[314]

LIKE FATHER, LIKE SON

Lamar Charles Quintero exhibited much of his father's casual disregard in journalistic practice at the *Daily Picayune*. His education included study under private tutors as well as at the local Jesuit College (most likely Immaculate Conception College, progenitor of Loyola University). His father still a potent figure at the *Picayune*, upon Lamar's 1881 graduation he joined the staid, family-oriented newspaper as a court reporter. Only two years later, this 20-year-old Crescent City native of Latin-Anglo descent secured vice-consul appointment by Costa Rica, as did his father before. In recognition for valuable services as one of this country's commissioners to the World Cotton Centennial Exposition, Lamar ascended to consul (1885) upon his father's death, and later consul-general for the South (1890) as well as positions his father had held since 1878, U.S. Commissioner and Notary Public.[315]

The *Daily Picayune* celebrated its semicentennial in 1887 and spoke highly of its promising "general reporter":

> Mr. Lamar C. Quintero, son of the poet and journalist, the late Don Joseph A. Quintero, who long illuminated by his genius the columns of the Picayune, is a bright young fellow and an excellent linguist. He was born in Matamoros, Mexico. He enjoys, in addition to his position on the Picayune, the dignities of being United States Commissioner and Consul for the Republic of Costa Rica.[316]

During these waning years of the century, Lamar also married Emma Peniston (1895) and studied law at Tulane, emerging a barrister in 1890. Clerking and working in the office of Judge John Clegg, his recently graduated brother John Marshall Quintero joined the firm in 1902. In 1912, Lamar and Marshall formed the law partnership of Caffery, Quintero & Brumby, associating with Robert E. Brumby and Donelson Caffery. Though Lamar served for a decade as attorney for the United Fruit Company's Tropical Division, he did not sever ties with his father's paper, the *Picayune*. In fact, Lamar naturally assumed the role of *Picayune* attorney; but, he also maintained a lifelong, somewhat loose commitment as its drama and music critic.[317]

The prolific self-appointed *Picayune* biographer John Smith Kendall also joined the *Picayune* during Lamar's tenure. He would write of this time, obliquely referring to Lamar: "When I became connected with the Picayune in 1891, there were several men who had been in the employ of the paper for some years, and remained on the staff for a long time subsequently." More than half a century later, Kendall wrote an amusing piece entitled "Old Days on the New Orleans Picayune" and furnished insight into the somewhat reckless journalistic style Quintero displayed:

> It must be confessed that [Lamar] Quintero did not take his reportorial responsibilities very much to heart. Once, in the early days of his career, he was sent to report a festival promoted by a local benevolent organization, one of those fraternal societies very numerous in New Orleans in those days, but which have since completely disappeared. The merry-making was to take place at one of the resorts on Lake Pontchartrain, and to attend it, as Quintero ascertained, would require a tedious trip in a "dummy" train and a lengthy stay in a not-very-congenial group. He decided not to go, but wrote a glowing account of what he imagined took place, including a speech by the president of the organization. The next day he was called on the carpet by Major Robinson, to explain how a dead man was able to deliver that oration. It seems that the president had died suddenly on the previous morning, and the festivities had been cancelled. There was nothing to do but confess, which Quintero did, and, after the tolerant, happy-go-lucky fashion of those pleasant days, was forgiven, on the understanding that he wouldn't do it again.[318]

In Kendall's short history of the old days appear many larger-than-life old-style reporters with whom Lamar Quintero had once associated, but Ernst Hoepner proved singular. The German newspaper artist led an interesting enough life, many adventures due to "his fondness for spirituous liquors," but his fame had more to do with a casual suggestion made in 1897. It seems an aspiring writer-editor named William Sidney Porter chanced upon Hoepner at a local newsman haunt, the Tobacco Plant Saloon. The barkeeper, Henry, always seemed to have wheedled useful information from customers, and he proved the real attraction to local reporters. Porter, just returned from self-imposed exile in Honduras, had been visiting the saloon for a few months, trying to gain the nerve to return to Texas to face more or less false charges of embezzlement at a bank he once worked for. Drinking with Hoepner and his colleagues, Porter treated the group to a round, demanding, "Oh Henry! Set 'em up again, will you?" Over these drinks he produced a freshly completed story manuscript. Probably thinking of his fate awaiting in Texas, he told his fellow imbibers to suggest a name to submit to a magazine, for he did not want to use his own. Hoepner casually suggested, "Oh, Henry?" He added, "You certainly say that often enough." The group no doubt laughed at this suggestion, but some time later in a cold, gloomy Texas jail cell Porter recalled the memory of this warm, friendly time. There he signed an early successful submission with a pseudonym more famous than any other during its day: O. Henry. No doubt O. Henry's story *Cherchez la Femme* is a tribute to these newshound friends; here, none other than a *Picayune* reporter solves the New Orleans theft of Madame Tibault's twenty thousand dollars.[319]

Regardless of newshound mischief and associations with colorful fellow reporters, as the new century arrived, Lamar Quintero increasingly served his county in the sensitive international arena, eclipsing even his father's name. After the Spanish-American War, in 1901 President William McKinley's Taft Commission appointed him as an associate justice on the Philippine Supreme Court — Quintero declined. In 1910, President William Taft himself appointed Quintero a U.S. Commission Delegate to the 4th International Pan American Congress, held that year in Buenos Aires. Headed by former Secretary of State Elihu Root — who would secure the Nobel Peace Prize just two years later — this conference rechristened the 20-year-old hemispheric association the Pan American Union, a bureau which yet exists, having also spawned the Organization of American States (OAS). In this same year, President Taft further assigned Quintero the role of special representative to the 1910 Chilean Centennial.[320] Said to have also served the republics of Nicaragua, Venezuela, Ecuador, as well as the King of Denmark, Quintero contributed significantly to New Orlean's international trade with Latin America. At the age of 58, he died on October 30, 1921.[321]

HONORING THE CAUSE

At Washington Artillery Assembly Hall in New Orleans on the evening of December 11, 1889, the largest meeting of Confederates since the end of the war occurred. Eight Southern governors and many thousands of soldiers had come to the funeral of Jefferson Davis, paying final respects to their onetime president. General John B. Gordon brought together these men that somber night under the auspices of the newly-formed United Confederate Veterans (UCV), which he headed; they not only underscored the dedication of veterans to the memory of their struggle, but cemented the leadership position of New Orleans within the UCV.[322]

Quintero's sons evidently treasured the service and memory of their father to the cause of the Confederacy. Their own service to the veterans exemplified Confederate General Stephen D. Lee's charge to the UCV successor organization, United Sons of Confederate Veterans, made at the 1906 convention in New Orleans:

> To you, Sons of Confederate Veterans, we submit the vindication of the Cause for which we fought; to your strength will be given the defense of the Confederate soldier's good name, the guardianship of his history, the emulation of his virtues, the perpetuation of those principles he loved and which made him

glorious and which you also cherish. Remember, it is your duty to see that the true history of the South is presented to future generations.[323]

In the pages of *Confederate Veteran* magazine, founded by the UCV in 1894, turn of the century articles frequently mentioned contributions of the Quintero family. The January, 1903, issue reported on the Confederate Reunion Committee of New Orleans, and its grand plans for the upcoming meeting to be held in the spring. The *Picayune* covered the important committee deliberations "at length," noting that Lamar Quintero served on the "Music Committee." In the following year, the September edition highlighted staff officers to Gen. Stephen D. Lee, the UCV's new commanding general. Apparently the UCV permitted positions of rank among its "sons," for listed under aides appeared "Capt. Lamar C. Quintero, New Orleans, La." Commander Lee further announced that he "commends most earnestly the action looking to a closer union of the U.C.V. and the U.S.C.V., and in the near future will add to his staff a proper representative from the Sons." The UCV continued in future numbers to recognize Lamar's contributions. By November of 1905, Don José's oldest son claimed the rank of Lt. Colonel and served in New Orleans as Aide-de-Camp.[324]

Lamar received mention a last time three years later, again in the November issue. In New Orleans, subscriptions for the Moorman monument, honoring the city's own past UCV Adjutant General and Chief-of-Staff, gained coverage in *Confederate Veteran*. Among the five-dollar contributors numbered Lamar C. Quintero. UCV rank and file credited Major General George Moorman's "zeal, energy and executive ability" for the phenomenal growth of their benevolent and patriotic association, in just the first decade, to a member roll of thousands organized under 1,250 camps.[325]

It would be three more years before another Quintero appeared in *Confederate Veteran*, in this case the younger brother, John Marshall. As the "thin gray line" of old veterans withered with age, the September, 1911, issue reported on Officers of Camp Beauregard, United Sons of Confederate Veterans (a designation shortened a year later to the current "Sons of Confederate Veterans"). The camp's chairman of the "Committee on Finance" proved none other than J. M. Quintero.[326]

CARRYING THE TORCH

Torn between the pen and the bench throughout his career, to his sons the Confederate Quintero bequeathed his lifelong passions: Lamar inherited Don José's journalistic impulse; Marshall fulfilled his father's unrealized pursuit of the law; both dedicated themselves to international service. Marshall had only reached the age of 14 when his father died at the helm of the *Picayune* in 1885. Lamar, by then, had entrenched himself in the paper, but his career shifted inversely to that of his father: from journalism to law. Never completely abandoning the *Picayune*, Lamar focused on the consular service and his calling as an attorney. The partnership he and Marshall formed — Caffery, Quintero & Brumby — dissolved by 1920 when Caffery withdrew after Brumby's death. They continued their practice in New Orleans as partners to Louis M. Hubert and Philip S. Gidiere, until Hubert, Gidiere and finally Lamar Quintero himself, died.

J. Marshall Quintero, as he styled himself, formed a new firm of Quintero & Ritter, with Quintero senior partner to August H. Ritter. To some extent his civil practice emphasized international law, specifically relating to Central and South America. In fact, Marshall embraced the long family tradition: He served Costa Rica as vice-consul beginning in 1906, ascended to consul in 1924, and by 1931 progressed to consul-general, a position he held to the end of his long life.

As a noted attorney, Marshall Quintero untangled extremely complicated property rights cases involving heirs subject to testamentary wills. The Abascal case, for example, proved typical of his adroit legal maneuvering, as summarized: "... [Quintero] plead that the clause in the will was merely a declaration of ownership and not a bequest and that since the testator at the time of making the will was not the owner of the said effects, he could not therefore bequeath property belonging to another." In many cases, the Louisiana Supreme Court reversed lower court decisions on appeal, siding with Quintero. A member of the New Orleans Bar Association for over half a century, in 1957 the society awarded him their certificate of merit.

Quintero's personal life in New Orleans proved as varied as his professional interests. An avid reader with an appreciation for music, he also claimed membership in the "Old Chess, Checkers and Whist and Pickwick clubs" located there. As no doubt his father before him, Marshall was Catholic and a Democrat. In Havana, Cuba on August 31, 1929, he wed Margot, the daughter of Cienfuegos mechanical engineer Andres Clemente Simo. Marshall and his wife had no children. Finally, almost a century after Louisiana seceded — and his father joined the Confederate diplomatic service — J. Marshall Quintero died on November 29, 1960.[327]

FINAL SOJOURN OF A PATRIOT

José Agustín Quintero's sons witnessed Victorian America's transition to global leadership, but the father himself belonged to a more Bohemian era. Even the *Picayune* seemed to cling to another time, waiting for the old newsman's passing, which finally arrived September 7, 1885. As if not to offend the old Cuban, the venerable lady of Camp Street finally installed electric lights one year later.[328]

At 8 o'clock on that Monday evening, September 7, at his home at 46 Dumaine Street, Quintero expired in the company of his two sons. He had been ill "for more than a year." The family invited "friends and acquaintances" to the funeral, beginning at half-past four o'clock the next day, Tuesday, at his home located between Royal and Chartres Streets.[329]

In the land of his birth, Quintero's obituary appeared in an 1886 issue of *Revista Cubana*. Ironically, the old Confederate appeared along with another veteran of the "late unpleasantness" who had also passed away in 1885 — George McClellan. Even in *la patria*, the press thus linked Quintero's memory to the North American War he served. Yet, the record also proved symbolic: Presaging how soon his own homeland would forget his life and passions, even the Yankee McClellan received a more substantial and glowing tribute than Quintero.[330]

At least his adopted Southern homeland accorded him quiet, lasting honor in death. The Cuban in Gray slumbers eternally at New Orleans Metairie Cemetery, buried near the monument to the Army of Northern Virginia.[331] The day of his funeral, Quintero's Southern comrades, affiliated under a predecessor organization to the United Confederate Veterans, did not forget the fallen defender of the cause. They viewed a respectful order placed in the *Daily Picayune* by their officers Walter H. Rogers, president, and Wm. E. Todd, secretary:

ARMY OF TENNESSEE, Louisiana Division —(Veterans)— The officers and members of the association are requested to attend the funeral of our late comrade, JOSEPH A. QUINTERO, aged 56 years, a member of the Quitman Rifles of Austin, Texas C.S.A.,....[332]

During his active, varied life, Quintero wrote innumerable poems, essays and articles, but they are widely scattered in the literature of Cuba, Texas, Boston and elsewhere. The more readily available items provide a fuzzy sketch of his life, but only hint at the breadth of his adventurous days. Some decades back, *The Handbook of Texas* noted that in the *Picayune* files "are many of his poems, political essays, and other fugitive pieces," but these, sadly, have now been lost track of.[333]

A larger than life figure — poet, duelist, revolutionary, diplomat, editor, attorney and author — José Agustín Quintero's accomplishments can only stir admiration. That he has been resigned to relative oblivion is a tragic oversight of history, hardly deserved by this patriot of no less than two causes and two nations. Perhaps John Smith Kendall, who worked with and knew the Quintero sons so well, captured this pathos best:

Quintero had the misfortune to live in one of the great, revolutionary moments of history, and in the turmoil of the time he (and not he only) was all but lost to sight. In such epochs the rush of political and military events sweeps away much that is merely beautiful, or elegant, or charming; and no one suffers eclipse so certainly as the poet. Alas that it should not be so![334]

El Banquete del Destierro
(The Banquet of the Exiled)

by José Agustín Quintero

Destino amargo y severo,
a tierra extraña nos lanza;
¡ved el cielo qué sombrío!
¡no hay ni un rayo de esperanza!
  ¡Mas ríamos de las penas,
¡a espumante copa alzad!
¡Un brindis por los que han muerto!
¡Hurra por la Libertad!

Severe and bitter destiny
to strange lands sends us;
look how dark the sky is!
There is not even a ray of hope!
  But let us laugh at the sorrows,
raise the foaming cup!
A toast for those who have died!
Hurrah for Liberty!

Tras noches de insomnio fiero
está la mejilla hundida,
mas pronto el bullente vino
ha de dejarla encendida.
  ¡Atrás el esplín amargo!
¡Diáfana la copa alzad!
¡Un brindis por los que han muerto!
¡Hurra por la Libertad!

After nights of fierce insomnia
the cheek is sunken,
but soon the sparkling wine
will make it inflamed.
  Put behind the bitter melancholy!
Raise the transparent cup!
A toast for those who have died!
Hurrah for Liberty!

Que no haya ni un suspiro,
ni una lágrima siquiera,
por los héroes que encontraron
un sudario en su bandera.
  ¡Oh, cuántas memorias tristes! ...
¡Mas vuestras copas llenad!
¡Un brindis por los que han muerto!
¡Hurra por la Libertad!

That there will be not a sigh,
nor even a tear whatsoever,
for the heroes that found
in their flag a shroud.
  Oh how many sad memories! ...
But fill your cups!
A toast for those who have died!
Hurrah for Liberty!

En el campo de batalla
yacen con airado ceño;
mas las lágrimas cobardes
no despiertan ese sueño.
Así la copa espumosa
al seco labio llevad.

In the battle field
they lie in angry ring;
but the cowardly tears
do not awaken that dream.
Therefore the foaming cup
put to dry lips.

¡Un brindis por los que han muerto!
¡Hurra por la Libertad!

Nuestro corazón oprime
pesada mano de hierro;
mas con júbilo venimos
al banquete del destierro.
¡La copa alzad! Nuestra orquesta
es la horrenda tempestad! ...
¡Un brindis por los que han muerto!
¡Hurra por la Libertad!

Dejad que a la triste madre
recuerde el alma sombría ...
¡Ja, ja, ja! ¿Quién aquí espera
volver a verla algún día?
Mas el corazón se hiela,
la bullente copa alzad ...
¡Un brindis por los que han muerto!
¡Hurra por la Libertad!

¿Qué es la vida? 1Grano leve
de arena que huella el paso,
¡la burbuja que en el vino
revienta al tocar el vaso!
¡Decepción por donde quiera!
¡Mas vuestras copas llenad!
¡Un brindis por los que han muerto!
¡Hurra por la Libertad!

¡Mirad! ¡Mirad el pasado! ...
Fuerza es que la fe sucumba ...
¿No véis? ¡Es un cementerio!
¡Cada esperanza una tumba!
Mas se enciden nuestras frentes ...
¡Otra vez la copa alzad!
¡Un brindis por los que han muerto!
¡Hurra por la Libertad!

Lejos de la patria, el alma
las emociones destierra;
muramos sin un gemido,
de emigración en la tierra.
Un brindis por el primero
que se hunda en la eternidad.
¡Hurra por los que murieron!
¡Hurra por la Libertad!

A toast for those who have died!
Hurrah for Liberty!

Our heart is pressed
by an iron hand;
with joy we come
to the banquet of the exiled.
Raise the cup! Our orchestra
is the horrendous tempest! ...
A toast for those who have died!
Hurrah for Liberty!

Let the sad mother
remember the melancholic soul ...
Ha, ha, ha! Who here would hope
to see her again one day?
But the heart turns to ice,
raise the bubbling cup ...
A toast for those who have died!
Hurrah for Liberty!

What is life? A trifling grain
of sand that treads the passage,
the bubble in the wine that
bursts when it hits the glass!
Deception is everywhere!
But, refill your cups!
A toast for those who have died!
Hurrah for Liberty!

Look, look to the past! ...
faith succumbs to the force ...
Do you not see? It is a cemetery!
Each hope is a tomb!
But our brows are aflamed ...
Again raise the cup!
A toast for those who have died!
Hurrah for Liberty!

Far from the motherland, the soul
its emotions banished;
let us die without a groan,
as we migrate from the earth.
A toast for the first
who sinks into eternity.
Hurrah for those that died!
Hurrah for Liberty![335]

Notes

While Quintero's life as a poet, revolutionary and journalist has received scant attention, biographers have given his Confederate diplomatic service significantly more consideration. Two excellent books on this subject are Ronnie C. Tyler's Santiago Vidaurri and the Southern Confederacy (Austin: Texas State Historical Association, 1973) and James W. Daddysman's The Matamoros Trade: Confederate Commerce, Diplomacy, and Intrigue (Newark: University of Delaware Press, 1984). The author wishes to thank Uncle Ted Beckingham for unexpected insights in Phillip Nolan, and to express appreciation to Dr. José A. Armillas of the Universidad de Zaragoza, Spain, for his efforts to locate Confederate correspondence related to Narciso Monturiol at Spanish archives in Barcelona and elsewhere. Thanks also to Myrian King for assistance with the translation of "El Banquete del Destierro." Finalmente, a mis abuelos Tomás Villanueva Vega y Monserrate Bonilla López.

1. *The Daily Picayune*, New Orleans, "Joseph A. Quintero (obit.)," Sep. 8, 1885, p. 4; José Manuel Carbonell, *Los Poetas de "El Laud del Desterrado"* (La Habana: Imprenta "Avisor Comercial," 1930), p. 14; Glenn R. Conrad, *Dictionary of Louisiana Biography* (Lafayette: Louisiana Historical Association, 1997), pp. 669–670.

2. John Smith Kendall, "New Orleans Newspapermen of Yesterday," *The Louisiana Historical Quarterly* 29 (July 1946): 779.

3. *La Enciclopedia de Cuba*, Tomo 1, *Poesía* (San Juan: Enciclopedia y Clásicos Cubanos, 1975), p. 417; Max Henrique Ureña, *Panorama Histórico de la Literatura Cubana*, Primer Tomo (New York: Las Americas Publishing Co., 1963), p. 327.

4. José Antonio Fernández de Castro, "Un Poeta Revolucionario al Servicio de Intereses Esclavistas," in *Ensayos Cubano de Historia y de Critica con Una carta de Fernando Ortiz*, Jesus Montero (ed.), (La Habana: Biblioteca de Historia, Filosofia y Sociologia, Vol. XIII, 1943), p. 123; Julian Divanco (Dir.), *El Primer Periodista y Un Gran Educador*, Vol. IV, Colección Cultura Ariquannabense (La Habana, Cuba:, Imprenta "El Sol," 1955), p. 5; Francisco Lagomaggiore, *América Literaria*, Tomo II (Buenos Aires: Imprenta de La Nación, 1890), p. 604.

5. Madame la Comtesse Merlin, "La Havane," *The Southern Quarterly Review* VII (Jan. 1845): 179; Enrique José Varona, "José de la Luz y Caballero," *Revista Cubana*, Tomo I (1885): 541–546.

6. Juan J. Remos y Rubio, *Historia de la Literatura Cubana* (La Habana, Cuba: Cárdenas y Compañía, 1945), II, p. 270.

7. Alfred Coester, *The Literary History of Spanish America* (New York: The MacMillan Company, 1950), pp. 407–408.

8. Merlin, "La Havane," pp. 179–180.

9. Coester, *The Literary History of Spanish America*, p. 396.

10. Fermin Peraza Sarausa, *Dicciónario Biografico Cubano* (Habana: Ediciónes Anuario Bibliografico Cubano, 1967), V, p. 7.

11. *The Daily Picayune*, Sep. 8, 1885, p. 4.

12. Fernández de Castro, "Un Poeta Revolucionario," p. 123; Rafael Estenger, *Cien de las mejores Poesias Cubanos* (Miami: Mnemosyne Publishing Co., 1969), p. 175.

13. Carbonell, *Los Poetas*, p. 18; Jose Lezama Lima, *Antologia de la Poesia Cubana*, Tomo III (La Habana, Cuba: Consejo Nacional del Cultura, 1965), p. 269.

14. *The Daily Picayune*, Sep. 8, 1885, p. 4; Clement Evans (ed.), *Confederate Military History: Vol. XIII — Louisiana* (Atlanta: Confederate Publishing Company, 1899), pp. 556–557.

15. Carbonell, *Los Poetas*, p. 18.

16. *The Daily Picayune*, Sep. 8, 1885, p. 4.

17. Kendall, "New Orleans Newspapermen of Yesterday," p. 780.

18. Divanco, *El Primer Periodista*, p. 5.

19. Coester, *The Literary History of Spanish America*, p. 397.

20. John Smith Kendall, "The Humors of the Duello," *The Louisiana Historical Quarterly* 23 (Jan.–Oct., 1940): 454; Ureña, *Panorama Histórico*, p. 327.

21. Dumas Malone (ed.), "Henry Wadsworth Longfellow," *Dictionary of American Biography* (New York: Charles Scribner's Sons, 1933), XI, pp. 382–384; Cecil B. Williams, *Henry Wadsworth Longfellow* (New York: Twayne Publishers, 1964) pp. 72–73; Herbert S. Gorman, *A Victorian American: Henry Wadsworth Longfellow* (1926; rpt. Port Washington, N.Y.: Kennikat Press, 1967), p. 228.

22. Gorman, *ibid.*, p. 228; Williams, *ibid.*, p. 81.

23. Francis H. Underwood, *Henry Wadsworth Longfellow: A Biographical Sketch* (New York: Haskell House Publishers, Ltd., 1973) pp. 74–75.

24. Malone, "Ralph Waldo Emerson," *Dictionary of American Biography*, VI, p. 137; Clarke F. Ansley (ed.), *The Columbia Encyclopedia in One Volume* (New York: Columbia University Press, 1946), p. 567.

25. Underwood, *Henry Wadsworth Longfellow*, p. 77.

26. José Agustín Quintero, "Lyric Poetry in Cuba." 1850(?) Manuscript in Department of Rare Books and Manuscripts, Boston Public Library, Boston, Mass., 21 pp.

27. Quintero, "Lyric Poetry in Cuba," pp. 2–3.

28. Carbonell, *Los Poetas*, p. 114.

29. Quintero, "Lyric Poetry in Cuba," pp. 16–17.

30. Remos y Rubio, *Historia de la Literatura Cubana*, p. 270.

31. Quintero, "Lyric Poetry in Cuba," pp. 12–13.

32. Coester, *The Literary History of Spanish America*, p. 379.

33. Ureña, *Panorama Histórico*, p. 331; Carbonell, *Los Poetas*, p. 79; "Pedro Santacilia y Palacios," *Enciclopedia Universal Ilustrada Europeo-Americana* (Madrid: Espasa-Calpe, 1964), LIV, p. 196.

34. Coester, *The Literary History of Spanish America*, p. 409.

35. Carbonell, *Los Poetas*, p. 19.

36. Quintero, "Lyric Poetry in Cuba," p. 21.

37. Ronnie C. Tyler, *Santiago Vidaurri and the Southern Confederacy* (Austin: Texas State Historical Association, 1973), p. 46; Ron Tyler, *The New Handbook of Texas* (Austin: Texas State Historical Association, 1996), p. 393.

38. Conrad, *Dictionary of Louisiana Biography*, p. 669; Donald E. Herdeck (ed.), *Caribbean Writers: A Bio-Bibliographical-Critical Encyclopedia* (Washington, D.C.: Three Continents Press, Inc., 1979), p. 852.

39. Vidal Morales y Morales, *Iniciadores y Primeros Mártires de la Revolución Cubana*, Tomo II (La Habana, Cuba: Consejo Naciónal de Cultura, 1963), p. 368; Fernández de Castro, "Un Poeta Revolucionario," p. 123.

40. Morales, *ibid.*, p. 368.

41. Cirilo Villaverde, *Cecilia Valdés o La Loma del Angel* (New York: Las Américas Publishing Company, 1964), p. 11.

42. Hortensia Pichardo, "El Club de La Habana en las Conspiraciones de la Epoca," in *Los Primeros Movimientos Revolucionarios del General Narciso Lopez*, Dir. Emilio Roig de Leuchsenring (La Habana: Cuadernos de Historia Habanera, 1950), pp. 59–68; Morales, *Iniciadores*, pp. 12–13, 367–368.

43. Teodoro Johnson (Pres.), *A Memoir of Five Years of Cultural Relations (1943–1948)— Informe Quinquenal* (La Habana: Instituto Cultural Cubano-Norteamericano, 1948), pp. 51–52; Pichardo, "El Club…", pp. 67–68.

44. Basil Rauch, *American Interest in Cuba: 1848–1855*, (New York: Columbia Press, 1948), pp. 78–79; Pichardo, *ibid.*, pp. 74–75.

45. Morales, *Iniciadores*, pp. 13–14; Pichardo, *ibid.*, pp. 67, 71; Robert Granville Caldwell, *The Lopez Expeditions to Cuba 1848–1851* [Published Dissertation], (Princeton: Princeton University Press, 1915), p. 66.

46. U.R. Brooks, "Ambrosio Jose Gonzales," *Stories of the Confederacy* (Columbia, S.C.: The State Company, 1912), p. 284; Lewis Pinckney Jones, "Ambrosio José Gonzales, A Cuban Patriot in Carolina," *The South Carolina Historical Magazine* LVI (April, 1955): 67.

47. Sarausa, *Diccíonario Biografico Cubano*, XI, p. 50; Betty Smith (ed.), "Narciso Gener Gonzales — Newspaperman Extraordinaire!," *Nuestro* 8 (August, 1984): p. 40.

48. Lewis Pinckney Jones, "Carolinians and Cubans: The Elliotts and Gonzales, Their Work and Their Writings," Ph.D. Dissertation, University of North Carolina, 1952, p. 77; O.D.D.O. (J. C. Davis), *History of the Late Expedition to Cuba* (New Orleans: Daily Delta Publishing, 1850), p. 59.

49. Pichardo, "El club…," p. 62; Coester, *The Literary History of Spanish America*, pp. 376, 391–392.

50. Divanco, *El Primer Periodista*, p. 5.

51. Morales, *Iniciadores*, p. 367.

52. *The Daily Picayune*, Sep. 8, 1885, p. 4.

53. Carbonell, *Los Poetas*, pp. 125, 135–136; Ureña, *Panorama Histórico*, p. 333.

54. Carbonell, *ibid.*, pp. 82–83, 87–90, 97; Brian Hamnett, *Juárez* (New York: Longman, 1994), p. 51.

55. Coester, *The Literary History*, p. 409; Carbonell, *ibid.*, pp. 143–145.

56. Pichardo, "El Club…," pp. 62–66; Hudson Strode, *The Pageant of Cuba* (New York: Random House, 1934), p. 93.

57. Ambrosio Jose Gonzales, *Manifesto on Cuban Affairs, Address to the People of the United States* (New Orleans: Daily Delta, 1852), p. 6; Brooks, "Ambrosio Jose Gonzales," pp. 285–286; Pichardo, *ibid.*, pp. 71–75; Ansley (ed.), *The Columbia Encyclopedia in One Volume*, p. 1925; Michael J. Mazarr, *Semper Fidel: America & Cuba 1776–1988* (Baltimore, Maryland: The Nautical & Aviation Publishing Company of America, 1988), p. 39.

58. Mazarr, *Semper Fidel*, pp. 39–40, 44; James M. McPherson, *Battle Cry of Freedom — The Civil War Era* (New York: Oxford University Press, 1988), p. 105;

Caldwell, *The Lopez Expeditions*, pp. 43–46; Brooks, "Ambrosio Jose Gonzales," p. 285; Jaime Suchlicki, *Historical Dictionary of Cuba* (Metuchen, N.J.: Scarecrow Press, 1988), pp.162-163; Trumbull White, *Pictorial History of Our War with Spain for Cuba's Freedom* (Freedom Publishing Co., 1898), pp. 152–153; Graham H. Stuart, *Latin America and the United States* (New York: Appleton-Century-Crofts, Inc., 1955), pp. 194–195.

59. Caldwell, *ibid.*, p. 45–46; Strode, *The Pageant of Cuba*, p. 92.

60. Morales, *Iniciadores*, p. 15; Caldwell, *ibid.*, p. 46; Carlos Márquez Sterling and Manual Márquez Sterling, *História de la Isla de Cuba* (New York: Regents Publishing Company, 1975), p. 131.

61. Carbonell, *Los Poetas*, pp. 41, 59, 72–73; Quintero, "Lyric Poetry in Cuba," pp. 17–18.

62. Villaverde, *Cecilia Valdés*, pp. 11–14; Pichardo, "El Club...," pp. 61–69, 118.

63. Mazarr, *Semper Fidel*, pp. 43–44.

64. Pichardo, "El Club...," pp. 67–72; Rauch, *American Interest in Cuba*, p. 76.

65. Mazarr, *Semper Fidel*, p. 40; Rauch, *ibid.*, pp. 77–78; Sterling and Sterling, *Historia*, p. 132; Brooks, "Ambrosio Jose Gonzales," p. 285.

66. Caldwell, *The Lopez Expeditions*, p. 46; Morales, *Iniciadores*, pp. 20–21; Sterling and Sterling, *ibid.*

67. Pichardo, "El Club...," pp. 119–122; Morales, *ibid.*, p. 15; McPherson, *Battle Cry of Freedom*, p. 105; Jefferson Davis, "Robert E. Lee," *Confederate Veteran* 37 (Jan. 1939): 14; Mollie H. Houston, "The Double Tribute," *Confederate Veteran* 34 (Jan. 1926): 46; Gonzalo de Quesada and Henry Davenport Northrop, *The War in Cuba* (Chicago: Wabash Publishing House, 1896), pp. 19–20.; James Hyde Clark, *Cuba and the Fight for Freedom* (Philadelphia: Globe Bible Publishing Co., 1896), pp. 218–221; Sterling and Sterling, *ibid.*, pp. 131–137.

68. Morales, *ibid.*, pp. 20–21; Caldwell, *The Lopez Expeditions*, p. 46; Brooks, "Ambrosio Jose Gonzales," p. 285; Pichardo, "El Club...," p. 71; Geraldine LeMay (Dir.), *Annals of Savannah, 1850–1937 — A Digest and Index of the Newspaper Record of Events and Opinions — Abstracted from the files of the Savannah Morning News*, V. I (1850), 1961, pp. 68, 170.

69. Ureña, *Panorama Histórico*, pp. 178, 330–333; Carbonell, *Los Poetas*, pp. 39–40, 145, 83; Johnson (Pres.), *A Memoir*, p. 51.

70. José María Chacón y Calvo, *Las Cien Mejores Poesias Cubanas* (Madrid: Ediciónes Cultura Hispanica, 1958), p. 177; Morales, *Iniciadores*, p. 367; Evans, *Confederate Military History: Vol. XIII — Louisiana*, p. 556.

71. Villaverde, *Cecilia Valdés*, pp. 11–14; Rauch, *American Interest in Cuba*, p. 79; Morales, *Ibid.*, pp. 21, 367; Carbonell, *Los Poetas*, pp. 38–39, 90, 136.

72. Divanco, *El Primer Periodista*, p. 6; Ureña, *Panorama Histórico*, p. 230; Carbonell, *ibid.*, pp. 18–19.

73. Divanco, *ibid.*, p. 6; Villaverde, *Cecelia Valdés*, pp. 11–12; Ureña, *ibid.*, pp. 226–229.

74. Villaverde, *ibid.*, pp. 47–48; Rauch, *American Interest in Cuba*, pp. 115–117; Chester Stanley Urban, "New Orleans and the Cuban Question During the Lopez Expedition of 1849–1851: A Local Study in 'Manifest Destiny'," *The Louisiana His-*

torical Quarterly 22 (Oct. 1939): 1106–1108; Consul Robert B. Campbell to Secretary of State John M. Clayton, July 31, 1849, in President Zachary Taylor, MESSAGE FROM THE PRESIDENT OF THE UNITED STATES, *Communication, In Compliance with the resolution of the Senate, Information in relation to the abduction of Rey, alias Garcia, from New Orleans,* June 14, 1850.

75. Caldwell, *The Lopez Expeditions,* pp. 51–52.; Urban, *ibid.*, pp. 1106–1120.

76. Divanco, *El Primer Periodista,* p. 6; Villaverde, *Cecelia Valdés,* p. 48; Caldwell, *ibid.*, p. 51; Zachary Taylor, MESSAGE FROM THE PRESIDENT OF THE UNITED STATES.

77. Urban, "New Orleans and the Cuban Question...," p. 107.

78. Carbonell, *Los Poetas,* p. 18; Divanco, *El Primer Periodista,* p. 6; Kendall, "The Humors of the Duello," p. 454; Fayette Copeland, "The New Orleans Press and the Reconstruction," *The Louisiana Historical Quarterly* 30 (Jan. 1947): p. 262.

79. Villaverde, *Cecelia Valdés,* pp. 47–48; Brooks, "Ambrosio José Gonzales," p. 286; Carbonell, *ibid.*, pp. 40, 79–83, 124–125, 142–145; Johnson, *A Memoir,* p. 51.

80. Caldwell, *The Lopez Expeditions,* p. 56; Urban, "New Orleans and the Cuban Question...," p. 1122; Robert E. May, *John A. Quitman — Old South Crusader* (Baton Rouge: Louisiana State University Press, 1985), pp. 236–242; Leo Wheat, "Memoirs of Gen. C. R. Wheat, Commander of the 'Louisiana Tiger Battalion,'" *Southern Historical Society Papers* XVIII (Jan.-Dec., 1889): 49–52; "Filibustering," *Encyclopedia Britannica,* 1994; T.R. Fehrenbach, *Lone Star, A History of Texas and the Texans* (New York: The MacMillan Company, 1968), pp. 115–116.

81. Evans, *Confederate Military History: Vol. XIII — Louisiana,* p. 556; Malone (ed.), "Mirabeau Buonaparte Lamar," *Dictionary of American Biography,* X, p.554; Divanco, *El Primer Periodista,* p. 10; Walter Prescott Webb and H. Bailey Carroll, *The Handbook of Texas,* Vol. II (Austin: The Texas State Historical Association, 1952), p. 424; Kendall, "The Humors of the Duello," p. 454.

82. "Mirabeau Buonaparte Lamar," *The National Cyclopaedia of American Biography* (rpt. Ann Arbor: University Microfilms, 1967), IX, pp. 66–67; Webb and Carroll, *The Handbook of Texas,* pp. 13–14.

83. Sanchez y Ynaga to Lamar, June 15, 1850 in Harriet Smither (ed.), *The Papers of Mirabeau Buonaparte Lamar,* VI (Austin: Von Boeckmann-Jones Co., 1926), p. 310; Caldwell, *The Lopez Expeditions,* pp. 73–74, 78; Rauch, *American Interest in Cuba,* pp. 147–149; Urban, "New Orleans...," pp. 1131–1136; May, *John A. Quitman,* pp. 240–241, 250–251; McPherson, *Battle Cry of Freedom* p. 106; Stanley Siegel, *The Poet President of Texas — The Life of Mirabeau B. Lamar, President of the Republic of Texas* (Austin: Jenkins Publishing Company, 1977), pp. 144–145; Robert E. May, *The Southern Dream of a Caribbean Empire, 1854–1861* (Athens, Ga.: The University of Georgia Press, 1989), pp. 261–262. 84. Gonzales to Lamar, March 14, 1851 in Smither (ed.), *The Papers of Mirabeau Buonaparte Lamar,* IV (Part 1), (Austin: Von Boeckmann-Jones Co., 1924), pp. 282–284.

85. Lamar to Gonzales, April 1851 in Smither (ed.), vol. VI, p. 314.

86. Lamar to Lopez, April? 1851? in Smither (ed.), vol. VI, pp. 314–325.

87. Caldwell, *The Lopez Expeditions,* pp. 91–113; Rauch, *American Interest in Cuba,* 159–161; Morales, *Iniciadores,* p. 16; Pinckney Jones, "Ambrosio José Gonzales," pp. 68–69; Brooks, "Ambrosio José Gonzales," p. 289; Jefferson B. Browne, *Key*

West— The Old and the New (1912; rpt. Gainesville: University of Florida Press, 1973), p. 116.

88. Lamar to Lopez, April? 1851? in Smither *The Papers of Mirabeau Buonaparte Lamar*, vol. VI, p. 318.

89. Siegel, *The Poet President of Texas*, p. 145; Malone, "Mirabeau Buonaparte Lamar," *Dictionary of American Biography*, pp. 553–554; *The Daily Picayune*, New Orleans, "Joseph A. Quintero (obit.)," Sep. 8, 1885, p. 4; Fernández de Castro, "Un Poeta Revolucionario," p. 128; Hamnett, *Juárez*, p. 128; Ralph Roeder, *Juarez and His Mexico* (New York: Greenwood Press, 1968), p. 110; Carbonell, *Los Poetas*, pp. 97–98, 165; Ureña, *Panorama Histórico*, p. 331; *New Orleans City Directory* (1849–1860), in New Orleans Public Library; James D. Atwater and Ramón E. Ruiz, *Out From Under— Benito Juárez and Mexico's Struggle for Independence* (Garden City, N.Y.: Doubleday & Company, 1969), p. 60.

90. Webb and Carroll, *The Handbook of Texas*, pp. 13–14; Siegel, *The Poet President of Texas*, p. 143.

91. Thrasher to Lamar, Jan. 10, 1855 in Smither, *The Papers of...*, vol. VI, pp. 327–328; Caldwell, *The Lopez Expeditions*, p. 32; Gavin B. Henderson, "Southern Designs on Cuba, 1854–1857 and Some European Opinions," *The Journal of Southern History* V (Aug. 1939): 374–380; May, *The Southern Dream of a Caribbean Empire*, pp. 280, 288–289; Alexander Humbolt, *The Island of Cuba* [Translated by J.S. Thrasher] (New York: Derby & Jackson, 1856), preface; Quintero to Lamar, Dec. 25, 1857 in Smither (ed.), vol. VI, pp. 355–356.

92. Siegel, *The Poet President of Texas*, pp. 146–148; Stuart, *Latin America and the United States*, pp. 197–198; Mazarr, *Semper Fidel*, pp. 54–55.

93. Marilyn McAdams Sibley, *Lone Stars and State Gazettes— Texas Newspapers before the Civil War* (College Station: Texas A&M Press, 1983), p. 215; Evans, *Confederate Military History*, p. 586; Kendall, "New Orleans Newspapermen of Yesterday," p. 780; Kendall, "The Humors of the Duello," p. 454; Jon L. Wakelyn, *Biographical Dictionary of the Confederacy* (Westport, Conn.: Greenwood Press, 1977), p. 359.

94. Carbonell, *Los Poetas*, p. 66.

95. Conrad, *Dictionary of Louisiana Biography*, p. 670; Kendall, "New Orleans Newspapermen of Yesterday," p. 780.

96. Sibley, *Lone Stars and State Gazettes*, p. 215.

97. John Hoyt Williams, *Sam Houston, A Biography of the Father of Texas* (New York: Simon & Schuster, 1993), pp. 283, 287, 294; Alan Brinkley, *The Unfinished Nation— A Concise History of the American People* (New York: McGraw-Hill, 1993), pp. 276–277; Sibley, *ibid.*, pp. 246–249.

98. Williams, *ibid.*, pp. 284, 289–292, 295; Sibley, *ibid.*, p. 248.

99. Sibley, *ibid.*, pp. 215, 251–253.

100. Vinton Lee James, *Frontier and Pioneer Recollections of Early Days in San Antonio and West Texas* (San Antonio: Artes Graficas, 1838), p. 106; Sibley *ibid.*, pp. 215–217, 251–252; James D. Rudolph (ed.), *Nicaragua— A Country Study* (Washington: U.S. Government Printing Office, 1982), pp. 12–13.

101. Quintero to Lamar, Dec. 25, 1857 in Smither (ed.), *The Papers of Mirabeau Buonaparte Lamar*, vol. VI, p. 335.

102. Ernest W. Winkler (ed.), *Check List of Texas Imprints 1846–1860* (Austin: The Texas State Historical Association, 1963), p. 152.

103. Winkler, *ibid.*, pp. 188, 190; Evans, *Confederate Military History*, p. 556.

104. *The Times-Picayune*, January 25, 1937, p. 17.; *The Daily Picayune*, Sep. 8, 1885, p. 4.

105. Williams, *Sam Houston*, pp. 296–297.

106. Quintero to Lamar, Dec. 25, 1857 in Smither, *The Papers of...*, vol. VI, pp. 335–336; Siegel, *The Poet President of Texas*, p. 148.

107. José A. Quintero Marriage License (No. 209), April 13, 1857, Parish of Orleans, Louisiana, in New Orleans Public Library.

108. "John Marshall Quintero," *National Cyclopaedia of American Biography*, XLIX (New York: James T. White and Co., 1966), p. 367.

109. Wakelyn, *Biographical Dictionary of the Confederacy*, p. 359; *The Daily Picayune*, Sep. 8, 1885, p. 4; Webb and Carroll, *The Handbook of Texas*, p. 424.

110. Ureña, *Panorama Histórico*, p 329; Remos y Rubio, *Historia de la Literatura Cubana*, p. 270; Estenger, *Cien de las mejores Poesias Cubanos*, p. 175; Herdeck, *Caribbean Writers: A Bio-Bibliographical-Critical Encyclopedia*, p. 852.

111. Quintero to Lamar, Dec. 25, 1857 in Smither, *The Papers of...*, vol. VI, p. 335.

112. J. A. Quintero, "Review of Verse Memorials," in Smither, *ibid.*, vol. VI, pp. 356–359.

113. Mirabeau B. Lamar, *Verse Memorials* (New York: W.P. Fetridge & Co., 1857), p. 5; Carbonell, *Los Poetas*, p. 40.

114. Johnson, *A Memoir*, pp. 51–52.

115. Lamar, *Verse Memorials*, pp. 49, 173, 176.

116. Quintero, "Review of Verse Memorials," pp. 360–361.

117. [José Elías Hernández (ed.)], *Ed Laud del Desterrado* (New York: Imprenta de "La Revolución," 1858), prólogo; Carbonell, *Los Poetas*, p. 73.

118. Tyler, *Santiago Vidaurri*, pp. 30–36, 47; James W. Daddysman, *The Matamoros Trade: Confederate Commerce, Diplomacy and Intrigue* (Cranbury, New Jersey: Associated Union Press, 1984), p. 44; Herbert Ingram Priestley, *The Mexican Nation, A History* (New York: Cooper Square Publishers, Inc., 1969), pp. 331–335.

119. Siegel, *The Poet President of Texas*, pp. 153–157; James Grant Wilson and John Fiske (ed.), "Mirabeau Buonaparte Lamar," *Appleton's Cyclopaedia of American Biography* (New York: D. Appleton and Company, 1894), p. 598; Webb and Carroll, *The Handbook of Texas*, p. 14; Malone, "Mirabeau Buonaparte Lamar," p. 554.

120. Conrad, *Dictionary of Louisiana Biography*, p. 670.

121. Quintero to Vidaurri, Oct. 27, 1860, Correspondencia Particular de Don Santiago Vidaurri, Archivo General del Estado de Nuevo León, Monterrey [Photocopy Courtesy Dr. Ron Tyler, Director, Texas State Historical Association, Austin].

122. Sarausa, *Diccónario Biografico Cubano*, V, p. 6; Estenger, *Cien de las mejores Poesias Cubanos*, p. 175; Evans, *Confederate Military History*, p. 557; Lima, *Antologia*, p. 269.

123. Evans, *ibid.*, p. 556; *The Daily Picayune*, Sep. 8, 1885, p. 4; Estenger, *ibid.*, p. 175; Kendall, "New Orleans Newspapermen of Yesterday," p. 780.

124. Villaverde, *Cecelia Valdés*, pp. 12–13.

125. Quintero to Vidaurri, Oct. 27, 1860, Correspondencia Particular de Don Santiago Vidaurri.

126. Quintero, "Lyric Poetry in Cuba"; Quintero, "Review of Verse Memorials," in Smither, *The Papers of Mirabeau Buonaparte Lamar*, pp. 356–359. 127. Johnson, *A Memoir...*, p. 54; Fernández de Castro, "Un Poeta Revolucionario," p. 125; Lima, *Antologia*, p. 270; Carbonell, *Los Poetas*, p. 26; Angel Minchero Vilasaro, *Dicciónario Universal de Escritores*, II (San Sebastian, España: EDIDHE, 1957), p. 500.

127. Johnson (Pres.), p. 54; Fernández de Castro, "Un Poeta Revolucionario al Servicio de Intereses Esclavistas," p. 125; Lima, p. 270; Carbonell, p. 26; Angel Minchero Vilasaro, *Dicciónario Universal de Escritores*, II (San Sebastiona, Expana: EDIDHE, 1957), p. 500.

128. Divanco, *El Primer Periodista*, pp. 6–11.

129. Ureña, *Panorama Histórico*, pp. 326–327; David William Foster (ed.), *Handbook of Latin American Literature* (New York: Garland Publishing, Inc.), p. 230; Hernández, *Ed Laud del Desterrado*, prólogo, pp. 9–12; Carbonell, *Los Poetas*, pp. 59, 69; Coester, *Literary History*, pp. 90–103.

130. Hernadez, prólogo, pp. 79–86; Carbonell, *ibid.*, pp. 19–20.

131. Carbonell, *ibid.*, p. 20.

132. Carbonell, *ibid.*, p. 22.

133. Carbonell, *ibid.*, pp. 26–28; Remos y Rubio, *Historia de la Literatura Cubana*, p. 275.

134. Carbonell, *ibid.*, pp. 24–26; Dr. Antonio Iraizoz y de Villar, *La Crítica en la Literatura Cubana* (La Habana: Imprenta "Avisador Comercial", 1930), p. 25; Johnson, *A Memoir*, p. 54; Ureña, *Panorama Histórico*, p. 329; Fernández de Castro, "Un Poeta Revolucionario," p. 122.

135. Divanco, *El Primer Periodusta*, pp. 5–7; Fernández de Castro, *ibid.*, pp. 121–122; Morales, *Iniciadores*, p. 371; Lima, *Antologia*, p. 269; Ureña, *ibid.*, p. 327; Vilasaro, *Diccionario*, p. 500; M. J. Fenwick, *Writers of the Caribbean and Central America*, vol. 1 (New York: Garland Publishing, Inc., 1992), p. 331; Castellanos G. Gerardo, *Panorama Historico Ensayo de Cronologia Cuba Desde 1492 hasta 1933* (La Habana: Ucar, Garcia y Cia, 1934), p. 352.

136. Morales, *ibid.*, p. 368; Coester, *Literary History*, pp. 390, 424, 453–455; Foster, *Handbook of Latin American Literature*, pp. 232–233.

137. Patricia L. Faust (ed.), *Historical Times Illustrated Encyclopedia of the Civil War* (New York: Harper Perennial, 1986), p. 750; Williams, *Sam Houston*, p. 23; Brinkley, *The Unfinished Nation*, pp. 189, 205–205, 230; Jefferson Davis, *The Rise and Fall of the Confederate Government*, vol. I (rpt. New York: Thomas Yoseloff, 1958), pp. 70–76; Hunter McGuire and George L. Christian, *The Confederate Cause and Conduct in the War Between the States* (Richmond: L. H. Jenkins, 1907), pp. 35–48.

138. Brinkley, *ibid.*, p. 365; Paul M. Angle and Earl Schench Miers (eds.), *The Living Lincoln* (New York: Barnes and Noble, 1992), pp. 381, 387.

139. McGuire and Christian, *The Confederate Cause*, p. 25.

140. Roger W. Hicks and Frances E. Schultz, *Battlefields of the Civil War* (Topsfield, Mass.: Salem House Publishers, 1989), p. 7.

132   Cubans in the Confederacy

141. *The Daily Picayune*, Sep. 8, 1885, p. 4.

142. *Ibid.*; Conrad, *Dictionary of Louisiana Biography*, p. 669; Evans, *Confederate Military History*, p. 557; Ted Alexander, *Hispanics in the Civil War* [pamphlet] (Washington, D.C.: National Park Service, U.S. Dept. Of Interior, 1991), p. 2; *The Daily Picayune*, "Died," Sep. 8, 1885, p. 4; Tyler, *The New Handbook of Texas*, p. 393; William Frayne Amann, *Personnel of the Civil War* (New York: Thomas Yoseloff, 1961), p. 124.

143. *Compiled Service Records* (microfilm), "John A. Quintero" and "Juan A. Quintero," National Archives, Washington, D.C.; Henry Putney Beers, *Guide to the Archives of the Government of the Confederate States of America* (Washington: The National Archives, 1968), pp. 73–77; Tyler, *Santiago Vidaurri*, p. 36; "Confederate Commissioners and Agents to Foreign Countries" in *Official Records of the Union and Confederate Navies in the War of the Rebellion [ORN]*, Ser. II, vol. 3, p. 11.

144. Ella Lonn, *Foreigners in the Confederacy* (1940: rpt. Gloucester, Mass.: Peter Smith, 1965), pp. 127, 143–144, 481–493.

145. Quintus C. Wilson, "Confederate Press Association: A Pioneer News Agency," *Journalism Quarterly*, 26 (June, 1949), pp. 160-161.

146. Louis Gruss (Trans.), "Jose Julian Martí on Judah Philip Benjamin," *The Louisiana Historical Quarterly* 23 (Jan.-Oct. 1940): 259–264.

147. Frank Lawrence Owsley, *King Cotton Diplomacy—Foreign Relations of the Confederate States of America* (Chicago: University of Chicago Press, 1959), pp. 87–89.

148. Emory M. Thomas, *The Confederate Nation: 1861-1865* (New York: Harper & Row, 1979), pp. 80, 103; Browne, *Key West—The Old and the New*, p. 115; *ORN*, Ser. II, Vol. 3, pp. 16- 17 (preface); Wakelyn, *Biographical Dictionary of the Confederacy*, "John T. Pickett," pp. 347–348.

149. Secretary of State Robert Toombs to John T. Pickett, May 17, 1861 in James D. Richardson, *A Compilation of the Messages and Papers of the Confederacy* (Nashville: United States Publishing Company, 1905), pp. 21–22.

150. Owsley, *King Cotton Diplomacy*, pp. 90–94, 97–100; Burton J. Hendrick, *Statesmen of the Lost Cause: Jefferson Davis and His Cabinet* (New York: The Literary Guild of America, Inc., 1939), pp. 124–138.

151. Owsley, *ibid.*, pp. 101–107; Hendrick, *ibid.*, pp. 119–122; Daddysman, *The Matamoros Trade*, p. 41; Roeder, *Juarez and His Mexico*, vol. 1, pp. 350–352.

152. Owsley, *ibid.*, pp. 104–112; J. Fred Rippy, *The United States and Mexico* (New York: F.S. Crofts & Co., 1931), pp. 256–257.

153. Tyler, *Santiago Vidaurri*, p. 79; Daddysman, *ibid.*, pp. 42–43, 53; Owsley, *ibid.*, pp. 113–114.

154. *The Daily Picayune*, "Joseph A. Quintero (obit.)," Sep. 8, 1885, p. 4; Ureña, *Panorama Histórico,* p. 328; Chacón y Calvo, *Los Cien Mejores Poesias Cubanas*, p. 177.

155. R. Toombs to J.A. Quintero, May 22, 1861 in *ORN*, Ser. II, vol. 3, p. 217.

156. R. Toombs to Governor Santiago Vidaurri, May 22, 1861 in *ORN*, Ser. II, vol. 3, pp. 217-218.

157. Tyler, *Santiago Vidaurri*, pp. 46–48; Daddysman, *The Matamoros Trade*, pp. 45–46; Lonn, *Foreigners in the Confederacy*, p. 81.

158. Tyler, *ibid.*, p. 48–49; Daddysman, *ibid.*, pp. 46–47, 77; Rippy, *The United States and Mexico*, p. 235.

159. Tyler, *ibid.*, p. 49; Daddysman, *ibid.*, p. 47; Owsley, *King Cotton Diplomacy*, pp. 94–95.

160. Tyler, *ibid.*, pp. 29, 49–51, 53; Daddysman, *ibid.*, pp. 47, 50–51.

161. Tyler, *ibid.*, pp. 54–56; Daddysman, *ibid.*, p. 51.

162. Tyler, *ibid.*, pp. 52–53; Daddysman, *ibid.*, pp. 49–50; Owsley, *King Cotton Diplomacy*, pp. 114–115.

163. Tyler, *ibid.*, p. 51; Daddysman, *ibid.*, pp. 47–48.

164. Tyler, *ibid.*, pp. 52, 54; Daddysman, *ibid.*, pp. 19–22, 48.

165. Daddysman, *ibid.*, pp. 47–52; Tyler, *ibid.*, pp. 52–56.

166. William M. Browne to [Josiah] Gorgas, August 29, 1861 in *ORN*, Ser. II, vol. 3, p. 252; Faust (ed.), "Josiah Gorgas," *Historical Times Illustrated Encyclopedia of the Civil War*, p. 316.

167. Owsley, *King Cotton Diplomacy*, pp. 115–116; Daddysman, *The Matamoros Trade*, pp. 51–52; Tyler, *Santiago Vidaurri*, p. 56; William M. Browne to J.A. Quinterro, Sep. 6, 1861 in Richardson, *A Compilation of the Messages and Papers of the Confederacy*, pp. 77–80; Thomas, *The Confederate Nation: 1861–1865*, p. 186.

168. William M. Browne to J.A. Quinterro, Sep. 6, 1861 in Richardson, *ibid.*, pp. 77–80; Rippy, *The United States and Mexico*, p. 235; May, *The Southern Dream of a Caribbean Empire, 1854–1861*, pp. 251–252.

169. Owsley, *King Cotton Diplomacy*, pp. 116–117; Tyler, *Santiago Vidaurri*, p. 58.

170. Daddysman, *The Matamoros Trade*, pp. 52–53; Tyler, *Santiago Vidaurri*, pp. 58–60.

171. Daddysman, *ibid.*, pp. 53–54; Owsley, *King Cotton Diplomacy*, p. 117.

172. Tyler, *Santiago Vidaurri*, pp. 16–24.

173. Tyler, *ibid.*, pp. 61–63; Daddysman, *The Matamoros Trade*, p. 55; Sid S. Johnson, *Texans Who Wore the Gray* (Tyler, Texas, 1907), p. 109.

174. Tyler, *ibid.*, pp. 63–64; Daddysman, *ibid.*, pp. 56, 85; Lonn, *Foreigners in the Confederacy*, pp. 424–425.

175. William Browne to J.A. Quinterro, Jan. 14, 1862 in *ORN*, Ser. II, vol. 3, pp. 316–317.

176. Tyler, *Santiago Vidaurri*, pp. 64–67; Daddysman, *The Matamoros Trade*, pp. 56–57; Priestley, *The Mexican Nation*, pp. 347–349.

177. J. A. Quinterro to W. M. Browne, March 4, 1862 in *ORN*, Ser. I, vol. 18, pp. 831–832; Robert W. Delaney, "Matamoros, Port for Texas during the Civil War," *Southwestern Historical Quarterly* LVIII (Apr., 1955): 485; Daddysman, *ibid.*, pp. 162–163; Alfred Jackson Hanna and Kathryn Abbey Hanna, *Napoleon III and Mexico* (Chapel Hill: University of North Carolina, 1971), p. 159.

178. Tyler, *Santiago Vidaurri*, pp. 63, 67–74; Daddysman, *The Matamoros Trade*, pp. 57–58; Owsley, *King Cotton Diplomacy*, pp. 121–122.

179. Tyler, *ibid.*, pp. 74–75; Daddysman, *ibid.*, pp. 58, 83, 102; Owsley, *ibid.*, pp. 122–123; John Salmon Ford, *RIP Ford's Texas* (Austin: U. of Texas, 1963), p. 404.

180. Tyler, *ibid.*, pp. 99–100; Daddysman, *ibid.*, pp. 54–55, 78.

181. Daddysman, *ibid.*, p. 59; Tyler, *ibid.*, p. 115.

182. Daddysman, *ibid.*, p. 63; Tyler, *ibid.*, p. 101–103, 107–108; Owsley, *King Cotton Diplomacy*, pp. 119–120.

183. Daddysman, *ibid.*, pp. 107–113; Tyler, *ibid.*, p. 104–105.

184. Tyler, *ibid.*, p. 105–106; Daddysman, *ibid.*, p. 108.

185. Tyler, *ibid.*, p. 108; Daddysman, *ibid.*, pp. 116–117.

186. Daddysman, *ibid.*, pp. 121–123; Tyler, *ibid.*, pp. 110–111.

187. Tyler, *ibid.*, pp. 98, 101–102; William Diamond, "Imports of the Confederate Government from Europe and Mexico," *The Journal of Southern History* IV (Nov. 1940): 499–500; Hanna and Hanna, *Napoleon III and Mexico*, p. 161; J. P. Benjamin to C.C. Memminger, Nov. 27, 1862 in *ORN*, Ser. I, vol. 19, p. 809; Daddysman, *ibid.*, pp. 60–64, 120.

188. Diamond, *ibid.*, p. 500; Rippy, *The United States and Mexico*, p. 239; Kimmey to Seward, Oct. 29, 1862 in *The War of the Rebellion: A Compilation of the Official Records of the Union and Confederate Armies [ORA]*, Ser. III, vol. II, pp. 949–951; Tyler, *ibid.*, pp. 127–128; F. H. Morse to William H. Seward, Nov. 28, 1862 in *ORA*, Ser. II, vol. II, p. 948.

189. Daddysman, *The Matamoros Trade*, pp. 155–159; Hanna and Hanna *Napoleon III and Mexico*, pp. 156–157.

190. Tyler, *Santiago Vidaurri*, pp. 91–95, 111; Daddysman, *ibid.*, pp. 87–88, 103; Albino Lopez to Headquarters of the Military Commander of the State of Tamaulipas, Feb. 28, 1863 in *ORA*, Ser. I, vol. XV, pp. 1126–1127.

191. Tyler, *ibid.*, pp. 86–90; Daddysman, *ibid.*, pp. 88–89; H. P. Bee to Albino Lopez, March 10, 1863, in *ORA*, Ser. I, vol. XV, pp. 1127–1128; J. A. Quintero to J. P. Benjamin, March 21, 1863 in ORA, Ser. I, vol. XXVI, Pt. II, p. 68; Albino Lopez [to H. P. Bee], March 17, 1863 [*sic* as 1868] in *ORA*, Ser. I, vol. XV, p. 1131; H. P. Bee to Albino Lopez, March 18, 1863 in *ORA*, Ser. I, vol. XV, p. 1137.

192. Diamond, "Imports of the Confederate Government…," p. 500.

193. Daddysman, *The Matamoros Trade*, pp. 89–91; Tyler, *Santiago Vidaurri*, p. 91.

194. "Lamar Charles Quintero," *Who Was Who in America: Vol. 1—1897–1942* (Chicago: The A.N. Marquis Company, 1943), p. 1005;. "Quintero (Lamar Charles)," *Enciclopedia Universal Ilustrada Europeo-Americana*, (Barcelona: Hijos de J. Espasa, Editores, 1922), XLVIII, p. 1390; *The Daily Picayune*, "The Picayune: Its Semi-Centennial," January 25, 1887, p. 10; Conrad, *Dictionary of Louisiana Biography*, p. 669; Tyler, *ibid.*, p. 91; J.A. Quintero to Pedro Santacilia, Jan. 29, 1864 in Jorge L. Tamayo (ed.) *Benito Juarez, Documentos, Discurosos y Correspondencia* (Mexico City: Editorial Libros de Mexico, 1974), p. 595.

195. Villaverde, *Cecelia Valdés*, p. 39.

196. J. A. Quintero, "The San Saba Gold and Silver Mines," and "Philip Nolan and His Companions," *The Texas Almanac for 1868* (Galveston: W. Richardson & Co., Publishers, 1867), pp. 60, 64, 83; Edward E. Hale, *The Man Without a Country* (Boston: Roberts Brothers, 1898), p. 104; Tyler, *Santiago Vidaurri*, p. 74.

197. Hale, *The Man Without a Country*, p. 81; Jean Holloway, *Edward Everett Hale, A Biography* (Austin: University of Texas Press, 1956), pp. 134–135.

198. J. A. Quintero to J. P. Benjamin, April 9, 1863, in *ORN*, Ser. II, vol. 3, p. 735.

199. Robert Hughes, *Barcelona* (New York: Alfred A. Knopf, 1992), pp. 267–271.

200. Almirante Director, Museo Naval, José Ignacio González-Aller Hierro to Dar-

ryl E. Brock, June 10, 1994 [personal communication]; Dr. José A. Armillas, Universidad de Zaragoxa, Espana to Darryl E. Brock, Nov. 11, 1994 [personal communication].

201. Diamond, "Imports of the Confederate Government...," p. 503; J. Thomas Scharf, *History of the Confederate States Navy* (1887: rpt. New York: The Fairfax Press, 1977), pp. 758–760; Milton F. Perry, *Infernal Machines: The Story of Confederate Submarine and Mine Warfare* (Baton Rouge: Louisiana State University Press, 1965), pp. 5–6, 81–84, 106–108; Robert F. Burgess, *Ships Beneath the Sea: A History of Subs and Submersibles* (New York: McGraw Hill, 1975), pp. 63–78.

202. J.A. Quintero to J.P. Benjamin, September 6, 1863 in *ORN*, Ser. II, vol. 3, pp. 899–902.

203. Daddysman, *The Matamores Trade*, pp. 91–96; J.A. Quinterro to J.P. Benjamin, Nov. 26, 1863 in *ORA*, Ser. I, vol. XXXIV, Pt. II, pp. 888–890.

204. Tyler, *Santiago Vidaurri*, p. 120–121; Daddysman, *ibid.*, p. 93–94; H.P. Bee to J.A. Quinterro, Nov. 9, 1863 in *ORA*, Ser. I, vol, XXVI, Pt. II, pp. 399–400; Marcus J. Wright (compiler), *Texas in the War 1861–1865* (Hillsboro, Texas: Hill Junior College, 1965), p. 121.

205. Daddysman, *ibid.*, pp. 137–141; Tyler, *ibid.*, p. 123–127; Clarence C. Thayer to Lt. Gen. Kirby Smith, Dec. 20, 1863 in *ORA*, Ser I, vol. III, pp. 930–931; Owsley, *King Cotton Diplomacy*, pp. 125–131; Patricio Milmo to S. Hart, Dec. 11, 1863 in *ORA*, Ser. I, vol. LIII, p. 936; J.A. Quinterro to Maj. S. Hart, Dec. 20, 1863 in *ORA*, Ser. I, vol. LIII, pp. 943–944; James, *Frontier and Pioneer Recollections*, p. 106; Johnson, *Texans Who Wore the Gray*, p. 105; J.A. Quintero to Pedro Santacilia, Jan. 29, 1864 in Tamayo, *Benito Juarez*, pp. 593–595.

206. H. P. Bee to Maj. Santos Benavides, Nov. 9, 1863 in ORA, Ser. I, vol. XXVI, Pt. II, pp. 398–399; Daddysman, *ibid.*, pp. 97–99; Walter L. Fleming, "Jefferson Davis's Camel Experiment," *The Popular Science Monthly*, LXXIV (Feb. 1909), pp. 141–152; Wright, *Texas in the War*, p. 162; Jerry Don Thompson, "A Stand Along the Border: Santos Benavides and the Battle for Laredo," *Civil War Times Illustrated*, XIX (Aug. 1980), pp. 26–33.

207. J.P. Benjamin to General William Preston, Jan. 7, 1864 in *ORN*, Ser. II, vol. 3, pp. 988–990.

208. Tyler, *Santiago Vidaurri*, pp. 129, 132, 140; Ivie E. Cadenhead, Jr. *Benito Juárez* (New York: Twayne Publishers, 1973), pp. 96–98; Roader, *Juarez and His Mexico*, pp. 546–550.

209. Tyler, *ibid.*, pp. 140–142; Roader, *ibid.*, pp. 549–550; Cadenhead, *ibid.*, p. 98.

210. Tyler, *ibid.*, pp. 142–145; Owsley, *King Cotton Diplomacy*, pp. 131–133; Daddysman, *The Matamoros Trade*, pp. 96–97; Quintero, "The San Saba Gold and Silver Mines," *The Texas Almanac for 1868*, p. 83; Hanna and Hanna, *Napoleon III and Mexico*, p. 163.

211. Owsley, *ibid.*, pp. 131–133; Hamnett, *Juarez*, pp. 51–53.

212. Hamnett, *ibid.*, pp. 51–52; J.M. Puig Casauranc (prologo), *Archivos Privados de D. Benito Juarez y D. Pedro Santacilia*, Tomo I (Secretaria de Educación Publica, 1928); "Santacilia y Palacios (Pedro)," *Enciclopedia Universal Ilustrada*, Tomo LIV, p. 196; J.A. Quintero to Pedro Santacilia, Jan. 29, 1864 in Tamayo, *Benito Juarez*, pp. 593–595.

213. Tyler, *Santiago Vidaurri*, p. 143; Carlos González Peña, *History of Mexican Literature* (trans. *Historia de la Literatura Mexicana*) (Dallas: Southern Methodist University Press, 1968), p. 219; Carbonell, *Los Poetas*, p. 98.

214. Tyler, *ibid.*, p. 143–145; Daddysman, *The Matamoros Trade*, pp. 97, 140; Malone, "Morehead, Charles Slaughter," *Dictionary of American Biography*, pp. 157–158.

215. Daddysman, *ibid.*, pp. 98–99.

216. Consul-General Thomas Savage to William H. Seward, July 8, 1864 in *ORA*, Ser. I. vol. L, Pt. II, pp. 904–906.

217. Tyler, *Santiago Vidaurri*, pp. 35, 145–147.

218. Tyler, *ibid.*, pp. 147–148; Daddysman, *The Matamoros Trade*, pp. 182–184.

219. Diamond, "Imports of the Confederate Government...," pp. 501–502; Daddysman, *ibid.*, p. 182.

220. Daddysman, *ibid.*, pp. 148, 153; Rippy, *The United States and Mexico*, p. 243; Owsley, *King Cotton Diplomacy*, p. 133.

221. Diamond, "Imports of the Confederate Government...," p. 502; Faust, *Historical Times Illustrated Encyclopedia of the Civil War*, p. 799.

222. Daddysman, *The Matamoros Trade*, p. 185; Tyler, *Santiago Vidaurri*, p. 149; Beers, *Guide to the Archives of the Government of the Confederate States of America*, p. 133; James E. Slaughter to General Tomas Mejia, Feb. 8, 1865, Tomas Mejia to General J. E. Slaughter, Feb. 9, 1865, James E. Slaughter to Tomas Mejia, Feb. 13, 1865, Tomas Mejia to J. E. Slaughter, Feb. 14, 1865 and J. A. Quinterro to J. E. Slaughter, Feb. 19, 1865, in *ORA*, Ser. I, vol. XLVIII, Pt. 1, pp. 1399–1401.

223. Daddysman, *ibid.*, pp. 184–185; Andrew Rolle, *The Lost Cause: The Confederate Exodus to Mexico* (Norman: University of Oklahoma Press, 1965), pp. 215–217; Ford, *RIP Ford's Texas*, pp. 388–389; Rippy, *The United States and Mexico*, pp. 266–267; Irving McKee, *Ben-Hur Wallace: The Life of General Lew Wallace* (Berkeley: University of California Press, 1947), pp. 93–94; Lew Wallace to U.S. Grant, January 14, 1865, Lew Wallace to J. E. Slaughter, March 10, 1865, Lew Wallace to U.S. Grant, March 14, 1865, J. G. Walker to J. E. Slaughter, March 27, 1865, J. G. Walker to [Lew] Wallace, March 27, 1865 in *ORA*, Ser. I, vol. XLVIII, Pt. I, pp. 512, 1280, 1166–1167, 1448, 1275–1276.

224. Rippy, *ibid.*, p. 244; Daddysman, *ibid.*, pp. 185–186; Ronnie C. Tyler, "Cotton on the Border, 1861–1865" in Ralph A. Wooster (ed.), *Lone Star Blue and Gray: Essays on Texas in the Civil War* (Austin: Texas State Historical Association, 1995), pp. 230–231; Ford, *ibid.*, pp. 389–396.

225. Daddysman, *ibid.*, p. 187; A. H. Cañedo to P. J. Osterhaus, June 4, 1865 in *ORA*, Ser. I, vol. XLVIII, Pt. II, p. 771.

226. Owsley, *King Cotton Diplomacy*, p. 133; Daddysman, *ibid.*, pp. 189–190; Tyler, "Cotton on the Border," p. 232; Tyler, *Santiago Vidaurri*, pp. 29, 145–146, 151–152.

227. Owsley, *ibid.*, pp. 120–129; Lonn, *Foreigners in the Confederacy*, pp. 440–441; Copeland, "The New Orleans Press and the Reconstruction," p. 262.

228. Wilson, "Confederate Press Association: A Pioneer News Agency," pp. 160–161.

229. Lonn, *Foreigners in the Confederacy*, pp, 143–144.

230. Remos y Rubio, *Historia de la Literatura Cubana*, p. 275.

231. Fernández de Castro, *Un Poeta Revolucionario*, pp. 129–130; Ureña, *Panorama Histórico*, p. 328; Lima, *Antologia*, p. 270; "José Agustín Quintero," *La Enciclopedia de Cuba—Poesía* (Enciclopedia y Clásicos Cubanos, 1975), p. 417; José Manuel Carbonell y Rivero, *La Poesía Lírica en Cuba*, Tomo III (La Habana: Imprenta "El Siglo XX," 1928), p. 286.

232. Tyler, *Santiago Vidaurri*, pp. 146–147.

233. Andrew Johnson via William H. Seward, May 29, 1865 "A Proclamation," in *ORA*, Series II, vol. VIII, pp. 578–580.

234. Rolle, *The Lost Cause*, pp. 17–18, 54–56, 136, 223; Rippy, *The United States and Mexico*, pp. 246–250; Robert McHenry (ed.), *Webster's American Military Biographies* (New York: Dover Publications, Inc., 1978), p. 194.

235. Tyler, *Santiago Vidaurri*, pp. 154–155.

236. Rolle, *The Lost Cause*, p. 134.

237. Carbonell y Rivero, *La Poesía Lírica en Cuba*, p. 887; Hamnett, *Juarez*, p. 259; A. H. Cañedo to P. J. Osterhaus, June 4, 1865 in *ORA*, Ser. I, vol. XLVIII, Pt. II, p. 771.

238. *The Daily Southern Star*, New Orleans, "Municipal Matters," Feb. 3, 1866, p. 8.

239. *The Daily Picayune*, New Orleans, February 2, 1866, p. 6.

240. *The Daily Picayune*, New Orleans, "Joseph A. Quintero (obit.)," Sep. 8, 1885, p. 4; *The Times-Picayune*, "Times-Picayune's Course Through Century Molded by Wise Leaders," January 25, 1937, p. 17; Enrique Jose Varona, "Necrologia de 1885—José Agustín Quintero," *Revista Cubana*, Tomo III (April, 1886), p. 328; Evans, *Confederate Military History*, pp. 556–557.

241. Ezra J. Warner and W. Buck Yearns, *Biographical Register of the Confederate Congress* (Baton Rouge: Louisiana State University Press, 1975), pp. 216–217; Robert Tallant, *The Romantic New Orleans* (New York: E. P. Dutton & Co., 1950), pp. 254–255.

242. Evans, *Confederate Military History*, p. 557; *The Times-Picayune*, January 25, 1937, p. 17.

243. *The Daily Picayune*, "Joseph A. Quintero (obit.)," Sep. 8, 1885, p. 4; Ansley, *The Columbia Encyclopedia in One Volume*, p. 1795.

244. *The Daily Picayune*, "Joseph A. Quintero (Obit.)," Sep. 8, 1885, p. 4; Copeland, "The New Orleans Press and the Reconstruction," p. 262; Stewart Sifakis, *Who Was Who in the Confederacy* (New York: Facts on File, 1988), p. 235; Kendall, "New Orleans Newspapermen of Yesterday," p. 780.

245. *La Enciclopedia de Cuba, Poesía*, p. 417; Estenger, *Cien de las mejores Poesias Cubanos*, p. 175; Kendall, "New Orleans Newspapermen of Yesterday," p. 780.

246. Copeland, "The New Orleans Press and the Reconstruction," p. 262; *The Daily Picayune*, "Joseph A. Quintero (Obit.)," Sep. 8, 1885, p. 4.

247. Quintero, "Philip Nolan and His Companions" and "The San Saba Gold and Silver Mines," *The Texas Almanac for 1868*, pp. 60–64, 83–85; W. Richardson & Co, Publishers, *The Texas Almanac for 1868*, preface; J.A. Quintero, "J.A. Quintero, Attorney and Counselor at Law" (advertisement), *The Texas Almanac for 1868*, p. 256.

248. W. Richardson & Co, Publishers, *The Texas Almanac for 1868*, preface & cover page.

249. John Smith Kendall, "Journalism in New Orleans Between 1880 and 1900," *The Louisiana Historical Quarterly* 8 (Jan.-Oct., 1925): 563.

250. Remos y Rubio, *Historia de la Literatura Cubana*, p. 271; Villaverde, *Cecelia Valdés*, p. 12; Carbonell, "Miguel Teurbe Tolón, Poeta y Conspirador" in *Los Poetas*, p. 66; Sarausa, *Diccionario Biografico Cubano*, p. 7; Remos y Rubio, *Historia de la Literatura Cubana*, II, p. 271; Carbonell y Rivero, *La Poesía Lírica en Cuba*, pp. 286–287; Esteban Roldán Oliarte (ed.), *Cuba en la Mano — Enciclopedia Popular Ilustrada* (La Habana, Cuba: Imprenta Ucar: García y cía, 1940), p. 989.

251. Eli N. Evans, *Judah P. Benjamin: The Jewish Confederate* (New York: The Free Press, 1988), p. 320; Francis Leigh Williams, *Matthew Fontaine Maury, Scientist of the Sea* (New Brunswick: Rutgers University Press, 1963), p. 418–420; Rolle, *The Lost Cause*, p. 226.

252. Rolle, *ibid.*, p. 188; Lonn, *Foreigners in the Confederacy*, p. 67; Stuart, *Latin America and The United States*, pp. 196–197.

253. Rolle, *ibid.*, pp. 120, 188.

254. Frank de Varona (ed.), "Federico Fernández Cavada: Loyal to Two Flags," in *Hispanic Presence In the United States: Historical Beginnings* (Miami: Mnemosyne Publishing Company, 1993), pp. 166–169; Mary Ruiz de Zárate, *El General Candela: Biografía de una Guerrilla* (La Habana: Editorial de Ciencias Sociales, 1974), pp. 26–27.

255. Carbonell, *Los Poetas*, pp. 28–29.

256. Carbonell y Rivero, *La Poesía Lírica en Cuba*, p. 287.

257. Ramón Emeterio Betances, "Cuba, revolución latinoamericana" (Paris: Sacado "Revista Latino-Americana," Tipografía Lahure, 1874), p. 20; Richard H. Bradford, *The Virginius Affair* (Boulder: Colorado Associated University Press, 1980), p. 21; W.A. Swanberg, *Sickles the Incredible* (New York: Charles Scribner's Sons, 1956), p. 320; Mazarr, *Semper Fidel*, p. 71.

258. Andrés A. Ramon Mattei, *Betances en el ciclo revolucionario antillano: 1867–1875* (San Juan: Instituto de Cultural Puertorriqueña, 1987), pp. 17, 72; Jorge Quintana, *Indice de Extranjeros en el Ejército Liberator de Cuba (1895-1898)* (La Habana: Publicaciónes del Archivo Nacional de Cuba, XXXV, 1953), pp. 342–384; German Dalgado Pasapera, *Puerto Rico: Sus Luchas Emancipadores* (1850–1898) (Río Piedras: Editorial Cultural, 1984), pp. 106–113, 133; Loida Figueroa, *History of Puerto Rico* (New York: L.A. Publishing Company, Inc., 1978), pp. 277–278; Mattei, *Betances en el ciclo revolucionario* , p. 18.

259. Mazarr, *Semper Fidel*, p. 71 73; Figueroa, *History of Puerto Rico*, p. 276, 286–290; Paul G. Miller, *Historia de Puerto Rico* (Nueva York: Rand McNally y Compañía, 1947), pp. 278–279; Bradford, *The Virginius Affair*, pp. 7–9; Sterling and Sterling, *Historia de la Isla de Cuba*, pp. 90, 95–96; Philip S. Foner, *Anonio Maceo: The "Bronze Titan" of Cuba's Struggle for Independence* (New York: Monthly Review Press, 1977), pp. 19–20; "Lersundi (Conde de)," *Enciclopedia Universal Ilustrada Europeo-Americana*, XXX, p. 163.

260. Carbonell y Rivero, *La Poesía Lírica en Cuba*, p. 287; N.G. Gonzales, *In*

Darkest Cuba (Columbia, S.C.: The State Co., 1927), pp. 7–15; Jones, "Ambrosio José Gonzales, A Cuban Patriot in Carolina," p. 72.

261. Varona, "Necrologia de 1885 — José Agustín Quintero," *Revista Cubana,* p. 328; Copeland, "The New Orleans Press and the Reconstruction," p. 255; Divanco, *El Primer Periodista,* p. 10; Fernández de Castro, "Un Poeta Revolucionario," p. 130.

262. Carbonell y Rivero, *La Poesía Lírica en Cuba,* p. 287.

263. Foner, *Anonio Maceo: The "Bronze Titan" of Cuba's Struggle for Independence,* p. 22.

264. Malone, "Thomas Jordan," *Dictionary of American Biography,* V, p. 216; Johnson, *A Memoir,* pp. 69–70; Victor Vega Ceballos, *Thomas S. Jordan: Jefe de Estado Mayor del Ejército Liberator de Cuba (1869–1870)* (La Habana: Socidedad Colombista Panamericana, 1953), pp. 5–19.

265. Frank de Varona, "Federico Fernández Cavada...," pp. 166–169; Ruiz de Zárate, *El General Candela,* pp. 26–27; Oliver Wilson Davis, *Sketch of Frederic Fernandez Cavada, A Native of Cuba* (Philadelphia: James B. Chandler, 1871), pp. 14–19.

266. McHenry, *Webster's American Military Biographies,* p. 194; Malone, "John Newland Maffitt," *Dictionary of American Biography,* VI, p. 196; Bradford, *The Virginius Affair,* pp. 46–47, 52–53; "Cuban Independence Movement," *Encyclopedia Britannica,* 1994; Mazarr, *Semper Fidel,* pp. 77–79.

267. Carbonell, *Los Poetas,* "Leopoldo Turla: Su Poesia y Su Actuación Revolucionaria," p. 116.

268. Copeland, "The New Orleans Press and the Reconstruction," pp. 256–261, 264–265.

269. "John Marshall Quintero," *National Cyclopaedia of American Biography,* XLIX, p. 367; Webb and Carroll, *The Handbook of Texas,* vol. II, p. 424.

270. *The Daily Picayune,* "Festal. Great Banquet at the Picayune Office," April 1, 1875, p. 1.

271. *The Daily Picayune,* April 1, 1875, p. 2.

272. *The Daily Picayune,* April 3, 1875, p. 4.

273. *The Daily Picayune,* "Public Calamity. Fall of the City Hall Front," April 1, 1876, p. 1.

274. Edward E. Hale, Jr. *The Life and Letters of Edward Everett Hale* (Boston: Little, Brown, and Company, 1917), p. 225.

275. Fehrenbach, *Lone Star,* pp. 116–118; Quintero, "Philip Nolan and His Companions," pp. 60–62; Williams, *Sam Houston,* pp.49–50.

276. Quintero, "The San Saba Gold and Silver Mines," p. 83.

277. Quintero, "Philip Nolan and His Companions," pp. 60, 64.

278. Holloway, *Edward Everett Hale,* pp. 136–137.

279. Hale, *The Man Without a Country,* p. 104.

280. Hale, *ibid.,* pp. 104–105; Hale, Jr., *Life and Letters,* p. 257.

281. Holloway, *Edward Everett Hale,* pp. 201–203.

282. Holloway, *ibid.,* pp. 203–206.

283. Edward Everett Hale, "Philip Nolan's Friends; Or, Show Your Passports!," *Scribner's Monthly,* XIII (17) (Nov. 1876 to Apr. 1877), p. 256.

284. Hale, Jr., *Life and Letters*, p. 227; Williams, *Henry Wadsworth Longfellow*, p. 72; Ansley, *The Columbia Encyclopedia in One Volume*, p. 781.

285. Hale, "Philip Nolan's Friends; Or, Show Your Passports!," p. 408.

286. Hale, *ibid.*, p. 260.

287. Divanco, *El Primer Periodista*, pp. 11–12.

288. Carbonell, "Leopoldo Turla: Su Poesia y Su Actuación Revolucionaria," pp. 116, 119.

289. Divanco, *El Primer Periodista*, p. 12.

290. Clement Eaton, *The Growth of Southern Civilization*, 1790–1860 (New York: Harper & Row, 1961), pp. 275; Virginius Dabney, *Richmond: Story of a City* (Charlottesville: University Press of Virginia, 1990), p. 215.

291. Emergy and Brewster (eds.), *The New Century Dictionary of the English Language*, p. 466; Kendall, "The Humors of the Duello," p. 453.

292. Kendall "New Orleans Newspapermen of Yesterday," p. 779; Kendall "The Humors of the Duello," p. 454.

293. Kendall, "The Humors...," p. 453; Copeland, "The New Orleans Press and the Reconstruction," p. 263.

294. J. A. Quintero. *The Code of Honour*, 2nd rev. ed. (1883; rpt. New Orleans: The Ruskin Press, 1911), p. 1.

295. Quintero, p. 3.

296. Quintero, pp. 3–4.

297. Quintero, p. 4.

298. Quintero, p. 5.

299. Quintero, p. 5–6.

300. Quintero, p. 8–9.

301. Quintero, p. 8, 10.

302. Quintero, p. 13–22.

303. Quintero, p. 11.

304. Kendall, "The Humors of the Duello," p. 452.

305. Rolle, *The Lost Cause*, pp. 192–193.

306. John Smith Kendall, "Old Days on the New Orleans Picayune," *The Louisiana Historical Quarterly* 33 (July 1950): 321–322; "Quintero (Lamar Charles)," *Enciclopedia Universal Ilustrada Europeo-Americana*, Tomo XLVIII, p. 1390; Kendall, "Old Days on the New Orleans Picayune," p. 321.

307. B.H. Gilley, "A Woman for Women: Eliza Nicholson, Publisher of the New Orleans *Daily Picayune*," *Louisiana History* XXX (Summer 1989): pp. 233–236.

308. Thomas Ewing Dabney, *One Hundred Great Years: The Story of the Times-Picayune From its Founding to 1940* (Baton Rouge: Louisiana State Press, 1944): p. 265; Copeland, "The New Orleans Press and the Reconstruction," p. 266; Gilley, *ibid.*, p. 236; Joy J. Jackson, *New Orleans in the Gilded Age* (Baton Rouge: Louisiana State University Press, 1969), p. 293.

309. Gilley, *ibid.*, pp. 236–237; Dabney, *ibid.*, pp. 264, 266; Lamar W. Bridges, "Eliza Jane Nicholson and the *Daily Picayune*, 1876–1896," *Louisiana History* XXX (Summer 1989): 266.

310. *The Times Picayune*, Dixie (Times-Picayune States Roto Magazine), p. 5.

311. Dabney, *One Hundred Great Years*, p. 266.

312. Bridges, "Eliza Jane Nicholson and the *Daily Picayune*, 1876–1896," pp. 266–271; Dabney, *ibid.*, p. 304; Copeland, "The New Orleans Press," p. 258; Gilley, "A Woman for Women...," pp. 237.

313. Bridges, "Eliza Jane Nicholson and the *Daily Picayune*, 1876–1896," pp. 266–269, 277.

314. Gilley, "A Woman for Women...," p. 236.

315. *The Times-Picayune*, January 25, 1937, p. 17; Ansley, *The Columbia Encyclopedia in One Volume*, p. 1073; *The Times-Picayune*, January 25, 1937, p. 17; "Lamar Charles Quintero," *Who Was Who in America: Vol. 1—1897–1942*, p. 1005; "Quintero (Lamar Charles)," *Enciclopedia Universal Ilustrada Europeo-Americana*, p. 1390; *The Daily Picayune*, Sep. 8, 1885, p. 4; Evans, *Confederate Military History*, p. 557.

316. *The Daily Picayune*, "The Picayune: Its Semi-Centennial," January 25, 1887, p. 10.

317. *Who Was Who in America: Vol. 1—1897–1942*, p. 1005; *The Times-Picayune*, January 25, 1937, p. 17; Kendall, "Old Days on the New Orleans Picayune," p. 321; "John Marshall Quintero," *National Cyclopaedia of American Biography*, XLIX, pp. 367–368.

318. "John Marshall Quintero," *National Cyclopaedia, ibid.*, pp. 320–322.

319. "John Marshall Quintero," *ibid.*, pp. 328–330; Ansley, *The Columbia Encyclopedia in One Volume*, pp. 817–818.

320. *Who Was Who in America: Vol. 1—1897–1942*, p. 1005; *The Times-Picayune*, January 25, 1937, p. 17; Kendall, "Old Days on the New Orleans Picayune," p. 321; Ansley, *ibid.*, pp. 1336, 1529.

321. "Quintero (José Agustín)," *Enciclopedia Universal Ilustrada Europeo-Americana*, p. 1390; *The Times-Picayune*, January 25, 1937, p. 17.

322. Michael Andrew Grissom, *Southern by the Grace of God* (Gretna, Louisiana: Southern Publishing Company, 1989), p. 511; Robert C. Wood, *Confederate Handbook* (1900; rpt. Falls Church, Va: Sterling Press, 1982), pp. 92–93; Faust, *Historical Times Illustrated Encyclopedia of the Civil War*, p. 773.

323. James Vogler (ed.), "A Letter from the Commander-in-Chief," *Confederate Veteran*, (3rd of 1996), p. 2; Grissom, *Southern by the Grace of God*, p. 513.

324. Faust, *Historical Times Illustrated Encyclopedia*, p. 773; S.A. Cunningham (ed.), "Confederate Reunion Arrangements," *Confederate Veteran*, XI (Jan. 1903), p. 1; Cunningham, "Staff Officers to Commander in Chief Gen. Stephen D. Lee," *Confederate Veteran* XII (Sep., 1904) 426; Cunningham, "Officers United Confederate Veterans," *Confederate Veteran* XIII (Nov. 1905): 502.

325. Cunningham (ed.), "Moorman Monument Fund," *Confederate Veteran* XVI (Nov. 1908): 594; Wood, *Confederate Handbook*, p. 93.

326. Grissom, *Southern by the Grace of God*, p. 513; S.A. Cunningham (ed.), "Officers of Camp Beauregard, U.S.C.V., New Orleans," *Confederate Veteran* XIX (Sep. 1911): 415.

327. "John Marshall Quintero," *National Cyclopaedia of American Biography*, XLIX, pp. 367–368.

328. Dabney, *One Hundred Great Years*, p. 307; *The Daily Picayune*, "The Picayune: Its Semi-Centennial," January 25, 1887, p. 7.

329. *The Daily Picayune*, "Died," September 8, 1885, p. 4.

330. Varona, "Necrologia de 1885 — José Agustín Quintero," *Revista Cubana*, p. 328.

331. Conrad, *Dictionary of Louisiana Biography*, pp. 669–670.

332. *The Daily Picayune*, "Died," September 8, 1885, p. 4.

333. Webb and Carroll, *The Handbook of Texas*, p. 424.

334. Kendall, "New Orleans Newspapermen of Yesterday," p. 780.

335. Estenger, *Cien de las mejores Poesias Cubanas*, pp. 177–179.

2

Two Flags, One Cause —
A Cuban Patriot in Gray:
Ambrosio José Gonzales

by Michel Wendell Stevens

There was an uneasy quiet in the dark Charleston harbor, a quiet rudely broken by the sounds drifting from the shore across the calm water. At 4:30 in the morning, a loud explosion and flash from the southern shore sent a long, bright arc of light through the night sky toward the center of the channel. A thundering concussion accompanied the burst of light that illuminated the red brick of the fort. Only a brief moment passed as the light faded, when from all points on the shore, the firing of cannons and mortars turned the picturesque harbor into a battleground.

The firing of guns continued through the darkness and into the light of morning. General Pierre G. T. Beauregard, the officer commanding the Confederate and state forces manning those guns, pointed his field glasses toward the fort. He thought of the long weeks of preparation, the hard and purposeful work of soldiers and civilians transforming this colonial town from a commercial center into a military base. He watched the shells arc through the night, then saw the flash from their explosion reflecting off the water and the stark high stone walls. Now as the morning light filled the sky, he focused his glasses on the isolated fortress to measure the success of those preparations. Now too, in the light of day, he could see the flag flying on its staff over the fort. He had served that flag for most of his life. Now he was responsible for the guns firing on it.

In a boat moving across the harbor, another observer took in the scene of the morning's battle with his own confused thoughts of national and personal loyalties. When forced from his Cuban homeland, he pledged his loyalty as a citizen of the nation whose flag flew over the harbor fort. Now he responded to the excitement of the call to arms. As Beauregard's longtime friend and recent business associate, he came in the early hours of the attack to volunteer his services to the general. He foresaw the coming division in his adopted land and now sought his part in this great adventure. Deep in his heart, though, he knew of the scars left on patriots when their adventures fail. He had already shed his blood serving another flag in another place, and he carried the scars of the bullets that wounded him. His service to that earlier cause made him an exile from his country of birth and brought a sentence of death should he return. Yet, he still believed, and would die believing, that his actions were correct. Now in his early forties, a South Carolinian by marriage and a Confederate by choice, his path brought him to Charleston harbor at one of the most critical times in the history of his adopted nation. On this new day, he felt hope for a new cause, a new nation and a new flag. His bond to that new flag would last for over four years of his life and for the full life of the Confederate nation.

A CHILD OF CUBA

History records the events in Charleston harbor that April day as the beginning of a great civil war. The exiled Cuban observing the historic event was Ambrosio José Gonzales. His path in life took its circuitous journey to this time and place just as his energy and desire for change earlier led him on the path of the patriot in his homeland.

The Cuba of Gonzales's birth was a well-established agricultural colony of Spain. Tropical rain and constant temperatures allowed agriculture to flourish, especially the cultivation of sugar cane, then a commodity crop in great demand. The potential bounty of the land brought a steady flow of settlers, including his grandfather who immigrated from the Canary Islands. Ambrosio's father, though born in the Canary Islands, received his education in Cuba. Settling in the Northern coastal town of Matanzas, 75 miles from Havana in the picturesque Yamuri valley of Cuba, his father established a busy life on the island. He was an engineer and sugar planter. He established the *Aurora*, the first daily newspaper in Matanzas. As a teacher, he established the city's first institution of learning. Here also, he married the daughter of a prominent Matanzas family. Ten months later, on October 3, 1818, he welcomed the arrival of his son Ambrosio José Gonzalez-Rufin.[1]

There is little information on Ambrosio's early years, but he must have lived the somewhat protected life as a child of a moderately prominent colonial family. Gonzales's early years in Cuba certainly did not appear to start his life on the path of revolution. Perhaps he developed the questioning instinct of his journalist father, or perhaps a spirit of discontent formed during his education and exposure to other worlds and other cultures. Tradition dictated that proper education of the island's youth came from formal education in Spain and Europe. Though starting his education in Europe, his father sent him to school in the United States at the age of nine. There in New York, he attended the "French school" run by the Peugnet brothers, both soldiers who served under Napoleon as captains of cavalry and artillery.[2] Advertised as a "commercial and mathematical" school, the brothers ran it in a semimilitary manner. While at the school, Ambrosio met another student who would strongly influence his later life. Young Pierre Toutant-Beauregard, who was the same age as Gonzales, arrived in New York in 1829. There may have been an understanding between them because of their common circumstances and difficulties — Gonzales arriving with his Spanish-speaking Cuban background, Beauregard with his French-speaking Louisiana Creole background — two "foreigners" struggling with the English language and culture. Ambrosio remained four or five years at the New York school.

Returning to Cuba to complete his education, young Ambrosio attended the University of Havana where he obtained a bachelor of law degree in 1839.[3] In the period which followed his university education, Gonzales became increasingly disheartened by the system of colonial government. He abandoned his pursuit of law to follow his father's profession as a teacher. Over time he became a professor at a Matanzas college, followed by a teaching position at the University of Havana, where he taught languages, mathematics and geography.[4] In May 1845, depressed by the death of his father, he embarked on two years of travel in Spain and the United States. After his world travels, he returned to teaching in Havana. In the academic and intellectual circles of Havana, he developed relationships with associates who would turn his path toward the cause of Cuban freedom.

CITIZEN AND PATRIOT

Spain's South American colonies successfully overthrew the colonial yoke as Spain struggled to regain its world position in the post–Napoleonic years. Between 1810 and 1825, political and military action in Mexico, Central America, Columbia and the rest of South America successfully established their independence from the Iberian thrones. Even Haiti successfully removed the French. Yet, the Spanish island possessions of Cuba and Puerto Rico still remained as tightly controlled colonies.

In 1823, several political events began the move toward Cuban freedom. In the United States, the proclamation of the Monroe Doctrine closed the

Americas to further European colonization.[5] However, the Doctrine brought little hope of immediate assistance to Cuban freedom since it declared that existing colonies of foreign nations were not subject to U.S. interference. In Cuba, members of a clandestine movement unsuccessfully sought the assistance of Simon Bolivar, the great South American liberator, in a plot to forcefully remove the Spanish from Cuba. In Spain, the reestablished monarchy took stronger control of the island by reinstituting an autocratic government, with a Military Commission, to govern Cuba. Spain took even tighter control in 1837 by suspending Cuban representation in the Cortes, the national governing body of Spain, and directing the island to be ruled by Royal decrees. Spain even took the legal position that their possessions were not subject to any treaties signed by Spain. This removed the protection of the foreign consular officials who became simple trade representatives for their home nations.[6]

The politics of their neighbor to the north, which had for decades indicated interest in acquiring the island, continued to complicate thoughts of liberation within Cuba. Cuban land owners had strong differences of opinion over the merits of becoming part of the young United States. Already a major trading partner of Cuba, the United States brought the promise of a strong market, and it brought the promise of democratic government. Still, a union could simply make the island someone else's colony. It was clear that the success of the United States in the Mexican War, which expanded their territory from ocean to ocean, also refocused interest on Caribbean expansion.

However, the change in the U.S. political climate due to the issue of slavery complicated any movement toward Cuban annexation. With the labor-intense agriculture of the island's sugar production, the institution of slavery easily entered and remained in Cuba. A successful revolt by slaves in Haiti and several uprisings in Cuba highlighted concerns for the stability of the slave population and brought about tighter controls. On the other side, the anti-slavery movement in Cuba called for an end to the oppressive institution. Increasingly, the voice of the antislavery movement split political positions in Cuba as it did in U.S. politics. By the 1840s, annexation of Cuba to the United States without abolition of slavery threatened to add Cuba to the proslavery camp of the Southern states. This could alter the balance of political power in the U.S. Congress and further damage the growing debate over control of slavery in new U.S. territories. For Cuba, it could mean that slavery remained in the culture. Thus for both countries, conflict between the economics and morality of slavery dramatically influenced political debate.

Now at the age of 30, Ambrosio Gonzales entered into this debate and tangled himself in the web of events that would direct the rest of his life. In the spring of 1848, a number of prominent Cubans formed a social group whose goal was the annexation of Cuba by the United States. The Club de la

Habana included a select group of aristocratic intellectuals.[7] Though primarily plantation owners, merchants, and attorneys, the group included journalists and novelists, with several members practicing multiple roles. There is evidence that the movement drew heavily on relationships developed in freemasonry.[8] Many of the members, like Gonzales, received all or part of their education in the States, as well as traveling widely to other countries. This gave them first-hand experience with other forms of government. The members of the Club sought the replacement of colonial government by democratic institutions like those of the United States. However, Cuba's continued dependence on sugar to drive its economy supported the need for the cheap labor provided by slavery. There was increasing concern that Spain might follow other European nations in banning slavery. Abolition could bring financial ruin to the island's plantation owners, and possibly to the island itself. Thus, overthrow of the colonial government, with subsequent annexation by the United States, carried the possibility of preserving, and even enhancing, the economic status of Cuba. However, not all of the members favored the continuation of slavery. They held the hope of U.S. annexation bringing new population movement, in turn leading an economic shift toward industrialization and eventually to the emancipation of the slave population. Already political debates within the United States sought resolution of the slavery issue. Resolution of this heated issue in the United States would resolve it for an annexed Cuba.

In their initial planning, the Club proposed a single quick and ambitious stroke — the overthrow of the government by an armed invasion. The junta proposed hiring American veterans of the recent Mexican War, now becoming available as the United States discharged their troops occupying Mexico. A quick military campaign by these men and their leadership would avoid the possibility of a prolonged and destructive civil war and prevent any opportunity for slave insurrection.

The Club focused its initial efforts on proper leadership. As their prime candidate, they identified U.S. Major General William Worth, who had a history of service in the U.S. Army with broad recognition as a hero of the War of 1812, the Seminole War, and now the Mexican War. He commanded prominently in the successful assaults and captures of Monterrey, Veracruz and Mexico City.[9] He also spoke openly on the expansion of U.S. territory into Mexico, Central America and Cuba. In May 1848, the Club dispatched Rafael de Castro to Mexico to meet with General Worth and offer him three million dollars to lead an expedition to liberate Cuba. With the loss of Worth's personal papers, no record remains from the General himself of the meeting in Mexico. However, others reported that he agreed to the proposal, to be formally accepted after resigning his miliary commission and disbanding his volunteer troops in Mexico.[10] The Club's plan appeared to be off to a good start.

As might be expected in the suppressed political climate of Spanish-controlled Cuba, the scheme of the Havana Club was not the only effort underway to remove the colonial government. In the Trinidad region of the island, former Spanish Major General Narciso Lopez began his own plot. Born in Venezuela, Lopez initially joined the Spanish army in Columbia to fight against the revolution of Simon Bolivar. Rising to the rank of colonel, he moved with the Spanish Army to Cuba in 1823 as Bolivar's success forced the Spanish out. There he married into the noble family of Count Pozos Dulces, who later aligned with the Havana Club. Lopez transferred to Spain, embroiled himself in Spanish politics and ultimately became involved in the Carlist War on the side of Queen Christina. He served as aide to General Valdez, commanded a cavalry brigade of 3,000 men, and served for a short time as Captain-General of Valencia and governor of Madrid. Lopez ended the war as a field marshal and became a senator in the Spanish Cortes. With the appointment of General Valdez as Captain-General of Cuba, Lopez moved back to the Caribbean as governor of Trinidad province in the central part of Cuba. He also became president of the Supreme Military Tribunal, or Military Commission, of Cuba.[11]

As early as 1842, Lopez contemplated the separation of Cuba from Spain, but he continued to support his associate and mentor General Valdez. Following a change in the Spanish government and the removal of Valdez from Cuba, Lopez quickly lost his offices and his political status. In addition, several business enterprises failed through mismanagement and, possibly, through his gambling. Perhaps out of dislike for the Spanish government, perhaps out of a quest for power, he formulated an insurrection that would separate a slaveholding Cuba from Spain and foster U.S. annexation. Lopez reported his interest in leading this insurrection to U.S. Consul Robert Campbell, apparently to seek U.S. support. Lopez set the uprising for June 24, 1848.

The Cuban liberation movement already had a strong foothold in the United States. In New Orleans, the newspaper *La Patria* stirred public support for Cuban freedom. In New York, the *Consejo Cubano* (Cuban Council), linked with the Cuban movement through the Havana Club, actively published a prorevolutionary newspaper, *La Verdad*. The distribution of *La Verdad* in Cuba created political friction between the United States and Cuba. The Spanish government attempted to control the island's newspapers, especially those containing articles critical of their government. Efforts to suppress import of foreign papers led to problems with the United States when the Cubans seized a civilian purser from the American frigate *Childe Harold* who attempted to bring copies of the Cuban Council's paper onto the island.[12]

The membership of the New York Cuban Council included Gaspar Betancourt Cisneros, an exiled landowner, Miguel Tolon, a poet and newspaper editor from Matanzas, and Cristobal Madan, now a naturalized U.S. citizen. Madan's wife was the sister of John L. O'Sullivan, the editor of the *United*

States Magazine and Democratic Review. O'Sullivan expressed the feelings of the young expansionist nation when he coined and published the phrase "Manifest Destiny." He became a primary supporter of the Cuban movement and a spokesman for the movement to the U.S. government. His concept of territorial expansion focused more strongly on the Caribbean islands following the establishment of the western and southern borders of the country following the success of the Mexican War.[13]

In May 1848, O'Sullivan and Senator Stephen Douglas visited with President Polk to encourage U.S. efforts to buy Cuba from Spain. With the experience of the Louisiana Purchase, the United States viewed the political and economic turmoil in Spain as an opening for a possible agreement with Spain that could improve the Spanish treasury and allow the United States to acquire peacefully the Caribbean territory. O'Sullivan received some Cabinet support for the proposal, especially from Treasury Secretary Robert Walker of Mississippi. President Polk indicated his preference for buying the island rather than taking actions that might risk war with Spain or other European nations. Information flowing in May and early June between President Polk, Consul Campbell in Cuba, and O'Sullivan disclosed an imminent Cuban insurrection. O'Sullivan also reported the pledge of support from a prominent U.S. general. In late June, Cuban Council members sought audience with the President. Gaspar Betancourt and Jose Iznaga, recently informed of the Lopez plot by his nephew in Cuba, met with Senator Jefferson Davis and others to seek their support for a meeting with President Polk. Little came of the various discussions when the President provided no encouragement for any Cuban revolt which might jeopardize possible negotiations with Spain. After conclusion of the treaty with Mexico, Polk instructed Romulus Saunders, the U.S. Minister to Spain, to negotiate with the Spanish for the purchase of Cuba, with 100 million dollars set as the upper limit on the offer.[14] However, U.S. and Spanish press releases discussing the possible sale, the questionable conduct of the U.S. consulate in Spain, and the misjudgment of the sentiments of the Spanish government ultimately prevented any possibility of acquiring the territory through this easier path during Polk's remaining term.

However, the politics of the Democratic party, the politics of the President, and the concern for pending negotiations with Spain pushed the President to disclose the Cuban plot to the Spanish authorities prior to the attempted negotiations with the Spanish. Information on the Lopez scheme passed from the U.S. government to the Spanish minister in Washington, the Cuban authorities in Havana, and the Spanish Crown government in Madrid. The government also ordered General Worth to come directly to Washington after taking his troops to New Orleans, no doubt to assure that the volunteers leaving Mexico would not "detour" to Cuba. Clearly, Washington sought to control U.S. involvement in any Cuban-based plot to free the island.

As these discussions occurred in Washington, General Lopez contacted and met with the Havana Club. To cooperate with them, he rather unwillingly delayed some aspects of his internal insurrection to coordinate with arrival of the planned invasion force. There was additional delay when Lopez failed to receive arms shipments he expected. As President Polk shared his information with the Spanish, there were information leaks in Cuba as well. Jose Sanchez Iznaga, a young Lopez coconspirator who described the plot in letters to his uncle Jose in New York, also revealed the plot to his parents.[15] Out of fear of reprisal, his parents informed the government. In early July, the province governor summoned Lopez for an important meeting. Already aware of other arrests, Lopez saw through the governor's plot and fled to the coastal town of Cardenas. There he boarded the ship *Neptune* and sailed to Rhode Island.[16] In response to the plot, the Governor General condemned Lopez to death but took only limited action against his coconspirators.

Undeterred by the setback to Lopez's plot, the Havana Club continued its active plan for an invasion based on General Worth's commitment to them. The United States drew the Cuban loyalists as a base of operations. There, safe from Spanish control, they could utilize the strong interest in Cuban freedom and the support for Cuban annexation to build the military forces needed for a successful invasion of the island. As they moved to advance their plan, Gonzales now became a major player in the Cuban movement. With his command of English and experience living in the United States, the Havana Club selected him to represent the Club and deliver their offer of three million dollars directly to General Worth.

On August 5, 1848, Ambrosio Gonzales left Cuba for the last time as a free Cuban citizen.[17] Boarding the *Crescent City* in Havana without a passport, a crime punishable by death if found by the Spanish authorities, Gonzales embarked for New Orleans. There Worth was in transit from Mexico after his recall by the Polk administration. He also faced a court of inquiry investigating charges, later dismissed, that his private letters violated orders concerning military disclosures. Arriving in New Orleans without passport or his credentials from the Club, Gonzales missed General Worth. He followed the general to Newport, Rhode Island, finally meeting with Worth to extend the Club's offer. Worth, also a freemason, invited Gonzales to accompany him to his home in Hudson, New York, and then to New York City to meet with Betancourt and the recently escaped Lopez. The trip continued to Washington, where Gonzales met with Navy Secretary Mason and with other government contacts. At Gonzales's suggestion, General Worth sent his aide, Colonel Henry Bohlin, to Havana to determine the Cuban organization's ability to furnish the money and support offered. Bohlin returned with appropriate assurances.

By November, the War Department altered the Cubans' plans when they ordered General Worth to Texas. In addition, the election of Whig candidate Zachary Taylor left little time to press the outgoing Democratic administration for support. Gonzales sought this support in Washington through various social contacts. One contact, the prominent Caleb Cushing, introduced him to President Polk.[18] Joined by Lopez and by the young Sanchez Iznaga, who fled in fear from Cuba after his disclosure of the Lopez plot, Gonzales met with a number of senators including John Calhoun of South Carolina, a former Vice-President, Secretary of State and supporter of Texas annexation. Several years later, Gonzales described the discussions with the influential politician and recalled his support for Cuban annexation: "You have my best wishes, but whatever the result, as the pear when ripe, falls by the laws of gravity into the lap of the husbandman, so will Cuba eventually drop into the lap of the Union."[19] Though there was considerable support from the Senator and other prominent Southerners, the politics of the time prevented any general Congressional support for Cuban annexation, especially as a potential slave territory.

As the new Taylor administration took its place in Washington, Gonzales continued his active support for the planned military expedition. However, he also began a quest which continued throughout his life, that of seeking a political patronage appointment. The possibility of obtaining a position with the Mexican Claims Commission encouraged Gonzales to become a U.S. citizen, which he successfully accomplished on March 26, 1849. Unfortunately, this did not help, since he did not receive the appointment.

A Change in Plans

In May, the Havana Club's plan received a major setback. General Worth contracted cholera and died in Texas. With the focus on Worth's leadership, there was little additional activity directed toward raising an invasion force while Worth was in Texas. There are no clear explanations for the inactivity, but some, including Sanchez Iznaga, reported that the Club was unable to raise appropriate funds.[20] The death of Worth certainly caused some wealthy Cubans to withdraw their promised support, hindering the future efforts of the Club.

It is probable during this period following Worth's death that the Cubans approached other Mexican War veterans. Lopez, who spoke little English, and Gonzales, acting as aide and translator, attempted to recruit Senator Jefferson Davis as a leader for the proposed expedition. Considered pro–Cuban, Davis declared in 1848 that "the island of Cuba must be ours."[21] This pro–Cuban stance, his political prominence and the military leadership experience of the Mexican War made him an attractive alternate. The offer, as later reported, even included $100,000 for Davis's wife to use while the invasion was underway. Davis declined the offer, but suggested they talk with a promising and experienced army officer, Captain of Engineers Robert E. Lee. Lee consulted with Davis, then, foreshadowing a decision he would face later, declined the Cuban offer, believing it wrong to accept a commission in a foreign army while he held a commission in the U.S. military.

Preelection interviews with Zachary Taylor already indicated little support for Cuban annexation from the major political parties. Even the anti-Masonic statements of Vice-President Fillmore threatened the plan. The Cubans began to focus more directly on Southern politicians and other proponents of the expansion of slavery. With its approximately one million population, Cuba was about 40 percent slaves. To the proslavery element in the Southern states, the island clearly had the prospect of becoming another proslavery state, or perhaps more than one state, expanding the slave labor population, the agricultural base and the political power of the South. The revolutionaries attempted to use these expansionist pressures to their advantage. While efforts continued in Boston, New York, and Baltimore in the north, New Orleans became a center of pro–Cuban activity in the South.

General Lopez, encouraged by the support of expansionists and proslavery politicians such as Calhoun and Claiborne, began the planning for an invasion of Cuba. In July 1849, open recruitment for an armed invasion force began. Public solicitations raised money in New York to supplement funds provided by the Havana Club. General Lopez became the identified leader of the planned expedition. In New York, the movement purchased two steamers to carry men, arms and supplies for the expedition. In New Orleans, a Colonel George White, who served with the Louisiana Regiment in the Mexican War, purchased the steamer *Fanny* to transport troops to Cuba. White organized some 600 recruits, who were given a $1,000 bond payable by the Cuban government to be established following a successful invasion. At the end of July, ships moved the recruits to Round Island, three miles off the Mississippi coast. Word of the effort to raise an expedition reached the U.S. government. Though the recruits claimed to be emigrants headed for California, rumors circulating in New Orleans readily identified the destination of the men as Cuba. Army General David Twiggs requested instructions from the government on how to deal with this body of men.

Meanwhile on Round Island, lack of discipline among the recruits lead to trouble with local inhabitants. The U.S. District Attorney requested naval assistance to control the rowdy new arrivals. The Navy Secretary dispatched the Pensacola fleet to suppress any effort by the force on Round Island to reach Cuba. Information from multiple sources reaching the State Department encouraged the Secretary of State to convey the invasion rumors to the Spanish minister. The message went out to investigate any Cuban recruitment efforts in key Northern cities. On August 11, President Taylor issued a proclamation directing activities by Federal authorities to prevent any Cuban invasion attempt. His declaration prohibited the invasion of any friendly country from American soil. By the 28th, naval vessels controlled Round Island, and the naval commander notified the men on the island that they were to disperse. Unaware of these events, General Lopez prepared to leave Washington to join the expedition at a "parting breakfast" given by Mrs. Rose Greenhow, the wife of a State Department translator.[22]

Though the Navy took little action following their notice, the blockade encouraged the volunteers to leave. By mid–October, all the men returned to the mainland. In New York harbor, the government boarded and seized the expedition's purchased ships. As the expedition dissolved by default, Lopez lost this opportunity to lead an invasion of Cuba.

In a show of general public support for the expedition and a show of anti–Spanish sentiment, Louisiana and Mississippi newspapers urged the senators from Mississippi to bring the matter before Congress. In January 1850, a Senate resolution introduced by Jefferson Davis requested the President to provide all correspondence related to the Round Island incident. Though the Senate made additional requests that year, the President never fully complied.[23]

The failure of the expedition and the damage to the finances of the Cuban movement caused disagreement within the leadership. Cristobal Madan, president of the Cuban Council, secretly negotiated with others for military leadership of any new expedition. Madan's personal style sought secrecy, signing all documents with a false name to shelter his work from the Cuban government and to protect his Cuban property. Excluded from the discussion and declared unnecessary, Lopez fired off his written resignation from the organization. The furor in the Cuban movement drew in Gonzales as a negotiator for Lopez with Madan. Just when negotiations appeared successful, Lopez sent another letter stating he would leave the New York and conduct his efforts for Cuban liberation elsewhere.[24] The disagreement split the Cuban movement, with Madan forming the Cuban Council of Organization and Government containing most of the Cuban Council/Havana Club members. The new group invited Lopez to join, but he refused, forming his own group, "Junta for the Promotion of the Political Interests of Cuba." This group issued a public proclamation written by Gonzales and signed by him and three other Cuban exiles — Jose Sanchez Iznaga, Cirilo Villaverde and Juan Macias.[25] The editorial comment of the New York *Herald* cited the problems with the previous expedition and concluded: "Upon the whole, this movement appears to be a matter beyond a joke. In fact it becomes *opera seria*." The Cuban government responded differently to the December announcement of Lopez's junta. The Captain-General of Cuba ordered an immediate review of possible charges against Gonzales and the other conspirators signing the published announcement.

Gonzales saw in Lopez the action and drive needed to force the liberation of his homeland and began to play a critical part in the Lopez organization. As stated previously, for all his experience and world travel, Lopez spoke no English. Gonzales thus became the primary contact for the Lopez organization, functioning as Lopez's translator or representative at most meetings. He now clearly set his course with Lopez, and that course would take him back to Cuba.

THE FILIBUSTER

A war of words and wills continued between the two Cuban factions. Attempts to reunite the separate groups failed, Lopez refused the offer of military command from the Council and the Council refused to provide Lopez with military supplies left from the Round Island expedition. Each side took direct steps to undermine the other's effort to obtain financial support for an invasion. In February, the Havana Club requested the two factions to attempt a reconciliation. Their request began splintering the Council.

With the unfavorable climate in New York created by the split in the Cuban factions, Lopez sought support from other sources in other cities. Washington became the initial focus. In late December 1849, Gonzales and Lopez took up residence in the capital. O'Sullivan joined them as did Colonel White from the Round Island effort. There were meetings with prominent politicians such as Senators Jefferson Davis and Henry Foote. In the course of making the political rounds in the city, Gonzales met John Henderson, a former Senator, a militia general, and a New Orleans lawyer. Henderson was a political ally of Mississippi governor and Mexican War hero, General John Quitman.[26] He agreed to support the movement.

At the end of February the following year, Lopez began to organize an expedition in the Southern states with New Orleans as a focus. He and Gonzales traveled through Louisville to meet with newly found Kentucky supporters including Colonel Theodore O'Hara,[27] Lieutenant Colonel John Pickett[28] and Major Thomas Hawkins, all of whom initially met Lopez in Washington. O'Hara agreed to form a regiment of troops for the invasion, and Gonzales issued him a commission in the newly planned expedition. In Cincinnati, they interviewed Captain Hardy, a Mexican War veteran requesting to join them. Moving down the Mississippi River, Lopez stopped in Vicksburg, Mississippi, while Gonzales continued to New Orleans to meet with Henderson, who had his law office in the city. There Gonzales met attorney Laurent Sigur, a supporter of Cuban annexation and editor of the New

Orleans newspaper *The Delta*. Henderson and Gonzales then returned upriver to meet Lopez in Vicksburg. The three men traveled to Jackson to meet with Governor John Quitman.

Lawyer, plantation owner, politician, fighter for Texas independence, brigadier general who led in the assault on Chapultepec in the Mexican War, Quitman was the newly elected governor of Mississippi. Lopez offered Governor Quitman the command of the expedition. It is clear that Quitman was interested, as shown by letters to his former aide Mansfield Lovell.[29] Still, in spite of his history of action and the urging of associates, he declined to lead an effort against Cuba until the people of Cuba had taken steps toward independence through their own efforts. His commitment to his newly elected position also prevented immediate actions. While meeting with Governor Quitman, three Mississippi justices, including Judge Cotesworth Smith, joined the discussions and provided legal advice on ways to circumvent the federal Neutrality Law prohibiting the use of U.S. soil for mounting or training forces for a foreign invasion. At the completion of the talks, Gonzales returned to New Orleans but maintained correspondence with Quitman. In a back-door ploy to undermine Lopez, Madan and the Council also offered the military command of their proposed expedition to the Governor.

During March and April, New Orleans became the focal point for the Cuban expedition. A steady flow of men interested in participating, or interested in raising forces to participate, met with Gonzales and the other parties now involved. Lieutenant Colonel Peter Smith, son of the Mississippi justice, requested authorization for recruiting in his home state. Mexican War veteran Chatham Roberdeau Wheat asked to accompany the expedition and became a colonel in the expedition after recruiting a unit of Louisiana volunteers.[30]

Lopez continued unsuccessfully to press the Council for release of the arms and equipment from the Round Island expedition. The local support the expedition garnered brought in money, and some funding came from Cuba. The organizers issued bonds signed by General Lopez which were sold or bartered in New Orleans and surrounding areas. In mid–April, with Henderson's backing in cash and notes, the expedition purchased the steamer *Creole* to provide transport to Cuba. The expedition obtained arms requisitioned from the State Arsenal in New Orleans based on bond provided by *Delta* editor Sigur and others. Quitman became involved using his contacts to get rifles from the Mississippi government. In bits and pieces, man by man, an expedition took shape.

The Spanish minister took due notice of these diverse activities. He began petitioning for U.S. government intervention like that which prevented the Round Island expedition. Rumors of an invasion force brought U.S. naval movements designed to guard against any invasion attempt from U.S. soil.

This action led to many editorials in papers openly supporting the annexation effort. Rumors led to a government raid against an uninvolved ship in the New Orleans port. The owners sued the Spanish Consul who provided the false information to the U.S. Attorney. Other misinformation reached Spanish ears, but the Spanish clearly knew that Lopez and Gonzales were the movement's leaders.

In the spring, the forces and the plan were in place. General Lopez led a force of about 500 men — 200 men from Kentucky and Ohio, and 300 men from Louisiana, Mississippi, and Tennessee. As their incentive, each recruit received the promise of a bounty of $4,000 and lands in Cuba for one year of service. Officers, many of whom were Mexican War veterans, received high rank and a promised bounty of $10,000. Gonzales served as adjutant general and second in command to Lopez. With the large number of non–Spanish-speaking men in the expedition, the verbal command of the expedition fell naturally to Gonzales. Governor Quitman's role in the expedition appeared to be his agreement to lead reinforcements to the island after Lopez's force established popular support among the island's population.[31] To this end, Quitman obtained information on Spanish troop movements from U.S. Navy Lieutenant Henry Hartstene.[32]

On April 4th, the *Martha Washington* carried the 120 Ohio men and the Kentucky contingent to New Orleans. Colonel O'Hara arrived in the city on April 11th, with Majors T. T. Hawkins and William Hardy and with Dr. Samuel Scott,[33] who assisted in raising the 225 Kentucky men, serving as surgeon of the Kentucky Regiment. A military expedition began to assemble for an invasion of Cuba.

ON TO CUBA

On April 25th, the men from Kentucky boarded the ship *Georgiana* with tickets misleadingly declaring their destination as Chagres, Mexico. A large crowd gathered to bid them farewell, including General Lopez, Adjutant Gonzales and General Henderson. At the mouth of the Mississippi, a fishing boat under the personal charge of Mr. Sigur met the expedition to transfer regulation army muskets, possibly acquired from the states of Louisiana and Mississippi, and 10,000 rounds of ammunition. A government revenue cutter circled the boat as it left the river but did not stop them. At sea, the captain set course for the island of Mujeres, the chosen rendezvous point off the Yucatan coast of Mexico. The Louisiana battalion of about 150 men under Colonel Wheat sailed from New Orleans on May 2 on the brig *Susan Loud*. Wheat chartered the ship when there was insufficient space for his men on the other vessels of the expedition. He planned to meet with the *Creole* at sea. Lopez,

Gonzales, Sanchez Iznaga, Juan Macias and Jose Hernandez, the only Cubans, boarded the *Creole* on May 5 and set sail with 150 men, only delaying down-river to load additional supplies.

There was little secrecy about the expedition, however. The local papers openly reported formation of an invasion force and speculated on when it would sail. Even the New York *Sun* reported that an invasion force was under-way and flew the first "Cuban" flag outside their office, drawing an immediate Spanish protest. The flag flown by the *Sun* was the banner adopted by the Junta from a design proposed by a group of exiles including Gonzales. One exile's wife stitched the first flag. Carrying three broad stripes of blue on a white field symbolizing the three departments of Cuba and a gold star on a red triangle signifying the blood which would be spilled in the fight for Cuban freedom, this simple but bold design developed by the planners of the first expedition to free Cuba survives today as the national flag of that nation.[34]

The lone star flag of Cuban liberation flew over the Gulf of Mexico for the first time on May 6, 1850, as the *Susan Loud* reached the appointed meeting spot. Following a patriotic speech, Colonel Wheat divided the men into 10 squads to serve as the core of future companies. On the 10th, the *Creole* joined the *Susan Loud* at sea. General Gonzales boarded Wheat's ship to greet the men. The expedition spent most of the next day transferring men and supplies to the steamer. Captain Pendleton of the *Loud* joined the crew of the *Creole* due to his familiarity with Cuban harbors. On the 12th, the men formally met their commander General Lopez, and the leadership agreed to distribute arms to the men to calm their worries about possible capture by the Spanish. The *Creole* then set sail for Mujeres.

The *Georgiana* was unsuccessful in making the island rendezvous. After an uneventful five days, she arrived off the Yucatan coast, about 80 miles west of the island of Mujeres. Unfavorable winds hindered the ship's movement, and it took four days to reach Contoy, a small island still 10 miles from the rendezvous point. They landed there on May 7 but found it uninhabited and without a water source. Building a signal fire to attract the *Creole*, they only drew the attention of three fishing boats. Using a pilot from one of the boats, the *Georgiana's* captain spent four days trying to get to Mujeres. The unexpected conditions of life on the ship and the island spread such discontent in the men that they almost mutinied. Fifty or sixty men signed a petition to return to New Orleans. Colonel O'Hara spoke to the men promising that they would return in eight days if Lopez did not arrive. There was still sufficient enthusiasm for the expedition since almost all the men signed an oath to the Articles of War of the United States Army and an oath to the Republic of Cuba represented by Lopez. The local fishing boats brought fresh provisions along with word of the arrival of another American vessel.

After almost missing the *Georgiana* at anchor at Contoy, the arrival of the *Creole* brought the full expedition together. After the leaders delivered a proclamation to the men of the expedition, the *Creole* sailed to Mujeres where Gonzales obtained water for the expedition. The discontent still present caused Colonel Wheat to address the troops again. Before leaving the island for Cuba, the leadership offered a last opportunity for anyone to return to the States, and 39 men requested permission to leave the expedition at the island. The *Creole* headed for Cuba with 521 men. During the voyage, the officers distributed the remaining arms and issued the men a uniform of sorts, consisting of a red shirt with a star over the heart. At sea, the commanders attempted to provide military drill for the men, though all movements had to be carefully staged to keep the overloaded ship in trim.

Several officers of the expedition later wrote their descriptions of life during the expedition. One of the writers reflected on Gonzales's personality and role as adjutant to the expedition:

> A casual observer would pronounce Gonzales a deep and powerful thinker.... Converse with him five little minutes and he will display to you the most erudite knowledge of character and the general world. I shall say that deep policy and mental activity were his distinguishing characteristics.... [On board the ship] He is the embodiment and incarnation of ubiquity — here, there, and everywhere — now ready to intervene, and palliate, and remove entirely, any acerbity of feeling that may spring up among the officers; and again, pausing for hours by the side of unclean privates, to afford every explanation and dissipate every doubt and fear ... I have seen him wearied with the cares and exertions of a hot tropical day, surrender his berth to some gaping officer, and with joy on his face betake himself to slumber upon the hard deck, without even the consolation of a knapsack for a pillow.[35]

Finally, Lopez disclosed his plans to the men of the expedition. They were to land on the north shore of Cuba at the unfortified town of Cardenas, seize the railroad, then move on Matanzas, Gonzales's birthplace 30 miles away. Lopez proposed Matanzas as their recruiting center. From the city, they could cut the roads and bridges to Havana hindering any government response. Lopez expected to recruit and train at least 5,000 Cubans to form five new regiments. In his vision, the army would grow to 30,000 with the expedition's attack on Havana.

Based on their new information, the Spanish sent two ships to intercept the filibusters. Weather conditions forced Lopez's expedition on a more northerly course, probably causing them to miss the Spanish warships searching for them. However, before the men who withdrew from Lopez's expedition on the island of Contoy could return to the United States, the Spanish found them and imprisoned them. The disposition of these prisoners created considerable political tension between the United States and Cuba.

On May 18, the *Creole* and its cargo of "emigrants" entered the Cardenas harbor.[36] In the early hours of the morning the ship moved cautiously through the shallow water approaching the wharf. Without a local pilot to guide the ship, the captain ran aground a few yards from the dock. Fastening a narrow board from the ship to the dock as a temporary walkway to the wharf, Gonzales and Lopez led the red-shirted men ashore. The Cuban port captain, initially captured by Lopez, escaped and spread the alarm. Notice quickly reached Matanzas and Havana. The alerted Spanish garrison in Cardenas set up their defenses. The Kentucky Regiment moved out in search of the local garrison as the Louisiana Regiment moved toward the town plaza and government buildings. Part of the Mississippi unit moved to occupy the train station.

In the plaza, Lopez's men exchanged fire with soldiers in the jail, which they mistook for the barracks. Fire from the guards wounded Colonel O'Hara in the leg. As Colonel Wheat approached the square with his men, an exchange of fire with fleeing soldiers left him wounded in the shoulder. The combined unit tried unsuccessfully to take the Capitular House on the city plaza. Lopez and Gonzales crossed the plaza at dawn to call for the surrender of the Governor, but they drew fire from the Spanish garrison. Two bullets struck Gonzales in the leg. While this incident took Gonzales out of the fighting, it did allow him to be identified as the first Cuban to shed his blood in the fight for Cuban freedom. Several of the soldiers took Gonzales back to the *Creole*.

In anger, Lopez set the torch to the building and then several others as the soldiers changed location to escape the fires. Eventually the garrison surrendered along with the Lieutenant Governor, a nephew of the island's Captain-General. Lopez raised the lone star flag of the expedition over Cuban soil for the first time and followed with a patriotic speech on the coming liberation to the men and the few remaining local citizens.

As they prepared supplies for the trip to Matanzas, Lopez's force faced and successfully repulsed attacks from relief troops throughout the day. However, there was no general uprising of local citizens, most of whom had already fled from the fighting. Reports came that 2,000 Spanish troops were marching to Cardenas in response to Lopez's attack. With several key officers wounded and few volunteers coming forward from the population to reinforce the overtaxed invaders, success appeared more and more unlikely for the expedition. Lopez made the decision to withdraw from the city and move the expedition to the Pinar del Rio region, based on reports of 2,000 Cuban rebels available there for support. Gathering the scattered forces, he ordered the men back to the *Creole*. Spanish relief forces arrived during the withdrawal and immediately attacked. The Kentucky unit effectively repulsed the assaults, allowing time for the men of the expedition to reach the ship. Unfortunately, the expedition left behind six wounded Americans, four of whom the Spanish executed.

The *Creole* was underway at dark, but the overweight ship again risked the possibility of running aground. Throwing out tons of ammunition and moving some men temporarily off the ship allowed it to float free of any obstacles. At sea, a vote of the men went against a second landing. Without the support of all his officers and with little support from the men, Lopez agreed to return to the States. The expedition released their prisoners, including the governor of Cardenas. As their vessel sailed north away from Cuba, they narrowly missed the Spanish warship *Pizarro* and, fortunately for the expedition, the Spanish ship initially overlooked the *Creole*. The Spanish quickly realized their mistake and set off in hot pursuit. Just off the Keys, the vessels sighted each other. Burning rosin, fat bacon, uniforms and the ship's furniture, the *Creole* ran for the harbor. On the 21st, the expedition arrived at Key West, Florida, just 25 minutes ahead, and in sight, of the Spanish war vessel.[37] Described by Gonzales, it was a shark chasing a minnow. Now in the port they appeared safe.

SANCTUARY AND ARREST

Key West, a wild and unsettled town typical of the Caribbean ports, survived on the seafaring life and the stories of ship wrecks and pirates and strange ports of call. It was an appropriate landing site for the Cuban adventurers. Stephen Mallory, the Collector of Customs and a prominent lawyer and longtime resident of the Keys, greeted their arrival.[38] He placed the wounded Gonzales in his own home, where with proper care by Mallory and his Spanish wife, Gonzales took three weeks to recover. The rest of the men settled into an old army barracks nearby.

Spanish Admiral Armero on the *Pizarro* demanded the surrender of the fugitives. Mallory, as captain of the militia, ordered Fort Taylor manned to resist any action by the Spanish. Out of concern that the government might surrender the filibusters to the Spanish, two local merchants held ships ready to carry the adventurers to safer waters if needed. However, on advice of the Spanish consul, the Spanish admiral left the harbor and returned to Cuba empty handed.

Moving quickly, and with the active encouragement from Spain, the U.S. government began discussing prosecution of the expedition's officers and supporters for violation of the Neutrality Law. In spite of the direct involvement of Cuban natives, the government viewed the expedition not as an independence movement but as an adventuristic and illegal effort to interfere in Cuban affairs. Officials of the government arrested Lopez on May 25, just one day after he arrived in Savannah from the Keys. The evidence available to the court was inadequate to detain Lopez, and the judge dismissed the charges.[39] Lopez continued to receive much popular support and vowed to continue his efforts for Cuban independence. The Spanish minister increased his pressure on the government to enforce the Neutrality Act. By the end of May, federal arrest warrants were issued naming most of the expedition organizers. The government again arrested Lopez in June and issued detention orders for Gonzales and the other leaders.

After his recovery, General Gonzales surrendered to Federal authorities in the Keys. The government sent him and 30 others to New Orleans to be formally charged with violation of the Neutrality Law. A New Orleans grand jury returned indictments against Lopez, Gonzales, O'Hara, Wheat, Henderson, Sigur, O'Sullivan, Governor Quitman and other leaders of the expedition. The government set the date for trial to be held in the city, with Henderson scheduled to be the first defendant.

The Spanish government also acted in response to the invasion. The hearings on the December, 1849, public newspaper announcement of the junta were pending, but Lopez's expedition reached the island before a government decision. Acting swiftly after the invasion, the captain-general of Cuba ordered an immediate review of charges related to the publication. Newspapers in the United States carried the official announcement that the Spanish military commission in Havana issued a death sentence for the signers of the notice, including Gonzales.[40] In addition, they ordered prison terms and banishment for four of the Cuban Council members, including Madan, who worked so hard to remain anonymous.

The energy and patriotic zeal of the coconspirators continued in spite of the failure of the expedition, the prospect of the Federal trial or the threats of the Spanish government. General Lopez immediately began a new effort to recruit the men and capital needed for a second invasion attempt. O'Sullivan met with Governor Quitman who still intended to wait for a popular uprising before acting. Gonzales met in July with Quitman to encourage him to lead the new expedition. Lopez and Gonzales traveled in late June and August to recruit in Savannah, building political and social links in the Georgia port and along the coast. In Texas, the movement induced Mirabeau Lamar to provide support.[41] Even during the upcoming trial, recruiting continued.

The trial finally began in late December. Henderson acted as his own attorney. Jury selection began and proceeded with difficulty, but a jury was in place in early January, 1851. The prosecuting attorney Judah Benjamin, later to become the Secretary of War for the Confederate States, opened the trial with an unfounded mischaracterization of the conditions in Cuba:

> Not a single movement has been made in Cuba; not a ripple disturbs the smooth current of life of that people; not a single proof is given of their dissatisfaction with their lot.... The rich are busily engaged in rolling their sugar cane, gathering in their rich crops; the poor are eating tortillas, smoking cigars, swinging

in hammocks, and sucking oranges. They do not appear to be at all troubled by their oppression or disturbed with their lot.[42]

This, no doubt, was an insult to the Cubans who fled their country because of their concern for Spanish rule.

Witnesses gave detailed testimony on the expedition and its background. Gonzales and Sigur were the only witnesses for the defense. Gonzales testified that all actions were taken in accordance with the Neutrality Act and that Henderson did not participate in the actual expedition. The strong cross-examination by Benjamin pressed Gonzales to stretch the truth and show a selective failure to recall events. Jury deliberation began January 20. After discussions that evening and the following day, they reported themselves deadlocked, forcing a mistrial. The government immediately requested another trial, leaving the charges hanging over Gonzales and Lopez as they continued to recruit.

Undaunted by the inability to get a decision from the first jury, the Federal District Attorney began a second trial in late January. Selecting a jury became increasingly difficult. Many citizens did not answer the jury call and, of those that did, most were dismissed due to opinions formed from the wide publicity and the open support shown locally for the Cuban movement. The second trial lasted little over a week with both sides calling few witnesses. General Quitman, after resigning his governorship, interrupted the trial to answer the government's charges and enter a "not guilty" plea in the court. Henderson, still defending himself, spent three hours delivering his concluding arguments. The jury spent only two days deliberating before reporting that they too were deadlocked. Again the government faced a mistrial. Immediately pressing for a third trial, the government began jury selection in mid–February. It took until March 1, and over 500 people, to select a jury. The testimony was similar to the previous trials, and the jury outcome was the same, though even more in support of the defendants.

At this point, the district attorney and Special Prosecutor Benjamin agreed to abandon the prosecution. The government dropped all charges against Henderson and then against Gonzales and the other defendants. The government's inability to obtain a favorable decision reflected the strong sympathy in the general population for national expansion in general and the annexation of Cuba in particular.

THE *CLEOPATRA* EXPEDITION

Success in the court only brought frustration to the expeditionaries due to their lack of accomplishments in other areas. Continuing their active planning for the next invasion, they solicited funds, sold bonds, and maintained strong recruiting programs. Efforts in Charleston, Savannah and other areas in Georgia and Florida drew many supporters and volunteers. Gonzales continued his work to obtain arms, soliciting support from local planters and businessmen. In March, he contacted General Mirabeau Lamar, a former Georgian who became President of the Texas Republic and was a supporter of the Lopez movement.[43] Gonzales reported his success selling bonds for the proposed Cuban Republic and acquiring artillery, men and arms to transport to Cuba. His letter also discussed the relationship with prominent planters and with a "high functionary" met through Lamar. Gonzales described information received on the conditions in Cuba from Sidney Lanier following a visit to Cuba. He reported promises of weapons and support within Georgia. The 1,800 men reported available included several hundred Hungarians and Poles. In a foretelling of his future role, Gonzales took it upon himself to learn the requirements for handling and firing the artillery acquired.

Clearly, arrangements were well in place for collection and transport of the troops, horses, and supplies to the invasion point in Matanzas, Cuba. In Georgia and South Carolina, local planters aided in the movement and storage of supplies and arms. In Florida, Henry Titus supported the expedition and assisted in arrangements, as Jacksonville became a staging area and proposed point of departure.[44] Support and funding for the expedition also came from New York, where John O'Sullivan provided a leadership role. In addition to recruiting men for the expedition, he acquired the ship *Cleopatra* to transport men, rifles and cannon to Savannah. Gonzales sent the money for the purchase in early April. Recruits continued to come forward, and the newspapers actively reported the gatherings of men headed for Cuba.

However, the work of the expeditionaries proceeded under the watchful eyes of both the U.S. and Spanish governments. The Spanish closely monitored all activities through general intelligence and through paid spies who infiltrated the plot. The Spanish spy network actively observed Lopez's activities in New Orleans, and the Spanish consul transmitted reports routinely from Charleston on Gonzales's Georgia activities. In February and March, the Spanish authorities in Cuba closed in on one of Lopez's couriers, intercepted coded letters and arrested several Cubans involved in plans to support the proposed invasion.[45] The Spanish continued to press the United States for action to suppress the filibuster activities. In New York, a Dr. Henry Burtnett introduced himself to the Cuban movement.[46] He persuaded Iznaga and O'Sullivan of his interest in the movement and agreed to act as their agent in acquiring transport vessels. Unfortunately, Dr. Burtnett was in the pay of the Spanish authorities. Within the movement, Lopez's old nemesis Cristobal Madan, whose efforts to control the Cuban movement removed critical support from the first expedition, returned to Cuba. It is unclear what agreement he had with the Spanish government or what information he provided to them which allowed him to return with his family to Cuba.

By the end of April, the grand plan for an invasion to liberate Cuba began to unravel. The Federal government took a more aggressive role in disrupting the movement. Disclosures by Burtnett in New York led to U.S. government seizure of the expedition's ship *Cleopatra*. O'Sullivan received a grand jury indictment, though a mistrial followed. In Georgia, searches by Federal authorities forced Gonzales to remain in the shadows, sheltered by supporters throughout the state. By early May, newspapers began announcing the disbanding of the expedition. In a matter of weeks, the actions of the U.S. and Spanish governments pulled apart what appeared to be the most widely supported, the best equipped, the most fully manned, and the best organized of Lopez's expeditions almost at the moment of its launch. It was a severe blow against Cuban liberation. Still, this latest setback did not break Gonzales's spirit or end his efforts for the Cuban cause.

TAKING THE WATERS

There was no question that the continued failures of the Cuban movement cast doubt on the ability of General Lopez to effectively mount an expedition to free Cuba. Yet the movement, though disrupted, remained strong. Organizations in New Orleans and New York maintained active programs of public awareness and planned for additional actions against Cuba. In New Orleans, Sigur sold his newspaper interest to purchase the ship *Pompero* to transport any future expedition. Lopez committed to another attempt in June, 1851, began gathering Cuban exiles as supporters and swore to be successful in this effort or return to Venezuela.

Remaining loyal to Lopez, Gonzales continued activities in Georgia where the stores of arms hidden there were critical to the new plan. In his travels across Georgia, he sheltered from a rain storm at a local plantation. The plantation owner, a revenue collector, told Gonzales that he had "an order for your arrest from the President" but, the collector did not execute the order, allowing Gonzales to leave the next day.[47] He judiciously completed his travels in Georgia and returned to South Carolina.

After the trip, Gonzales developed a severe fever, probably malaria. He responded to a letter from Cubans in New Orleans that he was taking quinine.[48] Lopez advised Gonzales to seek treatment in order to be ready for a fall expedition, so Gonzales traveled to Fanquier White Sulfur Springs, Virginia, in part because the order for his arrest for filibuster activities made the mineral springs in Georgia unsafe. In the mountains of Virginia, he sought the curative and recuperative therapy of the mineral waters as was the custom and belief of the times. Unknown to Gonzales, the visit to the Springs provided a greater than medicinal impact on his survival.

In July, Lopez received word of a local revolt in Camaguey, Cuba. A small group of citizens issued an independence proclamation, raised the Cuban flag of the Lopez expedition and skirmished with Spanish troops. Many U.S. papers carried the story. The revolt did not last through the month, but it provided a focus for the U.S.-based Cuban effort. Lopez moved to put his plan quickly in place. He sent urgent messages to supporters including those in Georgia and Florida. Strong local support in New Orleans at a Cuban rally encouraged Lopez to proceed with a hurried plan. Continued newspaper reports of rebellion in Cuba provided added incentive for rapid action. Lopez quickly recruited a small untrained force to launch an immediate invasion of the island. Efforts were underway to raise men from the Kentucky and Ohio Valley areas, but Lopez did not believe he could wait.

Then, as he learned from his sources that the *Pampero* was about to be seized by the government on the request of the Spanish consul, he ordered the ship to leave on the first of August. At midnight, Lopez boarded the *Pampero* in New Orleans. Joining him was Colonel William Crittenden, of the prominent Crittenden family of Kentucky, who was to command the Kentucky regiment. Crittenden also arrived at the dock accompanied by a Miss Lucy Holcombe.[49] At dawn, with about 500 men on board, the ship left the port bound for Cuba. A group of Cubans and Spaniards boarded the boat downstream. Off the coast of Belize, Lopez sent about 100 men back to New Orleans on a supply ship to allow room for the men and supplies expected in Georgia and Florida. Stopping in Key West for supplies, Lopez received word of an expanding revolt in Cuba, with the Spanish army moving into the interior to put down the uprising. Lopez digested the information, then committed himself to an invasion of Cuba. Rather than sail the lengthy voyage to Jacksonville for the stored arms waiting there, they sailed south for an immediate landing in Cuba.

Hastily formed, too quickly launched and acting on poor information, the expedition was ill-fated from the start. On August 11, the *Pampero* ran aground as the expedition attempted a landing at Morrillo, west of Havana. After disembarking the men and equipment, the refloated ship headed toward Jacksonville with orders for Gonzales, Iznaga and others to form an expedition to land at Puerto Prince further to the east.

Lopez sent a main force inland to obtain transportation while Crittenden secured the beach area with 120 men, later moving inland to follow Lopez. On the 13th a Spanish force attacked. A counterattack by Lopez mortally wounded the Spanish commander and sent the Spanish troops scurrying in retreat. A second Spanish attack on Crittenden's force also proved unsuccessful, but Crittenden decided to retreat back to the coast. Lopez, meanwhile, moved into the countryside. On the march they learned that the Spanish had already suppressed the reported uprisings.

The Spanish continued to harass Lopez's small force. One of their attacks cost the life of another Spanish general, but the Spanish eventually drove Lopez's force into the hills. After days without food and suffering from exposure, the bulk of Lopez's force surrendered. The Spanish pursuit finally captured Lopez on the 29th. Crittenden maintained his position on the coast for several days but could not link with Lopez in the interior. He and 49 of his men withdrew from the island and headed for Florida. Unfortunately, the Spanish captured them at sea and returned them to Cuba.[50]

While recuperating from his illness, Gonzales received word of Lopez's precipitous action and hurried south to assemble the expedition force. There was much dissension in Jacksonville and Savannah when the expeditionaries learned that Lopez landed without them. The *Pampero* reached Jacksonville around the 17th. Meanwhile in New Orleans, the Kentucky Regiment waited for transportation. Gonzales continued his efforts to recruit more men, even as the attempts continued to embark reinforcements for Lopez. While drumming up support in Charleston, he received the news of Lopez's capture. Then the U.S. government stepped in again by issuing a warrant for Gonzales's arrest.

In Cuba, the government moved swiftly to end any future threat from General Lopez and his followers. With Lopez already carrying a sentence of death from his earlier revolutionary efforts, there was little need for a trial. The Spanish sent him swiftly to Havana where, in the public square, they put him to death by garrote. At Atares Castle in Havana, Spanish soldiers forced Crittenden and his men from their cells and shot them down in the public yard outside the prison.

The invasion of Cuba caused international tension. In New Orleans, the news of Lopez's death led to riots, and a mob attacked and burned the Spanish consulate. The British and the French added to the tension when they sent a naval force into the Caribbean to prevent further landings in Cuba by what they called "adventurers."[51] Their primary concern was that Spain might lose the strategically important Cuban colony to the United States. The U.S. government responded strongly that it did not intend to have its citizens watched by these foreign nations. The tension between Spain and the United States continued for months as the United States attempted to negotiate for the survivors of the Lopez expedition. The Fillmore administration, through Daniel Webster and later Edward Everett, pleaded with Spain for release and return of the American prisoners.

In the United States, the supporters of Cuban independence voiced serious concerns about the motivations of the government. They questioned the Taylor and Fillmore administrations and challenged the repeated Federal government actions to prevent or hinder the filibuster expeditions. The movement depended in large part on the support it drew throughout the Southern states. In Congress, support from Southern senators and congressmen continued. Yet the Southern presidents and their administrations seemed obsessed with stopping the liberation of Cuba.

THE CAUSE OF OUR OWN DEAR LAND

The death of Lopez was a severe blow to the filibuster movement but not a fatal one. Since most of the major organizers missed Lopez's doomed invasion, the driving revolutionary spirit remained alive and well in the United States. The Lopez wing of the Cuban patriots allied with southern supporters to organize a secret society, "Order of the Lone Star," with John Quitman as a leader in the governing council and Ambrosio Gonzales, in New York, as the military leader. O'Sullivan and O'Hara continued active roles also. The Order planned a new invasion for June, 1852, to coincide with an internal Cuban insurrection planned by Lopez's brother-in-law. However, the Cuban revolt never occurred, and the Lone Star organization did not launch its proposed invasion.[52] Still, the group remained active in political movements, held public meetings and parades and organized and drilled military units. With their supporting newspapers and presses, they published broad appeals for public support.

On the anniversary of Lopez's death, Gonzales published a widely distributed pamphlet *Manifesto on Cuban Affairs Addressed to the People of the United States.* Written while Gonzales rested at the resort springs in Warrenton, Virginia, the manuscript was a political defense of the Cuban filibuster movement. His rhetorical argument openly compared the Cuban effort to the American Revolution and called for American support.

> Cuba, knowing no rights, and groaning under oppressions a thousand times more galling [than colonial America], has sought the individual aid of a neighboring republican people, heirs to the liberties won by the colonies, and to the destiny they were called to fulfill.[53]

The *Manifesto* provided a history of the liberation movement and the two Lopez expeditions to Cuba. The lengthy manuscript called for public support in the face of the U.S. government's resistance to the liberation of Cuba from the Spanish, which he characterized as a failure to support basic human rights.

In his inaugural address of March, 1853, newly elected President Franklin Pierce spoke openly and favorably of expansionism, providing encouragement to the Cuban movement. Yet Pierce appeared to dash any hope of governmental support for taking Cuba by force of arms. References in his speech to "the cultivation of relations of peace and amity with all nations" gave a mixed message against actions potentially damaging to future alliances with Spain or other European powers. Still, throughout 1853 the Cuban movement gathered money, arms and men. The effort centered on John Quitman and his willingness to lead an expedition. He reportedly signed a contract with the New York junta which provided a one million dollar bonus for a successful invasion. He continued a lengthy exchange of views with the Cubans and other associates. Quitman traveled to New York; Gonzales traveled to New Orleans and to meetings with Quitman. In meetings with President Pierce in mid–1853, Quitman seemed encouraged by apparent administration support. The Pierce administration's diplomatic appointments of Cuban liberation supporters Pierre Soule to Spain and John O'Sullivan to Portugal appeared to foster a proexpansionist position.

There was also considerable grassroots support for the filibuster effort. Politicians in Texas and Alabama openly spoke in favor of the movement. Alexander Stephens of Georgia supported U.S. action. John Thrasher, an American journalist who was an original member of the Havana Club, was now in New York drumming up support.[54] Mansfield Lovell, Quitman's former military aide, joined the effort. Many of the men from the 1851 expedition also remained active. O'Hara and Pickett continued their recruiting in Kentucky. Chatham Wheat continued to support an expedition even after moving to California to start a law practice. Macias maintained an active recruiting program in Savannah. The efforts accumulated perhaps the largest and potentially most successful force. Contemporary accounts reported that the plan called for 200,000 men, and, perhaps overly optimistic, reported three-fourths of this number available by 1854.

Actions of the Spanish government also raised concerns in the movement and pushed them toward action. Efforts in Cuba to control the illegal slave trade, along with certain freedoms granted to some social classes, gave the appearance of sympathy for emancipation of slaves on the island. This worried supporters looking to expand the political interests of the proslavery states. There were more direct insults also. The Spanish, well aware that the independence movement continued, built up and maintained an extensive spy network to obtain information. The Spanish passed appropriate information to the U.S. government to encourage its continued intervention in any actions against Cuba.

Political support for a Cuban invasion continued also. Within the Pierce administration, there was still the hope that the Spanish would agree to the purchase of the island or that an internal revolt in Cuba would throw out the Spanish. These actions did not satisfy the expansionists or their Cuban supporters. In the summer of 1854, John Slidell, a senator from Louisiana and brother-in-law of Pierre G. T. Beauregard, introduced a motion to suspend the Neutrality Law and remove the legal penalty for any invasion of Cuba launched from U.S. soil. He received support from fellow Louisiana Senator Judah Benjamin, the prosecutor in the earlier filibuster trials. The liberation movement appeared to be ready for its best attempt to free Cuba.

Then in May 1854, President Pierce issued a proclamation openly directed at the current filibuster movement. His administration exhausted itself in the debate and passage of the Kansas-Nebraska Act. Any perceived effort on his part to acquire territory that would change the delicate and strained balance of free and slave territory would severely damage support for Pierce and for his party. The proclamation was a severe blow to the movement. In June, the government brought Quitman, Henderson, Thrasher and others before a grand jury in New Orleans. Though the jury recommended no action, the judge took it upon himself to place the men under a legal bond which required compliance with the Neutrality Law for the next nine months.[55]

Regardless, preparations for an invasion continued. By September, the junta acquired a ship, artillery and further supplies. The expedition appeared to be ready to sail in November or early December. However, the political climate grew more and more unfavorable.

In October 1854 Ambassador Soule met in Ostend, Belgium, with James Buchanan, minister to Britain, and James Mason, minister to France. Out of this meeting came the "Ostend Manifesto," declaring that the security of the United States justified the acquisition of Cuba by other means if it could not be purchased from Spain. As the news of the document reached the European and American press, the dramatic and negative responses forced the Pierce administration to drop proposals to acquire Cuba. In the United States, the negative view of the Kansas-Nebraska Act and the Ostend Manifesto led to the Democrats' loss of 66 northern congressional seats and the accompanying damage to the party.

With the coming of the new year, the long-developing plans began to come apart. In Cuba, an informant provided names of Cuban supporters to the Cuban government. Arrests, and at least one execution, followed. In the United States, the Spanish continued active pressure on the government for action against the filibuster movement. Within the movement, various factions sparred for leadership. In Georgia, Domingo de Goicouria, a Cuban exile on the editorial board of *La Verdad*, interfered with recruiting and fund-raising efforts and launched an unsuccessful invasion of his own. The logistics of men and material provided its own drain on the leadership's energy. Quitman's interest though sincere was slow to develop. The focus of the junta on his leadership alone slowed the efforts to develop the expedition. The losses suffered by the Democrats in the 1854 election and the actions taken by the previously supportive Pierce administration added their adverse effects to the political environment.

In March 1855 the President summoned Quitman to the White House. Though the parties did not disclose the nature of the conference, the meeting had a telling effect on Quitman. He backed out of his arrangements with the Cubans and offered his resignation to the junta in April.[56] Millions of dollars raised from Cuban "bonds" remained unspent in support of the expedition and remained largely unaccounted for in available records. Financial backers who were promised refunds that did not come became alienated and distrusted any further requests for support. Even with the strong and wide-ranging support throughout the United States and Cuba, the plan collapsed. Perhaps it had simply taken too long, or perhaps it was lack of a strong and committed leadership. Though the movement for Cuban freedom continued, its strength and notoriety declined. It was soon overshadowed by the internal struggle within the United States. After years spent in preparation, the dream which drew so much of Gonzales's energy and effort faded.

BUREAUCRAT AND HUSBAND

While he immersed himself in the support for the Cuban independence movement, Gonzales was not without other directions for his energy. He continued to court personal political favor and patronage while seeking support for the Cuban effort. Following President Pierce's election in 1852, Gonzales began a personal effort to obtain a diplomatic post in the new administration, drawing support from his contacts acquired in the South. Drawing on his earlier associations with influential Southern politicians in Washington, he called on Jefferson Davis, the new Secretary of War, and Caleb Cushing, now Attorney General. He obtained the support of Senator Slidell, who unsuccessfully recommended Gonzales for a State Department post in early 1853.

Success seemed closer when Pierre Soule recommended Gonzales as the Secretary of the Legation to France while General Dix was under consideration as minister to France. In a letter to Secretary Davis, Gonzales thanked him for his earlier support of Lopez and indicated interest in becoming General Dix's secretary in Paris or in becoming the Charge to Venezuela.[57] However, O'Sullivan counseled Dix against accepting the post, and politics delayed a decision from the government. With O'Sullivan representing Dix in a meeting with the President, the discussions eventually led to the mutual decision not to appoint Dix to the post. This left Gonzales without the patronage position he sought.

Finally in 1854, Slidell, the future Confederate diplomat, was instrumental with others in getting a minor clerk, or possibly a translator, position for Gonzales at the State Department. This work occupied his time and provided a small income while he awaited the development of the grand scheme for Cuban independence.

Possibly during one of his early recruiting drives for the independence movement, or perhaps while hiding in South Carolina after the failure of the 1851 *Cleopatra* expedition, Gonzales established a friendship with William Elliott, a wealthy South Carolina low country planter. Elliott's father reportedly produced the first successful crop of cotton in South Carolina and, thus in the United States, on Hilton Head Island around 1790.[58] Gonzales exchanged correspondence with the family in 1854 at their plantation "Oak Lawn" near Adams Run, South Carolina. He visited with them at various locations around the country, including White Sulfur Springs, Sarasota, and Washington. In March, 1855, Elliott wrote to his wife during a visit to Washington where he and two of his daughters were spectators at the current legislative session: "We have seen Gonzales frequently. He visits in the best circles ... has some employment in the Secty. of State's office which gives him a moderate income — and appears to have the respect of the principle people."[59]

Gonzales's continental style no doubt impressed the Elliott daughters. There were two unmarried daughters closer to Gonzales's age of 37. However, at some point he developed an interest in Elliott's youngest daughter, whom he first met when she was only 15 years old. Despite the age difference, the correspondence they exchanged carried the classic marks of sincere love letters. Harriet, his "Hattie," received letters of longing and emotion from her "Gonzie." It appears she responded in kind. William Elliott did not discourage the relationship, and, in December 1855, Gonzales and Harriet Elliott became engaged.

Gonzales returned to his job, now at the Patent Office in Washington, maintaining his political and social connections there. In January he visited with Davis and his wife, met their new daughter and discussed Cuban politics. A few days later he visited with the President's wife at the White House.[60] He was a frequent invitee to diplomatic functions of the President.

In April, he visited South Carolina again. There at Oak Lawn, one of the Elliott plantations, he married his "Hattie," now a more mature 16 years old. For the next few years, they settled into Washington where Gonzales, who continued to be called "General," and his new wife moved in the city's social circle, visiting with associates and continuing efforts to acquire a political or diplomatic position. There were visits with President Pierce and Secretary Davis and political and social dinners to attend, with side trips to Virginia's mineral springs and other travels. In her letters home, his wife often described the social events with the President and Secretary Davis. She also reported the inside gossip she heard, such as the report that Gonzales was soon to be made governor of Cuba.[61]

In the spring of 1857, Hattie and Gonzie welcomed their first child, a son Ambrosio José, born at one of the Elliott estates. Through the summer, Gonzales continued his search for a political appointment with the new

Buchanan administration. His exchange of correspondence with Hattie showed the strain and frustration accompanying their separation and his unsuccessful efforts to find a position. He obtained endorsements for the diplomatic mission to Chile through letters of recommendation from senators, representatives and prominent citizens of nine Southern states, including endorsements of former associates Davis, Quitman, Mallory, Slidell and Beauregard, as well as new support from Robert Toombs of Georgia, Clement Clay of Alabama, Tom Rusk of Texas, and the mayor and alderman of Savannah. His father-in-law also used his Washington contacts, meeting with Mirabeau Lamar, now minister to Nicaragua. Gonzales only received offers of several minor positions but, apparently hoping for something better, he declined these offers.

Gonzales spent the summer of 1858 with his family on Edisto Island, the summer seaside retreat of the wealthy planter families. In August his second son arrived, but the infant's poor health required medical care. The welfare of his family appeared to be his primary concern. He remained on Edisto from May to November, apparently without any specific employment.

His active efforts for Cuban independence declined as his family, or perhaps his employment, placed demands on him. Still his correspondence and his letters to newspapers clearly show his thoughts were directed toward Cuba. Gonzales remained optimistic about his future and continued his correspondence with other Cuban expatriots and contacts. However, the increasing turmoil in the United States began to take on the appearance of a revolution itself. The political response to the Kansas-Nebraska Act, the vocal increase of the abolitionist movement, and the widening philosophical separation between the northern and southern states continued to raise the level of tension in the country. In his southern environment, the former revolutionary clearly saw the increased alienation that the southern states felt for the Federal government.

As a spirit of revolution pervaded the South at the close of the decade, there were business opportunities to be seized. Gonzales took advantage of this environment as he became a weapons salesman for the Maynard Arms Company of Massachusetts. He began showing and selling their newly designed rifle and other services to various Southern legislatures. He also became an agent of the LeMat revolver. Patented in 1856 by a New Orleans physician, this formidable weapon was a 42-caliber revolver with nine chambers and a second barrel for a single 12-gauge shotgun cartridge.[62] Captain Pierre Beauregard was an apparent partner in the enterprise. Though still in the Army and about to become the Superintendent of West Point, the old schoolmate expressed his excitement for the prospect of increased sales of the revolver "... now that southern blood is up...."[63]

In November 1860, a local newspaper reported Gonzales's demonstration of the Maynard repeating rifle and the LeMat revolver in Milledgeville, Georgia. He reported that sales there netted him a profit of $300.[64] He also worked with his brother-in-law Ralph Elliott, now a captain in the South Carolina militia, to encourage similar interest in their home state. Gonzales corresponded directly with Governor Gist of South Carolina, sending him a brochure from the Maynard Gun works concerning their technique for converting muskets to breech-loading rifles.[65]

Still, Gonzales — the "General" — felt that there was a calling for him in the military. The wounds from his Cuban adventure either faded from his memory or infected him with military adventure. With South Carolina becoming the center of action for the forthcoming drama, he wanted to play a part on that stage. On November 11, 1859, Gonzales offered his personal service to the State of South Carolina.[66]

In mid–December the South Carolina State Convention met in Charleston to consider secession. Gonzales, in his role as a businessman, quickly moved to the center of controversy. Arriving in Charleston as an "agent for the Maynard arms, and for the Le Mot [sic] grape shot revolver,"[67] he took the opportunity to obtain orders for his companies. He now worked with newly elected Governor Francis Pickens, whose wife had bid farewell to Crittenden and Lopez from the New Orleans dock as they embarked on their fatal voyage. By late December, Gonzales successfully sold almost $2,000 worth of Maynard rifles to the state.

On December 20, the South Carolina legislature dissolved "the Union now subsisting" with the United States. As the politics of secession swirled around him, Gonzales found himself allied with a new power. His long associations with the Southern states and with many Southern leaders, his long opposition to coercive political controls, and his new family of South Carolina lineage drew him to the Southern cause and the new Confederacy. Here he would find a new direction for his adventurous spirit.

THE VOLUNTEER

In January 1861, the arrival of the Federal steamship *Star of the West* in Charleston harbor drew fire from cannons manned by Citadel Cadets. The elevation of the political situation with the secession of additional states led to formation of the Confederate States of America. Gonzales knew well the newly elected President, his friend and associate, Jefferson Davis. He also knew well the new nation's Attorney General, Judah Benjamin, and its Secretary of the Navy, Stephen Mallory. As the new nation attempted to secure its stretched borders, newly commissioned Brigadier General Pierre Beauregard of the Provisional Confederate Army assumed command of troops in

Charleston. Beauregard faced the daunting task of coordinating the polyglot force assembled there to develop a cohesive defense of this important city and state against any Federal threat.

Gonzales immediately offered his services to his old friend. Gonzales's personal respect for his former schoolmate and partner was obvious. In May, 1860, he had named his third son Alfonso Beauregard. However, with the wealth of politically prominent men seeking Beauregard's favor, there was no immediate need for Gonzales's personal services. This situation was only temporary.

After months of political posturing, the disagreement that led to South Carolina's secession and the formation of the Confederate States moved to force of arms. Facing Beauregard militarily in Charleston harbor was U.S. Colonel Robert Anderson, who had served as Beauregard's artillery instructor at West Point.[68] Anderson inadvertently contributed to the political crisis by removing his troops from Fort Moultrie to the island fortification of Fort Sumter in the center of the harbor. The new U.S. president, Abraham Lincoln, threatened to supply and even reinforce the garrison there. This proved unacceptable to the new Confederate government.

In the early morning of April 12, 1861, Gonzales awakened to the sound of cannon fire from the direction of Charleston. Dressing quickly, he boarded a freight train passing close to the Elliott plantation where he resided. Without knowing how deeply the decision committed him, he hurried to Charleston with his Maynard rifle to offer his assistance to the Confederate commander and join the Southern cause.

Beauregard took advantage of the offer and assigned Gonzales as Assistant Adjutant and Inspector General on the staff of Major General Milledge Bonham, who commanded the Army of South Carolina. Bonham's assignment was to establish defensive positions on Morris Island for the expected Federal attack on the city. With Bonham, Gonzales crossed the harbor by boat during the bombardment of Fort Sumter to land at Cummings Point. From his position on Morris Island, Gonzales witnessed the surrender of the Federal fort. With the cease fire, Confederate naval Captain Hartstene, a native of South Carolina who as a Federal naval officer provided intelligence for General Quitman, piloted the boat which carried the Federal garrison out of the harbor.

Beauregard's novice but victorious force of militia, provisional army and civilian volunteers received the thanks of the city and the new nation. The Charleston papers duly recognized Beauregard and his regular army staff, which included future Confederate generals David Jones and S.D. Lee, and his volunteer staff John Manning, James Chestnut, Louis Wigfall, Roger Pryor, William Porcher Miles, Alexander Chisholm and Ambrosio Gonzales.[69] Beauregard also expressed his indebtedness for Gonzales's service in his official report to Confederate Adjutant General Samuel Cooper.[70]

Gonzales remained on special duty with Bonham until Bonham's appointment as Brigadier General in the Confederate Provisional Army and assignment to Virginia. Beauregard then appointed Gonzales as Acting Inspector General on Morris Island, where he toured defensive works with the commanding general and reported on the condition and needs of the forces serving there.[71] Shortly thereafter, Gonzales sought a more firm military position, the command of General Robert Rhett's brigade following Rhett's promotion to Quartermaster General for the state. Gonzales solicited Beauregard's support, and his friend forwarded the request with recommendations to Governor Pickens. He did not receive the appointment. Though still a volunteer, Gonzales took seriously the assignments from General Beauregard. In May, he accompanied Beauregard on an inspection tour of the coastal defenses[72] and later that month inspected the coast in the company of Captain F. D. Lee, Engineers,[73] who later had an active role in developing torpedo defenses and "David" boats for Charleston. Accompanying them was Major Edward Manigault, who later commanded the siege artillery. Gonzales received assurances from Beauregard that his services would be remembered.[74]

May also brought a change in assignment for General Beauregard. With a Federal army threatening the new capital in Richmond, the defense of northern Virginia fell on the popular officer. As a civilian volunteer, Gonzales remained behind. However in late May, he received a state appointment from Governor Pickens as special aide-de-camp, with full powers and rank of lieutenant-colonel, for the control, supervision, and direction of the broad seaboard defenses of South Carolina between Georgetown to the north of Charleston and Savannah to the south.[75] Gonzales even spoke on behalf of the Governor the following month, thanking the Calhoun Artillery for their service to the State.[76] In late June, Gonzales received an assignment to Richmond for two months to procure coastal guns from the Tredeger Iron Works for the defense of South Carolina. He stayed at the Arlington House on 6th and Main, just three blocks from Capital Square.[77] There is no report that he visited with President Davis, but he certainly experienced some of the more pleasant times of the war. During August and September, 1861, he met often with James Chestnut, now serving in the Provisional Congress, and his wife Mary. She recorded these meetings at the boarding house in her diary. When James Chestnut became ill, Gonzales offered quinine. On another occasion, Secretary Mallory joined the social gathering just two blocks from his house. The men spent a good part of the evening discussing President Davis. At the end of the evening as Mrs. Chestnut retired, Gonzales presented her with a small, and much appreciated, bottle of "cherry bounce."[78]

Mrs. Chestnut's writings provide one of the few contemporary descriptions of Gonzales. She identified him warmly as the "handsome Spaniard" who sings divinely and remarks on his "foreign, pathetic, polite, highbred way" of conducting himself. She also noted that the Cuban shared something besides friendship with his former schoolmate and commander General Beauregard. She recorded that he was so like Beauregard in appearance "as to be mistaken for him."[79] Later correspondence from an artillery officer in Charleston in 1863 echoed this view, stating that Gonzales looked more like General Beauregard "than any man alive."[80] Another diarist from Charleston, Miss Emma Holmes, also observed him while in Charleston during the war and noted the remarkable likeness as well as his singing ability:

> Col. Gonzales, who is an enthusiast in music, as I saw the mere play of his face, played & sang two or three spirited songs, ending with the Marseillaise, to which others sang the chorus; he has a fine voice & it was really delightful. I recognized him as soon as he entered by his likeness to Beauregard, of which I had often heard. Our beloved general was also there, so I had good opportunity of comparing them. I loved to look at Beauregard's quiet modest but determined face, so full of character, but so impenetrable. His square forehead, high cheek bones, dark impressive eyes & closely cut grey hair form a figure, once seen, never to be forgotten. Gonzales is a little taller & can be instantly recognized.[81]

Photographs and paintings show today the remarkable likeness between the two men. Perhaps in some ways, they were too much alike.

While in Richmond, Gonzales also gave serious thought to his responsibilities in defending his adopted state. On September 14, he sent a lengthy letter to President Davis presenting his ideas for a system of coastal defense based on mobile siege guns. Building on his experiences as Governor Pickens's inspector for troops and defenses, he proposed a "flying column"—a force of 1,200 men and 12 guns that could be quickly moved to any point of enemy attack along the South Carolina coast.[82] Davis recommended the letter to the Secretary of War with endorsement by Confederate Adjutant General Cooper. Gonzales proudly told his brother-in-law about his plan and its reception.[83] While he never saw his idea fully implemented, Gonzales became associated with the Charleston siege train for most of the war to come.

The artillery project in Richmond stretched into early October. Finally returning to Charleston, Gonzales received recognition for his work in Richmond and the "warmest thanks" for his effort.[84] Still holding only the position with his state, Gonzales continued his quest for appointment as an officer in Confederate service. His correspondence with the Richmond government finally netted him the offer of Adjutant and Inspector General with the rank of Major in the Provisional Army. Concerned that the position offered less than the position he currently held with the state, he declined the offer in a letter to General Cooper. He also appears to have written what must have been an indicting letter to President Davis giving his reasons for rejecting the offer. An October 16 reply to Gonzales from Davis strongly, and in typically defensive language, refutes Gonzales's criticism of Davis's position.[85] It was not a pleasant letter. After all the years of association with Davis, Gonzales had allowed his ego to show too openly in his correspondence, and Davis in his style responded in kind. Gonzales openly complained about the incident to James Chestnut.[86]

It is entirely possible that Gonzales's association with General Beauregard hindered his relationship with President Davis. Meetings between Davis and the General after Manassas, letters sent by the general to his former aides Chestnut and Miles in their current roles in the Confederate Congress and the refusal of Davis to support Beauregard's plan to invade Maryland widened the rift between the two men.[87] On October 22, Beauregard's complaint about the command structure of the army in Virginia led to a reorganization that left him dissatisfied as one of Johnston's subordinate commanders. By the end of October, the Davis-Beauregard quarrel reached the newspapers. In the midst of this acrimonious correspondence between Davis and Beauregard, Gonzales chose to send his complaints to the President.

In spite of the rebuff from Davis and the failure to obtain the desired commission, Gonzales actively continued to serve his state in the defense of Charleston. In November, he acted as volunteer aide to Brigadier General Roswell Ripley. Ripley himself almost resigned when he failed to receive a Confederate commission, but now was military commander in South Carolina.

The Union's capture of Port Royal Sound south of Charleston alerted the Confederates and forced them to strengthen the inner defenses in that area. General Gonzales, as others continued to refer to him, received command of the siege train on Huguenin's Neck on the Broad River, which flows into Port Royal Sound.[88] With four 8-inch howitzers manned by the Palmetto Guard and a small force of mounted troops, the unit protected the bridge for the critical rail line connecting Savannah and Charleston. Gonzales also commanded a "force of negroes" working on obstructions on the Coosawatchie River.

The Federal activity on the coast also stirred a response in Richmond. On November 5, the War Department created a coastal department from South Carolina, Georgia and east Florida with Davis's military advisor, General Robert E. Lee placed in command.[89] Lee arrived within days and placed his headquarters in the town of Coosawhatchie near the railroad line. He immediately faced a Union threat. In Port Royal Sound, the Federal fleet bombarded the Southern fortifications of Forts Walker and Beauregard. These quickly fell, and the fleet landed 12,000 troops under General Thomas Sherman to establish a base for future actions along the coast. Lee ordered evacuations and immediately began consolidating forces and building defenses against attack from Port Royal. He ordered General Ripley to Charleston, leaving the forces he placed in the Port Royal area, including Gonzales, reporting directly to General Lee. The new commander ordered entrenchments all along the threatened coastal areas. Where possible, he encouraged construction of river obstructions, favorably citing in one instance the work of General Gonzales on the Coosawhatchie.[90] These works no doubt received the direct attention and input of General Lee in his efforts to protect the rail line.[91] Lee's efforts also went into strengthening Savannah's defenses against the increased Federal threat. He worked long hours in planning and inspecting the coastal works. Finally able to travel to Charleston, Lee attempted a social evening only to be interrupted by the December fire that destroyed large portions of the city and forced the general and his guests from their hotel.

Lee continued his work in Charleston, moving guns and successfully encouraging the Governor to place more state troops under Confederate command. This did not proceed smoothly though, as General Ripley developed a strong dislike for the commander. Lee, in his easy style, managed to work through this internal tension. The Federal fleet applied external tension by sinking 16 old whaling ships filled with granite blocks in the harbor entrance. The Federal forces intended to block the port to Confederate trading vessels until the Union navy established a proper naval blockade. This December effort blocked the main channel off Morris Island, but runners still got through in other areas. In January, the Federals attempted to block another passage with a second "stone fleet."[92] South of the city, the Union forces expanded their hold on the Hilton Head and Port Royal Sound. For Gonzales, the loss of Port Royal also meant the loss of the Elliott family plantations on Hilton Head, a loss which they would never recover.

Gonzales remained busy supervising construction projects for the coastal defenses. He also busied himself with the search for a Confederate commission. In late 1861, he obtained recommendations for a brigadier general position from associates of his father-in-law and from officers with whom he served. This included a recommendation from Confederate General John Pemberton, Lee's second-in-command and commander of the military district around Port Royal. Gonzales had met the general years earlier when Pemberton served as aide to General Worth at the time the Havana Club solicited Worth's leadership for the invasion of Cuba. Gonzales also visited the state capital in Columbia, accompanied by former governor Manning, to actively pursue a commission through the South Carolina Executive Commission. The Executive Council of the state, in a rare move, requested that President Davis appoint Gonzales to a rank appropriate for the position of Chief of Artillery in the district.[93] The Richmond government failed to act on the request.

In March, decisions in Richmond brought Lee and Pemberton one step closer to their historical destiny. Lee received orders to return to Richmond, and General Pemberton became acting commander of the Department. The discussion of Lee's service in the Charleston area, as with other postwar analyses, created a continuing controversy concerning which commander played the greatest role in preparing the Charleston defenses. Lee received much credit for the defense of Charleston, in part promoted by his aide and biographer A. L. Long,[94] who also served as his chief of artillery in the district. Equal arguments for Beauregard came from his staff.[95] Lee's contributions to the Savannah defenses were clear,[96] and his development of interior defenses changed the nature of the fighting on the coast. There is little doubt that Lee's engineering skills and his accommodating personal style played an important part in the development of the structure and direction of the district. Regardless, the changing nature of the Federal threat continued to call on the engineering skills of all those assigned to the district.

For Gonzales, the change in command made little difference. In May, a pleasant and complimentary article appeared in the paper discussing Gonzales's work on behalf of the city's defense.[97] Yet, Richmond failed to respond to his entreaties for commission. While in Columbia in March, he met with James Chestnut and discussed the threat to the Savannah railroad.[98] In the conversation, Gonzales openly proclaimed his dislike for President Davis, reiterating the issues from his correspondence the previous year and stating, "Jeff Davis will be the sun — radiating all light, heat, and patronage. He will not be the moon reflecting public opinion. For he has the soul of a despot. And he delights to spite public opinion."[99] Such attitudes did not foster good will between Gonzales and the Confederate president. Still, that same day in Columbia, he sent a letter to Davis attempting to correct their earlier misunderstanding about the support provided Davis in 1854, and he requested that Davis reconsider the letters of recommendation sent on Gonzales's behalf.[100] Several weeks later, following the promotion of A. L. Long, the department's Chief of Artillery, to a position on Lee's staff in Virginia, Gonzales formally applied for the vacant position in a letter to Adjutant General Cooper.[101] He received support in this effort from Governor Pickens and General Ripley, and from Pemberton, whom he continued to serve in his civilian capacity.[102] Finally, as a result of this petition, Gonzales received recognition with a commission in the Provisional Army as a Lieutenant Colonel[103] and an immediate appointment from Pemberton in Charleston as the Chief of Artillery for the Department of South Carolina, Georgia, and Florida.[104] With his acceptance of the appointment, Gonzales officially joined the Confederate Army. The *Courier* declared its agreement with the appointment, stating that:

> No citizen, native or adopted, has labored more zealously, efficiently and disinterestedly for South Carolina since the opening of the war than General A. J.

Gonzales, as he is know to his friends.... [He] has accordingly served thus far without adequate commission or reward, beyond the conscientiousness of duty, and the flattering testimonials of all under whose commands he had acted. In the prosecution of the measures deemed necessary to obtain adequate supplies for this State he exhibited a perseverance and importunity which overcame difficulties that repelled others, and performed what was considered impossibilities.[105]

Gonzales now further committed himself to the life-and-death struggle for Charleston, for his adopted state and for the new nation.

LONG YEARS OF WAR

Gonzales hardly settled into his new position before Federal forces increased the pressure on the district's coastal defenses. Fort Pulaski guarding Savannah fell to Federal artillery in April, much as General Lee predicted it would. General Pemberton consolidated the Command's defenses in response to the Federal threat. As part of this reorganization, he ordered the removal of Confederate fortifications from the outer islands along the coast. These changes included the evacuation of Cole's Island on the Stono River. General Ripley openly disagreed with the commanding general's decision, feeling that it invited a Federal move against James Island through the Stono River. The disagreement ultimately led to his transfer out of Charleston, and service in Virginia until wounded at Antietam. In early June, Union General Hunter did take advantage of this controversial change, moving his Federal forces against Charleston by seizing Cole's and Folly Islands and landing troops on the tip of James Island. This again forced the Confederates into hasty modifications to the defensive positions around the city. Gonzales assisted in strengthening the James Island works and in placing siege guns being moved there from other locations.[106]

On June 16, 1862, Federal forces attacked James Island at Fort Lamar, an earthen-walled battery emplacement near Secessionville. Outmanned by the attacking Federal troops, the Confederate garrison of infantry and artillerymen held their defensive position and repulsed three Federal assaults. Hand-to-hand fighting occurred as the Union troops struggled to seize the fort. By midmorning, high casualties in the attacking troops forced the Union command to break off the assault and order a retreat. Heavy guns placed by Gonzales caused many of the casualties and contributed to the Federal withdrawal. The strong defensive positions caused General Hunter to delay plans for further attacks.

As the Confederates waited for the Union attack through the heat of Charleston's summer, Gonzales continued his oversight of the Department's artillery. He promoted his "flying battery" idea as a means to make the best use of the guns available for the lengthy coastal defense. The local papers recognized his idea "for the efficient use and application of barbette and siege guns" submitted to the Department commander.[107] He also continued his correspondence with Richmond. On August 11, Gonzales petitioned Secretary of War George Randolph for promotion to colonel. On August 14, Gonzales received notice of the success of his petition. He accepted the promotion on August 24, and the Confederate Senate confirmed the appointment October 4th.[108] This rank provided him with a salary of $210 per month, with a food and provision allowance. For the remaining course of the war, this salary did not change. Inflation, on the other hand drove the price of a cord of wood for his headquarters in Charleston from $7 in 1862 to $40 in 1864.[109] Fortunately, his family had greater security at the Elliott plantation at Adam's Run, 24 miles from Charleston.

There was less security for Gonzales's commander. Pemberton never received the popular or governmental support he needed to be truly effective in his command in the southern coastal district. Perhaps it was his officious manner acquired from years of military service. Perhaps it was just the pressure of "states rights" that prevented local cooperation with the central government that the district commander represented. Issues such as military conscription or the requisition of slave labor quickly became areas of friction. He angered South Carolina General Ripley with his order to evacuate Cole's Island. He failed to effectively develop a relationship with Governor Pickens, who constantly went to General Lee in Richmond with his complaints. Eventually, the Governor requested Pemberton's removal.[110] Richmond complied, replacing General Pemberton in late August. By the end of October, the general was in Mississippi and his assured place in history. Later in disgrace after Vicksburg and without a field command, he received a letter from Gonzales intended to boost his low spirits. Saluting Pemberton's "silent enduring," Gonzales stated:

> ... my pleasant duty to pay tribute to truth and justice, by meeting numerous attacks made on you [from the people of Charleston] ... and hope that these lines, even from so humble an individual as myself ... may prove to you that malignity and slander, if public, are not universal.

In the letter, he praised Pemberton's service in Charleston, developing defenses that still "hold the enemy at bay."[111]

Charleston's first Confederate commander also faced controversy. Beauregard's success at Bull Run failed to improve his status in the hierarchy of Confederate command. His transfer to the war's western theater again placed him in a subordinate position to Albert Sidney Johnston. Undisputed command of an army came on the second day at Shiloh following Johnston's

death, but the condition of the Southern forces and the reenforcement of
Grant's army forced Beauregard to order a retreat. His defense of Corinth did
not hold back the advancing Union army, forcing evacuation of the key Mississippi railroad center. In the summer of 1862, Beauregard became ill. Without the permission of Richmond, he turned command over to General Braxton
Bragg and took a leave of absence to recuperate. Already receiving President
Davis's blame for the failure at Shiloh, coupled with questions of his capa-
bility after Corinth, Davis took advantage of Beauregard's absence and dismissed the general from his command. This seemingly ungracious removal
from the army in Mississippi gave the Creole general an irreconcilable dislike, even open hatred, for Jefferson Davis. Following the recovery of his health,
Beauregard received an offer of a command in the Trans-Mississippi theater
or in Charleston. Prior to this offer, Davis laid the groundwork with Governor Pickens for his acceptance of Beauregard as a welcome replacement for
Pemberton. Beauregard considered his choices and his possible future, then
reluctantly chose the familiar post on the Carolina coast.[112] Gonzales and Beauregard, friends since childhood, and looking so much alike, were together again.

In early September, Gonzales wrote to Beauregard of "the delight with
which I look forward to renewed service under you."[113] He requested reten-
tion in his position as Chief of Artillery and, in addition, requested the position of Inspector General. While awaiting Beauregard's arrival, he served with
Brigadier General Johnson Hagood and Colonel James Cullough on a court
of enquiry for Colonel John Dunovant of the 1st Regiment South Carolina
Infantry. The court found him guilty of drunkenness while on duty, leading
to his dismissal from service. Richmond upheld the court's decision. However, his prior military experience and his apparent overall character led to his
reinstatement to command in South Carolina and later service in Virginia,
where he was killed shortly after promotion to brigadier general.

General Beauregard arrived in Charleston in mid–September with full
awareness of the increasing Federal activities along the coast. Discussions of
Union plans for the capture of the city by sea and land routinely appeared in
Northern newspapers. As Beauregard officially relieved Pemberton on September 24, 1862, his first orders recognized that the task ahead was "the
defence of two of the most important cities in the Confederate States against
the most formidable efforts of our powerful enemy...."[114] Beauregard immediately began an extensive six-day inspection tour of the defensive positions in
and around Charleston and Savannah, accompanied by Pemberton and Gonzales.[115] Beauregard and Gonzales also conducted a review of defenses north
of the city. The general's engineering eye noted the need for immediate
improvements. Pemberton's substitution of inner island defenses, modifying
the coastal defenses proposed originally by Beauregard and those later planned
by Lee, had left the defenses "vulnerable at various points, and necessitating

more labor and greater armament than we could command."[116] The most immediate need for the defense of Charleston was more and heavier artillery. In a September 19 letter to Colonel Josiah Gorgas, Chief of the Ordnance Bureau in Richmond, Gonzales discussed the need for more and better artillery in Charleston due to Federal naval action off the harbor which demonstrated "the formidable character of the iron-clad ships preparing for the attack of Charleston."[117] He also cited the difficulties the department had in obtaining guns from the Rome (GA) Arsenal. He requested that heavy guns for the defense of the city be sent directly from Richmond.

With his return to Charleston, Beauregard brought with him his Chief of Staff from the West, Brigadier General Thomas Jordan. Jordan had an interesting background. At West Point, he was the roommate of Union General William T. Sherman. Prior to his assignment in the western theater, he established a spy network in Washington, including the infamous Rose Greenhow, that reportedly provided intelligence to Beauregard prior to the battle of First Manassas. Jordan served at Shiloh and was present at Johnston's death. While well involved in staff intrigues, Jordan wrote in July, 1862, to Beauregard about General Bragg's appointment as the western theater commander. He discouraged the General from accepting "some small and inactive command, the Department of South Carolina for example, and the defence of Charleston and Savannah at a season when the climate will be better defence than casemate forts."[118] Jordan, nonetheless, offered his services to Beauregard and joined him in Charleston.

Beauregard also brought Charleston a new symbol of the Confederacy, the Confederate battle flag. Beauregard initially developed the historic standard during the defense of northern Virginia to aid recognition of Confederate troops on the battlefield. The new banner quickly became the pattern for flags used by the Army of Northern Virginia. Beauregard brought the new flag with him to Tennessee and Mississippi. Now, with its arrival in Charleston, the famous battle flag slowly replaced or supplemented the assortment of state flags to fly over the men and the fortifications on the South Carolina and Georgia coasts.[119]

Under the new command and the new flag, Gonzales actively planned and supervised the placement of available and newly acquired artillery. In addition, there was the constant repositioning of available weaponry to replace losses due to damage, to make repairs, and to rifle and reband outdated smoothbore weapons. On September 29, Gonzales participated in a staff meeting which included Commodore Ingraham, commander of the harbor naval forces, Brigadier General State Rights Gist, commanding the First District during the illness of General William Smith, and Captain Francis D. Lee of the Engineers. The meeting discussed the conditions of the harbor defenses and the possible outcome of a Federal ironclad attack. The discussion included plans for iron and chain boom obstructions across the harbor channel, placement of guns to defend the inner harbor, defense of Fort Sumter from direct naval attack, defense of area rivers, and evacuation plans for James Island in the event of a successful Federal attack.[120] Following the meeting, Gonzales offered a number of suggestions for correcting many of the concerns identified.[121] He obtained approval for construction of "service magazines" to improve James Island defenses.[122] Gonzales also became involved in the discussion of ironclad gunboats for defense of the harbor, offering written recommendations for shallow draft vessels. Beauregard forwarded the proposal to Richmond, but, reflective of the government's economic strain, Richmond approved the concept but offered no funding. Secretary Mallory reported prior commitment of all resources for such a project in Charleston.[123]

The role of Chief of Artillery under Beauregard was not without its problems, whether real or perceived. While Gonzales appeared an active participant in the new commander's administration, he viewed himself as being left out of many headquarters decisions. In an October letter to Jordan, Gonzales complained of being excluded from much information on the departmental artillery.[124] In his often offending style, he claimed that he was not receiving the full authority his title demanded. Still, his role kept him close to Beauregard. He joined the general on a lengthy inspection tour of the Savannah area in late October. In December, he received additional responsibilities as Chief of Artillery and Ordnance following the reorganization of Beauregard's staff.[125] Shortly thereafter, with Beauregard's approval, Gonzales again petitioned Richmond for promotion based on his new responsibilities. There is no evidence of a response from the government.[126]

The additional duties carried increased stress. In addition to the paperwork generated in recording and responding to the many requests for arms and ammunition from the limited stores of the district, Gonzales was responsible for replenishing and maintaining the armaments necessary to support the military mission on the district's broad defensive front. In response to the strained ability of the Confederacy to supply its national needs, the pressure increased to assure that Charleston and the coastal areas received proper consideration by the Richmond government. Beauregard later described his concern for the decreasing support received at that time by the district from the new Secretary of War James Seddon.[127] The correspondence between Gonzales and the Ordnance Bureau, in particular that with Colonel Gorgas, reflected the growing tensions arising from the South's limited resources. Gonzales reported that the district was without Enfield cartridges, which he could not requisition from the Atlanta arsenal without approval of Richmond. He also reported that Charleston foundries produced only 38 projectiles per day. At other sites in the district, Augusta had inadequate materials for production of shells, and Macon lacked even the engineering drawings needed to manufacture shells.

He reported that the guns of Forts Sumter and Moultrie had less than 50 rounds each, and several batteries, including the siege train, were without ammunition. Gorgas replied that Atlanta was fully committed to supplying the Army of Tennessee, though he would order cartridges from other sites. Gorgas also suggested slowing down the conversion of 32-pound smoothbores to rifled weapons if the appropriate projectiles could not be found. He indicated that he would do all he could to supply the district, but that Gonzales should limit his request "to, say, 150 rounds per gun."[128] Beauregard sent letters of complaint to the War Department in Richmond about the lack of support from the Ordnance Bureau. In late January, Gonzales provided a full list of the rifled guns of the district to Gorgas with a renewed request for the 150 rounds of promised ammunition. He also reported that requested ammunition failed to arrive with new guns received from Richmond "although [the shells were] packed and addressed in the presence of [my aide] Major Alston...."[129] The tension of the position and its extra duties showed in orders and correspondence he exchanged with other officers. In February, Gonzales requested relief from the new duties. Beauregard denied his request.

AN APPETITE FOR CHARLESTON

With these poor supply conditions, Beauregard and his staff faced their greatest challenge. As the war moved into its second year, Charleston continued to be a viable port for the Confederacy in spite of the Union blockade. The city served as a home port for many of the companies engaged in blockade running.[130] In January, 1863, reports of the harbor show vessels continuing to move between Charleston and the Bahamas.

Confederate spirits improved during January 1863 with two naval-related actions at the end of the month. Confederate forces captured the gunboat *Isaac Smith* in the Stono River on January 30. The inability to obstruct or defend the river allowed Federal blockading vessels to conduct routine raids up the river to engage the James Island defenses. To counteract this, the Confederates established a hidden battery and defensive emplacements which they revealed after the *Smith* moved past the positions. This effectively trapped the vessel and, after a heated exchange of fire, forced its surrender. The captured vessel, renamed *Stono* and commanded by Captain Hartstene, became the harbor's nighttime picket boat used to warn of the approach of Federal ironclads under cover of dark.[131]

The second naval action involved Confederate ironclads. At Beauregard's insistence, the unwieldy and poorly constructed ships moved against the blockading Federal fleet. On the night of January 30, the *Palmetto State* and the *Chicora* sailed from the harbor. Attacking several Federal ships, the two Confederate vessels forced the surrender of one ship and damaged another. Quickly, the blockading ships dispersed well out of range of the Southern guns, leaving no targets for the slow ironclads. While the foray against the Union fleet did not break or even lessen the blockade, it did provide a warning to the Federals that Charleston continued to be a difficult prize.

For the U.S. government, Charleston's survival continued to be a thorn. War plans called for the capture of the city as soon as Richmond fell to McClellan the previous year. Even with the failure on the Peninsula, the War Department sought the capture of the South Carolina port. Charleston's newspapers reported arrivals of each blockade runner, reminding the Federal commanders that their blockade was inadequate to stop Southern commerce. Viewed as the heart of the secession movement, there was also an emotional drive to seize and hold the city. As the Union naval blockade commander Rear Admiral DuPont stated, there was "a marked appetite" on the part of the government for possession of Charleston.[132] Though the task was foreboding, the Federal forces planned a spring attack to open the harbor to capture by Federal troops.

Even with their planning in place, the Federal army and fleet continued to delay the attack. This allowed much needed time to the Confederate defenders. Beauregard reported that he doubled the defense of the harbor while the enemy waited.[133] Gonzales continued his efforts adjusting locations of heavy guns, placing available guns in newly built works and improving the city and harbor defenses.[134] In late February and early March, Federal ironclads made several small attacks on Charleston fortifications. By the end of March, a major Federal attack was a certainty. Even the British, French and Spanish consuls fled the city. On March 31, Gonzales received orders to remove all unneeded ordnance and stores to "some safe place,"[135] and other commanders received orders to remove baggage and supplies from the city. The precautions were well founded.

The Union navy under Rear Admiral DuPont continued to add to the collection of ironclads in the blockading fleet. The bureaucrats in Washington, in opposition to the commander on the scene, insisted that these vessels be used to run past the guns of the harbor entrance and directly attack Fort Sumter. There was an untried faith that iron-walled vessels could withstand any threat from the Charleston defenses. DuPont became more and more convinced that the outgunned and mechanically flawed ironclads could not force the harbor, but felt pressured to continue with the plan.[136] Washington continued to send the newest monitors to DuPont at Hilton Head. This concentration of forces led to the loss of the USS *Monitor* in a storm off Hatteras as she sailed to join DuPont's fleet.

Finally on the clear afternoon of April 7, 1863, eight turreted ironclads and the ironclad frigate *New Ironsides* sailed across the still waters of the bay and into the main channel east of Morris Island. Their objective was Fort Sumter, which they planned to reduce to rubble. The *Weehawken*, under Captain John Rogers, took the lead with an antitorpedo raft, a monument to the concern for Confederate defensive measures. By three o'clock, the fleet passed within range of Fort Moultrie. The guns emplaced there began a continuous and accurate fire. As the vessels pressed further into the harbor, they drew fire from Fort Sumter. Soon all of the harbor guns that could be brought to bear fired on the Federal fleet. The slowness of the ironclads and the limited ability to maneuver in the tight channel put them at a clear disadvantage. For over two hours the Confederate guns pounded the Federal fleet, which could do little to respond effectively. The Confederates fired 2,209 rounds, of which over 500 struck the Union vessels. The Union ships, with their 32 guns, managed only 154 rounds in return. Still, the Federal guns left clear evidence of their power, with 34 hits on the fort causing a breach in one wall and craters over two feet deep at other locations. For this lack of success against Fort Sumter, the Federals paid with five ironclads seriously damaged and the *Keokuk* sunk off Morris Island. The damage kept the monitors under repair into January of the next year. At one point in the action, the *Ironsides* anchored over a large Confederate mine. However, accidental damage to the electrical wires used to trigger the device prevented even greater loss to the Union fleet. As a final insult to the Federal navy, the Confederate defenders recovered the guns from the sunken *Keokuk* and mounted one of them at Fort Sumter for future use against the fleet. The naval attack was a clear failure.[137]

In his battle report, Beauregard thanks Colonel Gonzales for his services in his department.[138] Beauregard and his command received the thanks of the Confederate Congress for the defense of the city. On the Federal side, the War Department in Washington, upset that their belief in the ironclad ships did not lead to immediate success in Charleston, blamed Admiral DuPont for the fleet's failure and then relieved him from command.

With the immediate threat of the Federal fleet removed, Gonzales requested a leave of absence in early May which he described as his first furlough request since the start of the war. Granted a seven-day leave, he visited with his family at Oak Lawn plantation.[139] Of note, his first daughter, Gertrude Ruffini, would arrive in February of the following year. Following his return to duty, he again sought and received relief from his Chief of Ordnance duties allowing him to concentrate on his continuing duties as Chief of Artillery for the District.[140] District returns from the end of May also show Gonzales to be in command of the siege train of the district, with 271 men present for duty.[141]

That month Gonzales wrote to a South Carolina officer to describe the plan he earlier submitted to Pemberton for improving the artillery defenses.[142] He proposed a double-track railroad along the coast and a rail line on James

Island. Cars towed by steam, horses or men with ropes could quickly move to the point of attack. He proposed building cars with siege platforms covered by iron-plated roofs, with loopholes in their walls for sharpshooters.

The successful defense by the Southern forces continued to keep Charleston open as a port for the Confederacy. In April and May, 15 vessels entered Charleston and 21 left with 10,000 bales of cotton, commerce worth over $138,000 to the Customs Office. The U.S. War Department's impatience with Admiral DuPont led to his replacement by Admiral Dahlgren in the summer of 1863. Major General Quincy Gillmore, who successfully shelled and captured Fort Pulaski in Savannah, assumed command of the land forces. The Union government expected immediate action to close the port.

In June and July, the Union forces fortified the northern end of Folly Island, taken from the Confederates earlier in the year. They quietly moved 11,000 men and 47 guns and mortars in position to move against Morris Island. The Confederates, in anticipation of possible Federal action, built Battery Gregg and Battery Wagner on Morris Island and strengthened fortifications on the southern end of James Island. They also strengthened Fort Sumter. The fort housed 68 guns and mortars, though their best guns were removed and placed in better locations throughout the harbor defenses, primarily under the supervision of Colonel Gonzales. All of this work to modify the harbor defenses continued with the day-to-day administrative tedium best illustrated by Gonzales's July 1 request for 200 blank forms for the Bureau of Artillery.[143]

Throughout these preparations, the Federals maintained a series of harassing raids with infantry, artillery, and gunboats that included burning bridges, houses and plantations along the various rivers. Guns from Gonzales's siege train provided defensive support against these raids.[144] On July 9th, Gonzales received orders to prepare the siege train to "move at a moment's notice," followed the next day by a request to place the train on James Island and to conduct a review of all heavy batteries on the island to determine their need for supplies.[145] Gonzales's siege train, under the command of Major Edward Manigault, took positions near Newtown Cut along the James Island Creek.[146] On the 11th, they received orders to move to Legere's Point, closer to Morris Island. Gonzales carried orders for Beauregard to the 1st Military District adjutant recommending movement of troops and guns to repel any Federal attack moving upstream from the Light House Inlet.[147]

The driving force for this urgent order was the Federal decision to seize Morris Island. After extensive preparations on Folly Island that included construction of hidden artillery positions within hearing distance of Confederate pickets, the Federals attacked on July 10. Brigadier General Truman Seymour, a former company commander at Fort Sumter during the 1861 attack, led the infantry units across the inlet in small boats. They seized three-quarters of the island in only four hours. The next day the Federals unsuccessfully attacked Battery Wagner at the northern end of the island.

After regrouping his forces, General Gillmore ordered a full-scale attack on the fortified position in mid–July. On July 18, an infantry force of 6,000 men moved out under cover of darkness toward the Battery. In the lead was the 54th Massachusetts Regiment, an African-American unit led by Colonel Robert Shaw. Though some men reached the parapets of the fortification, the defenders repulsed the attack with heavy casualties including Shaw.[148] The losses from the open attack across the beach into the face of the Confederate guns led to the Federal decision to begin a siege action that included extensive, time-consuming trenching operations.

Curiously, Gonzales played a role in the effective defense of Battery Wagner. In January, Gonzales wrote General Beauregard recommending that the area in front of the fortification be protected with "shells," or torpedoes (i.e., land mines).[149] Beauregard approved the plan and requested the area commander, the recently returned General Ripley, to take action on the plan. Federal forces documented losses from mines during the attacks on Battery Wagner, and during the construction of siege entrenchments. Gonzales also recommended the use of double-barrel shotguns, which he found in the Charleston arsenal, for defending the fort.[150] In addition, the siege train batteries, from positions at Legere's Point, directed flanking fire at the Federal forces attacking Battery Wagner throughout the attacks and the siege.

In late July, Gonzales inspected the battery positions with Major Manigault, after a breakfast joined by Captain Armand Beauregard, General Beauregard's brother and aide, and Captain Stephen Proctor, the general's brother-in-law and assistant quartermaster for the District. Gonzales obviously maintained his strong ties with the commanding general. On August 5, Gonzales received assignment to special service on James Island as the chief of artillery for Brigadier General William Taliaferro commanding the island.[151] There, at Beauregard's command, he assisted in strengthening the defenses and supervising the movement and placement of heavy artillery, some of which was taken from Fort Sumter.[152] He took the opportunity to suggest again his continuing idea for a railroad battery, this time as a single track which could be used to move between selected battery sites on Legere's Point. In this instance, Beauregard would describe the idea as "theoretically good, but practically impracticable."[153]

With the new duties on an active front, Gonzales again petitioned for an increase in rank. In a letter sent from James Island to Secretary of War Seddon, he described his responsibilities as the senior artillery officer on the island with responsibility for over 150 heavy and light guns.[154] This was well in excess of the 80 guns required by regulation for a brigadier general of artillery. Beauregard commented on Gonzales's "active, zealous and intelligent discharge of his duties" in his endorsement of the application. Gonzales followed this with a letter to President Davis which described the extent of his command in the defense of Charleston and informed the President of his request for promotion.[155] Gonzales, perhaps playing on the relationship between Davis and Pemberton, now disgraced after Vicksburg, commented that he "would have gone to Vicksburg with Genl. Pemberton" if he had not "devoted" himself to the defense of his home state. Secretary Seddon responded to the request but indicated he had no specific command to assign, even if the appointment was made. President Davis took over three months to forward Gonzales's letter to the War Department, with no specific recommendation for action.

Gonzales continued to serve on James Island for four months. During this critical time, the Federal forces began the direct bombardment of Charleston from a site on Gonzales's front known as the Marsh Battery. There, with marvelous engineering skill, they placed an 8-inch Parrott gun that became known as the "Swamp Angel." On August 21, the gun fired a 150-pound shell into the city and its civilian population. Other batteries of rifled guns set up by the Federals shelled Fort Sumter and Battery Wagner as Union troops continued to dig entrenchments closer to Wagner. Confederate batteries on James Island attempted to respond. There was little damage to the overall Federal activities by this defensive shelling, but the constant harassing fire continued to cause casualties and disruption among the besieging troops. Keeping the Confederate gun positions serviceable in the swampy terrain and keeping them supplied took continued effort from Gonzales and his staff. The "Swamp Angel" burst after firing only 36 rounds. However, the Federal fire on Fort Sumter from other batteries of heavy guns continued. Starting August 17, two weeks of Federal fire, including about 1,000 shells the first day and 5,000 in the week that followed, reduced Fort Sumter to "an infantry post."[156] The Federal navy joined freely in the attack on Fort Sumter, launching forays with their ironclads that, in one attack, almost cost them another ship. Finally, with the Union army's entrenchments reaching the face of Fort Wagner and under routine bombardment from land and sea, the Confederates ordered the abandonment of Morris Island. They successfully evacuated all troops on September 6.

The following day, Admiral Dahlgren demanded the surrender of Fort Sumter. Reportedly Beauregard responded, "Tell Admiral Dahlgren to come and take it."[157] And come he would. The first attempt on the afternoon of the 7th included five monitors and the *Ironsides*. The force attempted another excursion into Charleston harbor, exchanging fire with Fort Moultrie for over two hours. There was little gained by the fleet, and one monitor was almost lost when it ran aground. Only poor Confederate ammunition and the next morning's high tide saved the vessel.

The next action by the Federal navy fell directly on Fort Sumter. Under cover of darkness on September 9, a Federal force of 400 sailors and marines attempt to seize the fort by landing on Fort Sumter itself. Expecting only a token garrison of defenders after the shelling and damage the fort received, the Federal troops made an uncoordinated landing in small boats. Outnumbered Confederate troops commanded by Major Stephen Elliott, a former aide of Gonzales, repulsed and forced the retreat of the naval forces with severe losses. The Confederate ironclad *Chicora* assisted in repulsing the assault. Curiously, the Federal army commander planned a similar attack. However, interservice rivalries prevented appropriate coordination of the attacks, and problems in launching boats prevented the Union army troops reaching the fort.

After several weeks, the Federal forces responded by shelling what remained of the fort for another 23 days. Another 12-day bombardment from new batteries and from mortars firing 200-pound projectiles followed in an attempt to prevent any effective use of the fort. On October 26 the bombardment resumed, including the Federal battery at Cummings Point less than a mile away. Guns, Parrott rifles, heavy mortars, and two ironclads fired on the fort for 12 days. Confederate batteries on James and Sullivan's Islands returned fire. Gillmore stopped the bombardment on December 5. In the fort, there were only two casualties, and the position became stronger as debris piled up. The Union effort turned Sumter into a "shapeless and harmless mass of ruins." Yet, Admiral Dahlgren described the sight as a "heap of rubbish" that appeared "invincible."[158]

Following the evacuation of Morris Island, Gonzales joined Chief Engineer Colonel Harris and Major General Gilmer on a special board convened by Beauregard to review the armament of batteries for the new defensive lines on James Island and to recommend any appropriate changes in preparation for an expected Federal assault.[159] Much of Gonzales's work in the next few months consisted of inspections, changing the locations of heavy guns to place artillery in its best sighting on the enemy works, supervising labor on the gun emplacements, ordering rebanding of selected artillery tubes and assuring proper distribution of the limited stores of ammunition in the city.[160]

The torpedoes, or water mines, used in the entrance to the Charleston Harbor had some success in the defense of the harbor. Their presence caused the Union Navy considerable concern for the safety of the ironclads in attacks into the harbor. Gonzales supported the use of these new weapons and openly encouraged their use in blocking the various rivers in the Charleston area. In response to the requests for assistance from units along the Stono River, where Union vessels made routine raids, Gonzales developed, and Beauregard approved, another plan for hidden artillery and use of torpedoes to disable or capture any ship unexpectedly entering the prepared area.[161] He also supported the use of "David" boats, small steam-powered semisubmersibles, built in Charleston by Engineer Captain Francis Lee. The boats carried a small torpedo, also designed by Lee, on a long wooden spar on the bow of the vessel.[162] In early October, the small boats had their greatest success when a vessel commanded by Lieutenant Glassell of the Confederate Navy damaged the armored vessel USS *New Ironsides*. The damage, often reported as "slight," was sufficient to cause withdrawal of the ship from the area for extensive repairs. James H. Tomb, assistant engineer, saved the Confederate naval vessel and returned it to port.[163]

In the midst of the preparations of the James Island defenses, Gonzales took the time to prepare his letter of sympathy to General Pemberton.[164] In response to "the unparalleled warfare which has been so bitterly waged against you," Gonzales offered to "pay a tribute to truth and justice" by praising Pemberton for the work he did in Charleston during his service there. He credited Pemberton with the foresight to move guns from Fort Sumter to other locations where they strengthened the defense and which "contributed so largely to the repulse [of the Federal ironclads] of April 7th." He offered his regards to Pemberton's family and closed "trusting that a brighter day is still in store for you." While the relationship between Gonzales and Pemberton is not clear from available correspondence, this letter must have been one of the few bright spots in the otherwise trying times for Pemberton and his family.

Things were less cordial between General Beauregard and President Davis. The President arrived in Charleston in early November. He was returning to Richmond from a meeting with Bragg, held in response to the complaints filed by Bragg's subordinates after the Battle of Chickamauga. In Charleston, Davis addressed a large crowd, praising the defense of Charleston and Fort Sumter. He mentioned Major Elliott, commander of Fort Sumter, by name. Though Beauregard stood at his side, the President did not use Beauregard's name, simply calling for trust in the "commander" and commenting on the need to forget personal feuds. Beauregard was irate at Davis's perceived slight and at the comment on feuds. He did not attend the dinner given in Davis's honor, having refused an invitation prior to the President's arrival.[165]

In November, Gonzales requested his return to departmental duties from his James Island assignment. Orders of December 3 allowed him to resume his position as Chief of Artillery for the department.[166] He also requested and received a leave of 10 days to visit his family, whom he had not seen in the four months of his assignment on James Island. Even on leave, he did not get away from his work. A letter addressed to Beauregard from Oak Lawn discussed recommendations for the disposition of guns.[167] Later during the Christmas holiday Gonzales spent at Oak Lawn, he again wrote to Beauregard several times about artillery dispositions. This concern is not surprising, since he could no doubt hear the Federal guns continuing to bombard Charleston, killing one civilian and wounding another even on Christmas Day.

On Christmas Day, other Federal activity triggered the plan proposed by Gonzales to trap Federal ships on the Stono River. The USS *Marblehead*, commanded by Lt. Commander Richard Meade, the brother of General George Meade, commander of the Army of the Potomac, landed troops in the Legareville area. The Confederate batteries moved into their preplanned positions, then, in the morning light, opened fire on the vessel. Though it took some time for the Union ship to build up steam, the Confederate artillery appeared to have little success in hitting or damaging their target. Eventually supported with flanking fire by the USS *Pawnee*, the ships forced the withdrawal of the Confederate artillery forces, then landed troops which captured two 8-inch howitzers left by the Confederates. The Southern officers attributed their lack of success to the range and to generally poor gunnery due to lack of practice. In truth, the Confederate gunnery was reasonably accurate, as shown by the Union report of damage to the ship's foremast, some 12 shots in the hull, 18 hits on the upper works, and a 30-pound shell in the steerage which did not explode. In his review of the action, General Beauregard made it clear that the quality of the ammunition and supplies were to blame for the lack of success.[168] The quality of ordnance was to be a hinderance to Southern artillery in Charleston as it was on other fronts.

ANOTHER YEAR OF CHALLENGE

As 1864 began, Gonzales returned to Charleston and his department duties. With the decreased level of Federal activity in late 1863 and into 1864, the duties consisted of the usual round of inspection and inspection reports, of service on boards and of requisitions and paperwork.[169] His writings showed some interdepartmental rivalry following the inspection of the Florida district by Captain Jaquelin Smith of the Department's Ordnance Bureau, referred to Gonzales by Beauregard for action. In his return of the report, Gonzales used his flowing and polite writing style to remind the commanding general that inspection of artillery units was the responsibility of his department and not that of the Ordnance Bureau.[170] In this instance, Beauregard concurred. Gonzales also interjected himself into a minor controversy between one of his battery commanders and Brigadier General Wise, the Sixth District commander, which developed following a Union reconnaissance in force on Johns Island.[171]

On the personal side, Gonzales again took the opportunity to solicit his promotion. In a letter to President Davis, he highlighted his service on the Charleston front and the recommendations he received.[172] Davis passed the letter to General Bragg after his appointment as Davis's military advisor following his disastrous campaign in Chattanooga. After several months, Davis treated the correspondence as a personal letter that required no action. Gonzales again faced frustration in his attempt for promotion. Even Beauregard was sensitive to the situation of promotions in the Charleston command. In his April 1864 "Department of Refuge" letter,[173] he stated: "...My recommendations and applications for officers are seldom if ever heeded ... [except for three] not one of my officers has been promoted since the beginning of the siege of Charleston...." Even though critical to the survival of the South, the Department remained a backwater for Richmond.

The Federal navy continued its relative inactivity. With the strengthened harbor defenses and concern over harbor obstructions and torpedoes, Admiral Dahlgran refused to risk the only Federal "ironclad" fleet. Already the fleet had lost one monitor to bad weather, and living conditions on the metal-sheathed ships took their toll on the crews. Damage to the pride of the fleet, *New Ironside*, and other losses lessened the strength available for proper bombardment of the harbor. The Federals also became acquainted with another naval innovation in mid–February when the Confederate submersible craft, the CSS *Hunley*, sailed across Charleston harbor and with its spar torpedo, damaged and sank the Federal ship USS *Housatonic*. While the South's fragile craft was lost with all hands, the South again made naval history. As for the Union army, their efforts amounted to little more than continuing minor artillery fire directed at the city and its defenders. The reduction of Fort Sumter was visibly complete, but the Confederates simply moved the rubble and strengthened the position, even mounting a small battery there for its defense.

With Sherman moving toward Atlanta and Grant organizing for a spring campaign in Virginia, both sides began to reorganize in the Charleston area to face the coming action. For the Confederates, there was a change in command. Beauregard, recovering from the loss of his wife who died in Union-held New Orleans, requested a leave of absence.[174] He also tired of the squabbling with Davis and Bragg, the continued drain on the Department's manpower and the absence of a true field command in his "Department of Refuge." Unexpectedly, he received orders to another coastal command which covered all of North Carolina and the coast of Virginia up to the James River. By mid–April, he joined his new command; by mid–May, he was in the midst of the struggle for Petersburg. Major General Samuel Jones, who served as Beauregard's chief of artillery at Manassas, received the Departmental command after being relieved of his command in western Virginia. Again the shift in command brought little change for Gonzales. To the new commander, he reported 472 guns in position, 150 guns in movable batteries for a total of 622 guns in the department and under his supervision as the Chief of Artillery.[175] There would be steady work for the many guns and for the remaining Southern forces.

On the Federal side, the artillery siege of the city made little progress. There were no bloody infantry attacks or sieges like that which earlier took Morris Island from the Confederates. Federal attacks consisted of minor but steady raids still limited to burning houses and bridges. With the manpower demands of the proposed Federal spring campaigns, General Gillmore and 10,000 men moved to Virginia in May. Major General John G. Foster, the new Union army commander and former engineer officer at Sumter at the time of its surrender, began gathering troops for a major action directed toward Charleston. In early July, he launched a multipronged attack aimed at both ends of James Island and on Johns Island against the depleted defenders. The success on the southern end of James Island encouraged an amphibious attack on Fort Johnson on the northern shore of the island in Charleston harbor. This was a complete failure. The Federals failed to capitalize on the initial success of the other attacks, and the armies returned to a stalemate.[176] Washington then ordered Foster's best troops to Virginia.

On July 7, the Federal artillery opened another bombardment of the fort at the rate of 350 rounds per day. During July over 7,000 shells struck the fort. The defenders added wooden pikes and barbed wire entanglements in preparation for an expected landing to seize the fort. Failure of the War Department in Washington to provide the vessels needed for a landing force prevented a planned Federal attack. The bombardment continued into September. In the later part of the year, the limited ordnance supplies provided to the Union command prevented even effective reply to Confederate artillery and mortar fire. Confederate sharpshooters in the fort were even able to interfere with Union daily activities on the shore.

In one of the more perverse episodes of the war, the Federal command moved a large group of Confederate prisoners from Fort Delaware to an open and exposed stockade near the Union guns at the old Battery Wagner site on Morris Island. The Federal authorities claimed with a strange logic that this was in retaliation for the housing of Union troops in civilian areas in Charleston while the Union guns indiscriminantly shelled the Southern city. The Confederate prisoners, exposed to the defensive fire from Gonzales's guns, became known as the "Immortal 600."[177]

During the August bombardment of Fort Sumter, Gonzales went to Richmond on "business," though his purpose there in the midst of the continuing battle for Petersburg is unclear.[178] Still, while there, he took the opportunity once again to address the subject of promotion. In a letter to General Cooper, he restated his role in the military department and the breadth of his responsibilities which should be sufficient for his promotion based on the number of artillery pieces under his control, which at this time was about

620 guns. A letter of recommendation from Beauregard praised Gonzales for his effort and also acknowledged that the promotion should be granted if Gonzales had sufficient guns under his command.[179] John Pemberton, now serving as a lieutenant-colonel of artillery in the Richmond area, provided a letter of recommendation to Secretary of War Seddon on Gonzales's behalf.[180] There was no response until October 11th and, again, there was no promotion. Gonzales remained a colonel in the siege of Charleston.

General Beauregard maintained his connection with Charleston. In August from his position in Petersburg, he suggested that General Jones use rope barriers to increase harbor defenses following Farragut's success in Mobile.[181] In late September, Beauregard became directly involved in the district when President Davis sent him to Charleston to investigate charges against General Ripley. Based on allegations of intoxication, Richmond removed Ripley from command, and Beauregard recommended his engineering officer, Colonel Harris, as a replacement. In this case at least, with the President's concurrence, promotion seemed imminent. However, before the appointment, Colonel Harris succumbed to yellow fever, which was then killing about 20 people a day in Charleston.

In October, following controversy from General Beauregard's command in the Richmond area, his repeated clashes with Davis and Bragg and his dissatisfaction with his subordination to General Lee's command, Richmond offered and Beauregard accepted the questionable command of the Department of the West. There, in an area from Georgia to Mississippi, he faced scattered forces, the confused strategy of General Hood after his defeat in Atlanta, a Federal army under Sherman holding Atlanta and the threat to Mobile following Farragut's damaging naval attack.

At about the same time, the Department of South Carolina, Georgia and Florida again changed commanders. Another disagreement between generals, in this case between Lieutenant General William Hardee and General John Hood concerning the conduct of the Atlanta defense, finally pushed Richmond to resolve the problem. President Davis came to Georgia in late September, met with the commanders and finally agreed to relieve Hardee from his command with the Army of Tennessee. Hardee, a West Point classmate of Beauregard, received command of the broad coastal department on October 5th and moved to Charleston.

Gonzales continued his duties as Chief of Artillery for the new commander.[182] He took advantage of this new audience to forward his long-lived idea about a "flying column." He wrote to General Hardee's Assistant Adjutant General Thomas Roy[183] with his proposal for a force of about 2,000 trained men, with two picked batteries of artillery, to be transported as needed along the Charleston & Savannah railroad on dedicated trains to any point of conflict along the coast. The trains would have special cars with ramps to speed loading and unloading of artillery and horses in the absence of a station.[184] In this November letter, Gonzales claimed to have two locomotives already available, suggested the appropriate units to use from the current command, and even indicated the potential points of conflict where the forces might be needed. As before, the proposal received favorable review, but resources prevented implementation.

At this point in the war, there would be little time for new plans for the coastal defense. On November 8 and 9, General Sherman issued orders for the organization of his Federal army in a march to the sea, with Savannah as the target. By the 15th, he began his move across Georgia. To assist his effort, Sherman requested support from the forces along the South Carolina coast.[185] General Foster was to strike inland between Charleston and Savannah, cutting the rail line connecting the cities and depriving the Southern forces defending Savannah of supplies and reinforcements.

General Hardee in Savannah, faced with increasing activity from Kilpatrick's Union cavalry moving in advance of Sherman's army, worked to strengthen the city's defenses for the expected land-based attack. On November 27, he requested that Gonzales come to Savannah "for a few days" bringing with him entrenching tools and light artillery.[186] At about the same time, General Foster left his Hilton Head base with a force of 5,000 infantry, cavalry, and artillery and 500 naval and marine troops.[187] His destination was Boyd's Landing on the Broad River. From there the force planned an advance against the rail station at Grahamville, cutting the vital railroad line. These events brought Gonzales to his first field battle.

ACTION AT HONEY HILL

From the beginning, Foster's approach to the landing failed to go as planned. In the fog at the landing site, several ships ran aground. Confederate pickets observed the arrival of the Union troops and provided warning to the district headquarters of Colonel Charles Colcock and to Generals Hardee in Savannah and Jones in Charleston. Though the Confederates in Charleston hurriedly prepared troops to respond to the Union threat, the only troops immediately available were Georgia militia under the command of Major General Gustavus Smith. Smith earlier resigned his Confederate general's commission out of disgust for Jefferson Davis and now held a commission from the state of Georgia. Smith's forces arrived in Savannah after taking a circuitous and taxing route in their retreat from Griswoldville where they fought Sherman's advancing forces. Hardee ordered them to move immediately to Grahamville.[188]

Smith faced a command problem. His Georgia troops, as a state-controlled military force, were not authorized to leave the state of Georgia. In the early morning hours of November 30, he challenged General Hardee to justify orders which would send his fatigued troops across the South Carolina border. Hardee explained the Union threat to Savannah and apparently satisfied Smith who ordered his units north. Their trains reached Grahamville by eight o'clock that same morning.[189] Hardee assigned Colonel Gonzales as the artillery officer to accompany the Georgia troops. On arrival, Gonzales introduced Smith to the district commander, Colonel Colcock, who rushed to the site from an inspection trip after postponing his wedding scheduled this same day.[190] Based on the Colonel's knowledge of the railroad which he founded, and of the geography of the area under his command, Smith allowed Colcock to select an appropriate defensive site. The colonel selected a small rise called Honey Hill where prepared entrenchments of artillery emplacements and rifle pits already existed from the time of General Lee's command of the district. The commanders rushed artillery and men to the position.

The Federal forces had started their advance the day before. Under Commander George Preble, now reinstated in the Navy after the CSS *Florida* incident,[191] the naval units had left Boyd's Landing with howitzers in tow. After taking several wrong roads, the force eventually made contact with Confederate forces sent out by Colonel Colcock when he received word of the Union landing. Federal infantry and cavalry under Brigadier General Edward Potter eventually overtook the naval unit, recognized the error in the direction of march, and countermarched to the proper crossroads. However, a later error at another crossroad caused another countermarch. The delays provided much-needed time for the Southern forces to assemble at Honey Hill.

On the 30th, the Federal forces finally concentrated under their commander Brigadier General John Hatch, a former cavalry commander wounded at South Mountain. As they moved forward, they encountered units of Colcock's 3rd South Carolina Cavalry accompanied by a single 12-pound gun. The first fire by the Confederate force caused casualties and disrupted the Federal march. Federal guns dueled the lone Southern gun and forced the South Carolina troops to retreat to a second position. As the Federal forces pursued, they began to flank the Southern troops. Colonel Colcock responded by setting fire to the dry grass through which the Union forces now advanced. This forced the Federals back and again delayed their advance.

These delaying tactics provided the time for the main body of the Southern forces to move into the entrenchments. Gonzales, who also knew the region from his earlier work preparing defenses in the area, assumed the responsibility of placing, aligning and sighting the artillery which was to play a key defensive role in holding these works. He made certain that there were adequate fields of fire for each piece and that there would be adequate infantry protection for each piece if pressed by the Federal infantry. By 11 o'clock that morning, Colcock reported to Smith that the position was ready for the Federal assault forming to their front. Smith declined to command the field and retired to Grahamville leaving Colcock in full command.

The first response from the defending force caused considerable damage in the Federal artillery. The first Federal infantry assaults followed. General Potter, formerly Foster's commissary officer and the organizer of the 1st North Carolina (Union) Infantry, led his force of four New York and one Ohio regiment as well as a regiment of U.S. Colored Troops and the Marine Brigade. Attempting to press the flank of the Confederate defensive position, he ran into a regular Confederate unit just arriving as reinforcements from Charleston. A second attack, with Colonel Alfred Hartwell leading the now famous 54th Massachusetts and the 55th Massachusetts Colored Infantry, approached the Confederate positions to within canister range. As a result, casualties for troops and officers were severe and included the colonel. By midafternoon, General Hatch abandoned any hope of carrying the Confederate line and began a retreat to the landing area at dark. The Confederates found the field littered with equipment, including enough Enfield rifles to equip one of their regiments. General Hatch reported the battle as a draw, and Colonel Hartwell received a brevet to Brigadier General for his actions during the battle. Yet, casualties for the Federal force were 746 men out of the 5,500 available. For the Confederate force of 1,400, losses were eight killed and 42 wounded.[192] Most of the Union casualties, and the success of the battle, were due to the excellent placement and use of the Southern artillery.

In his report, General Smith praised the officers, including Colonel Gonzales, for successfully resisting the Federal attack. A news article in the Charleston paper reporting on the Battle of Honey Hill called Gonzales an active participant in the fight, responsible for posting guns as well as encouraging the troops.[193]

With the arrival of additional Confederate units from throughout the Department, Smith conferred with Hardee and obtained agreement to return his troops to Georgia. General Jones moved to Pocotaligo with troops from Charleston. Gonzales remained in South Carolina at Jones's headquarters. The Federal forces under General Hatch established a defensive position around the Boyd's Neck landing site and, on December 6th through 9th, launched a series of raids threatening the railroad, but they met with only limited success. However, with the victory at Honey Hill, the rail line remained open until after the evacuation of Savannah.

THE LONG RETREAT

The military threat to Savannah reached its critical stage in December, 1864. Sherman and his unstoppable troops rapidly approached the city, and

Hardee had few men to hold the broad defensive positions there. Beauregard went to Savannah where he directed Hardee to prepare for possible evacuation of the city if necessary to save the army. The evacuation came on the 20th when Hardee successfully moved his forces across the Savannah River and out of the historic city.

The northward retreat of Hardee's army required preparation of a new defensive line to face Sherman's expected move toward Charleston. Prior to the evacuation, General Hardee prepared orders endorsed by General Beauregard which assigned Colonel Gonzales the responsibility for placing the field artillery in South Carolina in "the most appropriate positions for the defence of the Fourth Sub-District and the Combahee River line." The actual order was issued December 22 while Gonzales was in Pocotaligo.[194] Hardee assigned four batteries of artillery for the command. The responsibilities of the Chief of Artillery for coordinating the movement of heavy and light artillery during the retreat continued well into the new year.[195]

The new year brought continued pressure from Sherman's army. It was clear that the limited southern troops available in the department could not halt the continued progress of the Federal army or remove the threat to the coastal defenses and to the city of Charleston. Additional Federal pressure on Beauregard's command came with the successful attack on Wilmington further north. General Howard's forces in Beaufort also moved inland from the South Carolina coast, with Pocotaligo taken by mid–January. In Charleston, the pressure continued through nightly maneuvers by Federal gunboats near the harbor entrance, though Confederate torpedoes claimed the monitor *Patapsco* on one of these excursions.

While Sherman's main force remained inactive through early January, 1865, the Confederates prepared for the onslaught to come. Sherman finally issued orders for the march through South Carolina into North Carolina on January 19. Skirmishes along the Confederate river defense lines maintained the visible threat to Charleston, though the Southern forces were unaware that the city was not Sherman's primary objective. The strength of his forces allowed feints toward Augusta and Charleston, while directing a main force toward Columbia. In February, the final campaign began, and a march of terror followed. Sherman's sweep through South Carolina spared little. Hardeeville and other towns along the march met the torch. The Federals occupied the former headquarters town of Coosawhatchie and burned Grahamville, which Gonzales had fought to protect just two months before. The swamp terrain and the rivers slowed Sherman's troops but could not stop them. As the advance turned inland toward Columbia, it was clear Charleston could not be held against an attack from the rear. With General Gillmore's return to command the Federal troops on the coast, the pressure on the city's front increased also. Richmond continued to hold out the hope that the city could be held, but Beauregard did not intend to allow the troops defending the city to be bottled up by the approaching Federal armies.

Gonzales also clearly saw the end approaching. In January, he joined other family members urging his mother-in-law to move from Oak Lawn plantation to a safer site. He admonished her not to delay, stating that she was "behind the times in every thing that has to be done" to prepare to move from Sherman's path.[196] This was also the last opportunity to move cotton from the family plantation to Charleston for export to Nassau. Gonzales's family moved to Charleston shortly thereafter, leaving his sister-in-law to make final preparations for the estates, while sending food and supplies to the family in Charleston. As the Federals breached another defensive line, Gonzales contacted Colonel Allan McFarlan, a friend of Gonzales's brother-in-law Ralph Elliott and president of the rail line running from Charleston to Cheraw (SC), requesting assistance in making arrangements for moving the family north of Charleston to the area of Cheraw.[197] The family eventually moved to the Darlington area. Unknown to Gonzales, the area his family chose stood in the path of the Federal army.

Since he was still serving as chief of artillery for the department, Gonzales took one final opportunity to obtain his long-sought-after promotion. When public clamor prevented his assignment to active duty, John Pemberton resigned his lieutenant generalship and accepted a position of lieutenant colonel of artillery serving in the Richmond defenses. Eventually removed from this post, he became the inspector of artillery for the army in January. He began his inspections in Charleston. In a letter of February 10th, he informed General Cooper in Richmond that General Hardee's department required "a general or field grade officer" to oversee the 106 artillery pieces of the department. He recommended that a brigadier general be appointed and recommended Colonel Gonzales for the position.[198] General Hardee endorsed the request stating: "... [Gonzales's] long experience, his thorough and practical knowledge of artillery, and his great industry and zeal, fully entitle him to the position of brigadier general of artillery." The request went to the Secretary of War, then to President Davis and then to General Gorgas, Chief of Ordnance. Gorgas's response destroyed the last opportunity for Gonzales's promotion. He instead suggested Brigadier General Francis Shoup [whose name Gorgas misspells], an officer with extensive field experience currently in Richmond without assignment. Gorgas also offered several other officers as possible candidates. In his comment on the request, he replied, "Col. Gonzales is, in my opinion, not fitted for the position, and in this opinion I am joined by Genl. Gilmer, Chief Engineer, who had better opportunities than myself to observe Col. Gonzales professionally."[199] The basis for this disparaging statement is never clarified, but, with these comments returned to the Secretary of War, there would be no promotion for Gonzales. Despite the scope of his command, his experience in that command, and the recommendation of two experienced senior generals, the decision of Richmond denied him the last hope of promotion. General Shoup received orders to assume the artillery command under General Hardee, then General Johnston, but Johnston requested the order be revoked before Shoup's arrival.[200] In the final irony, Gonzales continued the duties of Chief of Artillery in the department for the rest of the war without the rank requested or the status Richmond deemed appropriate for the command.

By the time the bureaucracy in Richmond processed the request, Charleston was no longer in Confederate hands. With Sherman's move toward Columbia, Beauregard and Hardee concurred that the army in Charleston risked being cut off from the other forces in the Carolinas. After setting fire to the cotton stored in the city, spiking heavy guns, and burning the three Southern ironclads, Confederate troops moved out of Charleston on the night of February 17. They quietly abandoned Fort Sumter and the other fortifications, leaving their flags still flying. In the morning of the 18th, the monitor *Canonicus* fired two shots into Fort Moultrie. Receiving no replay, the Federal forces confirmed the evacuation, and the siege of Charleston ended. By 9 o'clock in the morning, the Federal flag again flew over Sumter.

Hardee's army continued the retreat north from the city, following the railroad toward Cheraw. They learned on the march that Sherman occupied Columbia and that most of the South Carolina capital lay in ashes. In North Carolina, the city of Wilmington fell to Federal forces under General Schofield on the 23rd.

At this juncture, General Joseph Johnston received orders to take command of the Departments of South Carolina, Georgia and Florida, and of Tennessee and Georgia, to consolidate available forces to face Sherman. Beauregard, again a subordinate, reported to Johnston along with Hardee and with Bragg from North Carolina. General Wade Hampton, who took the reins of Lee's cavalry upon Jeb Stuart's death, received assignment to his home state. The remnants of the Army of Tennessee moved with orders to join Johnston in the Carolinas. The Confederate forces available in the area moved toward a concentration in central North Carolina, near Raleigh and Smithfield, actively pursued by Federal forces of Generals Sherman and Schofield.

The role that Gonzales played in the movement of the Confederate forces is not clear from the available records. Hardee reported on his move north toward Cheraw in late February, indicating that he had trouble concentrating his force due to transport and geographic problems, leaving his artillery in the rear as he marched north. By the first of March, he reported his infantry and light artillery were at Cheraw. By the 9th, Hardee was in Fayetteville. It is most likely that Gonzales was in direct charge of the movement of Hardee's artillery throughout the retreat from Charleston to Fayetteville. Johnston met with Hardee in Fayetteville. After this, as the Confederate forces concentrated in the Smithfield area, it appears that Gonzales had responsibility for the organization of the artillery reserves for Johnston's armies. Since Johnston arrived without staff, it is quite likely that Beauregard's influence placed Gonzales on Johnston's staff in the role that Beauregard, and Hardee, knew he could ably fulfill. On March 10, Johnston from Raleigh ordered Hardee to place his reserve artillery 15 miles to the rear of his main forces. On that same day, Hardee crossed the Cape Fear River at Fayetteville. On the 16th, as the Federals attacked Hardee at Averasboro, Johnston ordered Hardee to send all reserve artillery to Smithfield, repeating the order on the 18th prior to the attack on Sherman's flank.

The retreat took its toll on the spirit of the Confederate army, and on its strength. Desertions rose as the retreat moved north. Some of the South Carolina units disbanded. Georgia's Governor Brown called the Georgia militia home, and South Carolina's governor called on the state militia troops to protect areas within the state. Confused intelligence and confused orders created disruptions to the movement of men and materiel.[201] However, the fighting spirit still lived in the Southern armies. In early March, Bragg attacked unsuccessfully in an attempt to halt the Federal force moving from the North Carolina coast at Kinston. A cavalry raid by Wade Hampton caught, and almost captured, Federal cavalry commander Judson Kilpatrick literally with his pants down.

As Sherman moved north toward his planned junction with other Federal forces at Goldsboro, he found Hardee's army across his path. On the 16th at Averasboro, Sherman attacked and flanked Hardee's defensive position and forced a Southern retreat. Only a small battle by this war's bloody standards, it nonetheless delayed the advance of one wing of Sherman's force. As the Federal army spread out on its separate routes of advance, the wings became sufficiently separated to invite Confederate attack. Johnston organized the attack by his combined forces on Sherman's left wing units under command of Major General Henry Slocum. At Bentonville on March 19, the now consolidated Confederate forces struck two Federal corps on the march. After initial success in breaking the Federal defensive line, the veteran Union forces held their position on the field long enough for Sherman to order up reinforcements and counterattack. After a three-day battle, the Confederate forces retreated back to Smithfield.

After Bentonville, records show Gonzales's role as chief of artillery with orders received primarily from Beauregard, then serving as Johnston's second in command. The orders show Gonzales remained at Hillsboro for the last half of March and into April maintaining the artillery reserves of the army, shifting artillery to the various commands on orders from Beauregard's headquarters.[202] Gonzales also had the opportunity to work with Pemberton again.

On March 30, Johnston from Smithfield requested Pemberton in Hillsboro to have Gonzales prepare two batteries for distribution.[203] The following day, Beauregard ordered Gonzales to send batteries to Salisbury, and to prepare to move artillery to Raleigh or Smithfield to protect it from Federal cavalry under Major General Stoneman then moving into North Carolina from east Tennessee. Responding to the threat to the Confederate line of movement, and the threat to the Confederate government now retreating from Richmond through the area,[204] Johnston sent forces to hold Salisbury. In this action, Pemberton provided one last field service in the war commanding the batteries there, though he narrowly missed capture when Stoneman's cavalry attacked on April 12 and seized the Southern artillery.

While the maneuvering and skirmishing continued for several weeks after Bentonville, the heavy fighting stopped. As Sherman linked up with the other Federal forces, over 90,000 Federal troops were in the field to face Johnston's force of less than 20,000. Sherman went to Petersburg to confer with Grant, and neither side took any major action. The Federal army captured Smithfield and Raleigh. Then, with news of Lee's surrender in Virginia, Johnston sought an armistice. On April 14, Johnston requested and received a suspension of action from Sherman. On that same day in Charleston harbor, General Robert Anderson raised the same United States flag that Gonzales watched flying over Fort Sumter four years before. That evening John Wilkes Booth shot President Lincoln in Ford's Theater.

Johnston and Sherman signed an agreement effectively ending hostilities in North Carolina on April 18. The terms agreed to went beyond what the current government in Washington chose to accept, and Sherman had to renegotiate. Nonetheless, the fighting was over, and the Confederate army surrendered. In paroles issued by the Federal army at Greensboro, North Carolina on April 30, 1865, A. J. Gonzales appears on the list of surrendering Confederate officers as "Colonel, Chief of Artillery, Hardee's Corps, Johnston's Army."[205]

WAR'S END BRINGS NO PEACE

After four long years of war, the Confederacy was no more. After four tiring years of service to the Confederacy, the war was over for Ambrosio Gonzales. He was alive and physically unharmed. He had served his adopted land and the heritage of his new family with honor. Now he could go home. Like the South of the vanished Confederacy, like his home state, like the City of Charleston, Gonzales attempted to recover from the war in the society of family and friends. He found his family in Springville, South Carolina, where they had lived since their evacuation from Oak Lawn and Charleston. With the news of Oak Lawn's destruction, they remained in the Darlington area for some time.

During the summer after the war, Gonzales was a guest at the wedding of Mrs. Mary Gray Crockett. Mrs. Crockett described the "General" as a distinguished gentleman "who was a splendid performer on the piano and gave us some fine selections."[206] Mary Chestnut also described his singing at another party after the war. At least his social graces survived the trauma of war.

Still, the pleasantries of the social life and the comradery of former Confederate officers and soldiers did not alter the reality of the postwar situation for the South or for the Elliott-Gonzales family. The Union war effort and the occupation and destruction of property placed ruin at the doors of the Elliott families. Federal authorities confiscated some of their plantations under the questionably legal Federal wartime tax laws. Union troops destroyed other plantations. The first loss of four plantations and a home in Beaufort came with the capture of the Port Royal area; the last loss came with the burning of Oak Lawn during Federal movements after the fall of Charleston. During the war, investments in Confederate bonds, legal problems with the ownership of slaves the Elliotts rented to others, and the Federal sales of confiscated lands all damaged the Elliott finances. Confederate deserters murdered one of their sons-in-law, leaving his wife to raise a family alone. Also, in the common story of the war, Federal soldiers with the help of freed slaves stole hidden family silver. By late 1865, the Elliotts recovered title to some of their holdings, including Oak Lawn and Social Hall plantations. At least there was land to live on.

Gonzales, though of great service to his country in the war, could offer little immediate help to his extended family. He had no established profession before the war, so he had none to fall back on at the close of the war. He traveled to Charleston. Then, apparently taking advantage of a grand general amnesty offered in 1857 by the Spanish government, he traveled to Cuba to visit relatives and to seek financial support.[207] In early 1866 he established a business in Charleston with a former associate.[208] The Elliotts were none too happy about their Hattie living in Charleston and expressed concern for her health and safety, especially in April with the arrival of her fourth son Benigno.[209] The business survived only about six months, and Gonzales and his family searched for other means.

Using his wife's share of her father's inheritance, Gonzales acquired the Social Hall property from the Elliotts.[210] His initial efforts on the property appeared to be the improvement of the saw mill built on the river. He took his lumber business to Cuba, attempting to negotiate contracts for wood with Cuban railroads.[211] In the spring of 1867, for whatever reason, Gonzales and his family abandoned the city and moved to Social Hall. Problems with labor, equipment failures, defaulted payments by customers and canceled orders made the mill little more than a break-even effort.[212]

In the spring of 1868, Gonzales traveled to Cuba again with his family. While there, they met with Jefferson Davis, who was vacationing on the island. Whatever animosities developed between them during the war appear to have been put aside by the former Confederates.[213]

The environment for economic recovery of ex–Confederates remained poor under the reconstruction governments. Taxes continued to plague land owners, and business continued to be poor. In 1869, Cuba called Gonzales again. He packed up his wife and five children and set sail for his island homeland. The trip took them through the Florida Keys where they visited with Stephen Mallory and informed him that he was the godfather of their son Alfonso.[214] The Gonzales family's arrival in Cuba was not without incident, however. With the *Grito de Yara*, a recent revolt in the eastern provinces of the island, the Cubans questioned all arriving passengers concerning their reason for visiting Cuba. This was especially true for someone with a history like Gonzales. He remained under surveillance for his first few months on the island.[215]

As Gonzales arrived, his friend and former commander Pierre Beauregard wrote a letter of recommendation to Thomas Jordan, Beauregard's wartime Chief of Staff, who was in the process of being hired by a Cuban junta to become the commander of the revolutionary army on the island.[216] Beauregard stated his opposition to filibustering efforts, perhaps referring to the earlier Cuban liberation efforts. This was a strange position considering Beauregard's threat in 1856 to resign his army commission to become the second in command for William Walker's filibuster expedition in Nicaragua.[217] Still, he informed Jordan that Gonzales was in Cuba and might provide assistance. It is reasonable to conclude that Gonzales considered participating in the current rebellion, but he was too closely watched by a suspicious Cuban government. No doubt, the safety of his family came first. Jordan served for about a year before he was replaced by Cuban Maximo Gomez. Despite their long association through the war years, there is no evidence that Jordan and Gonzales exchanged correspondence while they were in Cuba.

Through the support of relatives and associates, Gonzales maintained himself and his family in Havana, then moved to Pueblo Nuevo in Matanzas province. He reestablished himself through teaching positions at two local colleges. He also gave private language lessons which increased his time away from his family but provided additional income for them.[218] The family finally seemed to be moving toward financial recovery. In May, his wife gave birth to a second daughter, Anita Rosita. The children received formal schooling and appeared acclimated to their new environment. There were social visits to Gonzales's relatives, and the older boys exchanged affectionate letters with their Elliott relatives in the States.

Then in September, tragedy came when yellow fever struck the family.

Though several of the children were ill, they recovered. Their mother, only 29 years old, did not. Hattie's death was emotionally devastating to Ambrosio. Friends described the deep love that he had for his wife in spite of their age difference. There is no question that her loss continued to haunt Gonzales, and the loss of her love and companionship may have contributed to the lack of direction in his later life.

For reasons not recorded, the loss of his wife led to his decision to return to South Carolina and to the Elliott family at Oak Lawn with four of the children, temporarily leaving the older and more independent boys, Narciso and Alfonso, in Cuba with the Dalcour family in Matanzas. In South Carolina, Gonzales left his four younger children in the feminine hands of their grandmother and maternal aunts at Oak Lawn while he struggled to find employment in the States. He sought employment as a teacher in Savannah, then moved to New York to seek similar employment. There, while living in tenement conditions, he found some work in assorted jobs. He also became a member of the St. Bartholomew's Episcopal Church choir.

In December 1870, the remaining sons returned from Cuba to join the Elliotts, though Gonzales was not informed of their departure or arrival. His absence from his children and his apparent problems in finding steady employment strained and then broke the relationship with the Elliotts. The Elliott family also worked to turn the children against their father, and in this they were quite successful. Raised on the stories of the Old South and its antebellum traditions and living through the social and political upheaval of Reconstruction, they lost connection with the heritage and traditions of their absentee father. In time the children dropped their Spanish names to adopt English ones — Ambrosio became Ambrose, Benigno became William Elliott, and Anita, the last born, assumed her grandmother's name of Harriet Rutledge after the elder Mrs. Elliott's death.

Personal success continued to be out of reach for the former adventurer and soldier. Through his fairly constant correspondence with the Elliotts, his children and especially his son Ambrose, the family followed his wanderings and shared the plans that never seemed to become reality. Gonzales held a number of different jobs, all short term — an agent for a New York business firm, a minor clerkship on Wall Street, a private teacher and an interpreter, and even singing in the church choir. In 1872, he moved to Baltimore where he found employment as a teacher and found time to become a member of an Episcopal choir. While in Baltimore, he learned from family members of the arrival of his oldest boys from Cuba. He authorized brother-in-law Ralph Elliott to sell his rifle and use the money for the children's well-being, but the Elliotts refused the proposal. They also refused a check that Gonzales sent.[219] During the summer of that year, he spent a month outside Warrenton at the farm of his former commander John Pemberton.[220]

Over the next few years, Gonzales moved between teaching, assorted jobs and various financial schemes while living in New York. He even applied for a position with the Grant administration. None of this work provided the kind of income that he needed to return to care for his children or stop his transient life. While several of his financial schemes centered on the Social Hall plantation, his neglect of the South Carolina property put it in jeopardy of confiscation by the government through nonpayment of taxes. In June 1874, J. D. Warren wrote to Gonzales in New York that the land was sold for back taxes and that Warren had acquired it for about $84, which Gonzales could repay in 90 days to retain the title. The letter was returned unclaimed.[221]

Gonzales lived for about a year in Washington, then returned to Cuba in 1879 to work for the railroad. During this period, he inherited $10,000 from an aunt, part of which he sent to the Elliotts for education of his younger children, payment of back taxes and construction at Oak Lawn plantation. With this, family relations warmed somewhat.

After travels to Paris, he returned to the United States in early 1883. He apparently found limited employment as a private tutor and translator. In the two years which followed, he petitioned for a university professorship in New Orleans, calling on the support of his former associate William Porcher Miles, the former Confederate congressman from South Carolina and now a prominent Louisiana sugar planter. He also sought Miles's support for a diplomatic appointment to a mission in "Spanish America."[222] He reported that he had the support of the governor and congressional delegation of South Carolina and the recommendation of a New York supreme court justice.

Gonzales supported the Democrats in the elections of 1884 in the hope that they would provide him with a diplomatic posting to Latin America. Just as he had over the last 30 years, Gonzales obtained recommendations from prominent supporters for his petition for a patronage position with the government. He moved to Washington to lobby for his request with the Cleveland administration. As with the previous efforts, the hoped-for position never materialized.

In this life of frustration, Gonzales sought the comfort of spiritualism, then a rising movement in the United States. He developed a relationship with P.L.O.A. Keeler, who specialized in seances, slate writing and "spirit" photographs — trick photos of his clients purporting to show the spirits of the dead surrounding the living subject. Gonzales involved himself in the belief, receiving written messages from his beloved Hattie from beyond the grave. He ultimately published a report of the spirit messages from his dead wife in order to show to others the connection that he believed existed with the world beyond.[223]

A DREAM OF CUBA

Even in the midst of his postwar struggle to rebuild his life, to obtain gainful employment and to maintain his tenuous link to his children, Ambrosio Gonzales continued his activities for Cuban independence. Throughout, the cause of Cuban freedom occupied his thoughts and energies. He continued to write and speak openly on Cuban freedom — "Cuba Libre." He wrote editorials and letters to various publications and prepared newspaper articles describing in detail the Lopez expeditions.[224] He participated in Cuban celebrations and appeared to maintain contact with the Cuban movement in New York and Baltimore.

There is no documentation that Gonzales played a role in the establishment of the Junta Central Republican de Cuba y Puerto Rico. This society linked the independence movement for the two islands and provided a lobbying organization for the independence movements for both Spanish-held territories. The group organized in New York during the time that Gonzales resided there. It is certainly likely that he knew or was associated with the people responsible for the movement, even if he was not himself actively involved.

In late 1889, he became involved in the First International Conference on American States, serving as a translator at the conference. This once again involved him in the question of independence for Cuba and other Spanish Caribbean territories. The idea for the conference developed out of the brief Garfield administration when Secretary of State James Blaine proposed an 1881 Pan-American conference of the nations of the western hemisphere. The plan collapsed with Garfield's assassination. Blaine, though out of office, finally succeeded in influencing Congress which forced the conference on outgoing President Cleveland. The conference took place under the new Harrison administration, with Blaine returned to the role of Secretary of State. Even though there was considerable disagreement between the various nations on the role of the conference, the meeting brought together the leaders of the American nations for the first time. The meeting also provided a focus for discussion of the future of Cuba by the leaders of the Cuban liberation movement.

José Marti, the hero and martyr of Cuban independence now in exile from his Cuban homeland, attended the conference as Uruguayan consul from New York. Expelled from Cuba in 1879, Marti came to the United States to continue his quest for Cuban freedom from Spain. Moving in the circle of Cuban activists built on the foundation established by Gonzales and his contemporaries, Marti wrote articles, published the revolutionary paper *Patria* and established links to the movements seeking Cuban and Puerto Rican independence. At the conference, he established a strong friendship with

Gonzalo de Quesada, a fellow Cuban serving as the secretary to the Argentine delegation. Other Cubans served as delegates, as alternates or, like Gonzales, as translators. This provided a core of attendees focused on uniting the
hemisphere's nations for the expulsion of Spain.[225] There is little doubt that
Gonzales took every opportunity to retell the stories of the Lopez movement
and his role in that great adventure to the young and enthusiastic Cubans
attending the conference.

At the meeting, Gonzales joined other patriots in promoting a project
proposed by Hamilton Fish in 1869 — Cuban independence from Spain in
return for a cash payment to Spain. The money for such a project was to come
from private funds but with payment guaranteed by the U.S. government.
Though there was not wide support, Gonzales persuaded his friend Senator
Wilkinson Call of Florida to introduce a resolution, authored by Gonzales,
supporting such a plan. Resistance to the proposal within Congress prevented
any action on the resolution.

In the year following the conference, Gonzales's health began a steady
decline. Now in his seventies, there were problems with his eyes and development of a slow paralysis which curtailed participation in the then active
Cuban freedom movement. He moved to Columbia, South Carolina, where
his sons owned a newspaper. The family correspondence shows little respect
for the senior Gonzales, even with his age and infirmities. His poor health,
and the strained relationship with the Elliott family, caused him to leave after
only a few months. He traveled to Key West where he hoped to find a more
favorable climate for his recovery. Also in the Keys, there was an established
colony of Cubans dedicated to their home island's liberation from Spain.
Within the circle of Cubans, Gonzales held a place in the history and legacy
of the movement. During the summer of 1892, Gonzales met with José Marti,
the leader of the current revolutionary movement, and other movement organizers. A very ill Gonzales attended a meeting between leaders of the 1868
Cuban revolution and current delegates of the Cuban Revolutionary Party.
As the assembly greeted him, he rose from his chair to call, "I salute the sav-
iors of the Homeland."[226]

Even with the open and friendly surroundings, Gonzales was forced to
leave the Keys. The lack of proper hospital facilities and a yellow fever outbreak encouraged him to move to New York for special medical care. There
Gonzalo de Quesada, now serving as Marti's secretary, visited him in an inva-
lid hospital in late 1892. Gonzales was sleeping when Quesada called to him
softly. Gonzales awoke, opened his eyes and to his visitor said, "I was dream-
ing of Cuba."[227]

In spite of the care Gonzales received, his health continued to deterio-
rate. After spending so much of his life and energy in the cause of Cuban
freedom, Gonzales did not live to see his homeland cast off the Spanish yoke.

Ambrosio José Gonzales died in New York City on July 31, 1893, at the age of 75. Burial was two days later in Woodlawn Cemetery, the Bronx, New York.

A LEGACY OF CHILDREN

The story of Ambrosio Gonzales and his legacy does not stop with his death. He was less than successful in his business pursuits and in his role as a father — his own son described his father's material success as a life that "does not tempt to imitation."[228] Yet, he gave of his spirit and energy to two great causes of the time. Perhaps it was this spirit or his ideas for these causes that continued after his death. Whatever the force, the Cuban patriot and Confederate citizen and officer left his legacy with his children.

In an obituary notice for Gonzales in the *Greenville News* of August 3, 1893, the paper stated that Gonzales's life

> ...was a very stormy and eventful one. Its fruits will, perhaps, be gathered when ... the country he loved and strove for takes her place among the free nations. He has left sons here who will do his name honor and his adopted state good service.[229]

This epitaph was surprisingly prophetic.

Like many children, the Gonzales offspring moved away from the heritage of their father, a father they so seldom saw. The children knew little of Cuba in their young lives, and, for the older boys, the war they saw in South Carolina brought simple memories of horses and swords and uniforms. With Gonzales's lengthy absences, they grew up in the ways of their mother's family, listening to the tales of the plantation South and the traditions of the Elliotts' heritage. They saw first hand the struggle for life and livelihood in the postwar reconstruction South. Their Cuban heritage became a symbol of their father's neglect, fed in part by the bitterness of their Elliott relations. The decisions to change their Spanish given names, even taking on Elliott family names outwardly expressed their childhood bitterness to their rarely seen father.

As their father moved from job to job, his children grew up. Ambrose received little formal education, only a few years in public or private schools. At 16, he learned telegraphy and spent four years at the Grahamville (SC) station on the Charleston and Savannah Railway, the very site that his father fought to save from Union forces at the Battle of Honey Hill. For several years, he moved around the country as a telegraph operator. William was slightly more fortunate. He attended Kings Mountain academy for a short period and, later, The Citadel in the city his father fought to defend. Unhappy with their jobs, these brothers gravitated toward the interests of their Cuban grand-father and became journalists.[230] Over time, brothers Narciso, Ambrose, and William Gonzales achieved some measure of local prominence. They became involved in South Carolina politics, in writing, and then in publishing. They established the newspaper *The State* in Columbia, South Carolina, in 1891.

Then as so often happens, their adults' view of the world led to an increased respect for their heritage, their heritage from Cuba and from the South. Indeed, Gonzales left his children the dream of an independent Cuba. They began to assume their father's dedication to this cause. They used their paper's editorial power to become more and more outspoken on the issue of Cuban freedom. They demanded U.S. intervention against the Spanish in Cuba. With the loss of the USS *Maine*, the Gonzales brothers took up the cry for war with Spain. They volunteered their services and became a part of the invasion of Cuba in the Spanish-American War. William led a unit of the 2nd South Carolina militia as a Captain, serving under General Fitzhugh Lee, the former Confederate general. Narciso, who published his experiences,[231] joined the Cuban army of General Emilio Nunez, a leader of filibustering expeditions to Cuba from Tampa. Then he served under Cuban General Maximo Gomez, who in 1870 replaced former Confederate Thomas Jordan as a leader in the Cuban Revolution of 1869. Ambrose served as a major in the occupation army at Santiago.[232] Fifty years after their father struck a blow for Cuban freedom and shed his blood for Cuban independence, the Gonzales children were part of the force which finally removed the Spanish from the island.

After the war, the Gonzales brothers continued their support for the Cuban cause by campaigning against United States involvement in Cuban affairs. William, then editor of *The State*, received the appointment as U.S. Minister to Cuba in 1913 from President Woodrow Wilson. He served for six years, during this time trying to resolve the Cuban revolt of 1917. In 1919, he became ambassador to Peru where he served about two years. He received the diplomatic appointments that his father so vigorously but unsuccessfully sought. Narciso continued his active role in the editing of their newspaper. His positions on state politics ultimately led to his assassination by a former lieutenant governor of South Carolina. A monument honoring this Gonzales brother stands across from the state capital grounds.[233]

Though Gonzales's children had little involvement in the events of the war, they became active in Confederate veterans affairs. Perhaps through the stories they heard of the war, they began to connect to their father and his role in this great struggle. They perhaps remembered the stories about the strength of their young mother struggling to survive with her husband away at war. They remembered the scenes of reconstruction life and the privations and struggles of the women in their adopted family during the postwar years. William Gonzales supported the proposal to build a statue respectfully honoring the women of the Confederacy. He provided leadership to the effort and ultimately had his proposal chosen as the inscription for the monument. The monument stands today on the South Carolina State Capital grounds. He also contributed inscriptions which adorn other sites in the capital.[234]

Gonzales's youngest daughter Harriet (or Anita Rosita, her given name), born during the ill-fated trip to Cuba, married Frank Hampton linking the heritage of the Elliotts and the Gonzaleses to the long history of the Hampton family of South Carolina. She lies today only a few feet away from the grave of Confederate General Wade Hampton, near the site of her murdered brother's monument.

Thus the Gonzales children, though once estranged from their father, carried on the dream of their father. They played their role in freeing Cuba from the yoke of Spain, opening one of the last sites of European colonialism in the Americas to the potential of democracy. They assisted in returning to Cuban soil the revolutionary flag that their father carried and bled for, the flag that is the symbol of Cuba today. They worked to honor the struggles and losses faced by the Confederacy's soldiers and civilians. They also carried on their father's tradition of influencing the course of free people and their governments through their newspaper work, their strong editorials and their dynamic political activities. Gonzales did not live to see their work, but, unquestionably, he would have been proud of his children.

A LIFE OF CAUSES

Ambrosio José Gonzales reflects the color and energy of Cuba and the United States in the nineteenth century. Educated and secure, he abandoned his life to fight for the abstract idea of freedom. Involved in a bold adventure, he sailed to free his Cuban home only to shed his flood in the failed cause. He spent the prime years of his life working without success to obtain Cuba's freedom from Spain. José Marti, who gave his own life for Cuba and is considered by many historians to be the "father of Cuban independence," stated in an article following Gonzales's death that "in the history of his people, Gonzales has written his name with characters that will never be erased."[235]

Gonzales moved in the highest circles of U.S. leadership, meeting with presidents, statesmen, and prominent politicians at national and local levels — the men of the nineteenth century who set the course for a nation and ultimately for a world. He shared his vision as he moved across the breadth of the nation, from its established coastal cities of New York, Washington, Charleston, Savannah, New Orleans and to its new lands and peoples in Texas, Kentucky, Mississippi and Florida. He watched with disappointment as the plans to free a homeland collapsed. Then, somewhere in his travels, he found a love that perhaps changed his direction in life. As the world around him and his new family erupted in war, he placed his life in the cause of the people he had come to know through his struggles for Cuba. He served in the defense of his adopted state, first as a simple volunteer, then as an officer for the new Confederate nation. He served loyally and with great energy on the staffs of the most famous Southern commanders — Beauregard, Lee, Pemberton, Hardee, Johnston. He was the artillery commander for a battle front sustained by the strength of its artillery, serving his important role in the most successful Confederate defensive action of the war. Yet, he received little notice for his years of service. He is not mentioned in Major Johnson's first-hand history of the defense of Charleston; he is unnamed in the memoirs, and rarely mentioned in the biographies, of his famous commanders and fellow officers; and he produced no personal memoirs or reflections on the war to tell his story. Even his role in the successful defense at Honey Hill is not mentioned in contemporary or modern descriptions of the battle. Despite the scope of his command and his experience in his job and in spite of the recommendations of prominent senior generals, decisions by Jefferson Davis and by the Richmond government denied him on six separate occasions the posterity and historical notoriety accorded even the most insignificant or notorious of the Confederate generals. Like so many heros of this massive war, his years of service to the Confederate cause faded into obscurity in the broad history of the conflict.

Cuban patriot and freedom fighter, military adventurer, soldier for the Southern cause, and often absentee father, Ambrosio José Gonzales lived the adventures of the nineteenth-century world. Like so many other adventurers, he died without the realization of his dream. His son Narciso summed this life simply. Ambrosio Gonzales was "a soldier under two flags but one cause; that of community independence."[236]

Notes

During preparation of this manuscript, the author became aware of a dissertation from West Virginia University which deals with the life of Ambrosio José Gonzales. Dr. Antonio Rafae De La Cova, a Cuban by birth and an exile from his homeland by politics, has written an excellent and detailed biography. His work covers in depth the Cuban movement in the United States during the filibuster period. It provides much insight into the misinterpretation of information about the Lopez movement and on the role of freemasonry in organization of the expeditions. It is highly recommended to anyone interested in further information on the roots of the movement for Cuban freedom.

1. U.R. Brooks, "Ambrosio José Gonzales," *Stories of the Confederacy* (Columbia, The State Company, 1912), pp. 284–299; Lewis Pinckney Jones, "Ambrosio José Gonzales, a Cuban Patriot in Carolina," *South Carolina Historical Magazine*, LVI, No. II (April 1955), pp. 67–76; Lewis Pinckney Jones, "Carolinians and Cubans: The Elliotts and Gonzales, Their Work and Their Writings," Ph.D. dissertation, University of North Carolina, 1952.

2. T. Harry Williams, *P.G.T. Beauregard: Napoleon in Gray* (Baton Rouge, Louisiana State University Press, 1955), p. 5; Hamilton Basso, *Beauregard: The Great Creole* (New York, Charles Scribner's Sons, 1933), p. 17.

3. Jones, "Carolinians and Cubans," p. 77.

4. O.D.D.O. (J. C. Davis), *History of the Late Expedition to Cuba* (New Orleans, Daily Delta Publishing, 1850), p. 59.

5. Samuel Flagg Bemis, *Diplomatic History of the United States*, 5th Edition (New York, Holt, Rinehart and Winston, 1965), p. 313.

6. Robert Granville Caldwell, *The Lopez Expedition to Cuba, 1848–51* [Dissertation] (Princeton, Princeton University Press, 1915), pp. 10–11, 17.

7. Herminio Portell Vila, *Narciso Lopez y su Epoca*, I (Havana: Cultural, S. A., 1930), pp. 242–245.

8. Portell Vila, *Narciso Lopez y su Epoca*, I, p. 76.

9. Alfred Hoyt Bill, *Rehearsal for Conflict* (New York: History Book Club, 1947). Worth also managed to involve himself in the unseemly affair of Gideon Pillow and in accusations questioning the leadership of General Winfield Scott.

10. Ambrosio José Gonzales, *Manifesto On Cuban Affairs Addressed to the People of the United States* (New Orleans: Daily Delta, 1852), p. 6.

11. Caldwell, *The Lopez Expedition to Cuba*, pp. 43–46; Portell Vila, *Narciso Lopez y su Epoca*, I, pp. 14ff.

12. Caldwell, *ibid.*, p. 10.

13. Vidal Morales y Morales, *Iniciadores y Primeros Martires de la Revolucion Cubana*, II (Havana: Consejo Nacional de Cultura, 1963), p. 12.

14. Caldwell, *The Lopez Expedition to Cuba*, p. 33.

15. Morales, *Iniciadores*, pp. 19–20.

16. *Ibid.*, p. 21; Caldwell, *The Lopez Expedition*, p. 46.

17. Ambrosio José Gonzales, "On To Cuba," *The Times Democrat*, March 30, 1884, p. 9.

18. The copy of Gonzales's pamphlet "Manifesto on Cuban Affairs" in the Library of Congress carries a personal handwritten dedication from the author to Caleb Cushing.

19. Ambrosio José Gonzales, "The Cuban Crusade; A Full History of the Georgian and Lopez Expeditions," *Times Democrat*, April 6, 1884, p. 2.

20. Morales, *Iniciadores*, pp. 193–194.

21. James T. McIntosh, ed., *The Papers of Jefferson Davis*, vol. 3 (Baton Rouge: Louisiana State University Press, 1981), pp. 292–293.

22. Basil Rauch, *American Interest in Cuba: 1848–1855* (New York: Columbia University Press, 1948), pp. 113–119. Mrs. Greenhow became a famous Confederate spy, working in a network established by Gen. Thomas Jordan, who also served with Gonzales on Gen. Beauregard's staff.

23. Lynda Crist, ed., *Papers of Jefferson Davis*, vol. 4 (Baton Rouge: Louisiana State University Press, 1983), pp. 58–59.

24. Portell Vila, *Narciso Lopez y su Epoca*, II, pp. 450–458.

25. "Revolution in Cuba — New and Important Movement," New York *Herald*, December 6, 1849, p. 2.

26. Robert E. May, *John A. Quitman: Old South Crusader* (Baton Rouge: Louisiana State University Press, 1985), p. 237.

27. Theodore O'Hara, a lawyer, served as a Captain in the army, receiving a brevet to major in the Mexican War. He later served with the filibuster William Walker. As the editor of the Louisville *Democrat*, he authored the famous poem "Bivouac of the Dead." With the outbreak of the Civil War, he raised the Alabama Light Dragoons in Mobile and occupied Fort McRee. He served as aide to Confederate General Johnston at Shiloh and later to General Breckenridge.

28. John Pickett served the Confederate government as consul to Veracruz and then as Confederate representative to the Juarez government. Strongly expansionist, his intercepted dispatches to Richmond offended the Mexicans with discussions of Confederate acquisition of Mexican territory.

29. May, *John A. Quitman*, p. 238. As a Confederate general, Lovell was responsible for the defense of New Orleans during the naval attack by Union Admiral David Farragut.

30. Charles Dufour, *Gentle Tiger: The Gallant Life of Roberdeau Wheat* (Baton Rouge: Louisiana State University Press, 1957), p. 33ff. Wheat afterward joined the filibuster expedition of William Walker which attempted to take Nicaragua. He left the service of Garibaldi in Italy at the start of the Civil War to recruit and lead the famous Louisiana Tiger Battalion. He was killed at Gaines Mill in the Peninsula Campaign.

31. May, *John A. Quitman*, p. 238.

32. *Ibid.*, p. 238. Hartstene became a Commander in the Confederate Navy. Assigned to Charleston, he commanded the boat that transferred the Federal defenders of Fort Sumter to the waiting U.S. Navy vessels. He served in Charleston with Gonzales during the War.

33. At the start of the Civil War, Scott worked to draw Kentucky into the Confederacy, replacing General Hodges on the "Council of Ten" provisional government; he served as a regimental, brigade, division and departmental surgeon, surrendering with Breckenridge at the end of the war. *Confederate Veteran*, vol. XI, July, 1903, pp. 331–332.

34. Sources differ as to the actual credit for the design of the flag. Some sources, citing Cirilo Villaverde, credit Miguel Tolon, others credit Lopez himself. Vidal Morales credits Lopez, Gonzales, and Iznaga.

35. O.D.D.O., *History of the Late Expedition to Cuba*, pp. 60–61.

36. Gonzales, "On to Cuba"; Lieutenant Hardy, *History and Adventures of the Cuban Expedition* (Cincinnati: Lorenzo Stratton, 1850), 94 pp.; O.D.D.O., *History of the Late Expedition to Cuba*.

37. Hardy, *Cuban Expedition*, pp. 46–49.

38. Gonzales, "On to Cuba"; O.D.D.O. *History of the Late Expedition*, pp. 76–79.

39. Gonzales, "On to Cuba"; Savannah (GA) *Morning News*, March 10, 1935, p. 4.

40. Gonzales, *Manifesto on Cuban Affairs*, p. 9.

41. Charles Gulick, Jr. and Winnie Allen, ed., *Papers of Mirabeau Bonaparte Lamar*, vol. IV (Austin: Von Boeckmann-Jones Co., 1924), p. 310.

42. Eli N. Evans, *Judah P. Benjamin* (New York: Macmillian, 1988), p. 42.

43. Gulick, "Letter of A.J. Gonzales to M.B. Lamar, Mar. 14, 1851," *Papers of Mirabeau Bonaparte Lamar*, vol. IV, p. 282.

44. Portell Vila, *Narciso Lopez y su Epoca*, III, p. 482. Titus, who may have served in Lopez's Matanzas expedition, fought with Walker in Nicaragua, became a Confederate blockade runner, and was the founder of Titusville, FL.

45. Portell Vila, *Narciso Lopez y su Epoca*, III, p. 62.

46. L. M. Perez (ed.), "Lopez's Expedition to Cuba, 1850-51; Betrayal of the *Cleopatra*, 1851," *Publications of the Southern History Association*, vol. X, 1906, pp. 345–362.

47. Gonzales, "The Cuban Crusade; A Full History ...," p. 9.

48. Portell Vila, *Narciso Lopez y su Epoca*, III, p. 228.

49. The young lady accompanying Crittenden wrote of her experiences [H. M. Hardiman, *The Free Flag of Cuba: or the Martyrdom of Lopez. A Tale of the Liberating Expedition of 1851*]. She later became the wife of South Carolina Governor Francis Pickens and was the only woman to have her portrait on currency of the Confederate States. As governor, Pickens gave Gonzales his first military commission in the Civil war.

50. Caldwell, *The Lopez Expedition*, pp. 91–113.

51. Bemis, *Diplomatic History of the United States*, pp. 315–320.

52. Rauch, *American Interest in Cuba*, pp. 228–230.

53. Gonzales, *Manifesto On Cuban Affairs*, p. 3.

54. John S. Thrasher had a long history of support for Cuban independence. His trade newspaper published in Cuba so offended the Cuban government that they jailed him on one occasion. Thrasher also translated and published a travelogue on Cuba which received wide readership in the United States. During the war, Thrasher served as General Superintendent, Press Association of the Confederate States formed in 1862.

55. May, *John A. Quitman*, pp. 290–295.

56. *Ibid.*, p. 295.

57. Crist, "From Ambrosio Gonzales," *Papers of Jefferson Davis*, vol. 5, pp. 54–55.

58. Brooks, *Stories of the Confederacy*, p. 290.

59. William Elliott to his wife, March 2, 1855, Elliott-Gonzales Papers, Southern Historical Collection (SHC), Manuscript Department, Wilson Library, University of North Carolina, Chapel Hill.

60. Gonzales to Hattie (Elliott), Jan. 20, 1856, Elliott-Gonzales Papers, SHC.

61. Hattie (Gonzales) to Mama (Elliott), Oct. 23, 1856, Elliott-Gonzales Papers, SHC.

62. William B. Edwards, *Civil War Guns* (Harrisburg: Stackpole Company, 1962), p. 362.

63. P. G. T. Beauregard to Gonzales, Dec. 1, 1860, quoted in Jones, "Carolinians and Cubans," p. 108.

64. Gonzales to Ralph Elliott, Nov. 28, 1860, Elliott-Gonzales Papers, SHC. This letter also included a news clipping from the Milledgeville (GA) *Record* of the same date reporting the event.

65. Gonzales to Governor Gist, Nov. 11, 1859, Combined Service Records (microfilm), National Archives, Washington, D.C.

66. Gonzales to Governor Gist, *ibid..*

67. Charleston (SC) *Courier*, Dec. 20, 1860, p. 2.

68. Basso, *Beauregard: the Great Creole*, p. 65.

69. Charleston (SC) *Courier*, April 12, 1861; May 6, 1861. Gonzales served in good company with the volunteer staff. Its members later served important roles in the Confederacy, with Wigfall, Miles, Chestnut and Pryor serving in the Confederate Congress. Chestnut and Pryor became Brigadier Generals, and Chisholm became a colonel, in the Confederate Army.

70. *The War of the Rebellion: A Compilation of the Official Records of the Union and Confederate Armies* (OR), Series I, Volume 1 (Washington: Government Printing Office, 1880), pp. 30–35.

71. Gonzales to Beauregard, April 17, 1861, Elliott-Gonzales Papers, SHC; Charleston (SC) *Courier*, May 15, 1861.

72. *OR*, Series I, vol. 53, p. 167.

73. *OR*, Series I, vol. 53, p. 171.

74. Gen. Beauregard to Gonzales, May 1861, Record Group 109, Chapter II, vol. 263, p. 267, National Archives, Washington, D.C.

75. Charleston (SC) *Courier*, May 28, 1861.

76. Charleston (SC) *Mercury*, June 24, 1861.

77. Richard M. Lee, *General Lee's City* (McLean: EPM Publications, 1987), pp. 150–151.

78. C. Vann Woodward, ed., *Mary Chestnut's Civil War* (New Haven: Yale University Press, 1981), pp. 143, 185–186.

79. *Ibid.*, p. 143.

80. Brooks, *Stories of the Confederacy*, p. 298.

81. John F. Marszalek, ed., *The Diary of Miss Emma Holmes, 1861–1866* (Baton Rouge: Louisiana State University Press, 1994), pp. 273–274.

82. *OR*, Series I, vol. 6, pp. 278–283.

83. Gonzales to Ralph Elliott, September 23, 1861, Elliott-Gonzales Papers, SHC.

84. Charleston (SC) *Courier*, October 8, 1861; Charleston (SC) *Mercury*, October 8, 1861.

85. Dunbar Rowland, ed., *Jefferson Davis Constitutionalist: His Letters, Papers and Speeches*, vol. V (Jackson: Mississippi Department of Archives and History, 1923), p. 143.

86. Woodward, *Mary Chestnut's Civil War*, p. 227.

87. Williams, *P.G.T. Beauregard*, pp. 96–105.

88. *OR*, Series I, vol. 6, p. 324.

89. *OR*, Series I, vol. 6, p. 309.

90. *OR*, Series I, vol. 53, p. 196.

91. A. L. Long, *Memoirs of Robert E. Lee* (New York: J.M. Stoddard & Co., 1886), pp. 138–139.

92. *OR*, Series I, vol. 6, pp. 42–43.

93. Charles E. Cauthen, *Journals of the South Carolina Executive Councils of 1861 and 1862* (Columbia: South Carolina Archives Department, 1956), p. 94.

94. A. L. Long, "Seacoast Defenses of South Carolina and Georgia," *Southern Historical Society Papers*, vol. 1, No. 2 (February, 1876), pp. 103–107; vol. 2, p. 239; Long, *Memoirs of Robert E. Lee*, pp. 134–144. This position is echoed in some later works such as Clifford Dowdey, *Lee* (Boston: Little, Brown & Co., 1965), p. 178.

95. Thomas Jordan, "Seacoast Defenses of South Carolina and Georgia," *Southern Historical Society Papers*, vol. 1, No. 6 (June, 1876), pp. 403–407; Alfred Roman, *The Military Operation of General Beauregard*, vol. II (New York, Harper & Brothers, 1884), p. 6.

96. Douglas Southhall Freeman, *R. E. Lee: A Biography*, vol. 1 (New York: Charles Scribner's Sons, 1934), p. 629.

97. Charleston (SC) *Courier*, May 2, 1862. This letter written March 15, 1862 from Winnsboro, SC, from a tentmate on Morris Island thanks the paper for its notice on Gonzales.

98. Woodward, *Mary Chestnut's Civil War*, p. 290.

99. *Ibid.*, p. 315.

100. Gonzales to Jefferson Davis, March 20, 1862, Davis Papers, Duke University.

101. Gonzales to Gen. Cooper, May 8, 1862, Compiled Service Records.

102. *OR*, Series I, vol. 14, p. 548. Pemberton's order of June 2, 1862, refers to "Mr. A.J. Gonzales."

103. War Department to Gonzales, June 4, 1862, Combined Service Records.

104. *OR*, Series I, vol. 14, p. 556. General Order No. 26.

105. Charleston (SC) *Courier*, June 16, 1862.

106. *OR*, Series I, vol. 14, p. 561; p. 565.

107. Charleston (SC) *Courier*, June 27, 1862.

108. *Journal of the Congress of the Confederate States of America, 1861–65*, vol. II (Washington: Government Printing Office, 1904), p. 422.

109. Gonzales's pay vouchers and supplies requisitions, Combined Service Records.

110. Michael B. Ballard, *Pemberton, A Biography* (Jackson: University Press of Mississippi, 1991), pp. 83–113. The author provides a broad general discussion of the many problems encountered and created by Pemberton during his tenure in South Carolina.

111. Gonzales to Pemberton, Sept. 17, 1863, Pemberton Papers, SHC. Also cited in Ballard, *Pemberton*, p. 112.

112. Williams, *P.G.T. Beauregard*, pp. 162–66.

113. Gonzales to Beauregard, Sept. 6, 1862, Ambrosio Gonzales Papers, South Caroliniana Library (SCL), U. South Carolina, Columbia, South Carolina.

114. *OR*, Series I, vol. 14, p. 609.

115. *Ibid.*, pp. 610–613.

116. G. T. Beauregard, "The Defense of Charleston," *Battles and Leaders of the Civil War*, vol. 4 (New York: Thomas Yoseloff, 1956), p. 2. This view of the changes instituted by Pemberton demonstrates the active role that General Beauregard played in Charleston. While Lee and Beauregard both deserve credit for developing critical defensive plans for the coastal district, Pemberton negated much of the design, forcing Beauregard to reorganize a defense when he returned to command in the district. Union army and naval actions made this an ongoing process.

117. *OR*, Series I, vol. 14, p. 604.

118. *OR*, Series I, vol. 27, Part II, pp. 640–641.

119. Beauregard to Capt. George H. Preble, January 24, 1872, Papers of P. G. T. Beauregard, Reel 1, Frame 709, Library of Congress, Manuscript Division, Washington, D.C.

120. *OR*, Series I, vol. 14, pp. 621–623.

121. Gonzales to Department Headquarters, Sept. 29, 1862, Ambrosio Gonzales Papers, SCL.

122. Gonzales to Beauregard, Oct. 8, 1862, Ambrosio Gonzales Papers, SCL.

123. *OR*, Series I, vol. 14, p. 673.

124. Gonzales to Brig. Gen. Thomas Jordan, Oct. 17, 1862, Ambrosio Gonzales Papers, SCL.

125. *OR*, Series I, vol. 14, pp. 726–727.

126. Gonzales to Beauregard, Jan. 27, 1863, Record Group 109, II, (30), 391, National Archives.

127. Beauregard, "Defense of Charleston," p. 4.

128. *OR*, Series I, vol. 14, pp. 745–747.

129. *OR*, Series I, vol. 14, p. 755. Major Alston was an artillery commander in the District, later commander of the South Carolina Siege Train.

130. Stephen R. Wise, *Lifeline of the Confederacy* (Columbia: University of South Carolina, 1988), pp. 122–124.

131. Beauregard, "Defense of Charleston," pp. 7–9.

132. James M. Merrill, *Dupont: The Making of an Admiral* (New York: Dodd, Mead & Company, 1986), p. 282.

133. Beauregard, "Defense of Charleston," p. 5.

134. *OR*, Series I, vol. 14, pp. 811, 834.

135. *Ibid.*, pp. 851–852.

136. Merrill, *Dupont*, pp. 280–289.

137. Beauregard, "Defense of Charleston," pp. 10–13; C.R.P. Rogers, "DuPont's Attack at Charleston," *Battles and Leaders of the Civil War*, vol. 4, pp. 32–47.

138. *OR*, Series I, vol. 14, pp. 240–243.

139. Special Order No. 97-10, Combined Service Records.

140. General Order 72/1, Combined Service Records.

141. *OR*, Series I, vol. 14, p. 953.

142. Gonzales to Col. R. G. M. Dunovant, May 29, 1863, Ambrosio Gonzales Papers, SCL.

143. Requisition Form, July 1, 1863, Combined Service Records.

144. *OR*, Series I, vol. 14, p. 963.

145. *OR*, Series I, vol. 28, Part II, p. 185.

146. Warren Ripley (ed.), *Siege Train* (Columbia: University of South Carolina Press, 1986), pp. 1–3. This is the diary of Major Edward Manigault, brother of Confederate General Arthur Manigault. He volunteered for service to South Carolina in November 1860 and was appointed colonel and Chief of Ordnance for the state. In May 1863, he petitioned for command of the District siege train when Major Alston resigned. He received the command with rank of Confederate major serving under Colonel Gonzales.

147. *OR*, Series I, vol. 28, Part II, p. 192.

147. Peter Burchard, *One Gallant Rush* (New York: St. Martins Press, 1965). For the interested reader, the story of this unit and its attack on Fort Wagner were portrayed in the movie "Glory," released by Tri-Star Pictures, 1989.

149. Beauregard to Gen. Roswell Ripley, Jan. 27, 1863, Record Group 109, II (30), 387, National Archives.

150. Beauregard to Gen. Ripley, July 25, 1863, Record Group 109, II (26), 255, National Archives.

151. *OR*, Series I, vol. 28, Part II, p. 259.

152. *Ibid.*, pp. 284–285, 287, 289.

153. *Ibid.*, pp. 269–270.

154. Gonzales to James A. Seddon, Aug. 19, 1863, Combined Service Records.

155. Gonzales to Jefferson Davis, Aug. 25, 1863, Combined Service Records.

156. Stewart Woodford, "The Story of Fort Sumter," *Personal Recollections of the War of The Rebellion* (New York: New York Commandery (MOLLUS), 1891), p. 277.

157. Roman, *Military Operations of General Beauregard*, vol. II, p. 155.

158. Frank Barnes, *Fort Sumter* (Washington: National Park Service Historical Handbook, 1952), p. 34.

159. *OR*, Series I, vol. 28, Part II, pp. 359–360.

160. *Ibid.*, pp. 266, 406, 415, 486, 505; Ripley, *Siege Train*, pp. 61, 64, 76, 78.

161. *OR*, Series I, vol. 28, Part II, pp. 435–438.

162. Milton F. Perry, *Infernal Machines* (Baton Rouge: Louisiana State University Press, 1965), pp. 81–89.

163. *OR*, Series I, vol. 28, Part I, pp. 731–735; Navy OR, vol. 15, pp. 10–21. After the Civil War, Tomb used his experience in the service of the Emperor of Brazil during South America's bloody War of the Triple Alliance (see Darryl Brock, "Naval Technology from Dixie," *Americas*, July/August, 1994, pp. 6–15.) Tomb joined ex–Confederate engineer F.D. Lee, then an established architect, in running a hotel in St. Louis at the turn of the century.

164. Gonzales to Pemberton, Sept. 17, 1863, Pemberton Papers, SHC.

165. Roman, *Military Operations of General Beauregard*, vol. II, p. 167; Williams, *P.G.T. Beauregard*, p. 199.

166. Gonzales to Jordan, Nov. 24, 1863, Combined Service Records; *OR*, Series I, vol. 28, Part II, p. 539.

167. Gonzales to Beauregard, Dec. 3, 1863, Combined Service Records.

168. Navy *OR*, Series I, vol. 15, pp. 188–209; *OR*, Series I, vol. 53, pp. 16–23; Ripley, *Siege Train*, pp. 99–104. Ripley reports that the captured 8-inch howitzers are on display at the Washington Navy Yard.

169. *OR*, Series I, vol. 35, Part II, pp. 382–388, 398–401.

170. *Ibid.*, Part I, pp. 588–590.

171. *Ibid.*, pp. 607–612.

172. Gonzales to Davis, Feb. 7, 1864, Record Group 109, Letters received by the Adjutant and Inspector General, Roll 113, Frame 542, National Archives.

173. *OR*, Series I, vol. 35, Part II, pp. 422–423.

174. Williams, *P.G.T. Beauregard*, pp. 203–207.

175. *OR*, Series I, vol. 35, Part II, pp. 462–468.

176. E. Milby Burton, *The Siege of Charleston 1861–1865* (Columbia: University of South Carolina Press, 1970), pp. 284–295.

177. Rod Gragg, *Illustrated Confederate Reader* (New York: Harper & Row, 1989), p. 163.

178. Special Order 184/2, July 20, 1864, Combined Service Records.

179. Beauregard to General Samuel Cooper, Aug. 13, 1864, Combined Service Records.

180. Pemberton to James Seddon, Aug. 16, 1864, Combined Service Records.

181. *OR*, Series I, vol. 35, Part II, p. 617.

182. General Order 76, Oct. 6, 1864, Combined Service Records.

183. Roy started the war as a clerk in Jordan's office while Jordan was on Beauregard's staff in Virginia. Moving west with them, he received Jordan's recommendation for a staff position with General Hardee, with whom he remained for the rest of the war. [Nathaniel Hughes, Jr., *General William J. Hardee, Old Reliable* (Baton Rouge: Louisiana State University Press, 1965), p. 116.]

184. Gonzales to Lt. Col. T. B. Roy, AAG, November 11, 1864, Ambrosio Gonzales Papers, SCL.

185. *OR*, Series I, vol. 39, Part III, p. 740.

186. *OR*, Series I, vol. 44, p. 902.

187. *Ibid.*, pp. 420–421.

188. *Ibid.*, p. 906.

189. *Ibid.*, pp. 413–418.

190. Gonzales knew Smith from his filibuster days. General Worth introduced the men when Gonzales traveled with Worth through New York, where Smith was an instructor at West Point. Smith may have participated in the Cuban liberation movement. Gonzales, of course, knew Colonel Colcock as one of the area commanders, but also because his nephew, Captain William W. Elliott, served as an aide to Colcock.

191. From a historical naval family, Preble commanded a vessel under Farragut which ran the New Orleans forts and the Vicksburg batteries. In command of a naval force off Mobile, he allowed the raider CSS *Florida* to enter the port through his blockade. To serve as an example, he was immediately dismissed from the Navy without even a trial. Later reinstated to his rank, he patroled for commerce raiders before

assignment to the Federal Department of the South. He was the recipient of Beauregard's letter on the Confederate battle flag cited above.

192. William R. Scaife, *The March To the Sea* (Saline: McNaughton & Gunn, 1993), pp. 71–84.

193. Charleston Daily *Courier*, Dec. 5, 1964, p. 1.

194. *OR*, Series I, vol. 44, pp. 971–972, 974–976.

195. *Ibid.*, p. 1007; *OR*, vol. 47, Part II, pp. 986, 992.

196. Gonzales to Anne H. Elliott, Jan. 18, 1865, Elliott-Gonzales Papers, SHC.

197. Gonzales to Col. Allan McFarlan, Feb. 10, 1865, McFarlan Papers, SCL.

198. *OR*, Series I, vol. 47, Part II, pp. 1153–54; Pemberton to Cooper, February 10, 1865, Combined Service Records.

199. Endorsement of Gorgas, Feb. 26, 1865, Combined Service Records. Francis Shoup, whose name Gorgas misspells, was a West Point graduate, who served as chief of artillery for General Hardee at Shiloh, adjutant general for General Hindman at Prairie Grove, a brigade commander at Vicksburg with General Pemberton, artillery chief for General Johnston in the Atlanta campaign, and chief of staff for General Hood. He and Gorgas taught at Sawanee College in the 1870s.

200. *OR*, Series I, vol. 47, Part II, pp. 1239, 1374, 1398.

201. Hughes, *General William J. Hardee*, pp. 273–285.

202. *OR*, Series I, vol. 47, Part III, pp. 710, 725–726, 744–745, 769, 780.

203. *Ibid.*, pp. 720, 726.

204. Davis, Mallory, Breckinridge and other Cabinet members were in Greensboro on April 12–15. Davis met with Johnston and Beauregard and agreed, after hearing Johnston's dismal forecast, to allow discussions with Sherman for the surrender of Johnston's army.

205. Brooks, *Stories of the Confederacy*, p. 291, Report of Adj. Gen Office, July 10, 1911; Record of Service, Combined Service Records.

206. "Reminiscences of Mrs. Mary Gray Crockett," *Recollections and Reminiscences, 1861–1865 through World War I*, vol. 1 (South Carolina: United Daughters of the Confederacy, 1990), pp. 544–546.

207. Elliott Johnstone to Anne Elliott, Aug. 3, 1865, Elliott-Gonzales Papers, SHC.

208. Advertisement for "Gonzales, Woodward & Co.," Charleston Daily *Courier*, Jan. 22, 1866, p. 2.

209. Ralph Elliott to Emily Elliott, Jan. 28, 1866, Elliott-Gonzales Papers, SHC.

210. Gonzales to Ralph Elliott, Oct. 25, 1866, Elliott-Gonzales Papers, SHC.

211. Gonzales to Mrs. Gonzales, Dec. 6, 1866, Elliott-Gonzales Papers, SHC.

212. Hattie Gonzales to Emily Elliott, March 27, 1867; May 3, 1867; Oct. 2, 1867; Dec. 16, 1867; Elliott-Gonzales Papers, SHC.

213. "Jefferson Davis in Cuba," Greenville (S.C.) *Southern Enterprise*, April 22, 1868, p. 2.

214. Hattie Gonzales to Mrs. A. H. Elliott, Jan. 23, 1869, Elliott-Gonzales Papers, SHC.

215. N. G. Gonzales, *In Darkest Cuba* (Columbia: The State Company, 1922), pp. 12–13.

216. Beauregard to Jordan, Jan. 24, 1868, Papers of P. G. T. Beauregard, Reel 1, Frame 594, Library of Congress.

217. Williams, *P.G.T. Beauregard*, p. 42.

218. Hattie Gonzales to Mother (Mrs. W. Elliott), Aug. 14, 1869, Elliott-Gonzales Papers, SHC.

219. W. C. Bee to Gonzales, March 6, 1872, Elliott-Gonzales Papers, SHC.

220. Gonzales to Ambrosio Gonzales, Jr., Aug. 28, 1872, Elliott-Gonzales Papers, SHC.

221. J. D. Warren to A. J. Gonzales, June 6, 1874, Ambrosio Gonzales Papers, SCL.

222. Gonzales to William Porcher Miles, May 23, 1885, William Porcher Miles Papers, SHC.

223. A.J. Gonzales, *Heaven Revealed, A Series of Authentic Spirit Messages from a Wife to Her Husband, Proving Sublime Nature of True Spiritualism* (Washington: McQueen & Wallace, 1889).

224. Gonzales, "On To Cuba"; "The Cuban Crusade."

225. Jones, "Ambrosio José Gonzales," pp. 73–74; Jack Childs, "The 1889–1890 Washington Conference Through Cuban Eyes: Jose Marti and the First International American Conference," *Revista Interamericana de Bibliografia*, Vol. XXXIX (No. 4), 1989, pp. 443–456.

226. Gonzalo de Quesada, "Ambrosio José Gonzales," *Patria*, December 31, 1892, p. 3.

227. *Ibid.*

228. "Ambrosio José Gonzales: Death of a Cuban and Confederate Patriot," Columbia (SC) *The State*, August 2, 1893.

229. Brooks, *Stories of the Confederacy*, p. 297.

230. Jones, "Ambrosio José Gonzales," p. 74; Gonzales, *In Darkest Cuba*, pp. 17–26.

231. Gonzales, *In Darkest Cuba*.

232. Gonzales, *In Darkest Cuba*, pp. 39ff; Brooks, *Stories of the Confederacy*, p. 299.

233. "Narciso Gener Gonzales — Newspaperman Extraordinaire," *Nuestro*, vol. 8 (August 1984), pp. 39–42.

234. Samuel L. Latimer, *The Story of the State* (Columbia: The State Printing Company, 1970), p. 256; Brooks, "To Mark Women's Monument," *Stories of the Confederacy*, p. 17.

235. José Marti, "Ambrosio José Gonzalez," *Patria*, August 5, 1893, p. 2.

236. N.G. Gonzales, quoted in Brooks, *Stories of the Confederacy*, p. 299; "Ambrosio José Gonzales: Death of a Cuban and Confederate Patriot."

3

Loreta Janeta Velazquez: Civil War Soldier and Spy

by Richard Hall

Just before the first battle of Bull Run on July 21, 1861, a dapper young Confederate lieutenant stood surveying the terrain, elated at the prospects for participating in a great battle. "The field was one of marvelous beauty and grandeur," Lieutenant Harry T. Buford reported in memoirs published more than ten years after the war. "I cannot pretend to express in words what I felt, as I found myself one among thousands of combatants, who were about to engage in a deadly and desperate struggle. The supreme moment of my life had arrived.... I was elated beyond measure, although cool-headed enough.... Fear was a word I did not know the meaning of."

Lieutenant Buford actually was Loreta Janeta Velazquez, a young woman from New Orleans, who fought in four battles wearing male disguise during the early years of the Civil War. After her disguise failed her and she was arrested several times on suspicion of being a woman, she became a spy and detective for the Confederacy, even infiltrating the operations of Northern spymaster LaFayette C. Baker and acting as a double agent. Velazquez was a spirited and resourceful advocate of the Confederate cause. Despite numerous personal setbacks she persisted to the very end, often discouraged but never entirely losing hope, applying her considerable talents in any way she could in support of Southern independence.

Velazquez was born in Havana, Cuba, on June 26, 1842, the sixth and last child of wealthy parents. Her father, serving as an official in Cuba, was Spanish and her mother was the daughter of a French naval officer and an American woman, who was the daughter of a wealthy merchant. In 1844 her father inherited a large cattle ranch in Mexico and moved to San Luis Potosi. When the U.S.-Mexican war broke out, her father joined the Mexican army, and the family was sent to live in St. Lucia, British West Indies. However, the estate in Mexico was destroyed during the war and, bitter toward the United States, her father moved back to Cuba and settled in Santiago.

Later her father inherited the Puerto de Palmas estate, a thriving sugar, tobacco, and coffee trade, and his wealth increased. In her early years, Loreta had an English governess. In 1849, when she was seven years old, she was sent to live with an aunt (her mother's sister) in New Orleans in order to attend a school run by the Sisters of Charity. There she became fluent in English. On April 5, 1856, when she was near 14 years old, Loreta secretly married an army officer from Texas, whose first name was William. However, she continued living with her aunt until they quarreled, then left to be with her husband. She converted to the Methodist Church, became estranged from her family, and lived in St. Louis for a while. Because of her husband's occupation, she spent time at various frontier posts where she learned about military life.

At the outbreak of the Civil War Loreta's husband, who defected to the Confederate army, was killed in a training camp accident. Before his death she had already begun acting on life-long fantasies of being a second Joan of Arc and having adventures in male disguise. She practiced walking and talking like a man, and purchased a custom-made girdle-like contrivance designed to conceal her female figure. Against her husband's wishes she joined the army, serving as an independent officer with her husband in Pensacola, Florida, paying for all of her own equipment. To impress her husband, she traveled to rural northeast Arkansas opposite Memphis, Tennessee, and recruited a battalion of soldiers which she then brought back to Pensacola, Florida, and turned over to him for training. After his death she decided to go to war.

GONE FOR A SOLDIER

The first battle of Bull Run was Loreta's first combat experience. There she served under the command of Brig. Gen. Barnard E. Bee, stationed near the center of the Confederate line. Following that Confederate victory she fought at the battle of Balls Bluff, October 21, 1861, attached to the 8th Virginia Infantry, describing as an eyewitness the ultimate scene when the Federal force, in full retreat, tumbled down the high bluff, many drowning in the Potomac River and others shot down like fish in a barrel. This carnage soured her on the "glory" or "nobility" of the war, but she campaigned on for a while.

Velazquez experienced her first military defeat February 13–16, 1862, during the defense of Fort Donelson when the fort fell to a Union siege led by Union commander U. S. Grant. There she volunteered for picket duty, but she had trouble adjusting to the bitter winter weather. "I confess" she said, "that, as the sleet stung my face, and the biting winds cut me to the bones, I wished myself well out of it, and longed for the siege to be over in some shape, even if relief came only through defeat." When the fort fell she managed to escape, but she was rapidly becoming disillusioned. "Immediately after [this defeat]," she said, "I was greatly depressed in spirit, and it was long before I could shake off the disposition to shudder, and the feeling of intense melancholy, that overcame me to such an extent, that I almost resolved to give up the whole business, and to never allow myself to be put in the way of witnessing anything of the kind again."

At Shiloh, April 6–7, 1862, the Confederate defeat after near victory galled her. "Although I had escaped from the two days' fighting unhurt [she was seriously wounded next day by an explosion while helping bury the dead from the battlefield], I was so utterly worn out and wretched, that I really did not care a great deal what became of me, and was almost as willing to be taken prisoner by the Federals as to return to Corinth, with a view of again undertaking to exert myself in what was now beginning to appear the hopeless cause of Southern independence."

Although Velazquez continued off and on in soldier disguise, she tired of combat and military life. After being arrested in Richmond in 1863 on the charge of being a woman in soldier's uniform (her disguise was "not in good order"), she noted:

It seemed to be an impossibility for me now to avoid getting into continual trouble about my disguise. Not only were a number of people fully informed of all the particulars of my career since the outbreak of the war, but it began to be whispered about among the soldiers and citizens that a woman dressed as a man had been discovered, and some highly-exaggerated rumors with regard to my exploits were diligently circulated.... I was credited with exploits of unparalleled heroism.

Also later that year in Atlanta: "My secret was now known to a great many persons, and its discovery had already caused me such annoyance that I hesitated about assuming my uniform again.... I had seen enough of fighting, enough of marching, enough of camp life, enough of prisons and hospitals." At this point she was inclined to give up her unorthodox life for a more conventional one. After he husband's death she had become informally engaged to another officer who had served with him, Thomas C. DeCaulp, but he did not know about her soldier life, and their military assignments had kept them apart. When she found DeCaulp recovering from an illness in an Atlanta hospital, she confessed her secret to him and they were married.

They had not been married long before DeCaulp, while returning to his regiment, relapsed and died in a southern hospital. Distraught by his sudden death, Velazquez found herself at loose ends, not wanting to resume military life but unable to face routine civilian life alone. Gradually she shifted to a career in spying behind Union lines, masquerading as a bereaved Union wife or as a Southern woman who had been mistreated by Confederate authorities and wished to make a new life in the north. At times she freelanced, but at other times she apparently served as a Confederate secret service agent duly authorized by officials in Richmond. Her missions included penetration of Union lines to deliver money or information to Confederate agents and to gather intelligence information about Union forces. In this service she used various names and cover stories.

One of her most dangerous feats was her service as a double agent in Colonel LaFayette Baker's Federal detective corps, convincing him that she was penetrating Confederate operations on his behalf while actually doing everything in her power to advance the Confederate cause. She had several close escapes, and Baker even confided in her about his difficulties in catching up with a female Confederate spy (her) who had been eluding his network of spies and informants. Toward the end of the war, Baker actually gave her the assignment of tracking down the elusive female spy. Concerned about being detected and apprehended by the Federal secret service chief, she fled to Europe with one of her brothers and his family and traveled extensively in the British Isles and on the continent. The trip apparently was paid for by money she had made selling counterfeit bonds in one of her undercover operations, with large sums of money going to finance Confederate spying and counterintelligence operations.

After the war she was part of an expedition of Confederate emigrés seeking a new home in Venezuela. Later, giving up on the colonization plan, she returned to the United States, apparently having exhausted her wartime profits, and traveled around the West seeking a new fortune in gold and silver mining. She married a mining entrepreneur who was her third husband and the father of her son, but she eventually became fed up with mining schemes and struck out on her own again, apparently separating from her husband.

This is the broad outline of her story as reported in her 1876 memoirs.[1] No biographies of her have been written, and all published references to her are derived from the memoirs with the few exceptions cited below. The life of her son (whose name is not on record) and the date and place of her death are unknown. Despite all her efforts to win fame and fortune, she ultimately vanished from the pages of history and died in obscurity. No record exists to tell whether she also died in poverty or managed, with the resourcefulness she so often displayed, to obtain the financial resources that allowed her to live out her life comfortably.

ASSESSING HER CLAIMS

Many Civil War writers and historians, and at least one prominent Confederate general, have expressed strong skepticism about Velazquez's story. This essay is a preliminary report of ongoing historical detective work attempting to assess the credibility of her claims, and thus is a work in progress. More details of her story and earlier findings are reported in the present author's 1993 book about Civil War female soldiers.[2] Research since then in cooperation with colleagues has turned up additional historical evidence that tends to confirm important segments of her story. Many questions remain, however, and certain portions of her memoirs suggest some fabrication or misleading reporting on her part.

One contemporary who considered Loreta Velazquez a fraud was Confederate General Jubal A. Early, with whom she exchanged barbs in 1878 in regard to the authenticity of her book.[3] Upon reading her book, Early declared that it contained "several inconsistences, absurdities, and impossibilities" that caused him to consider her "a mere pretender." Some of his objections are trivial and obviously based on gender stereotyping, and some could easily be attributed to a faulty memory 11 years after the war. Others are difficult or impossible to refute. Since her letter to him contained poor spelling and grammar, Early doubted that she had written the book. (Very possibly it was written by the editor, C. J. Worthington, based on her verbal narrative.)

Her description of recruiting a battalion of soldiers in Arkansas early in the war depicts her as acting without any state or Confederate government authority, Early noted. (Also, no record can be found of the small town she names or of a unit from that area by the designation she reports.) Her accounts of flitting from one army to the other in the Confederacy defied Early's knowledge and experience and seemed unlikely to him. At one point Velazquez reports taking a train from South Carolina to Richmond in 1861, passing through Lynchburg en route. Early correctly observed that there was no link to Lynchburg on this line until 1870. (Still, this could be an instance of faulty memory rather than false reporting.) Early also met Velazquez face to face one time and thought her speech and mannerisms belied her claim of Hispanic origin and of being a native southerner. He suspected she was a northern woman.

It is important to note in light of Early's skepticism that in the preface to her memoirs Velazquez said: "The loss of my notes had compelled me to rely entirely upon my memory; and memory is apt to be very treacherous, especially when, after a number of years, one endeavors to relate in their proper sequence a long series of complicated transactions. Besides, I have been compelled to write hurriedly, and in the intervals of pressing business [of] earning my daily bread." (In fact, she does report several incidents or battles out of their proper historical sequence and some events are garbled.) She also states forthrightly that she badly needs the money she hopes the book will bring her.

Various writers have characterized her memoirs in terms such as "unbelievable"; "mythical"; "the most fantastic ... sensational exaggerations"; "an air of the tawdry and the unreal."[4] Stuart Sifakis's estimation presented a challenge that spurred this investigation: "If there has ever been a case of exaggeration with a hidden element of truth, it is likely to be in the claims put forward by Loreta J. Velazquez.... *Little in her work can be even circumstantially supported.* [Emphasis added.] Yet there may be an element of truth. She may have done some of the things she claimed, but this will never be definitely known due to her penchant for exaggeration."[5]

Contrary to the widely accepted skeptical view of Velazquez by historians and others, an investigation has shown that a lot of her story can be "circumstantially supported," and some of it can be and has been fully authenticated. Despite some flaws in her narrative and some remaining problems, the evidence is increasing that her memoirs contain a basically true story. Intensive checking of specific details that she reports of battles, places (e.g., Atlanta during the war), names and official positions, commanders, and unit designations show, in general, a high degree of accuracy on her part. What errors she does make probably are attributable to faulty memory and careless mistakes made in haste rather than to deliberate fabrication. Overall, the internal evidence suggests that she was not consciously fabricating.[6]

Aside from Jubal Early's questions about her ability to recruit soldiers without government authority and to flit from army to army, two bothersome discrepancies remain — one comparatively minor but still difficult to explain in terms of memory lapse, and one major. In describing her experiences at the battle of Balls Bluff she reports looking down from atop the bluff at the Potomac River which she said was "very wide." The description in her memoirs makes no mention of the large sand bar island called Harrison Island that all but fills the river and dominates the view even today, leaving only a narrow channel. How she could simply forget this prominent geological feature is difficult to imagine.

The major discrepancy that cannot by any stretch of the imagination be accounted for by a memory lapse is her story of knowing and later marrying Thomas C. DeCaulp, a Confederate officer from Arkansas. There was a Thomas C. DeCaulp from Arkansas who was at some of the places at some of the times she reports, but his official records from the National Archives strongly contradict much of her alleged interactions with him, do not mention any marriage, and have him deserting to the North and becoming a so-called "galvanized Yankee" instead of dying in a southern hospital as she claims. Calvin Collier, a historian of Arkansas Civil War units, also noted that DeCaulp could not have been at Pensacola, Florida, or the battle of Shiloh (two places where she claimed to interact with him) because official records clearly show that he was elsewhere at the times in question.[7]

On the face of it, this appears to be a clear-cut instance of fabrication on her part, perhaps incorporating someone she knew or knew of into her story in a partly fictional manner. Since overall evaluation of her credibility tends to indicate that she was basically telling a true story, if somewhat garbled at times, what explanation might there be for this fabrication? A parallel example of a woman in male disguise who fought in combat and served as a spy for the North is Sarah Emma Edmonds, who took on the identity of "Franklin Thompson," a soldier in the 2nd Michigan Infantry.[8] Her memoirs disguised the fact that she was a soldier in the 2nd Michigan and used fictional devices to protect some of her comrades from being identified or embarrassed by publicity.[9] Could Velazquez have been trying to protect someone (possibly DeCaulp)?

In a letter dated May 18, 1878, her retort to Jubal Early's criticisms of her book, Velazquez said that she "ought to have given names connected with the facts" but was motivated by a desire to protect the family members of Civil War soldiers from publicity about the "misdeeds" of their soldier relatives. "I did not wish to taint their innocent names with their parents misdeeds. They may read the statements. While their names were not exposed to the public it would not offend the innocent for none of us want our parent's faults heralded to the world."[10] She expressed concern that his criticism would harm her book sales and prevent her from obtaining money she needed to raise her young son. Velazquez apparently acknowledges here disguising some information out of a desire to protect innocent parties. Even if she did have some noble motive for misleading her readers about DeCaulp, however, this remains an incomplete and inadequate explanation. There is little doubt that, for whatever reasons, she engaged in false and misleading reporting about her alleged relationship with DeCaulp.

CONFIRMATIONS OF HER MEMOIRS

A number of subtle points of her memoirs have proved to be accurate upon thorough investigation:

1. Describing her detention in the Lynchburg, Virginia, jail she mentions hearing footsteps coming up the stairs. A researcher in Lynchburg was

able to confirm that the jail, during the Civil War, had been on the second floor of a two-story building that also housed the mayor's office.

2. During her recruiting of soldiers in northeast Arkansas, she reported riding on a short spur of railroad starting at a place called Hopefield (opposite Memphis, Tennessee) that ran about 80 miles to the White River. At the suggestion of the conductor, she got off at a tiny town called Hurlburt Station. Calvin Collier determined that Hopefield did exist and was the railroad terminal on the west bank of the Mississippi River opposite Memphis. It showed on contemporary maps, and the railroad spur had been torn up in 1862 to make ironclad for a Confederate vessel. Collier could not find any place called Hurlburt Station.

3. Arriving in New Orleans in April 1862, after Shiloh, she reports meeting "a number of old friends, James Doolan, Frank Moore, Captain Daugherty, and others...."[11] A Frank L. Moore was captain of Co. D, 5th Louisiana Infantry later in 1862.[12] Major Davis G. Daugherty was an officer of the 31st Arkansas Infantry organized in early summer of 1862.[13] Late in 1863 when she was in Atlanta for medical care, Velazquez named several officers she encountered there including a Major Bacon and a Lieutenant Chamberlain, friends who helped take care of her.[14] E. H. Bacon, Jr., was a major and later lieutenant colonel of the 32nd Georgia Infantry.[15] Lieutenant D. C. Chamberlain in 1863 was an aide-de-camp to Maj. Gen. John P. McCown.[16] Although it is not certain that these are the correct identifications of the officers she named, in most cases there is no ambiguity — no other candidates with the same last names that would engender any doubt.

4. While visiting her brother who was in a Union prison at Camp Chase, Ohio, she reported meeting the "one-armed Major" in charge of Tod Barracks, who kindly allowed Loreta to use his personal quarters to talk privately with her brother. Historical research on Camp Chase by a colleague, Jennie Zeidman, resulted in finding a contemporary newspaper story about the commandant, a one-armed major whose name was John W. Skiles.[17] His military records subsequently were obtained from the National Archives. The Camp Chase prison, furthermore, was not a well-known one and would seem to be an unlikely choice for someone creating a fictional story.[18]

5. The names of buildings and places she reports in war-time Atlanta were verified by the Atlanta Historical Society.[19]

6. A photograph and story in a 1906 book about Confederate spying operations in Canada[20] apparently confirmed another portion of her

memoirs. The section dealt with Confederate efforts to free prisoners in northern prison camps later in the war. Some time after the Confederate raid on St. Albans, Vermont, in 1864, some Confederate officers were imprisoned in Montreal, Canada. A young woman, whose name the grateful prisoners had forgotten by the time the book was written long after the war, had shown up as a Confederate secret service agent and offered to try to obtain badly needed documents for the prisoners' defense from Richmond, and did so.

The mystery woman was said to be from Kentucky, according to the story, and was honored by the Kentucky legislature during a break from official business after the war. Her photograph bears a very strong resemblance to the engraving of Madame Velazquez that appears in her memoirs. At the corresponding point in her memoirs while on other business in Columbus, Ohio, Velazquez reports receiving an urgent dispatch directing her to go to an unspecified location in Canada at once. She does not further explain or elaborate on this sudden detour. Considering the sensitive nature of the mission in Montreal, she might well hold back the details from her book even long after the war while some of the formerly imprisoned veterans were still living. In other words, her curiously abbreviated account in the memoirs dovetails with reports by independent parties.

OBJECTIVE EVIDENCE OF LIEUTENANT BUFORD

Since so much of Velazquez's claim to have served the Confederate army in male disguise and to have been a Confederate secret service agent rests solely on her own word, objective references by third parties who witnessed her activities are especially important in verifying her story. They include the following (in chronological order):

Louisville *Daily Journal,* October 9, 1861. Reports the arrest in Lynchburg, Virginia, of a "Mrs. Mary Ann Keith" of Memphis, Tennessee, who had registered at the Piedmont House dressed in soldier's clothes as "Lieutenant Buford." (Velazquez reports in her memoirs being arrested and detained in Lynchburg, but at a later date.)

A Rebel War Clerk's Diary by John B. Jones, Vol. I (Philadelphia: J. B. Lippincott & Co., 1866, p. 94), November 20–21, 1861 entries. A "diminutive lieutenant" came to Jones's office to apply for a passport and transportation without orders from the adjutant general. This and certain feminine mannerisms aroused his suspicions. "Instead of the usual military salute at parting, he *courtesied* [sic]. This, when I reflected on the fineness of his speech, the fullness of his breast, his attitudes and his short steps, led me to believe the person was a woman...." When he told the provost marshal about it shortly afterwards, the latter person had the lieutenant arrested next day on the western route "and proved, as I suspected, to be a woman." But the provost marshal was ordered by the Secretary of War, Judah Philip Benjamin, to have her released. (Velazquez reports an incident of being arrested while traveling on the western route under similar circumstances.) The dates and destination match the general time frame when she would have been going west to join in the Mississippi campaign and the defense of Fort Donelson in February.

Richmond *Whig*, June 19, 1863 (from the Jackson *Mississippian*). Reports the presence in Jackson, Mississippi, of "Mrs. Laura J. Williams," recently arrived from New Orleans. She is described as a former resident of Arkansas who had served in the Confederate army as "Henry Benford." Her husband was said to be in the Union army.

Lynchburg *Daily Virginian*, July 4, 1863 (from the Richmond *Enquirer*). Reports the arrest in Richmond of a woman dressed in Confederate uniform, using the name "Lieutenant Bensford." She told authorities that her name was "Mrs. Alice Williams" and that her husband was in the Union army.

A reference to "Loretta Janeta Valesquez" [sic] and her imprisonment in Castle Thunder is included in the Richmond *Examiner*, July 25, 1863, and *Castle Thunder: The Confederate Provost Marshal's Prison, 1862–65* by Allan Golden (Richmond, 1980); both cited in *Richmond's Civil War Prisons* by Sandra V. Parker (Lynchburg, Va.: Virginia Battles and Leaders Series, 1990, pp. 26–27). (In her book, Velazquez reports fleeing from New Orleans to Jackson, Mississippi, in 1862 or 1863, there resuming her male disguise, and then going on to Richmond where she was promptly arrested and detained in Castle Thunder.)

Confederate Agent: A Discovery in History by James D. Horan (New York: Crown Publishers, 1954). In a section on Union counterspy Felix Stidger, who infiltrated the Copperhead movement (northerners sympathetic to the South), Horan reports that in the summer of 1863 Stidger went to St. Louis "where he saw the beautiful Madam Valesque [sic], the Confederate spy whose black eyes bewitched passes from Union generals" (p. 106).

Official Records, Series I, vol. 24, part 1, p. 634. Memo dated March 15, 1864 from H. Winslow to Gen. Leonidas Polk in Mobile, Alabama, about placing a female secret service agent who will travel in the West and North gathering information, and will report to Richmond in April. (Major H. Winslow was an aide to Gen. Polk. If not Velazquez, this would have to be someone else who fits her story exactly. In her memoirs on pp. 345–353, she reports traveling to Mobile with a letter of recommendation from the Richmond provost marshal, and there receiving a secret service assignment that took her to the West and North.)

Official Records, Series II, vol. 8, p. 936. Correspondence dated 1865 refers to "Miss Alice Williams" who served in the Confederate army as "Lieutenant Buford."

New Orleans *Picayune*, January 5, 1867, and other references cited in a 1960 Civil War centennial study.[21] The *Picayune* reported that "Mrs. Mary de Caulp has appeared as agent for the Southern states for a Venezuelan emigration company.... During the war she fought [in a Texas cavalry regiment] for the Confederacy as Lieutenant Bufort [sic] until her sex was discovered.... This woman was Loreta Janeta Velasquez, a New Orleans girl of Cuban extraction." (The account in her memoirs of the Venezuelan expedition, pp. 537–552, dovetails completely with the 1960 centennial study as to details of the voyage and circumstances of the planned colony. It is interesting that she was still using a version of the married name DeCaulp at this point even though she had since remarried.)

This scholarly study constitutes an extremely important independent confirmation of that portion of her memoirs. There can be little doubt that her account of the Venezuelan colony was truthful and accurate. In their preface, the authors note, "Of the various proposals for Confederate settlements abroad after the American Civil War, the colony in Venezuela is probably the least known." Again, how likely is it that a writer of creative fiction would have chosen — or even been aware of— the most obscure of settlement schemes to use in her claim to have been a participant?[22]

NEW EYEWITNESS REPORT

Late in 1993 a colleague, C. Kay Larson (who is researching the various roles of women in the Civil War and shares an interest in Velazquez), discovered an important new reference to Lieutenant Buford by an officer who encountered Velazquez as Buford in the field. Bromfield L. Ridley, who at the time was aide-de-camp to Lt. Gen. A. P. Stewart, reported in his history of the Army of the Tennessee[23]:

> I recollect another heroine, a Lieutenant Buford of an Arkansas regiment. She stepped and walked the personification of a soldier boy, had won her spurs on the battlefield at Bull Run, Fort Donelson, and Shiloh, and was promoted for gallantry. One evening she came to General Stewart's headquarters, at Tyner's Station, with an order from Major Kinloch Falconer to report for duty as a scout, but upon his finding that "he" was a woman, she was sent back and the order rescinded. She has written a book.[24]

Internal evidence indicates that the incident in question happened in the last half of 1864. Velazquez in her memoirs describes arriving at Tyner's Station

(Stewart's headquarters) by train at some uncertain date (she was often vague about exact dates) and after talking with friends in the 10th Tennessee infantry, deciding to make different plans.[25] This may have been her last attempt to obtain a military assignment. Shortly afterwards she resumed spying activities. The 10th Tennessee was part of the Army of Tennessee from September 1863 until the end of the war.[26]

SUMMARY AND PRELIMINARY CONCLUSIONS

Many loose ends remain, including important leads that could shed new light on the Civil War escapades of Loreta Janeta Velazquez. To date, the evidence strongly supports the view that she did serve in male disguise, in Confederate uniform, using the name Lieutenant Harry T. Buford (or a variant thereof), and that she did engage in spying operations on behalf of the Confederacy, at least part of the time with official authorization from Richmond. Exactly how many of the adventures she reports in her memoirs can be accepted as factual is more problematical.

The Woman in Battle clearly was written in haste, as she admits, and often reports events out of sequence. There is no internal evidence of deliberate embellishment or exaggeration in order to make her story more interesting or sensational. To the contrary, it documents her failures and frustrations in convincing fashion. Rather than tales of derring-do and constant successes, her story comes across as (for the most part) an honest and conscientious effort to tell the truth, and a lot of the truth was something other than she desired. It also tracks the rising or falling fortunes of war from the Confederate perspective very well.

On the other hand, her constant practices of deception as Lt. Buford and in her spying activities may have come back to haunt her when she tried to set the story straight in 1876. Giving her the benefit of the doubt, she may have tried to protect some people implicated by her story. On the other hand, she may have been so imbued with deceptive practices that she was constitutionally incapable of being completely forthright and honest.

The objective evidence of newspaper stories and other historical records show that she regularly used cover names such as "Alice Williams," "Laura Williams," and "Mary Ann Keith," and after the war, as we have seen, "Mary de Caulp." (In her memoirs she reports using the names "Mrs. Williams," "Mrs. Fowler," and "Mrs. Sue Battle," and after her alleged marriage to Thomas DeCaulp she would have been Loreta DeCaulp.) The variants on Buford ("Bensford," "Benford," and "Bufort") may have been phonetic misspellings, or they may have been deliberate on her part. The fact that in 1863 she twice told authorities that her husband was in the Union army is interesting in light of the DeCaulp story (official records state that he deserted to the North in 1863 and served in the Union army under an assumed name). Yet, in her memoirs she reported that DeCaulp died in a southern hospital that year. At various times she claimed to be (or was reported to be) from Arkansas, Kentucky, Tennessee, or Texas. In some versions, she led Texas troops in combat. However, her memoirs state that her home base was New Orleans, Louisiana, and that she recruited a battalion in rural Arkansas and served with them at Shiloh. Assuming that she was trying to set the story straight in her memoirs, other versions become either garbled or part of her cover stories.

Velazquez may have covered her tracks so successfully in her efforts to mislead Union authorities that she has inadvertently complicated the problem of trying to document her career in retrospect. Inevitably she brings to mind the epigram attributed to Walter Scott: "O, what a tangled web we weave, when first we practice to deceive!"

Because of all the unanswered questions about her, it is important to suspend judgment and await more evidence. We must not overlook the fact that, in general, and in many small particulars, historical evidence supports her story. How could she have imagined the details of hotels and streets in Atlanta, Lynchburg, and other places? How did she accurately describe the long-since-vanished railroad spur in northeast Arkansas? And how could she have known of the one-armed major who commanded the obscure Union prison at Camp Chase, Ohio?

Additional historical research may resolve some of the remaining questions. Information is invited that will contribute to the ongoing investigation.

Notes ─────────────────────────────────

1. C. J. Worthington (ed.), *The Woman in Battle* (Hartford, Conn.: T. Belknap, 1876). The book's long subtitle is "A Narrative of the Exploits, Adventures, and Travels of Madame Loreta Janeta Velazquez, Otherwise Known as Lieutenant Harry T. Buford, Confederate States Army." Quotes about First Bull Run, p. 100; Fort Donelson, pp. 167, 172; Shiloh, p. 218; arrests as woman in soldier's uniform, pp. 283, 339; Lafayette Baker, pp. 394–402.

2. Richard Hall, *Patriots in Disguise: Women Warriors of the Civil War* (New York: Paragon House, 1993). See chapters 9–11, chapter notes, and research notes.

3. The Early-Velazquez correspondence is in the Tucker family papers, Southern Historical Collection, Chapel Hill, North Carolina. See also Sylvia D. Hoffert, "Madame Loreta Velazquez: Heroine or Hoaxer?" in *Civil War Times Illustrated*, June 1978, pp. 24–31.

4. In order, see Patricia L. Faust, *Historical Times Illustrated Encyclopedia of the*

Civil War (New York: Harper, 1986), pp. 779–780; E. Merton Coulter, "The Confederate States of America 1861–1865" in *A History of the South*, vol. VII (Baton Rouge: LSU Press, 1950), p. 420; Mary Elizabeth Massey, *Bonnet Brigades* (New York: Alfred A. Knopf, 1966), p. 195; Francis B. Simkins and James W. Patton, *Women of the Confederacy* (Richmond: Garrett and Massie, 1936), p. 81.

5. Stuart Sifakis, *Who Was Who in the Civil War* (New York: Facts on File, 1988), p. 290.

6. See Hall, *Patriots in Disguise*, chapter notes and research notes.

7. Thomas C. DeCaulp regimental records from National Archives; personal communication from Calvin Collier, March 21, 1991.

8. Sylvia Dannett, *She Rode with the Generals* (New York: Thomas Nelson and Sons, 1960). A biography of Sarah Emma Edmonds.

9. S. Emma E. Edmonds, *Nurse and Spy in the Union Army* (Hartford, Conn.: W. S. Williams & Co., 1864). See Hall, *Patriots in Disguise*, chapters 4–7 and chapter and research notes for analysis of *Nurse and Spy* and Edmonds's life story.

10. Tucker Family Papers, Southern Historical Collection, *op cit.*

11. Worthington, *The Woman in Battle*, p. 230.

12. Arthur W. Bergeron, Jr., *Guide to Louisiana Confederate Military Units 1861–1865* (Baton Rouge: LSU Press, 1989), p. 82.

13. Joseph H. Crute, Jr., *Units of the Confederate States Army* (Midlothian, Va.: Derwent Books, 1987), pp. 56–57.

14. Worthington, *The Woman in Battle*, pp. 315–316.

15. John M. Carroll, *List of Field Officers, Regiments & Battalions in the Confederate States Army 1861–1865* (Mattituck, N.Y.: J. M. Carroll and Co., 1983), p. 7.

16. Joseph H. Crute, Jr. *Confederate Staff Officers 1861–1865* (Powhatan, Va.: Derwent Books, 1982), p. 137.

17. Delaware, Ohio, *Gazette*, Aug. 24, 1863. Story about Maj. John W. Skiles, the one-armed commandant of Tod Barracks at Camp Chase, Ohio.

18. In *The Story of Camp Chase* by William H. Knauss (Columbus, Ohio: The General's Books, 1990 reprint) the author states: "It is remarkable that in all the official reports and records of 1861–65 of the Governor of Ohio, his Adjutant General, or his subordinate officers no mention is made of the Confederate [sic] prison at Camp Chase except a brief reference made in 1861 by Gov. William Dennison." (p. 122.)

19. Personal communication from Franklin M. Garrett, June 12, 1990.

20. John W. Headley, *Confederate Operations in Canada and New York* (New York: Neale Publishing Co., 1906). The photograph of an unidentified Kentucky woman that strongly resembles Velazquez appears opposite page 376.

21. Alfred Jackson Hanna and Kathryn Abbey Hanna, *Confederate Exiles in Venezuela*, Confederate Centennial Studies #15 (Tuscaloosa, Ala.: Confederate Publishing Co., 1960).

22. The better-known colonization plans included a reasonably successful one in Brazil. See William Clark Griggs, *The Elusive Eden: Frank McMullan's Confederate Colony in Brazil* (Austin: University of Texas Press, 1987).

23. Bromfield L. Ridley, *Battles and Sketches of the Army of the Tennessee* (Mexico, Mo.: Missouri Printing and Publishing Co., 1906), p. 495.

24. Velazquez never claimed to have been promoted for gallantry; this apparently is an error by Ridley.

25. Worthington, *The Woman in Battle*, p. 292.

26. Stewart Sifakis, *Tennessee: Compendium of the Confederate Armies* (New York: Facts on File, 1992), pp. 106–108.

Index

241